# DE-CENTRING
# SEXUALITIES

An enormous amount of literature exists which explores and discusses sexuality in urban and 'colonized' spaces, but there is little which documents these issues in the marginal or 'in-between' places. These places have great significance with respect to representations and politics of sexuality, for it is in these spaces that hegemonic sexualities may be least stable.

*De-centring Sexualities: Politics and Representations Beyond the Metropolis* is an exploration of material and metaphysical geographies of sexualities outside of the urban arena. The 'marginal' sexualities are furthest from the movements that seek to liberate them, and sexual subjects are least stable in these marginal regions.

The book explores these issues in four parts: Non-metropolitan Sexualities; Beyond the Metropolis; Deconstructing Metropolitan Models; and Devolving Sexualities. The strong team of contributors from a range of different fields (including cultural studies, literature and history), investigate themes ranging from religion, to hierarchies of power, constructions of rural sexualities, politics of pastoral representation and sexual persecution.

# CRITICAL GEOGRAPHIES

Edited by **Tracey Skelton**, *Lecturer in International Studies, Nottingham Trent University,*
and **Gill Valentine**, *Professor of Geography, The University of Sheffield.*

This series offers cutting-edge research organised into four themes of concepts, scale, transformations and work. It is aimed at upper-level undergraduates, research students and academics, and will facilitate inter-disciplinary engagement between geography and other social sciences. It provides a forum for the innovative and vibrant debates which span the broad spectrum of this discipline.

1. MIND AND BODY SPACES
Geographies of illness, impairment and disability
*Edited by Ruth Butler and Hester Parr*

2. EMBODIED GEOGRAPHIES
Spaces, bodies and rites of passage
*Edited by Elizabeth Kenworthy Teather*

3. LEISURE/TOURISM GEOGRAPHIES
Practices and geographical knowledge
*Edited by David Crouch*

4. CLUBBING
Dancing, Ecstasy, Vitality
*Ben Malbon*

5. ENTANGLEMENTS OF POWER
Geographies of domination/resistance
*Edited by Joanne Sharp, Paul Routledge, Chris Philo and Ronan Paddison*

6. DE-CENTRING SEXUALITIES
Politics and Representations Beyond the Metropolis
*Edited by Richard Phillips, Diane Watt and David Shuttleton*

7. GEOPOLITICAL TRADITIONS
Critical Histories of a Century of Political Thought
*Edited by Klaus Dodds and David Atkinson*

8. CHILDREN'S GEOGRAPHIES
Playing, Living, Learning
*Edited by Sarah L Holloway and Gill Valentine*

9. THINKING SPACE
*Edited by Mike Crang and Nigel Thrift*

10. ANIMAL SPACES, BEASTLY PLACES
New Geographies of Human–Animal Relations
*Edited by Chris Philo ad Chris Wilbert*

# DE-CENTRING SEXUALITIES

Politics and representations beyond the metropolis

*Edited by Richard Phillips,
Diane Watt and
David Shuttleton*

London and New York

First published 2000
by Routledge
11 New Fetter Lane, London EC4P 4EE

Simultaneously published in the USA and Canada
by Routledge
29 West 35th Street, New York, NY 10001

*Routledge is an imprint of the Taylor & Francis Group*

© 2000 Richard Phillips, Diane Watt and David Shuttleton

Typeset in Perpetua by
Ponting–Green Publishing Services, Chesham, Buckinghamshire
Printed and bound in Great Britain by
Biddles Ltd, Guildford and King's Lynn

All rights reserved. No part of this book may be reprinted or
reproduced or utilized in any form or by any electronic,
mechanical, or other means, now known or hereafter
invented, including photocopying and recording, or in any
information storage or retrieval system, without permission in
writing from the publishers.

*British Library Cataloguing in Publication Data*
A catalogue record for this book is available from the British Library

*Library of Congress Cataloging in Publication Data*
A catalogue record for this book has been requested

ISBN 0–415–19465–2 (hbk)
ISBN 0–415–19466–0 (pbk)

# CONTENTS

*Notes on contributors* vii
*Acknowledgements* ix

**Introduction** 1
RICHARD PHIILLIPS AND DIANE WATT

## PART I
## Non-metropolitan sexualities 19

1 **The production of gay and the return of power** 21
   ALAN SINFIELD

2 **Marginality on the tropic** 37
   DENNIS ALTMAN

3 **Region, religion and sexuality: pilgrim through this barren land** 49
   KATE CHEDGZOY

4 **Margins of the city: towards a dialectic of suburban desire** 64
   BARRY LANGFORD

## PART II
## Beyond the metropolis 81

5 **Eroticizing the rural** 83
   DAVID BELL

6 **Imagined geographies and sexuality politics: the city, the country and the age of consent** 102
   RICHARD PHILLIPS

v

## CONTENTS

7  The queer politics of gay pastoral — 125
   DAVID SHUTTLETON

8  Skirting the margins: Anne Lister, self-representation and lesbian identity in early nineteenth-century Yorkshire — 147
   ANIRA ROWANCHILD

### PART III
### Deconstructing metropolitan models — 163

9  Marginalization and resistance: lesbians in Mexico — 165
   SUE WILLMAN

10  Remapping same-sex desire: queer writing and culture in the American heartland — 182
    WILLIAM J. SPURLIN

11  Getting your kicks on Route 66!: stories of gay and lesbian life in rural America, c. 1950–1970s — 199
    ANGELIA R. WILSON

12  Mapping decolonization of male homoerotic space in Pacific Canada — 217
    GORDON BRENT INGRAM

### PART IV
### Devolving sexualities — 239

13  Devolutionary desires — 241
    LYNNE PEARCE

14  On the borders of allegiance: identity politics in Ulster — 258
    VINCENT QUINN

15  Transgression in Glasgow: a poet coming to terms — 278
    EDWIN MORGAN

*Author index* — 292
*Subject index* — 296

# NOTES ON CONTRIBUTORS

**Dennis Altman** is senior lecturer at La Trobe University, Melbourne. His many books include *The Homosexualisation of America* (1982), *AIDS and the New Puritanism* (1986), *Homosexual Oppression and Liberation* (1971) and *Defying Gravity* (1996).

**David Bell** is senior lecturer in cultural studies at Staffordshire University. His publications include *Mapping Desire* (1995) and *Consuming Geographies* (1997) (both co-edited). He is also the co-author of *The Sexual Citizen* (2000) and co-editor of a *Cybercultures Reader* (2000).

**Kate Chedgzoy** is senior lecturer in English at the University of Warwick. She is the co-editor of a number of books about gender and sexuality in early modern culture, and the author of *Shakespeare's Queer Children: Sexual Politics and Contemporary Culture* (1996).

**Gordon Brent Ingram** is a queer activist and environmental designer, who has made his home *outside* of Vancouver, San Francisco and Rome. He is the editor of *Queers in Space: Communities/ Public Places/ Sites of Resistance* (1997), and an associate lecturer at the University of British Columbia.

**Barry Langford** is lecturer in Film and Television Studies in the Department of Media and Arts at Royal Holloway, University of London. He has published on film and the Holocaust, and is currently writing a book on media, identity and urban space.

**Edwin Morgan** is an internationally acclaimed Scottish poet. His recent publications include *Collected Poems* (1990), *Sweeping out the Dark* (1994), *Collected Translations* (1996) and *Virtual and Other Realities* (1997).

**Lynne Pearce** is senior lecturer in English at Lancaster University. She has published extensively on women's writing and feminist theory, most recently in *Devolving Identities: Feminist Readings in Nation, Class and Region* (1999).

## NOTES ON CONTRIBUTORS

**Richard Phillips** lectures in Geography at Salford University. His publications include *Mapping Men and Empire: A Geography of Adventure* (1997). He is currently writing a book about the cultural politics of decolonization.

**Vincent Quinn** lectures in English at the University of Sussex. His publications include *Luxurious Sexualities* (1997), an edition of *Textual Practice* which he co-edited, and numerous essays in the fields of literary criticism and gay and lesbian studies.

**Anira Rowanchild** is a tutor in Literature at the Open University, and a long-time activist in lesbian and feminist politics in the border counties of England and Wales.

**David Shuttleton** lectures in English and Film at the University of Wales, Aberystwyth. He has published on eighteenth-century and modern literature, and is the author of *Queer Pastoral: Nature, Homosexuality and Modernity* (forthcoming).

**Alan Sinfield** is Professor of English at Sussex University. His publications include *The Wilde Century* (1994), *Cultural Politics/Queer Reading*, *Literature, Politics and Culture in Post-war Britain*, and *Gay and After* (1998).

**William J. Spurlin** is based at Columbia University, New York. His publications include *Reclaiming the Heartland: Lesbian and Gay Voices from the Midwest* (1996).

**Diane Watt** is senior lecturer in English at the University of Wales, Aberystwyth. She has published an edited collection and a book, both about women's writing and history. She has also written a number of articles about gender and sexuality, and recently contributed to *Queerly Phrased: Language, Gender and Sexuality* (1997).

**Sue Willman** is a legal practitioner in London, specializing in equality and human rights cases. She is also a freelance journalist, whose essays on travel and sexuality have appeared in *Diva* and numerous other publications.

**Angelia R. Wilson** is the author of *Below the Belt: Sexuality, Religion and the American South* (forthcoming), the editor of *A Simple Matter of Justice?* (1994) and the co-editor with Joseph Bristow of *Activating Theory*. She is senior lecturer in the School of Social Policy at the University of Manchester.

# ACKNOWLEDGEMENTS

We would like to express our gratitude to the Departments of Geography and English at the University of Wales, Aberystwyth, and in particular to Professor John Lewin and Professor Lyn Pykett, for their encouragement and assistance. We would also like to thank the administrators of the College Research Fund for their generous financial support. This project had its origins in an interdisciplinary reading group which met regularly in the academic year 1995–6, and which was attended by staff and students from the university colleges at Aberystwyth and Lampeter, staff from the National Library of Wales, and members of the Aberystwyth community. In July 1997 we organized the Non-Metropolitan Sexualities Conference at Aberystwyth, and thanks are owed to everyone who took part, but in particular to the plenary speakers Dr David Bell, Professor Edwin Morgan, Professor Alan Sinfield, and Professor Greg Woods. Finally, thanks are due to all the contributors to this volume for their effort and their enthusiasm.

The editors, contributors and publishers would like to thank the following for their permission to reprint the following: Faber and Faber Ltd for an extract from Thom Gunn's 'The Missing' originally published in *The Man With Night Sweats*; Carcanet Press Ltd for Edwin Morgan's 'Glasgow Green', and for extracts from 'Je Ne Regrette Rien', 'Grendel' and 'The New Divan' all published in *Collected Poems*, for 'Il Traviato' from *Sweeping Out the Dark*, and for 'Venetian Sonnet 14' published in *Collected Translations*; and the Scottish Book Trust for an extract from Edwin Morgan's piece 'Fog City' originally published in *Reading Glasgow* by Moira Burgess. Despite every effort to trace and contact copyright holders prior to publication this has not been possible in every case. We apologize for any apparent infringement of copyright and if notified, we will be pleased to rectify any errors or omissions at the earliest opportunity.

# INTRODUCTION

*Richard Phillips and Diane Watt*

## De-centring sexualities

Sexualities and sexual discourses, both hegemonic and emancipatory, have traditionally been structured around centres and margins. Foucault's *'history* of sexuality' has a (hidden) geography: the legal, medical, religious and other institutions, which discursively constitute and regulate sexualities, are concentrated in geographical and political centres, broadly speaking in metropolitan centres (Foucault 1978). Critical discourses and emancipatory movements, notably those of lesbian and gay activism, are concentrated in broadly the same spaces. For example, the English legal and political establishment is shadowed by the lesbian and gay rights organization Stonewall, based in central London, which lobbies politicians and fights legal battles, but does so on the terms and in the geographical and institutional terrain of the establishment. Organizations such as Stonewall, and its more radical counterparts, seek rights or 'liberation' for 'homosexuals' and other groups, sexual subjects that official discourses have already constituted. Their critical project is in this respect limited.

Investigations of real and imagined geographies of sexualities are limited for similar reasons. They tend to be polarized, focused either on sexualized metropolitan centres such as New York and Berlin (see, for example, Bell and Valentine 1995; Ingram 1997), or on differently sexualized, marginalized and colonized spaces including the Orient and Africa (Bleys 1996; Hyam 1990; Kabbani 1986; McClintock 1995). Much less has been said about other liminal (Turner 1969) or in-between spaces (Bhabba 1994), including the small towns and rural parts of Europe, Australia and North America (preliminary studies include Fellows 1996; O'Carroll and Collins 1995; Riordan 1996). Yet these spaces may be of great significance, with respect to representations and politics of sexualities, for it is in such spaces that hegemonic sexualities may be least stable.

At some material and metaphorical distance from both the regulation and the liberation of the centre, in-between spaces on the margins of sexual geography are simultaneously spaces of sexual 'power and danger' (to borrow a phrase from Mary

INTRODUCTION

Douglas 1966: 121). Here, the power of the centred institutions and politics may be open to challenge, and may, for example, be resisted as a form of colonialist intrusion, perhaps within a broader politics of resisting internal colonialism. On the margins, away from the assured hegemony of institutions that constitute sexual subjects and away from the movements that seek to liberate them, sexual subjects are least stable. This means that critical sexual politics can go further, and may critically transform not only sexuality rights but, more fundamentally, sexualities. But since sexual subjectivity is less stable on the margins, sexual subjects may be vulnerable, less able to speak for or defend themselves, or to participate in liberatory politics. Sexuality politics and representations, in these liminal or in-between spaces, are therefore ambivalent, sites of critical power but also of danger.

*De-centring Sexualities* is at once an exploration and a political project. It is an exploration of material and metaphorical geographies of sexualities. It is also an attempt to create such spaces. The politics of exploring and creating such spaces is necessarily ambivalent, for the in-between spaces of sexuality are zones of often very concrete danger as well as potential critical power. To illustrate the ambivalence of de-centring sexualities, and to open up a series of broader questions for this book, we now turn to two texts that explore and de-centre sexualities: *Brokeback Mountain* (1998) by Annie Proulx and *Places Far From Ellesmere* (1990) by Aritha van Herk.

## Questions of power and danger

There was some open space between what he knew and what he tried to believe, but nothing could be done about it, and if you can't fix it you've got to stand it.

(Proulx 1998: 58)

*Brokeback Mountain*, Annie Proulx's short story about two Wyoming cowboys (Ennis del Mar and Jack Twist) who love each other but marry women (Alma Beers and Lureen) and father children, opens up space in which representations and politics of sexuality may be resisted and reconfigured, but also a space of sexual vulnerability and danger. More generally, it opens up questions about sexuality and space, with specific reference to the significance and potential of material and metaphorical spaces that lie beyond the metropolis.

*Brokeback Mountain* foregrounds tensions between metropolitan and non-metropolitan sexualities, posing questions about the legitimacy and stability of metropolitan sexualities in geographical and social margins by disrupting the imperializing tendencies of metropolitan sexual voices. The story was first published in the *New Yorker* (on October 13, 1997), and it is easy to imagine how some metropolitan readers might have interpreted it: a sadly familiar story of repressed

## INTRODUCTION

homosexuality and redneck homophobia, set incidentally if eloquently in Wyoming. Indeed, it would be easy to read *Brokeback Mountain* as the story of gay men, situated in a time and place that had yet to come to terms with homosexuality. However, mainstream reviewers, impressed with the 'universal' qualities of the book, have insisted that it is not gay literature – at least, not *just* gay literature. They are right, if possibly for the wrong reasons. For, while gay literature can resonate as widely as any other, there is no mention of 'gay' or 'homosexual' in *Brokeback Mountain*. The characters in this story are not gay for they are not possessed of sexual orientations that are transferable and generalizable to others of their sex – the relationship between Jack and Ennis is a one-off, love between two people, and Ennis likes the same kind of sex, irrespective of the gender of his partner. Nor is the story or any of its characters translatable or transplantable to a different setting, urban or otherwise. It would be inconceivable for Jack and Ennis to get up and go to New York or San Francisco, for example, for they are of Wyoming, as is their love. For *Brokeback Mountain* resists metropolitan terms. Ennis has not necessarily chosen his fate, but he has to 'stand it', and this means not only putting up with things as they are, but also standing his ground, refusing outsiders' identities and politics, discourse and practice. This is specific, not generic ground. Proulx has lived and worked in Wyoming, and she writes of places and people she knows with a strong sense of landscape and dialect. The love and sex she describes is framed within this landscape and dialect, with its earthy language and cowboy-speak. As perhaps only a Wyoming cowboy could put it, to his sexual partner, 'Christ, it got to be all that time a yours a-horseback makes it so goddam good' (Proulx 1998: 24). In all of this, *Brokeback Mountain* challenges and relativizes dominantly metropolitan voices, which advance powerful but limited sexuality politics and representations. Proulx does not idealize rural Wyoming; on the contrary she presents a textured picture of its beauty and its cruelty, its contradictions. There remains much, not only in the life of Ennis del Mar but also in Wyoming, that is not satisfactory. As Jack put it, 'fuck-all has worked the way I wanted. Nothin never came to my hand the right way' (Proulx 1998: 41). But if sexual life in Wyoming is to be fixed, it must be on Wyoming's own terms, in its own language. And, in fixing Wyoming, it is possible that Wyoming might speak to other places, disrupting and reconfiguring politics and representations of sexuality that have assumed hegemonic status; or, at least, asserting a militant particularism that disrupts the imperializing tendencies of metropolitan (regulatory and liberatory) voices.

*Brokeback Mountain* is in part a story of violence and danger, and the book poses more general questions about how and why people who live in such marginal spaces may be vulnerable. Jack and Ennis are marginal, socially as well as geographically. They both come from small ranches on the Wyoming borders – 'Jack Twist in Lightning Flat, up on the Montana Border, Ennis del Mar from around Sage, near

# INTRODUCTION

the Utah line' (Proulx 1998: 2–3) — and as adults they live in cheap rented houses and in trailers. High-school drop-outs with few prospects, Jack and Ennis are marginal, and this contributes to their vulnerability in a dangerous space where a man might be killed for his sexuality. As Ennis puts it:

> Jack, I don't want a be like them guys you see around sometimes. And I don't want a be dead. There was these two old guys ranched together down home, Earl and Rich … I was what, nine years old, and found Earl dead in a irrigation ditch. They'd took a tire iron to him, spurred him up, drug him around by his dick until it pulled off, just bloody pulp.
>
> (Proulx 1998: 30)

Jack and Ennis have to keep quiet about their love, for fear of physical violence. When Jack is killed in an accident, Ennis has good reason to suspect that he has been beaten to death because of his sexuality. Since their sexuality could not be named, it could not be asserted or defended.

In Proulx's Wyoming, sexualities exist but are not always put into words, or constituted through language. When Jack and Ennis were still theoretically able to be together (before they married and started families), 'They never talked about the sex, let it happen, at first only in the tent at night, then in the full daylight with the hot sun striking down, and at evening in the fire glow, quick, rough, laughing and snorting, no lack of noises, but saying not a goddam word.' (Proulx 1998: 14). These are not men of language; they prefer to leave things open. Ennis in particular belongs in open space, with its silent distances, rather than in the closed, circumscribed space of words: 'he was farsighted enough to dislike reading anything except Hamley's saddle catalogue' (Proulx 1998: 6).

For all this silence, this dangerously open space, there remains possibility. The cowboys meet and fall in love when they are working on Brokeback Mountain, and their love and sex is from then on situated in and associated with that mountain, and natural settings and open spaces more generally. On the mountain they have sex in the tent, by the fire, and in the open. Later, when they meet up, it is ostensibly to hunt or fish, and again they find natural settings accommodate their love in a manner that society, with all its towns and farms, could not. The mountain, with its height and its distance, provided separation from society and an apparently utopian male homosocial space.

> There were only two of them on the mountain, flying in the euphoric, bitter air, looking down on the hawk's back and the crawling lights of vehicles on the plain below, suspended above ordinary affairs and distant from tame ranch dogs barking in the dark hours.
>
> (Proulx 1998: 14)

# INTRODUCTION

The unnamed quality of love in this story parallels the unnamed quality of the landscape. As the critic William New once put it, to name the West would be 'to find words to articulate it, paradoxically at once to create and limit it. In the act of articulation, the endlessness of possibility is circumscribed, for an actual identity is announced' (New 1972: xii). Leaving spaces and sexualities at least partially unmapped, *Brokeback Mountain* retains some of the possibility that words (discourse, more generally) would erase.

*Brokeback Mountain*, while not a gay story, is then a story about love between two men set in an almost exclusively masculine world. A crisis point in the story occurs when Alma opens the door and fleetingly glimpses her husband passionately embracing his friend on the threshold. In this scene, two worlds which are usually kept separate clash: the external masculine world and the feminine domestic sphere. *Brokeback Mountain* says little about Alma and Lureen, or their children. The marginality of the women, and the very fleeting attention paid to their own sexualities and emotions, has its own significance. For Alma, sex appears to be for producing babies rather than pleasure. Presumably this is one reason why she objects to her husband's preference for having anal sex with her (and of course this is a practice which is often not acknowledged to be heterosexual). The reader learns very little about Alma's desires or feeling, about her lonely marriage to a man who loved another.

In direct contrast to *Brokeback Mountain*, Canadian novelist Aritha van Herk's *Places Far From Ellesmere* (van Herk 1990) deliberately concentrates on female selfhood and sexuality to the exclusion of male desire. This example of what van Herk herself refers to as *geografictione* brings together geography, fiction and personal experience (a combination which reflects the scope of this volume). Landscapes and cityscapes, distanced from the metropolitan centres of North America, serve as sites of self-exploration, rediscovery and discovery. Writing largely in the second person, van Herk revisits scenes of her childhood and adult life, rural Edberg and the provincial centres of Edmonton and Calgary, all on the Western edges of the Canadian Prairies. In the final section of the book she travels to the island of Ellesmere in the extreme North of Arctic Canada.

These various locations are maps of the mind which enable van Herk to trace her own fictions of the self, and they are also discursive spaces which allow her to investigate past and present, Old and New World constructions of women's sexuality. In this exploration, van Herk draws on the familiar trope of the migration to an urban centre as a necessary stage on the route to sexual maturity (the sort of journey eschewed by Ennis and Jack in Proulx's story). She tells us that adolescent sex is avoided because '[you] figured it was smart to wait until you hit the big city' (van Herk, 1990: 26). None the less in this country/city opposition, the rural areas are not themselves desexualized, but like the Wyoming of *Brokeback Mountain* they are associated with both purity and sexuality, even, in this case, depravity. We are told, for example, that 'the furtive gropings of Edberg boys were dangerously innocent' (van Herk 1990: 26), but, in relation to the local population of Mennonites, that 'innocence becomes its own corruption' (van Herk 1990: 28). If sex is associated with the city, there are still contradictions inherent in such representations of the countryside.

While van Herk focuses on female sexuality, she none the less appears anxious to avoid foregrounding her *own* experiences, and consequently her text shares the reticence traditionally associated with the prairie novel (Kroetsch 1989). However, her motives for holding back about her personal experiences may be rather complex. Sexual geographies cannot be divorced from gendered histories. Throughout history women have been represented either as objects of masculine heterosexual desire, or, if exceptionally as desiring subjects, then as culpable. Van Herk is responding to this stereotyping. This is not to say that she ignores her own (hetero)sexuality altogether, but rather reduces its significance. She evades the crude sensationalism of autobiography and the voyeuristic eroticism of female revelations when she passes over much of her young adult life and marriage, 'swearing you will never return to your sites of seduction and rage' (van Herk 1990: 53). Encounters in Calgary ('You need to encounter practice in the geography of lust' (van Herk 1990: 73)) occupy only two paragraphs inserted between descriptions of the city's 'crossword puzzle of street' (van Herk 1990: 72) and of its freeways, apparently leading nowhere. Paradoxically, female sexuality is both the central focus of van Herk's text, and, in relation to herself, an issue which she chooses to address only indirectly.

In the final section of *Places Far From Ellesmere* van Herk rereads and reappropriates *Anna Karenin* – a classic representation of woman as culturally oppressed and blameworthy – through both the landscape and her own experiences, and rereads the landscape and her own experiences through Tolstoy's novel. Ellesmere Island becomes therefore a space in which van Herk can not only reinvent herself, but also Anna Karenin, and at the same time re-examine her own society and its values. As she observes, 'Terror of women = terror of the north' (van Herk 1990: 123). In this section of the book, van Herk responds most directly to the fear of women as desiring sexual subjects. She equates the marginalization of female sexuality with the geographical margins, which may then function as sites of resistance.

In her depictions of the landscape, van Herk exploits and adapts familiar tropes and stereotypes of gendered landscape. Women are conventionally associated with the landscape: they are there to be conquered and explored, colonized and exploited. But Ellesmere is represented as being beyond such abuses. By rereading the novel in this context, van Herk hopes to liberate its heroine. This frozen landscape at the extremities of the world is not reinterpreted as frigidity but rather equated with the sort of freedom, remoteness and unpossessibility which van Herk wants to ascribe to women. It is in this sense that the landscape has transformative power. In the final section of *Places Far From Ellesmere*, *Anna Karenin*, its heroine, and the clearly feminized landscape (described variously as 'no one's mistress' (van Herk 1990:

# INTRODUCTION

139) or as 'this islanded woman' (van Herk 1990: 143)) become themselves the objects of the author-narrator's desire. For example, after describing the windswept and unruly Arctic poppies, van Herk continues:

> If this were a novel you would spend an afternoon picking them, picking them, hours and hours of gathering enough to strew, to cover thickly the bed, the sleeping bag, the pallet fit for a middle-heighted, middle-weighted woman to recline, and when you do, lie together, those flowers pressed against your skin will stain it with their Arctic ink, a bluish-black, the blood of permafrost. A bed of Arctic poppies on Ellesmere, and a lover to read their ink.
> 
> (van Herk 1990: 106–107).

Van Herk's stream-of-consciousness technique allows her to make loose associations between the sensuous pleasures of reading, exploration, and self-discovery. The sexuality of this imaginary encounter is only *suggested* by the metaphorical language of the narrative. It is not commented upon explicitly. Either deliberately or unconsciously, van Herk holds back from drawing conclusions. The longing described here is not fully articulated, and it seems she may not take it with her when she leaves.

Unlike the Wyoming of *Brokeback Mountain*, Ellesmere is represented by van Herk as uninhabited space, which has no language or culture of its own. It is, in a sense, a blank canvas. For van Herk it is full of possibilities. Yet, like her rereading of *Anna Karenin*, this representation is an act of reappropriation, although in this case a potentially exploitative one. In much of her fictional and critical writing, van Herk has been concerned with reclaiming *as a woman* the male colonized spaces of the West and the Arctic (see van Herk 1981, 1986, 1992; and also Howells 1996). There is a complex and layered centre–margin dynamic at work in *Places Far From Ellesmere*. Van Herk is responding to Canada's marginal position within North America, and to the marginality of Edmonton and Calgary in relation to central Canada. Yet at the same time the Arctic is itself marginal to southern Canada. In *Places Far From Ellesmere* the island's Inuit history is completely ignored, as is its status as a park reserve in the Nunavut Settlement Area (a status which is currently still under negotiation). Indeed Ellesmere seems to be regarded in this text almost as if it were simply Canada's 'backyard'. This representation of the Arctic might be contrasted to that in Percy Adlon's 1991 film *Salmonberries* (set in Alaska) in which a cultural encounter between the Old and New Worlds is once again figured as an erotic encounter between two women, but one in which ethnicity is addressed rather than pushed aside (illustrated for example in the scene in which the central character, a woman called Kotzebue, stands on a table in a crowded Berlin bar and falteringly shouts out 'Hey! Hey! I understand you. I'm Eskimo. I'm Eskimo. I'm an Eskimo').

# INTRODUCTION

These two examples, both taken from contemporary fiction, are by no means representative of the many different kinds of de-centred sexualities which the essays in this volume will explore. But they are illustrative of the complex relationships which can exist between marginal spaces and sexualities, and of just some of their dangers as well as power. Both *Brokeback Mountain* and *Places Far From Ellesmere* challenge masculine heteronormativity. In both texts, culturally marginal locations – the North American West, the Arctic – are represented as spaces in which sexualities can be powerfully articulated or rearticulated. Before drawing out these questions in more abstract terms and relating them to the contents of the book, we need to outline some of the broader points of comparison between the two texts.

Both of these texts reveal some of the dangers of simply replicating the hierarchies of power of the geographical and cultural centres: *Brokeback Mountain* in its marginalization of women; *Places Far From Ellesmere* in its appropriation of territories belonging to another people. Neither text fully contests all of what is referred to, in a different context later in this volume, as the 'defining orthodoxies' or exploitative politics of the dominant discourse(s). Both to some extent replicate hegemonic power structures. Furthermore, if we accept Alan Sinfield's controversial criticisms of the democratizing tendencies of metropolitan relationships (in the first essay in this collection), neither text offers examples of relationships which accommodate hierarchies of power – Ennis and Jack in *Brokeback Mountain* are both of similar age, class and education; Aritha van Herk is concerned to emphasize the points of resemblance rather than difference between herself, Anna Karenin, and the feminized and sexualized Ellesmere Island.

Furthermore, while our own readings of these texts draw out the similarities between them – we argue that in both texts, location is crucial to the exploration of sexuality – we have to be aware of the limitations of our own approach. Certainly both *Brokeback Mountain* and *Places Far From Ellesmere* focus on in-between spaces – areas of North America beyond the metropolitan centres which have not been adequately represented politically or culturally. Such in-between zones have often hitherto been stereotyped as either desexualized or as degenerate, or even as both at the same time; they have been unevenly or even contradictorily eroticized. Yet it is crucial that this book tries to avoid replicating the same old blind-spots and drawing artificial and distorting parallels between spaces and localities which, while they may offer us an opportunity to step outside of the dominant ideologies of the centre and to resist colonizing or globalizing impulses in the representation (political and cultural) of sexualities, are in fact very different from each other. It is, as we have suggested, a failing on van Herk's part that she represents Ellesmere Island as being in some sense 'beyond' the political and cultural parameters of central Canada even as she draws implicit parallels between the Arctic and the prairies. The essays in this volume focus on what might be seen as 'core' countries, but not upon core positions within those countries. The book examines a wide range of marginal spaces and in-between zones, from the American South and Midwest to Canada and Mexico, from rural and provincial England in the nineteenth and early twentieth centuries to the Celtic fringes of the post-devolution United Kingdom, from the industrialized regional centres of modern Britain and the London suburbs of the late 1970s to the Australian outback. Each of these localities has to be considered in its own right, and the strengths of this volume must lie in the militant particularism of the individual essays.

Our readings of *Brokeback Mountain* and *Places Far From Ellesmere* have raised a series of questions – questions of power and danger, of the ambivalent politics and representations of de-centring sexualities – which will be investigated at greater length in the course of this volume. These questions can be summarized as follows. How are sexualities structured around centres and margins? What dialectical relations exist between different spaces, and between centres and margins? What political tensions operate between sexual centres and margins? (This question relates not only to politics of sexuality but also to gender, class, ethnicity and nationality.) What role do (or could) spatial margins play in a broader economy of sexualities? This in turn raises questions about the legitimacy and stability of metropolitan sexualities in geographical, social and political margins. What are the dangers of de-centring sexualities? Where does its power lie, and how can de-centring sexualities be critically transformative?

## Politics and representations beyond the metropolis

*De-centring Sexualities* is a multi- and cross-disciplinary volume, which brings together new research on politics and representations of sexualities in non-metropolitan contexts from a range of different fields, including cultural geography, social and legal studies, environmental planning, cultural studies, literature and history. Its central focus is on North America (Canada, the United States and Mexico) and Western Europe (particularly Britain and Ireland), but it extends as far as Australia. And perhaps inevitably, given the importance of queer contributions to recent theoretical debates, the emphasis falls on homosexuality rather than heterosexuality (although the simple opposition of homosexuality and heterosexuality is often challenged).

The chapters in Part I are concerned with socio-spacial hierarchies and dynamics in representations and constructions of sexualities. In Chapter 1, Alan Sinfield focuses on the transformative potential of non-metropolitan sexualities. Sinfield argues that although contemporary gay and lesbian culture defines sexuality in metropolitan terms, this is a limitation rather than a strength. He suggests that, at least in the metropolitan context, two apparently contradictory models of sexuality dominate, which he terms the assimilationist (seen most clearly in same-sex marriages) and the transgressive (typified by the promiscuity of the ghetto). Sinfield

# INTRODUCTION

posits that both models assume that gayness is a question of identity and promote interaction only amongst equals. Non-metropolitan cultures, on the other hand, are more likely to recognize the existence of, and thus accommodate hierarchies of, class, race, gender and age. Sinfield's conclusion is itself dangerous, in the sense of controversial – he contends that if gay culture begins to move away from 'democratic' metropolitan models and acknowledge that power is sexy, it can finally begin to understand fully and thus to combat exploitation.

A crucial point raised by Sinfield in the course of his essay, is the dominance of the United States in gay ideology – in global terms, the position occupied by northwest Europe is a marginal one. Yet if, as Dennis Altman suggests in Chapter 2, the gay centre has shifted in the last few decades to North America from Britain, the real impact of this transfer on the rest of the world may not actually be all that great. Altman's approach is very different to Sinfield's: Altman illustrates his argument not by looking at hierarchies of power *per se* but by examining what he calls the 'triple marginality' of gay people in the Australian provinces such as Queensland. There, people are marginalized because of their sexuality, because of their remoteness from Sydney and the other centres of Australian gay culture, and because of Australia's colonial legacy, which constructed it as a country on the margins. In the last two decades, increasing toleration of gay people within Australian society has paralleled the emergence of Australia as an important nation within the Asia-Pacific. Altman believes that in this context the transformative power of multiculturalism – the acceptance of diversity – can counteract the negative impact of consumerism and globalization. Urban centres still serve important imaginary functions for geographically marginalized gays, but the reality is that with more toleration, gay ghettos, and even gay 'identities' of the type criticized by Sinfield, need no longer exist.

Chapters 3 and 4 approach the issue of sexual hierarchies and dynamics from a rather different direction to either Sinfield's or Altman's. Both address postmodernist challenges to stable notions of subjectivity and sexual identity. Kate Chedgzoy looks at the interaction of religion, region and sexual identity in two very different sorts of texts: the narrative of her own childhood in a Baptist community in South Wales and the independent film *Butterfly Kiss* set in the North of England. She examines the significance of religious motifs in these texts: in particular the centrality of desire and longing, and the importance of 'confession', the quest or pilgrimage, and spiritual and sexual transcendence. Chedgzoy's study of the similarities between religious fervour and lesbian sexuality enables her to explore the often treacherous territory of sadomasochism, and to offer her own formulation of what constitutes the 'lesbian sublime'.

The dangers rather than transformative possibilities of marginality provide the starting point for Barry Langford's study of suburbia. Langford illustrates that surburbia is often constructed negatively as feminine or emasculated (debased, repressed and perverse) and in opposition to the positive masculinity of the metropolitan. Langford

# INTRODUCTION

is concerned with subject formation, and the motif of the journey (in this case from the suburb to the city) re-emerges. Centring his argument on Hanif Kureishi's novel *The Buddha of Suburbia* (1990), Langford suggests that Kureishi does not rehabilitate the suburban as a site of resistance, but rather celebrates its ambiguity and hybridity which is paralleled in the protagonist's ethnicity and (bi)sexuality. None the less, while the metropolitan is itself sexualized – it functions as the fugitive or elusive object of desire – Langford's reading indicates that the novel ends by destabilizing the suburban/metropolitan opposition. Paradoxically suburbia can be seen as more metropolitan than the city it ostensibly seeks to imitate. Ultimately the suburbs are revealed to be at the heart of the city.

David Bell's essay (Chapter 5), which broadens the volume's focus to include heterosexuality as well as homosexuality and bisexuality, can be usefully read as a counterpoint to Sinfield's emphasis on what Bell dismisses as 'metrosex'. It introduces a short subgrouping of essays which shift the book's focus onto negative and positive representations and constructions of rural sexualities in North America and Britain. Concentrating on various manifestations of what he calls white-trash erotics, as well as on bestiality and naturism, Bell shows us that, depending on the perspective of the viewer, the rural can be seen as either naive or depraved, straight or queer. He concludes, however, that it is not enough simply to describe the way certain socio-sexual sexualities are represented – we also have to consider who is responsible for the representation, and for whom it is aimed. Taking this further, we also need to address the question of why a representation occurs, and what effect it has.

This is what Richard Phillips does in Chapter 6 in his exploration of imagined geographies and sexual politics in two case studies taken from the nineteenth and twentieth centuries. Phillips examines parallels between W.T. Stead's 'Maiden Tribute' Campaign of 1885, which helped secure the success of the Criminal Law Amendment Act in which the age of consent for girls was raised to 16, and John Willis's 1975 documentary *Johnny Go Home* which ostensibly functioned to draw attention to the plight of homeless young people, but which, Phillips reveals, indirectly contributed to the maintenance of a differential age of consent for homosexual males. As strategies devised to gain reader/audience sympathy for their political interventions, both media campaigns drew on popular stereotypes of the metropolitan as dangerous and corrupt and adapted narratives of sexual journeys which formulate migration to the city as a descent from innocence into depravation. Phillips pays attention to the specific socioeconomic factors that contributed to the migration of young people in both of his case-studies, factors which were underexplored by the journalists and television producers at the time. By pointing out the way in which the excessive regulation of those who are marginalized by society – those who are young, working class, female and/or homosexual – can be seen as a form of scapegoating, Phillips is able to conclude that discursive constructions of the metropolitan and the rural/provincial/suburban/regional have dangerous political implications and are part of a larger economy of power and exploitation.

Like Phillips's chapter, the essays by Shuttleton and Rowanchild (Chapters 7 and 8) also address issues of representation and appropriation, although in both these essays the emphasis is on the literary and the autobiographical rather than the strictly historical. Taking up Bell's observations concerning the meanings of nature within popular sites of rural erotics, Shuttleton illustrates how a pastoral discourse has served both to authenticate and to disrupt (through camp irony) the counter-assertion that male–male love is natural. Focussing upon Edwardian to immediate post-war literature (Firbank, Reid, Forster and Vidal), but within a framework addressing recent cinematic nostalgic reworking of pastoral as 'gay heritage', he acknowledges the importance of pastoral conventions for the representation of male same-sex romance, but questions any simplistic representation of pastoral as a transhistorically 'gay' liberatory genre. He suggests that a queer historicism should not flinch from exposing the diverse politics of gay pastoral, which has served a diversity of ideological functions from an elite romantic Hellenism to the utopian socialists, and from the liberal humanist or democratic, to the conservative, the anti-feminist, effemophobic and even fascist.

The politics of pastoral representation link Shuttleton's argument to the next chapter. Here we see how Anne Lister, a wealthy female landowner living in Halifax, a provincial centre in early nineteenth-century England, fashioned her own sexual experiences in her complex negotiation of social hierarchies and power relations. Rowanchild demonstrates that Lister's economic and social privileges were crucial to her exploration of her lesbian identity. None the less, while Lister cultivated her public role in society, not only playing an active part in the management of her estate but also, as a staunch conservative, openly engaging in political debate, both her sexual fantasies and her landscaping projects reveal a desire for privacy and rural retreat. This apparent contradiction can be explained by the dangers to which Lister was exposed by her marginal sexuality. As Rowanchild's study reveals, in this case pastoral fantasies serve a transformative function, offering a defence against the very real threats of condemnation, harassment or even incarceration.

Sue Willman looks at marginalization of Mexican lesbians, not only in relation to North America but also within the humanitarian, feminist, and gay liberation movements and the left-wing political groups within Mexico itself. Her essay (Chapter 9) is based on interviews with three members of the Mexican lesbian network, Entace Lesbico: an activist, the editor of the national lesbian magazine, and the founder of the national lesbian archive. Willman looks at the particular geographical, religious, social, economic and political factors which have resulted in the 'semi-clandestine' nature of lesbian activity in Mexico in particular, and Latin America in general. Although the familiar pattern of migration to metropolitan centres and coastal resorts emerges in this context (partly as a result of US influence), this is less typical

# INTRODUCTION

of lesbians than gay men, while within the provinces, poverty, lack of funding and the presence of the military are cited as contributing to lesbian invisibility. Fear is another factor – Mexico has one the highest rates of homophobic murders in the world, and the police intimidation is largely unchecked. However, cultural isolation is also crucial – Willman notes the marked absence of lesbian writing available in Spanish. Willman pays particular attention to ways in which lesbians have used their marginal positions as sites of resistance. She describes their ambivalent relationship with metropolitan (United States and European) models of sexual identity and sexuality politics. On the one hand Mexican lesbians have empowered themselves by borrowing from Western models, on the other hand they have resisted simple emulation of those models. She concludes that one possible way out of the margins for Mexican lesbians is joining forces with other groups such as the Zapatistas (the political movement for the indigenous peoples).

Migrations from the country to the city, discussed in rather different contexts by Altman and Phillips, form a starting point for William J. Spurlin's essay (Chapter 10). Spurlin challenges the cultural domination of the US seaboard cities from within North America through his analysis of queer literature and culture in the American South and Midwest. If New York, San Francisco and Los Angeles are perceived as the metropolitan centres for lesbians and gays from the American Heartland it is none the less the case that rural queer culture and politics are often marginalized or completely ignored. The urban coastal centres are constructed as the primary or possibly the only locations from which lesbians and gays can articulate an 'authentic' queer identity or fully participate in queer life. Spurlin's central argument is that queer identity should not be reduced to sexual difference alone, and that it is now imperative to theorize the role of what he refers to as geopolitical spatialization. In order to do this, he not only looks at the dangers of stereotyping the cultural landscape of the Midwest as pastoral, innocent, 'wholesome' and conservative, but also outlines some of the historical and social factors which led to the formation of queer communities in the seaboard cities and considers the dynamics of oppression and privilege which have resulted in their position of dominance. Spurlin's examination of reformulations of Midwestern location in literature and culture illustrates some of the multiplicity of ways in which it can function as a site of political resistance to heterosexism and homophobia and also as a mode of critique against the coastal/mid-continent opposition which often divides North American queers.

Angelia R. Wilson's study of homosexual life in rural America (Chapter 11) follows on from Spurlin's, but concentrates largely on individual experiences of homosexual life between the 1950s and the 1970s put together from gay and lesbian archives (letters and publications), along with some personal interviews. Like Spurlin, she considers the historical and social contexts (the impact of the Second World War, the findings of the Kinsey Report, the conservative backlash and the Civil Rights Movement). And again, like Spurlin, Wilson traces a pattern of rural

# INTRODUCTION

isolation, exclusion and homophobia along with migration to urban centres. Complementing Bell's study of the homosexual and homophile naturist movements, Wilson looks at the lesbian communes which were established in rural areas at a time when the Women's Movement was at its height. She points out that while such women-only communities often functioned to empower their members, the dangers of such existences include the extent to which they operated a policy of exclusion (often extending even to male children), and also their vulnerability to harassment from the local population (unless a state of interdependence was carefully and deliberately negotiated). However, Wilson concludes that escape to the city and separatism were not the only alternatives available to lesbians and gay men – many people in rural areas continue to live either fully of partially integrated into society.

Gordon Brent Ingram (Chapter 12) considers marginalization, racism and homophobia in Canadian history and its implications for public planning policy. Like Mexico, Canada can be seen to be influenced by developments in the United States, but the situation there is none the less radically different. In his study of British Columbia and Pacific Canada, Ingram reveals how non-metropolitan or 'hinterland' societies did not escape from Victorian controls of sexuality, but rather reproduced centre/margin dynamics. He argues that in this context the sort of homosexual isolation discussed by Spurlin and Wilson in relation to rural areas in the United States was in part the result of the marginalization of people of non-British and non-European origin. Charting social and cultural maps, and what he refers to as 'contests over homoerotic spaces', Ingram examines the transitions through colonialism, neocolonialism, nationalism, globalization and post-colonialism. One of the effects of racism is that intercultural alliances proved impossible until very recently. For example, one of the failings of the gay liberation movement (and the gay activist groups which were its immediate successors) was that it did not challenge anglophile dominance. Ingram coins the term 'pretty-near-talk' to describe the sort of communication and sexual contact necessary for forming cultural and subsequently political alliances. Unlike Altman, Ingram does not regard globalization as a danger, but argues that it has and still does work alongside multicultural queer culture in countering homophobia and dismantling colonialism and neocolonialism. Although, as Ingram suggests, public policy on sexuality issues currently progresses unevenly, it is this combination of globalization and multiculturalism, along with an established historical tradition of activism, which has resulted in British Columbia providing some of the best conditions for sexual minorities in the world.

Part IV concentrates on the British and Irish experience, politics and literature. In 1997 Scotland and Wales voted for political devolution; Northern Ireland voted for its own assembly the following year. These events provide a context for the essays by Lynne Pearce, Vincent Quinn and Edwin Morgan. As Pearce explains in Chapter 13, such studies are a crucial but under-researched aspect of the larger post-colonialist project, because historically Great Britain not only exploited other nations, but, as

# INTRODUCTION

the so-called United Kingdom, also artificially brought together disparate smaller countries under one flag. All three of these studies suggest the extent to which regional differences within Britain and Ireland can inflect sexual identities.

Pearce examines representations of romantic relationships and speculates on the impact of devolution on sexual politics. Like Quinn in the following essay, Pearce notes that the rhetoric of colonialism depends on heterosexual tropes, but she also argues that the discourse of desire is crucial to notions of patriotism and nationalism. National identity is validated within many 'marginal' cultures above sexual or gendered identity and is often apparently threatened by what are perceived to be deviant sexual choices. Literature from the so-called Celtic fringes can be read on one level as promoting or endorsing heterosexual reproductive sexual endogamy. This provides Pearce with her vision of the dangers of a devolution in which countries or regions retain a defensive marginal identity, characterized by exclusionary (sexual) politics and no capacity for change. On the other hand Irish writing in particular (but some Welsh writing also) supplies Pearce with examples of literature which depicts more transgressive sexual collaborations both behind and across the various borders. As Quinn also points out, preconceptions about racial or national purity can result in the victimization of individuals (figured as traitors) who are involved in homosexual and/or mixed-religion sexual relations. Certainly much of the writing which Pearce discusses tends to exclude homosexual relationships except at a token level (suggesting tolerance rather than conceptual refiguration of the interaction of national and sexual desires). This exposes what Pearce considers to be the greatest challenge to the nations on the threshhold of devolution, how to avoid simply reproducing the ideological and material assumptions and prejudices of the historical centre.

Quinn's essay (Chapter 14) develops key themes raised by Pearce, in particular the tension created between national allegiances and other forms of self-definition. Looking at the gendering of national identities in Ireland, seen for example in the poetry of Seamus Heaney (in which Ireland is represented as feminine, England masculine), or in the sexualized narratives centred around Derry/Londonderry as the maiden city, Quinn suggests that what he calls the myths of Irishness have marginalized gay men. He goes on to ask what space can exist for the exploration of sexual identity when other forms of political, religious and gendered identity are overdetermined. It is in this context that the concept of coming-out re-emerges and is redefined. Challenging, or at any rate refining an earlier contention by Sinfield that coming out is a metropolitan phenomenon, Quinn dismisses the idea that it has the same meaning throughout Britain (far less throughout the world). In a specifically Ulster context, coming out – which Quinn argues is a process rather than an end – creates lesbian and gay identities which may involve the reformulation although not the abandonment of sectarian loyalties. Quinn's study also responds to Altman's, in that he argues that consumerism and globalization are not equally pervasive in all

Western countries and regions – even within the United Kingdom very different patterns emerge.

(Male) fantasies of possessing a city gendered as masculine connect Langford's earlier study of suburbia with the final chapter, Edwin Morgan's autobiographical account of his life as a gay man in Glasgow. The attractions of the late night encounter with the Glasgow 'hard man' become almost a symbol of its power and the danger. This essay combines an account of Morgan's own life with a discussion of the changing attitudes towards homosexuality in Glasgow in the twentieth century. Morgan uses examples of his previously published and forthcoming poetry to illustrate his retelling of his childhood in Glasgow, his experiences as a gay man in the armed forces during the war, and his post-war experiences as an academic and internationally acclaimed poet. Morgan's essay, like Quinn's, also connects back to Altman's: once again North American and centralized models of sexuality are challenged. Morgan's description of life in a Scottish city distanced culturally as well as geographically from London, the metropolitan centre of the British Isles, charts its transformation from a site of repression into a cosmopolitan civic centre in which homosexuality is becoming more widely accepted and accommodated. Once again the in-between spaces and geographic margins become sites of transformation.

Together, the chapters in this volume explore a range of representations and experiences, linked by degrees of divergence from centred sexualities and by a complex mixture of differences and power relations. The chapters flesh out our claim that de-centring sexualities charts an ambivalent politics, marked both by danger and power, in a post-liberatory politics which does not simply shadow hegemonic sexualities.

## References

Bell, D. and Valentine, G. (eds) (1995), *Mapping Desire*, London: Routledge.
Bhabba, H.K. (1994) *The Location of Culture*, London: Routledge.
Bleys, R. (1996) *The Geography of Perversion. Male-to-Male Sexual Behaviour Outside the West and the Ethnographic Imagination 1750–1918*, London: Cassell.
Braidotti, R. (1994) *Nomadic Subjects: Embodiment and Sexual Difference in Contemporary Feminist Theory*, New York: Columbia University Press.
Butler, J. (1991) *Gender Trouble: Feminism and the Subversion of Identity*, London: Routledge.
Douglas, M. (1966) *Purity and Danger: An Analysis of Concepts of Pollution and Taboo*. London: Routledge and Kegan Paul.
Fellows, W. (1996) *Farm Boys: Lives of Gay Men From the Rural Midwest*, Madison: Wisconsin University Press.
Foucault, M. (1978) *The History of Sexuality, Volume 1*, London: Penguin.
Fuss, D. (ed.) (1991), *Inside/Out: Lesbian Theories, Gay Theories*, London: Routledge.
Howells, C.A. (1996) 'Aritha Van Herk's *No Fixed Address*: An Exploration of Prairie Space as Fictional Space', *The London Journal of Canadian Studies* 12: 4–19.

# INTRODUCTION

Hyam, R. (1990) *Sexuality and Empire*, Manchester: Manchester University Press.

Ingram, B. (ed.) (1997) *Queers in Space*, Seattle: Bay Press.

Kabbani, R. (1986) *Imperial Fictions*, London: Pandora.

Kroetsch, R. (1989) 'The Fear of Women in Prairie Fiction: An Erotics of Space', reprinted in *The Lovely Treachery of Words*, Toronto: Oxford University Press: 73–83.

McClintock, A. (1995) *Imperial Fictions: Race, Gender and Sexuality in the Colonial Contest*, London: Routledge.

Mason, M. (1985) *The Making of Victorian Sexuality*, Oxford: Oxford University Press.

Milbourne, P. (ed.) (1997) *Rural Others*, London: Cassell.

New, W.H. (1972) *Articulating West*, Toronto: New Press.

O'Carroll, I. and Collins E. (1995) *Lesbian and Gay Visions of Ireland*, London: Cassell.

Probyn, E. (1993) *Sexing the Self: Gendering Positions in Cultural Studies*, London: Routledge.

Proulx, A. (1998) *Brokeback Mountain*, London: Fourth Estate.

Riordan, M. (1996) *Out Our Way: Gay and Lesbian Life in the Country*, Toronto: Between the Lines.

Turner, V. (1969) *The Ritual Process*, Chicago: Aldine.

Van Herk, A. (1981) *The Tent Peg*, Toronto: McClelland and Stewart-Bantam.

—— (1986) *No Fixed Address: An Amorous Journey*, London: Virago.

—— (1990) *Places Far From Ellesmere, A Geografictione: Explorations on Site*, Alberta: Red Deer College Press.

—— (1992) 'Women Writers and the Prairie: Spies in an Indifferent Landscape', reprinted in *A Frozen Tongue*, Sydney: Dangaroo Press: 139–51.

Young, R. (1995) *Colonial Desire: Hybridity in Theory, Culture and Desire*, London: Routledge.

# Part I

# NON-METROPOLITAN SEXUALITIES

# 1

# THE PRODUCTION OF GAY AND THE RETURN OF POWER

*Alan Sinfield*

The scope of 'metropolitan' at the present time is not altogether precise, but that, I think, makes it the right term:

(1) It refers to a city in relation to its colonies; lately, in post-colonial contexts, it means the global centres of capital.
(2) However, it is used also to designate a capital or principal cities in a nation-state, and thus permits an awareness that global interaction has produced local versions of the metropolis in large cities all over the world – so the metropolitan gay model will be found in Johannesburg, Rio de Janeiro and Delhi, as well as New York and London, in interaction with traditional local, non-metropolitan, models.
(3) Conversely, subordinated groups living at or near the centres of capital, and specially non-white minorities, may be in some aspects non-metropolitan; a Filipino living in New York may share some ideas and attitudes with people living in the Philippines.

Overwhelmingly, we sense the metropolitan as powerful and imperialist, but actually there is movement in both directions. For we are talking about a relation. Metropolitan and non-metropolitan define each other – not just semantically, but in the real-world circulation of imperialism, commerce, tourism, and cultural exchange.

I want to explore some of the possibilities that appear when we bring into focus the *junctures between* metropolitan and non-metropolitan. This will entail abstracting from the fulness of experience, and dealing briskly with sensitive and intimate matters. If such a project can be justified, it will not be through its fidelity to people's immediate lives but in terms of the extending of the conceptual frameworks through which diverse peoples organize their experience.

If there is one thing that characterizes metropolitan lesbian and gay identities, it is 'coming out'. However, the term is misleading, in so far as it allows the supposition that this kind of gayness was always there, waiting to be uncovered. It suggests that we really always knew about it, individually and as a culture, but failed to own up to it. However, for Filipino culture, as Martin F. Manalansan IV has observed it, coming out is not the move that people are waiting to make; it is specifically foreign. Filipinos regard declarations of sexual involvements as not just shaming but unnecessary; one informant says: 'I know who I am and most people, including my family, know about me – without any declaration' (Manalansan IV 1995: 434). A similar point is made by Connie S. Chan about lesbian relations among East-Asian American women, for whom there is no identity outside the family and 'no concept of a sexual identity or of external sexual expression in the Asian part of the culture beyond the familial expectation of procreation' (Chan 1997: 244).

It is easy to see the limitations in this way of thinking, but in Chan's view there may be some advantages: 'the East Asian cultural restrictions upon open expression of sexuality may actually create less of a dichotomization of heterosexual versus homosexual behavior. Instead, given the importance of the concept of having only private expression of sexuality, there could actually be more allowance for fluidity within a sexual behavioral continuum' (p. 247). Provocatively, Chan deploys in her title phrases used to prevent gays in the US military from coming out: 'Don't Ask, Don't Tell, Don't Know'.

My thought here is not that these ways of regarding same-sex passion are better, or even that they are properly described. But they do indicate that non-metropolitan modes of relating may be validated in other cultures. Metropolitan gay and lesbian concepts should be regarded, therefore, not as denoting the ultimate achievement of human sexuality, but as something we have been producing – we homosexuals and we heterosexuals – in determinate economic and social conditions. Filipino and East-Asian modes also, of course, are produced. The means of this production is that urgent circulation of contested representations which we call culture. I approach my topic initially through a text set in the metropolitan heartland of New York: David Leavitt's *The Lost Language of Cranes*. This influential novel was published in 1986 and filmed for television in 1992; Leavitt's evident project is to sort out the good gays from the unfortunate approximations.

The older generation in the novel finds it hard to benefit from recent improvements in gay selfhood. Owen, who is married to Rose, is unable to talk to anyone about his yearning for gay sex; even at a pornographic cinema, which he visits regularly, he is too ashamed and frightened to speak to anyone or to follow up potential contacts. Two less prominent characters, Derek and Geoffrey, are old-style queens reminiscent of Oscar Wilde; they cultivate British accents, speak of men as 'girls', prepare a dinner in which all the food is blue, and include in their circle cultured Europeans who go to Tangiers where it's easy to buy young boys.

All this is regarded with a mixture of distaste and disbelief by the younger generation, represented centrally by Philip, the gay son of Owen and Rose. He had difficulty coming to terms with himself as an adolescent but, the narration suggests, he's doing it more or less right now. He postpones coming out to his parents until he believes he has achieved a gayness he can be proud of: 'I wanted to wait until I could show you that a homosexual life could be a good thing' (Leavitt 1987: 169). This involves, above all, having a presentable partner – 'he had counted on Eliot's presence in their living room to justify all he had said to them, to justify his life' (p. 198). For Philip finds little satisfaction in cruising or porn movies; he meets partners among friends at dinner parties. He has a favourite gay bar, but there is no backroom. It is 'a friendly place, very social, a place where people go who really are comfortable with being gay, and know it's a lot more than a matter of who you sleep with' (p. 155).

Eliot, Philip's prized partner, proves unreliable. Probably he is damaged by a prematurely queer upbringing – it is possible to become too casual about gayness, to the point of irresponsibility. Also there is unease around Eliot's superior wealth and connections. However, the resolution, for Philip, is already to hand. Brad, an old school friend, is of the same age, class, race and educational background; they enjoy spending time together. In due course they find that sex is a natural part of that, so no sticky, sexually explicit pick-up scene is required. When they first kiss, 'long and lovingly', it is 'spontaneous, without thought' (p. 311).

In outline, the same principles are disclosed through Jerene, who is African-American. Her adoptive parents – black, middle-class Republicans – reject her when she tells them she is a lesbian. She remains none the less nice, good and wise. However, her new partner is perceived by Philip and Brad as rather a pain, in the manner of characters in Tennessee Williams's *The Glass Menagerie*: 'If Laura's looks were Laura Wingfield – fragile and transparent as a tiny glass animal – her temperament was pure Amanda: loud and brash and indiscreet; full of hype and bombast; good-natured, loving, easy to hurt' (p. 251). This positions Laura as dominating mother posing as needful daughter; Jerene is subdued and silenced by her. These women have not yet (the reader is likely to conclude) arrived at a fully compatible, happy-ever-after partnership.

Meanwhile Owen, prompted by Philip's coming out, does his best to catch up. He tries out the idea that everyone is bisexual. No, Philip says; some people are, but 'I think this whole bisexual thing can become an excuse, a way of avoiding committing yourself, or admitting the truth. It means you can duck out when the going gets rough' (p. 232). Owen comes out to Rose. It goes badly, but he is now determined, and takes up with another married man of comparable age and class. So he too has an 'appropriate' partner. He wants to go on living with Rose nonetheless, but it seems unlikely that she will allow this. Philip, before he knew of Owen's gayness, told him: 'you're basically heterosexual, and that should be what defines your lifestyle' (p. 233). If Owen is going to be gay, his lifestyle will have to change accordingly.

If Leavitt's version of the metropolitan gay model appears strenuously devised, it is because he is promoting one position in a cardinal, ongoing dispute. The contrary position values multiple and anonymous partners. The two poles may be schematized as:

monogamy vs. promiscuity
lifestyle vs. sexual explicitness
assimilation vs. the ghetto.

Currently in the metropolis the dispute is often framed as a question about 'gay marriage'.

Positive representations of the right-hand column are not so easy to find as one might suppose. Pornography tends to promote the idea of multiple and anonymous partners, but it does so from a less prestigious sector of the gay cultural apparatus, thereby allowing the inference that the opposition is between good and bad, or at least respectable and dissolute. Samuel R. Delany, in *The Motion of Light in Water*, seeks to validate the right-hand column. There was a bar, cottage and truck scene in the 1950s, he says, but a post-Stonewall orgy at the baths was qualitatively different:

> what *this* experience said was that there was a population – not of individual homosexuals, some of whom now and then encountered, or that those encounters could be human and fulfilling in their way – not of hundreds, not of thousands, but rather of millions of gay men, and that history had, actively and already, created for us whole galleries of institutions, good and bad, to accommodate our sex.
>
> (Delany 1990: 267)

Leavitt's pitch is that we should have grown out of all that now, though he and Delany share a supposition that gays are a distinct population and that they can and should justify themselves.

Of course, these matters have become considerably more difficult since the onset of HIV and AIDS. Oscar Moore's *A Matter of Life and Sex* (1991) is one of many texts which suggest a correlation between the delights of multiple and anonymous partners and the fate, as it appears in the novel, of infection and death. For this reason, the most impressive anti-Leavitt representations are principled reassertions of multiple and anonymous partners in the face of AIDS. Larry Kramer, despite his own hostility to sleeping around, lets Mickey in *The Normal Heart* voice the case against abstention:

> I've spent fifteen years of my life fighting for our right to be free and make love whenever, wherever ... And you're telling me that all those years of being what gay stood for is wrong ... and I'm a murderer. We have been

so oppressed! Don't you remember how it was? Can't you see how important it is for us to love openly, without hiding and without guilt?

(Kramer 1986: 67)

Thom Gunn in his poem 'The Missing', in *The Man with Night Sweats* (1992: 80), reasserts a vision of unfettered sexual congress:

> Contact of friend led to another friend,
> Supple entwinement through the living mass
> Which for all that I knew might have no end,
> Image of an unlimited embrace.

Conversely, although characters in *The Lost Language of Cranes* mention AIDS, it doesn't bulk as large as one might expect. I think this is because Leavitt does not want readers to conclude that companionate sexual relations are good just because of the AIDS emergency.

Metropolitan lesbian and gay identities are strung out between these two extreme positions, then. However, I want to point out that the two parties share underlying beliefs. First, gayness should be boldly declared as an identity – contrary to, for instance, the Filipino and Asian assumptions I briefly invoked above. Second, this identity is so compelling that it makes *difference* irrelevant and inappropriate – at best invisible, at worst undesirable.

In *The Lost Language of Cranes* the ideal partner is similar to oneself – same class, background, income, age, ethnicity. In this respect, the Leavitt model is very like the dominant ideology of straight sexual pairing: the companionate marriage, as it has evolved from the 1920s endorsement of reciprocity in sexual pleasure through the 1950s pram-pushing hubby to the 1980s new man. Jerene is expected to have the same priorities as Philip. She does experience more difficulty, because unfortunately (as it appears) black families may be even less enlightened than white ones. Jerene takes on a white partner, but that is not presented as an issue or shown as creating any tension.

The counter-position, which I have elaborated through Mickey, Delany and Gunn, is strangely similar. Gayness is, again, an absolute condition, and the abundance of multiple and anonymous relationships submerges the particularity of this or that partner. Of course, among so many people there must be innumerable differences, but they are not significant. Not everyone is rich or beautiful on the dance floor in Andrew Holleran's pre-AIDS novel, *Dancer from the Dance*, but it doesn't matter:

> Archer Prentiss, who had no chin or hair; Spanish Lily, a tiny, wizened octoroon who lived with his blind mother in the Bronx and sold shoes in a local store – but who by night resembled Salome dancing for the head of

John the Baptist in peach-colored veils; Lavalava, a Haitian boy who modeled for *Vogue* till an editor saw him in the dressing room with an enormous penis where a vagina should have been; another man famous for a film he had produced and who had no wish to do anything else with his life – all of them mixed together on that square of blond wood and danced, without looking at anyone else, for one another.

(Holleran 1979: 43)

There may be plenty of difference, but it doesn't make any difference.

It is not incidental that the examples I have adduced are 'American'. The metropolitan imagery of gayness derives generally from the United States – or, to be more exact, from major cities there. It is common to observe that the word for 'gay' in countries such as Mexico is 'gay'; so it is in Europe, including Britain: the word was imported gradually, initially through privileged travellers such as Noël Coward, and then via GIs in the Second World War. Blue-jeans and T-shirts, short hair and moustaches are appropriated in the USA from ordinary male usage and specifically 'American' imagery – pioneer, rural, working-class, military. In Europe, these accoutrements of male gayness are second-hand, from 'American' gay culture. Drinking beer out of a can or a bottle is another recent instance. When the BBC got round to financing a gay film, in 1992, it was *The Lost Language of Cranes*, transposed by director Nigel Finch into a London context. Metropolitan/non-metropolitan, I have said, is a relation, and north-western Europe, even, is relatively marginal. Conversely, part of Philip's discovery of a proper gayness is the repudiation of English and European influences manifested by Derek and Geoffrey.

'America' supplies the ideology for the metropolitan gay model. The effacement of difference is founded in an ideology of opportunity, democracy and rights, which crosses into gay culture all too conveniently via Walt Whitman in the guise of a comradely, manly, sexual democracy. I argue in my book *Gay and After* (Sinfield 1998: chapter 2) that lesbians and gay men, in the USA particularly, have constituted themselves as something like an ethnic group claiming rights. As Steven Epstein observes, this ideology of rights appeals to 'the rules of the modern American pluralist myth, which portrays a harmonious competition among distinct social groups' (Epstein 1992: 282). How far that myth is to be trusted is a question far wider than queer politics: it is about how much we expect from the institutions through which capitalism and hetero-patriarchy are reproduced.

Lesbians have developed these topics in distinctive ways. The notion that women should be basing their relationships in reciprocity comes from some of the same sources and also, more importantly, from negotiations with feminism. In the 1970s feminists defined lesbianism as the way for women to abrogate traditional dependence on men and male power. 'Women-loving-women meant gentler, non-possessive, non-competitive, non-violent, nurturing and egalitarian relationships',

# THE PRODUCTION OF GAY AND THE RETURN OF POWER

Lynne Segal says (Segal 1994: 51–2). In the early 1980s still, Judith Halberstam observes, women

> tended not to represent their sexual practices, in lesbian feminist venues at least, as anything other than thoroughly proper, romantic, mutual and loving. … Even radical and fringe feminists like Valerie Solanas tended to cede sex to men, equate femininity with intimacy rather than sexuality and argue for the purity of lesbian sex as a full expression of feminism, egalitarianism and the joys of mutual desire untainted by the power dynamics inherent in patriarchal heterosexuality.
> (Halberstam 1997: 335–6)

What the egalitarian model is disallowing, for lesbians and gay men, is the realities and productivities of power in sexual relations. To be sure, few people suppose that it is possible to have a totally egalitarian relationship and, in practice, differences based on age, gender, class and race remain important. But the dominant ideology says that differentials are unfortunate and should be either avoided or overcome. That is the assumption I want to challenge.

The relevance of non-metropolitan sex–gender systems to all this is that elsewhere difference signifies differently. David F. Greenberg in *The Construction of Homosexuality* trawls through history and anthropology and finds more various opportunities for same-sex relations. He isolates three models, one of which he calls *egalitarian* – allowing the inference that metropolitan gay culture has been moving towards this. The other two models are structured on differences of *age* and *gender* (Greenberg 1998: Introduction). Stephen O. Murray takes up this tripartite framework: 'The "gay" or "modern" organization of homosexuality' is a change from traditional models. It 'breaks from assigning one partner to the inferior role of "boy" or "wife", and – without regard to their sexual behaviour – insists that both are men who should have equivalent privileges, not the least of which is autonomy' (Murray 1992: 29).

I want to indicate, necessarily briskly, something of how difference works in some non-metropolitan sex–gender systems. As well as age and gender, I invoke hierarchies of *class* and *race*, for they also may structure sexual relations. I will argue that it is unrealistic to suppose that we can simply sidestep the power structures that prevail in both metropolitan and non-metropolitan societies. Indeed, I suspect that it is because those structures involve primary social and political hierarchies that they are sites of erotic investment. Power is sexy.

A key aspiration of metropolitan gay men has been to rehandle the effeminacy ascribed to them, sometimes by defiantly asserting its transgressive potential, mostly by repudiating it or playing it down. Neither Leavitt, Holleran nor Gunn is inclined to reckon that gendering might have much to do with male same-sex practices.

Kramer in *The Normal Heart* presents camp gay men, but they are not allowed to be authoritative. Ned, his spokesman, wants the straight-acting Bruce on television: 'You're the kind of role model we need, not those drag queens from San Francisco who shove their faces in front of every camera they see' (Kramer 1986: 50).

There is nothing 'frilly or feminine' about Brad in *The Lost Language of Cranes* (Leavitt 1987: 249); nothing in Philip's appearance 'betrayed his homosexuality' (p. 33). Yet at school some boys 'routinely called him "faggot" or "fairy", though he hardly fitted the stereotype of the sensitive, silent, "different" boy who knows how to sew, is friends with the teacher and subject to colds' (p. 74). The element of inconsistency here is revealing: while Leavitt doesn't want Philip to be effeminate, he does need him to be a plausible gay man. For, of course, effeminacy didn't go away. In *The Farewell Symphony* (1997) Edmund White speaks of himself as like a girl and of a partner as a 'hubby'; like most men on the scene, he says, he preferred to be 'bottom' (White 1997: 416). The disposition of the culture was nonetheless masculine: 'Courtship was a con, again part of female culture. ... Even "love" was a suspect word, smelling of the bidet. Guys just sort of fell in with each other, buddies rubbing shoulders. We wanted sexual friends, loving comrades, multiple husbands in a whole polyandry of desire' (p. 298). To observe this ideology of 'Whitmanesque camaraderie' (p. 415) is not, of course, to validate it, in principle or as historical actuality.

In non-metropolitan sex–gender systems, gendering of same-sex relations is very often crucial, to the point where only the insertee – the 'passive', 'feminine' partner – may be regarded as truly deviant. Only he provokes what metropolitan gay culture apprehends as homophobic hostility; the 'active' partner is adequately manly.

In Latin America we have ample reports of a such a system (see Sinfield 1998: chapter 3; Kulick 1997). Manuel Puig's novel, *Kiss of the Spider Woman*, makes best sense in this light. Molina has been convicted of a sexual offence and prefers to imagine himself as a woman. Even so, argues his fellow-prisoner, the progressive Valentin, Molina doesn't have to 'submit' to a man, to be 'a martyr'. Molina replies: 'But if a man is ... my husband, he has to give the orders, so that he will feel right. That's the natural thing, because that makes him the ... man of the house.' No, Valentin insists, they have to be 'equal with one another'; otherwise this is 'a form of exploitation'. 'But then there's no kick to it' Molina insists. 'The kick is in the fact that when a man embraces you ... you may feel a little bit frightened' (Puig 1984: 243–4). The power difference is not an unwanted embarrassment; it is the turn-on.

Commentators whose expectations are framed within the metropolitan sex–gender system tend to disapprove. For Rebecca Bell-Metereau, William Hurt's portrayal of Molina in the film version (Hector Babenco, 1985) is 'problematic'. He 'applies makeup, wraps his hair in a towel, simpers and bats his eyelashes in imitation of his favorite movie star', and it all 'serves to reinforce many stereotypes about homosexuals' (Bell-Metereau 1993: 290).

# THE PRODUCTION OF GAY AND THE RETURN OF POWER

*Skesana* boys in the context of mine-labour in South Africa also glorify in their femininity and assume that it will attract partners:

MARTIN: I think in a relationship the woman must attend to her man. Like a woman she must clean the house, and he must be treated like a man.
THAMI: There must be a 'man' and a 'woman' in a relationship. A man must act mannish in his behaviour and his talks and walks. But a female must be queenish in every way.

(McLean and Ngcobo 1995: 164)

The *skesana* (like a wife) gains protection and favours in a violent and uncertain system; also, Hugh McLean and the late Linda Ngcobo add, he 'attains pleasure by flirting with power' (p. 165).

Gender hierarchy in lesbian sexuality is broached by Chicana writer Cherríe Moraga in *Loving in the War Years* (1983):

What the white women's movement tried to convince me of is that lesbian sexuality was *naturally* different than heterosexual sexuality. That the desire to penetrate and be penetrated, to fill and be filled, would vanish. That retaining such desires was 'reactionary', not 'politically correct', 'male identified'. And somehow reaching sexual ecstasy with a woman lover would never involve any kind of power struggle.

(Moraga 1983: 125–6)

In Moraga's play *Giving Up the Ghost*, Marisa and Amelia perceive and express their sexualities differently. Marisa's way of relating to women derives from her history as a Chicana tomboy under pressure – the play shows her childhood-self negotiating between her family and the other children in a neighbourhood in the Los Angeles basin, alongside her adulthood as a committed lesbian. Amalia is a generation older, was born in Mexico and needs to return there to feel whole, and that includes accepting her feeling for her male lover, Alejandro. Amalia's involvement with a man makes Marisa wildly jealous, but it is not entirely unfitting, since her 'passion' is 'to beat men at their own game': 'I never wanted to be a man, only wanted a woman to want me that bad. And they have, you know, plenty of them, but there's always that one you can't pin down, who's undecided. (*Beat.*) My mother was a heterosexual, I couldn't save her. My failures follow thereafter' (Moraga 1994: 8–9).

Moraga acknowledges that competing with men for dominance over women colludes with heterosexual, non-egalitarian patterns in Chicana/o society. 'Women do not usually grow up in women-only environments. Culture is sexually mixed', she says. 'The fact that some aspects of that culture are indeed oppressive does not

29

imply, as a solution, throwing out the entire business of racial/ethnic culture' (Moraga 1983: 127). Judith Halberstam comments: 'Chicana lesbians cannot suddenly be expected to cast off these sex roles in favour of a lesbian feminist egalitarianism' (Halberstam 1997: 335; see Moya 1997).

Lesbians in the metropolis have challenged the effacement of gendered models more directly than gay men, especially since Joan Nestle's demonstration in *A Restricted Country* of the historical and political provenance of the butch/fem model (Nestle 1988). For an ardent repudiation of this tendency, see Sheila Jeffreys's essay 'Butch and Femme: Now and Then' (Jeffreys 1993). Among advocates of butch/fem role-play it is unclear whether cross-dressing is to be regarded as a parodic assault on convention, or as a retrieval of misaligned but authentic gender identity. The former claim is made by Sue-Ellen Case, for whom the perverse, performing butch/fem duo are 'playfully inhabiting the camp space of irony and wit, free from biological determinism, elitist essentialism, and the heterosexist cleavage of sexual difference' (Case 1993: 305). However, for commentators on transgender, cross-dressing is an earnest matter. For Jay Prosser, it is 'crucial that we credit the lure of passing, account for the very human desire to belong, be accepted and be seen for who one feels oneself to be' (Prosser 1997: 320).

Age difference, everyone knows, structured same-sex male relationships among the ancient Greeks. More precisely, those peoples positioned all subordinates, including boys and women, as insertees. In fact, hierarchies of gender and age are often found in interaction: time and again, when we think we see a model based on age difference it transpires that the boys are regarded as feminine, and when we think we have a model based on gender difference we find that the feminized partners are younger. *Skesanas* are normally young, and may become *injongas* ('active' partners) as they become more senior and experienced. What we are observing, I believe, is a *conflation of subordinations*: since both boys and women figure subordination, they can be blurred together. In fact, one attraction of same-sex relations may reside in their potential to invoke, simultaneously, such major hierarchies. If, as I have suggested, the crucial point is power difference, then the specific social categories through which it is articulated may well be, to some degree, interchangeable or reinforcing; or they may significantly complicate each other.

If youth often co-occurs with femininity, it may do the opposite when it is inflected by class. This was generally the case in the dominant metropolitan model between Oscar Wilde and Stonewall, in which (stereotypically effete) middle-class men admired the putative masculinity of working-class young men. Jeffrey Weeks sums this up as an 'avidly exploitative sexual colonialism, which marched, point counter-point, with the dream of class reconciliation' (Weeks 1977: 44). But class difference for many was not just a convenience or an ideal – it was a turn-on. So Denton Welch in *Maiden Voyage* (1945) presents his sixteen-year-old self, defiantly, as a 'sissy', fascinated by working-class men: 'When he bent forward with a lighted match cupped in his hands, I saw how horny and broad they were. They were nice, and strong, with dirty nails. I wished I had hands like them' (Welch 1945: 110; see Sinfield 1997: 69). Many middle-class homosexuals recognized that their sexuality had been shaped by the prevailing social hierarchy. Michael Davidson records how as a youngster he was forbidden to play with 'ragged' village boys. 'There wasn't, that I know, a grain of sexuality in this childish friendship; yet I've wondered since whether the denial of it to me mayn't have helped to engender that predilection for "lower-class" boys which has guided my searches. Asiatic, Arabian, and African boys are "class-less" in my erotic manual' (Davidson 1977: 37–8). For Davidson hierarchies of class and race overlap.

In the metropolitan model today, race constitutes the most sensitive of these eroticized differences. As Isaac Julien's film *Looking For Langston* (1989) shows, relations between blacks and whites were regarded quite positively by gay men in the Harlem Renaissance of the 1920s and 1930s. A recent essay displays photographs taken at that time by Carl Van Vechten, of black and white men in sexual scenarios (Smalls 1997). These pictures have a good deal in common with the work of Robert Mapplethorpe, but a hierarchy that was perhaps taken for granted earlier on has now become highly controversial. Yet Gary Fisher, an African-American, writes in his journal in 1987: 'The racial humiliation is a huge turn on. I enjoy being your nigger, your property and worshipping not just you, but your whiteness' (Sedgwick 1997: 421).

African-American and Afro-Caribbean British gays today share many of the expectations of white gays, but have every reason to reassess the reluctance in the metropolitan model to acknowledge difference of race. As Julien says in his poem 'Gary's Tale' (1986; no relation to Gary Fisher), racial difference has got into the psyche:

> Because the last fight, the last battle, territory, will be
>     with one's self, the most important terrain, the psyche.
> The mind will be the last neo-colonialised space to be
>     decolonialised, this I know because I have been there, backwards
>     and forwards.
> 
>              (Mercer and Julien 1988: 128; see Chu 1997)

Marlon Riggs in his film *Tongues Untied* (1989), written around Riggs's poem of the same name, expounds his personal negotiation of sexuality and racial difference. He experienced oppression in his own community, as a sissy, more immediately than oppression as a black man; it was

> A whiteboy came to my rescue.
> Beckoned with gray/green eyes, a soft Tennessee drawl.
> Seduced me out of my adolescent silence.

Riggs found his way to San Francisco, the Castro:

> I learned the touch and taste of snow.
> Cruising whiteboys, I played out
> adolescent dreams deferred.
> Patterns of black upon white upon black upon white
> mesmerized me. I focused hard, concentrated deep.
> (Riggs 1991: 202)

Riggs was playing out racial relations as sexual relations. But it dawned upon him that this was not making him the person he sought to be: in the Castro he was 'an invisible man'; the available black images were racist sterotypes. 'I was a nigga, still.' He 'went in search of something better', he says, listening to 'Rhythms of blood, culture, / history, and race': black men must love one other (pp. 203–4).

The film *Tongues Untied* is about self-empowerment – 'Who dares to tell us we are poor and powerless?' Riggs stakes out new ground for black gays, with new authority. However, another way of looking at it would be to say that he has rediscovered and reaffirmed, not a distinctive African-American way of relating but a purer, sharper version of the metropolitan ideology itself. The Castro, he sees, blazons the principle that difference doesn't count, but actually repeats the racist assumptions of US society generally. Riggs's demand, therefore, is that the egalitarian ideology should work properly for black men, and the best way to achieve that will be to avoid racially mixed relations.

These assumptions appear in reverse in more optimistic versions of the metropolitan ideology, such as the films *My Beautiful Laundrette* (UK 1985) and *The Wedding Banquet* (Taiwan 1993). In these films a miraculously egalitarian, racially blind gay relationship is presented as a magical opportunity for the overthrow of racial difference. However, it is not so easy. As Riggs admits, the 'absence of black images' occurred not only in books, posters and films but in his 'own fantasies'. And he was embarrassed when commentators noted that his own partner was white (Riggs 1991: 202–3; see Simmons 1991).

Contributors to the British compilation *Lesbians Talk: Making Black Waves* (1993) approve of relations between different black peoples; for Araba Mercer they may be 'a learning and growing thing', for Linda Bellos they 'can make a relationship richer'. Even so, say the editors, Valerie Mason-John and Ann Khambatta, 'Black lesbians in Britain find themselves within a system which places our races in a hierarchy. For example, African-Caribbeans are seen as illiterate, aggressive, troublesome; South and East Asians as intelligent, passive and submissive. At times we have colluded with this' (Mason-John and Khambatta 1993: 28–9). Relationships with white women are rated as vastly more problematic because, with the best will in the world, hegemonic white racism is so insidious. Some of the women canvassed eschew them altogether.

Yet they may be 'healthy', Mercer, Mason-John and Khambatta say; probably by that they mean that racial difference is surmounted. One contributor, Madge, declares: 'I don't think making love to a White woman is any different from making love to a Black woman. All my life in this country I've had four beautiful relationships. Three were with White women and the fourth was with a Black woman' (p. 30).

These comments display the pattern we have seen elsewhere: difference is all right so long as it doesn't make any difference. The pattern appears again in a substantial, candid and courageous (late night!) television discussion among three black lesbians and three black gay men, *Doing It with You Is Taboo* (SOI for Channel 4, 1993). Some of the contributors were in or ready to contemplate relationships with whites, some not. Either way, two main alternative propositions emerge: (a) black/white couples are to be avoided because between such people race is bound to be important; (b) a black/white couple may be all right when, for these two people at least, race is unimportant. A third proposition, that black/white difference will be important and may be rewarding, is not entertained.

As I said at the start, I am touching here upon people's most intimate emotions; certainly it is none of my business to say how black people might conduct their love-lives. However, I think it is legitimate, and may be salutary, to observe that many non-metropolitan peoples work on different assumptions. For it is arrogant to suppose that the egalitarian model is superior, even if we don't yet all live up to it, and that other peoples should be 'developing' towards it (on the analogue of 'developing nations'). When it was decided that the New York Stonewall anniversary march of 1994 should start at the United Nations building, this was a well-meaning gesture – aspiring to free everyone, not just 'American' people. However, Manalansan remarks, this is all too familiar as an assumption of US imperialism. He notes 'capitalist expansion' also in the programme of the International Lesbian and Gay Association, which he accuses of propounding 'a universalized and formulaic picture of the future of all gay and lesbian political and cultural efforts' (Manalansan IV 1995: 429). He shows that New York Filipinos are uncomfortable with metropolitan constructs – indifferent to Stonewall and its anniversary, for instance, though one of Manalansan's informants was actually at the riot in 1969.

If metropolitan lesbians and gay men had in fact succeeded in wiping out power in relationships, all we would have to do is enjoy our egalitarian practice and let everyone else in on the secret. But that is far from the case. The prevailing sex–gender system, we have every reason to know, is geared to the production of hierarchy and, as part of that, to the production of anxious, unhappy and violent people. It produces us and our psychic lives – straights and gays – and it is not going to leave us alone. It is a liberal-bourgeois delusion to suppose that 'private' space can be somehow innocent of and protected from the real world. In actuality, none of the power hierarchies that I have been highlighting is insignificant in metropolitan sexual practice. But, unlike people in non-metropolitan systems, we prefer to pretend otherwise. It would be better, at the least, to acknowledge what we are doing.

Instead, we try to hive off power into special categories. Pornography, by definition, is the place where we position the sexiness we can't handle within more authorized patterns of relating. So we find plenty of power differentials there. Then there is s/m. The specialization and ritualizing of power in s/m allows us to suppose that it necessarily involves distinctive gear, dedicated bars and playrooms; and that in other contexts, conversely, we are egalitarian. Indeed, some SMers declare that they too are actually egalitarian. Lynda Hart and Joshua Dale note that in some quarters s/m 'has become less a polarized expression of a master's power over a slave than a mutual exchange of power'. Already in the 1970s, 'some practitioners began to refer to s/m as "sensuality and mutuality"'; by the early 1980s the 'mutualists', as Geoff Mains calls them, had become a principal element in the leather community (Hart and Dale 1997: 345–6).

Once more, all this is dangerous territory, so let me try to be clear. I'm not saying that we should be plunging into reactionary and complacent relations which exploit oppressions of class, age, race and gender, and abandoning politics, morality and responsibility. Thinking even for a moment about the reality of those oppressions should restore our commitment to fight them. At the same time, it cannot be realistic to suppose that we can simply, through good intentions, sidestep the hierarchies of capitalism and patriarchy. They inform our daily interactions, the language through which we come to consciousness, our psychic formations. That is why power is sexy. Islands of individual serenity are a strategic aspiration for therapy, but finally we must be talking about damage limitation; socialism in a single psyche must be a chimera.

As Halberstam puts it, 'while people may well invest in values like equality and reciprocity in their political lives, they may not want those same values dominating their sexual lives' (Halberstam 1997: 333). We should not expect to see an uncomplicated match between politics and fantasy, therefore. As Leo Bersani observes, 'Our fantasy investments are often countered by more consciously and more rationally elaborate modes of reaching out to others, such as liking or admiring people we don't desire. In that tension lies an important moral dimension of our political engagement' (Bersani 1995: 64). The task is to find ways of engaging fantasy without disempowering other people.

Nor do I suppose (to anticipate other objections) that everyone has been doing the same thing and that no one else has been pondering these issues. I am writing about a dominant ideology from which none of us is free, and which all of us may assess, adapt and resist.

My plundering of non-metropolitan sex–gender systems reveals the metropolitan model as a local and temporal creation, tending to disavow, repudiate or repress large areas of actual sexual experience. If we don't address power differentials, we don't begin to get a hold on exploitation – including that which we perpetrate ourselves. Besides, hierarchy is sexy. While the political priority of resisting actual oppressions must be maintained, power imbalances in lesbian and gay personal relations may be refigured as potentially rewarding, though inevitably troubling. We should be exploring ways to assess and recombine power, sexiness, responsibility and love.

## Acknowledgements

With special thanks to Andil Gosene, Rachel Holmes, Vincent Quinn and Pratap Rughani.

## References

Bell-Metereau, R. (1993) *Hollywood Androgyny*, 2nd edn, New York: Columbia University Press.
Bersani, L. (1995) *Homos*, Cambridge, Mass.: Harvard University Press.
Case, S.-E. (1993) 'Towards a Butch-Femme Aesthetic', in H. Abelove, M. A. Barale and D. M. Halperin (eds) *The Lesbian and Gay Studies Reader*, New York: Routledge.
Chan, C.S. (1997) 'Don't Ask, Don't Tell, Don't Know: The Formation of a Homosexual Identity and Sexual Expression Among Asian American Lesbians', in B. Greene (ed.) *Ethnic and Cultural Diversity Among Lesbians and Gay Men*, London: Sage.
Chu, W-c.R. (1997) 'Some Ethnic Gays Are Coming Home; or, the Trouble with Interraciality', *Textual Practice* 11: 219–36.
Davidson, M. (1977) *The World, the Flesh and Myself*, London: Quartet.
Delany, S.R. (1990) *The Motion of Light in Water*, London: Paladin.
Epstein, S. (1992) 'Gay Politics, Ethnic Identity', in E. Stein (ed.) *Forms of Desire*, New York: Routledge.
Greenberg, D.F. (1998) *The Construction of Homosexuality*, Chicago: Chicago University Press.
Gunn, T. (1992) *The Man with Night Sweats*, London: Faber.
Halberstam, J. (1997) 'Sex Debates', in A. Medhurst and S. Munt (eds) *Lesbian and Gay Studies*, London: Cassell.
Hart, L. and Dale, J. (1997) 'Sadomasochism', in A. Medhurst and S. Munt (eds) *Lesbian and Gay Studies*, London: Cassell.
Holleran, A. (1979) *Dancer from the Dance*, London: Cape.
Jeffreys, S. (1993) 'Butch and Femme: Now and Then', in Lesbian History Group (ed.) *Not a Passing Phase*, rev. edn, London: Women's Press.
Kramer, L. (1986) *The Normal Heart*, London: Methuen.
Kulick, D. (1997) 'A Man in the House: The Boyfriends of Brazilian *Travesti* Prostitutes', *Social Text* 52–3: 133–60.
Leavitt, D. (1987) *The Lost Language of Cranes*, Harmondsworth: Penguin.
McLean, H. and Ngcobo, L. (1995) 'Abangibhamayo bathi ngimnandi (Those who fuck me say I'm tasty): Gay Sexuality in Reef Townships', in M. Gevisser and E. Cameron (eds) *Defiant Desire*, London: Routledge.

Manalansan IV, M.F. (1995) 'In the Shadows of Stonewall: Examining Gay Transnational Politics and the Diasporic Dilemma', *GLQ (Gay and Lesbian Quarterly)* 2: 425–38.

Mason-John, V. and Khambatta, A. (eds) (1993) *Lesbians Talk: Making Black Waves*, London: Scarlet.

Mercer, K. and Julien, I. (1988) 'Race, Sexual Politics and Black Masculinity: A Dossier', in R. Chapman and J. Rutherford (eds) *Male Order*, London: Lawrence and Wishart.

Moore, O. (1991) *A Matter of Life and Sex*, Harmondsworth: Penguin.

Moraga, C. (1983) *Loving in the War Years*, Boston: South End Press.

Moraga, C. (1994) *Giving Up the Ghost*, in C. Moraga, *Heroes and Saints and Other Plays*, Albuquerque: West End Press.

Moya, P.M.L. (1997), 'Postmodernism, "Realism", and the Politics of Identity: Cherríe Moraga and Chicana Feminism', in M.J. Alexander and C.T. Mohanty (eds), *Feminist Genealogies, Colonial Legacies, Democratic Futures*, New York: Routledge.

Murray, S.O. (1992) 'The "Underdevelopment" of Modern/Gay Homosexuality in MesoAmerica', in K. Plummer (ed.) *Modern Homosexualities*, London: Routledge.

Nestle, J. (1988) *A Restricted Country*, London: Sheba Feminist Press.

Prosser, J. (1997) 'Transgender', in A. Medhurst and S. Munt (eds) *Lesbian and Gay Studies*, London: Cassell.

Puig, M. (1984) *Kiss of the Spider Woman*, trans. Thomas Colchie, London: Arena.

Riggs, R. (1991) 'Tongues Untied', in E. Hemphill (ed.) *Brother to Brother*, Boston: Alyson.

Sedgwick, E.K. (1997) 'Gary Fisher in Your Pocket', in J. Oppenheimer and H. Reckitt (eds) *Acting on AIDS*, London: Serpent's Tail and ICA.

Segal, L. (1994) *Straight Sex*, London: Virago.

Simmons, R. (1991) *'Tongues Untied*: An Interview with Marlon Riggs', in E. Hemphill (ed.) *Brother to Brother*, Boston: Alyson.

Sinfield, A. (1997) *Literature, Politics and Culture in Postwar Britain*, 2nd edn, London: Athlone.

Sinfield, A. (1998) *Gay and After*, London: Serpent's Tail.

Smalls, J. (1997) 'Public Face, Private Thoughts: Fetish, Interracialism, and the Homoerotic in Some Photographs by Carl Van Vechten', in T. Foster, C. Siegel and E. E. Berry (eds) *Sex Positives?*, *Genders* 25: 144–93.

Weeks, J. (1977) *Coming Out*, London: Quartet.

Welch, D. (1945) *Maiden Voyage*, London: Routledge.

White, E. (1997) *The Farewell Symphony*, London: Chatto.

# 2

# MARGINALITY ON THE TROPIC[1]

*Dennis Altman*

## Prologue

This piece grew out of a desire to bring together several themes which have preoccupied me over the past decade or so: the debate over Australian identity, both in terms of multiculturalism and our relationship to Asia, the role of intellectuals in this debate, the existing position of homosexuals in a post-gay liberation and, some would say, post-AIDS world. The essay arose from a visit to Rockhampton, a provincial city of 60,000, which sits on the Tropic of Capricorn, some 300 miles north of Brisbane. In a sense, though I didn't know this when I originally wrote the piece in 1994, it was a sketch for what would become my most recent book, *Defying Gravity* (Altman 1997a; see also Dessaix 1998).

The piece captures in part some of my immediate responses to what might be called the triple marginalization of being gay in a provincial town in the Antipodes.[2] I have argued elsewhere that the 'cultural cringe' of Australians is particularly apparent in its gay culture (Altman 1994b); I suspect the same is true for New Zealand as suggested in this quote from Peter Wells:

> Like many a provincial pouf (of which, if the truth be dreadfully told, most of us are, and must be: the great cities of the world are endlessly replenished by new arrivals on every bus, every plane) I made my pilgrimage to the homosexual Rome of my day – the sultry and sardonic London depicted in *The Swimming Pool Library*.
> 
> (Wells 1994: 200–201)

Over the past decade I've been increasingly interested in the ways in which this pilgrimage is both replicated and complicated in the current world, with its mass movements of people and its diasporas, linking, say, lesbians in Mumbai and Minneapolis, gay men in Seoul and Stuttgart. (There's a large literature on this, but think of recent films such as *Wedding Banquet* or *Together*.) How this might further complicate the discourse of marginality is something worth thinking about.

It is worth noting that since this piece was originally written Australia has experienced a change of government, with the replacement of a 'dry' Labor government, which was none the less supportive of various social changes, by a far more ideologically right-wing Liberal/National coalition and the emergence of a noisy anti-immigration rabble led by Independent Queensland MP Pauline Hanson (Brett 1997). The caution against over-optimism with which I ended the piece might today seem even more deserved – though I would note that Pauline Hanson failed in her attempt to enter the House of Representatives in the 1998 elections, and her One Nation Party has so far only been able to win seats in Queensland. Even so it is my sense that both the recognition of multiculturalism and the basic acceptance of lesbian/gay communities within this framework represents an irreversible change in Australian life.

Rockhampton is, of course, in the state of Queensland and an Australian readership would automatically therefore situate this article in the context of certain national mythologies which have cast Queensland as 'the deep north' of Australia. Like Tasmania – which I've used elsewhere as a fictional metaphor for the old Australia (Altman 1993) – Queensland is more decentralized and has experienced less diverse immigration than the rest of Australia. Like Tasmania, too, it has a long history of Labor governments (the Australian Labor Party was born amongst the sheep-shearers of Queensland) which was dramatically broken by the right-wing government of Joe Bjelke-Petersen (1968–86). Thus while the rest of Australia was undergoing dramatic social change during this period, the Bjelke-Petersen government defiantly resisted these changes, and adamantly opposed any recognition of homosexuality. Also, while the Australian governmental response to AIDS has been in most cases exemplary, and involved the creation of 'partnership' with gay community organizations (Altman 1994a; Ballard 1989), this was more difficult in Queensland where special arrangements had to be made for the funding of the Queensland AIDS Council by the federal government to get round the quite overt homophobia of the state government, and where quite sizeable provincial centres had no AIDS-specific services. This, again, would have contributed to the sense of isolation I describe in Rockhampton.

The National Party was out of power by 1989, but even when I visited Rockhampton there were echoes of its legacy in some of the attitudes I discuss. The new Labor government decriminalized homosexuality in 1990, leaving Tasmania the last state to retain criminal sanctions (now repealed). In 1996 Labor was replaced by a Conservative state government, but two years later the state election saw a hung Parliament, with Labor just short of a majority and Hanson's One Nation Party holding the balance of power.

## Notes from the Tropic of Capricorn

Going to Rockhampton was like entering a time warp back to the Australia of thirty years earlier. Of course the appurtenances of modern consumerism are everywhere apparent; video shops have largely replaced cinemas, there is now a café serving espresso coffee just off the inevitable City Mall, a welcome relief from that peculiarly Australian provincial invention, the cappuccino made with Nescafé. But Rockhampton remains the centre of a rich pastoral society, whose daughters and sons come to town to attend boarding school and then return fifty years later to retire. Life-size statues of bulls guard the entry roads, proclaiming the city's pre-eminence as a centre of the cattle industry, and its population is older and considerably more Anglo-Celtic than most of Australia. Far more about Rockhampton reminds one of its past than is true for other Australian tropical centres such as Cairns, with its tourist boom, or Darwin, which was largely rebuilt in the twenty years since it was flattened by a cyclone.[3] With its riverside buildings bearing the mark of late nineteenth century prosperity, Rockhampton retains much of the atmosphere of pre-multicultural Australia.

I had been invited to Rockhampton to speak at a conference called 'Voices From the Margin'. The conference posed questions about marginality in ways which cut across the academic/activist divide, bringing together the voices of women, the disabled, the transsexual, the Aboriginal in ways which challenged both their marginality and the certainty of identities based on a shared oppression. But during my time in Rockhampton I was conscious of rather different questions of marginality: those based on geography and distance. Despite constant stories of how electronic media and technological developments have abolished the 'tyranny of distance' – I read the *Time* cover story on cyberspace while I was in Rockhampton – old preoccupations about centre and periphery constantly resurfaced. The same sense of missing out on cultural/intellectual life which was so strong when I was growing up in Hobart seemed very present in Rockhampton. Like Hobart in the early 1960s this did not seem a good place to live outside the constraints of what mainstream television and the women's magazines define as 'normality'.

In Rockhampton the sort of gay/lesbian/queer assertion which produces Mardi Gras or 'queer theory' seemed far distant. Apart from the inevitable country 'beat', in this case centred on one of the city's parks shared by Aborigines, the homeless, waiting taxi drivers and those men in search of each other, public gay life seemed restricted to one night a week at a local pub where two local lesbians run a 'gay night' known as Club Venus. Nowhere was I so starkly reminded of the ways in which the past lives on as in this club which replicated, but with some complex differences, pre-1970s gay life. The club meets in the back lounge, and entry is limited to those who can convince the doorwoman of their bona fides. When I was there the crowd was remarkably mixed: at least as many women as men, ages from twenty to sixty, a small group of deaf gay men, immediately apparent from the vitality of their signed conversations, a handful of sympathetic straights. For a few hours at least it was possible to feel that there was a space in central Queensland where one could live openly outside the rules of compulsory heterosexuality.

For lesbians and gay men who feel particularly marginal in Rockhampton the centre is not, as it was for Australian homosexuals twenty years ago, overseas; rather it is in the perceived gay meccas of Sydney and Brisbane. 'It's absolutely necessary for us to visit a couple of times a year to get our fix of gay life' one man told me, much as earlier Australians thought of the grand trek to Britain as a way of countering the intellectual and artistic void of everyday life back home.

'Marginality' has become a fashionable word of late, being used to describe virtually anyone who can claim not to be part of the 'dead white heterosexual male' culture which is believed to overwhelm all other voices, and whose hegemony needs to be broken. Although this language is largely encountered in American 'political correctness' it has a particular resonance in Australia, which defines itself as marginal, the country at the bottom of the map in danger of being left off altogether. 'Marginality' is a particular part of the settler Australian experience; unlike the indigenous peoples we have always imagined ourselves as doubly marginal, displaced from the Atlantic centre of the world by Geoffrey Blainey's 'tyranny of distance' (Blainey 1996) while clinging to the coast of a largely inhospitable land mass as if unable to move away from the sea which unites us yet cuts us off from 'the real world'. For intellectuals there is yet the further marginalization of believing this to be a country particularly inhospitable to intellectual life, even though there are few countries in which the reality is much different.

Despite the rhetoric of Australian national assertion and our new place in the Asia/Pacific world the cultural cringe seems to me alive and well in intellectual circles. We still crave the approval of overseas – more accurately, of New York, London and Paris – and we reveal this in our exaggerated respect for the foreign guru; surely few are as deferential to French intellectual fashion as Australian graduate students in the humanities. Even more striking is our obeisance to the successful expatriate, to whom we defer even when, as seems true of the occasional pronouncements of a Clive James or a Jill Conway, they appear to have learnt nothing and forgotten nothing since they left Australia several decades ago.

Almost without our noticing, Australia has become one of the more diverse and genuinely tolerant societies in the world. (I think the shift began sometime in the last few years of the post-Menzies Liberal era, which is one of the ideas I tried to suggest in my novel *The Comfort of Men*.) I am not sure that we Australians always recognize this about ourselves: we are too used to self-criticism to recognize that there are certain things in which we can take pride. Although a deep strand of racism, particularly *vis-à-vis* Aborigines, remains it should not lead us to deny the extent to which the growing acceptance of Australia as a multicultural society has meant a greater awareness of recognition of diverse groups and values in society.

The most exciting changes going on in Australia at the moment are those which are leading us to re-imagine our place in the world, for the shift in emphasis from the Atlantic world to the Pacific brings with it a psychological shift which questions all those truculent assumptions of insignificance which have characterized settler Australia. Paul Keating may have been our first Prime Minister who genuinely did not believe that 'the centre' is located somewhere between Washington and London.[4] The melding of our European (largely British) culture with influences from newer immigrants and growing links with our region is beginning to produce something which is uniquely Australian, and hence something which ends our own perceptions of geographic marginality.

Within any given nation-state particular groups and subcultures will bear the mark of the larger political culture. Thus one can see in the particular experience of, say, Australian wharfies or Vietnamese immigrants or women cricketers certain aspects which set them apart from their counterparts in Canada or Sweden or even New Zealand, and help define what is peculiarly Australian. So it is with the homosexual world(s). It is worth considering the interplay of this one particular marginal group within the context of the larger sense of marginality which is such a central part of Australian self-definition.

Those for whom homosexuality is not a major concern—and those who are under forty years of age — may not realize just how fast things have changed. In the past two decades we have lived through the shift of homosexuality from something defined as an individual problem – deviance, sin, illness – to the view of it as a sexual preference, basis for a public identity and a visible community. Whether it be politicians acknowledging the importance of the gay vote, images of chic lesbians in up-market women's magazines or the mix of drag and macho connected with Mardi Gras, Madonna and fashion shows, homosexuals and homosexual imagery has become part of larger social life in a way unimaginable even twenty years ago.

Most comments on the development of contemporary gay identities over the past two decades would apply to the bulk of the western world; gay/lesbian/queer life in Melbourne, Munich and Minneapolis is remarkably similar (as indeed it is in provincial centres such as Rockhampton, Little Rock and Blackpool). But there are certain aspects of this which take on a particularly Australian character, which bear, as it were, the mark of our traditional cultural cringe. There is no question that the very creation of a 'gay' – then 'gay/lesbian' – community in Australia was very much influenced by overseas, overwhelmingly American, influences. Indeed, the first stirrings of a homosexual political movement in Australia came in the wake of a larger cultural shift, one which saw the centre of cultural influence move from Britain to the United States, a shift particularly reflected in the anti-war and sexual liberation movements. As a commercial gay world grew in Australia during the 1970s and 1980s American influences were solidified, with bars, discos, bookshops and publications reflecting a heavily American-centric view of what constituted this new identity.

Of course, these influences could only take hold because they matched what was happening in Australia. Indeed they masked some distinctively Australian features of the new community(ies), such as the stronger links with political radicalism and a lesser emphasis on respectability than was true of the US movement. Ten years of AIDS organizing, in very different political climates, has further increased those differences. Yet in some ways the Australian gay/lesbian world remains remarkably shaped by the American, largely through the dominance of US gay cultural representations. Writers such as Rita Mae Brown and Edmund White are seen as telling us the story of our lives, with no acknowledgement of their essential Americanness.

The last Mardi Gras festival was dominated by imported performers from the United States, and both gay and straight press gave the visitors far more attention than they did the locals. (This has changed a little, though the pattern remains.) In the same way an ABC documentary on the impact of AIDS on culture blurred any distinctions between Australia and the United States by its heavy reliance on the comments of Americans such as Larry Kramer and Armistead Maupin, despite the very different history of the epidemic in the two countries. In such an environment it becomes difficult for writers, performers and artists to develop a self-confident response which makes sense of the Australian experience. The same comments might be made about feminism, and the way in which second-rate American feminist thinkers, such as Naomi Wolfe and Susan Faludi, are hyped by the Australian media which is far less interested in our own very impressive feminist scholarship.

Perhaps the easiest way of understanding the development of a particular form of gay/lesbian identity within Australia is through the combination of two interrelated phenomena: globalization and multiculturalism. By the former I understand the complex networks of transnational economic power and electronic media which are rapidly turning the world into a single marketplace, whose most common features are McDonald's, Coca-Cola and American movies. (My male students now come to class wearing US baseball caps rather than AFL sweaters.) Globalization has helped create an international gay identity, which is by no means confined to the Western world: there are many signs of what we think of as 'modern' homosexuality in countries such as Brazil, Mexico, Malaysia and Thailand. Indeed the gay world – less obviously the lesbian, which is a mark of the extent of women's lesser freedom – is one of the best examples around of emerging global 'subcultures', whereby members of particular groups share far more across national and continental boundaries than they do with others in their own geographically defined societies.

Multiculturalism is a more contested term, but in Australia it has come to be an essential part of our evolving national self-definition, meaning both the preservation of immigrant cultures *and* the creation of a new Australian identity. There is undoubtedly some internal contradiction between using the term in both a static sense – the deep freezing of imported ethnicities – and a more fluid one – the constant remaking of Australian identity – but the ideology of multiculturalism has been of enormous value to the lesbian/gay community, allowing us to claim a place alongside every other ethnic group. (Indeed for many 'old' Australians the gay world of Oxford Street is probably far less threatening than suburban mosques.[5]) The growth of a gay/lesbian/queer identity heavily influenced by the pressures of globalization has been eased in Australia by the simultaneous development of a particular form of multiculturalism which has allowed some space for increasing acceptance of diversity.

Let me now admit that I was too cursory in my discussion of gay life in Rockhampton. Club Venus may have looked like something out of the pre-Stonewall 1960s, but the posters and publications available linked it clearly to the larger gay worlds of Brisbane and Sydney, there were moves in place to establish a campus gay society, and at least one newsagent stocked the magazine *Outrage*. This was not the subterranean world of pre-gay Tasmania in the 1960s, in which the very idea of homosexual community was almost literally unimaginable. Certainly there is very limited public space for lesbians and gay men in the town; probably the experience of growing up homosexual in Gladstone or Emerald or North Rockhampton is difficult and lonely. But so it is, too, for teenagers in the suburbs of Sydney and Melbourne (and equally of Berlin, New York and San Francisco). The changes in attitudes towards (homo)sexuality are both widespread and limited, nor are they confined to the yuppie inner-city. The barriers against full acceptance for most homosexuals remain everywhere.

Even now, three decades after the birth of the modern gay movement, the biggest problems facing homosexuals are those of self-esteem and self-acceptance. 'Coming out' as gay in public still remains the greatest obstacle for most homosexuals in a town such as Rockhampton. Their lives are neatly if painfully segmented, so that their sexual/emotional world is kept apart from family, jobs, even (straight) friends. Theirs is largely a self-imposed marginality, policed by probably exaggerated fears of the consequences of disclosure. (Not that I would want to discount these consequences: people do lose jobs, face persecution and encounter violence every day as a result of being – or being believed to be – lesbian or gay.)

Yet at the same time people can and do cling to the idea of a gay identity, even if it seems something that can only be taken up on Saturday nights and a once a year visit to the big city. It is the ability to imagine that one is part of a larger society where one does not have to live in secret which separates gay life today and that of thirty years ago. This in turn, as Marx would have put it, has created the conditions for the disappearance of that very identity. In big cities the growing acceptance of homosexuality has made the need for gay separatism less important, a contributing factor to the fashionability of 'queer' among younger homosexuals. Ultimately the end of marginality means that diversity can become a matter of individual choice rather than collective affirmation. If society no longer seeks to patrol the boundaries of sexual desire the need to create a specific and ghettoized lesbian/gay world will largely disappear.

The need to assert identity is usually born of a sense of insecurity; Australians devote considerable energy to a search for a national identity precisely because we are very conscious of our dependent state *vis-à-vis* North Atlantic culture and control. In part this search can be a fruitful one if it creates myths and goals which help us, both individually and collectively, to live better. Individuals, communities and even nations need a sense of self-esteem, and the creation of a secure sense of identity is important. Usually this is understood in essentialist terms: we use concepts such as 'discovering the real you' as if identity was something inherent and inborn within each of us.

But individuals, communities and nations invent their identities, and constantly remake them as their lives change. In my own life I have been marked above all by two great shifts in social identity: the development of a lesbian/gay community and the redefinition of Australia as a multicultural nation in Asia/Pacific. The former is a shift which is evident through the developed world, but it also shares a particular link with the latter in the ways in which Australia has incorporated some recognition of diverse communities into its own evolving sense of national identity. Both of these shifts demand new ways of thinking about what is marginal and what is central; visiting Rockhampton came as a reminder that social change is always uneven, that aspects of the old continue to co-exist with the new, and that this can produce considerable tensions (including resistance, sometimes ugly and violent, from those who feel threatened by change.)

In the development of an Australian gay world we can see in microcosm the Australian itinerary of borrowing heavily from overseas, transforming those borrowings into something uniquely and successfully Australian – and refusing to recognize our own achievements in so doing. There is still an Australian tendency to measure ourselves against the Old World, and to believe we are failures when we inevitably fail; our intellectuals still deplore the lack of café society a la Vienna and Paris, failing to notice that at least in our large cities we have a vibrant café culture of our own. The gay community reveals its essential national character when it follows suit.

If homosexuals have carved out some space for themselves in this country precisely because of the ideology of multiculturalism, this is surely a far healthier reaction to the forces of globalization than the religious and ethnic fundamentalism characteristic of many other societies. In contrast to the United States gay-bashing has not proved good politics in Australia. Partly this is due to the much lesser importance of fundamentalist Christianity. (Fred Nile for all the media attention he provokes is at least as marginal as his opponents.[6]) But partly, too, I suspect it is because Australians know that our national/social/cultural identity is in the process of constantly being remade, and that intolerance against any group represents a threat to all. The acid test of this proposition is post-Mabo responses to Aboriginal Australia, who face yet more deeply entrenched hostility and prejudice than do homosexuals.[7]

One of the marks of postmodern theory is the suggestion that there are no longer any centres, whether geographic or intellectual. If Australia need no longer feel on the margins of an increasingly de-centred world, so, in the same way, differences of ethnicity and sex/gender no longer define one within a fixed hierarchy which makes some experiences more significant or more authoritative than others. This is an attractive proposition: if it is to stand up it need apply to the everyday life of lesbians and gay men in Rockhampton as much as to the academics of inner Sydney and Melbourne.

I am often accused of being too pollyannaish in my optimism about this country. Optimism seems to me justified when the broad direction of change is moving towards the goals one seeks, which does not ignore the fact that change will produce some very unpleasant tensions along the way. As Australia's sense of itself becomes one of a country less marginal to the outside world so, too, change within Australia is making us a more diverse and tolerant society, in which marginalized groups feel more able to assert themselves and demand recognition and respect. Increasingly, if sometimes with difficulty, we are coming to redefine ours as a society without a centre, in the sense of one dominant racial, religious or sex/gender ideology. Twenty years ago there was no university in Rockhampton – and if there had been it is inconceivable that it would have sponsored a conference featuring 'voices from the margin'. In twenty years' time maybe the whole concept of marginality will seem far less relevant as our culture becomes increasingly more fluid and less dependent on any notion of 'the centre', geographic or ideological.

## Afterword

How might these notes relate to the larger theme of this book? Partly I suppose by emphasizing the double marginality of lesbigay life in a provincial city in Australia, which itself, despite its large gay world, even despite Mardi Gras, remains peripheral to the North Atlantic centre. American queer theory for all its theoretical enthusiasm for deconstructing borders remains relentlessly limited to its own geographic frontiers, symbolized by the parentheses in Spurlin's complaint about the privileging of American coastal cities 'over other geographic locations in the US (and elsewhere)'.

Thus the marginality of lesbigay life in Rockhampton must be understood as both part of the continued dominance of heterosexual hegemony outside the big cities and a reflection of the marginality which many Australians continue to feel *vis-à-vis* the larger world. This latter sense has the potential to change in quite dramatic ways due to the technologies of globalization, which provide links of communication sufficiently dense to allow for previously unimaginable ways for those in 'the provinces' to participate in global gay life. Videos and the internet make contact with 'the centre' possible in ways we are only beginning to fully understand. (Note for example the proliferation of lesbigay internet sites in East Asia.)

Not only do these changes make for a new relationship between 'centre' and 'periphery' *within* countries, they are also eliding differences *between* countries. Globalization, understood as both economic and cultural interpenetration, is an important factor in the creation of gay/lesbian communities and identities in most parts of the world, and over the past decade there has been a marked growth in individuals and groups organizing around sexual identity in every part of the world where there is sufficient political and economic space to assert oneself (Drucker 1996; McKenna 1996; Parker 1998; Polsky 1995).

I have written a great deal about these developments (Altman 1997b; 1996a; 1996b) so there's little point in repeating my arguments here. In terms of this book the changes which are going on at a global level suggest that we need be far more sensitive to the interplay between socioeconomic structures and cultural traditions in discussing the development of lesbigay/queer worlds. Perhaps the greatest marginalities are those we impose upon ourselves, and that the great bulk of recent G/L/Q scholarship – read that as you will – has itself contributed to an Atlantic-centrism which perpetuates marginalities within the queer world. I am constantly struck, for example, by the sheer ignorance of lesbigay writing which comes out of many parts of the non-Atlantic world, that even as scholarly a book as Gregory Woods's *A History of Gay Literature* (Woods 1998) can totally ignore writers from countries as diverse as Brazil, New Zealand and Singapore. Yet in recent years since I wrote this piece there has been a marked increase in Australian gay and lesbian literature, and its publication by mainstream houses.

The very idea of marginalities implies that somewhere there is a centre, rather in the sense that Sinfield speaks of the metropolitan. One of the paradoxes of globalization is that this is increasingly not the case, even as the economic concentrations of global capitalism mean less and less is locally owned or controlled. Yet it is also true that modern communications have in part obliterated distance, so that people in Rockhampton, Little Rock and Port Elizabeth can speak to each other through the illusionary immediacy of the internet, which allows for the removal of at least some of the loneliness of provincial (or outer suburban) life. Lesbians and gay men in Rockhampton may still be isolated from the big cities, but increasingly they will find ways of carving out meaningful ways of living in provincial centres which were unimaginable in the past.

During the 1990s Tasmania, the smallest Australian state, was also the home of its most active gay/lesbian movement, as international human rights law was invoked to bring about the belated decriminalization of homosexuality (Morris 1995). In the same way the last section of Jeff Buchanan's novel, *Sucking Feijoas*, invokes the possibility of a gay movement in New Plymouth, a provincial town in New Zealand. Over the next decade it seems very likely that we will see an increased visibility of lesbigay life in provincial centres, as the metropolitan ceases to be the only available definition for life beyond the heterosexual norm.

## Notes

1 An earlier version of this paper appeared in L. Rowan and J. McNamee, *Voices of a Margin*, C.Q.U.P., Rockhampton, 1995, and I am grateful to the Press for permission to republish here.
2 'Provincial' is a term commonly used in Australia to describe cities of 50,000-plus outside the state capitals. Here it has also the more general sense of non-metropolitan.
3 Cairns is now a major tourist centre, with numerous international flights, and Darwin is the capital of the Northern Territory, also with direct international airlinks. With Townsville, also on the Queensland coast, these are the only cities in the tropical third of Australia.
4 Paul Keating was Labor Prime Minister 1994–6, when he was defeated by the Liberal/National Coalition led by John Howard.
5 Oxford Street, which runs from the city of Sydney towards the Eastern suburbs, is the centre of Australia's most visible gay area, and the route of the annual Mardi Gras parade (see Wotherspoon 1991).
6 Fred Nile is a fundamentalist Protestant whose political party, the Call to Australia, recently renamed Christian Democrats, has some representation in the New South Wales upper house and is strongly opposed to homosexual rights.
7 In 1992 the Australian High Court (in *Mabo & others v. State of Queensland*) ruled that indigenous Australians had certain rights to land which had not been extinguished by white settlement. The response to this – and the subsequent Wik case – has made Aboriginal land rights central to political debate since.

## Bibliography

Altman, D. (1993) *The Comfort of Men*, Melbourne: Heinemann.
—— (1994a) *Power and Community: Organisational and Cultural Responses to AIDS*, London: Falmer.
—— (1994b) 'Multiculturalism and the Emergence of Lesbian/Gay Worlds', in R. Nile (ed.) *Australian Civilisation*, Melbourne: Oxford University Press, 110–24.
—— (1996a) 'Rupture or Continuity? The Internationalization of Gay Identities', *Social Text* 48.14: 77–94.
—— (1996b) 'On Global Queering', *Australian Humanities Review*, 2 July (electronic journal: www.lib.latrobe.edu.au).
—— (1997a) *Defying Gravity: A Political Life*, Sydney: Allen & Unwin.
—— (1997b) 'Global Gaze/Global Gays', *GLQ: A Journal of Lesbian and Gay Studies* 3: 417–36.
Ballard, J. (1989) 'The Politics of AIDS', in H. Gardner (ed.) *The Politics of Health: The Australian Experience*, Melbourne: Churchill.
Blainey, G. (1996) *The Tyranny of Distance*, Melbourne: Sun Books.
Brett, J. (1997) 'Pauline Hanson, John Howard and the Politics of Grievance', in G. Gray and C. Winter (eds) *The Resurgence of Racism*, Monash Publications in History No. 24, Melbourne: Monash University, 7–28.

Buchanan, J. (1998) *Sucking Feijoas*, Auckland: Tandem.

Dessaix, R. (1998) *Speaking their Minds: Intellectuals and the Public Culture in Australia*, Sydney: ABC Books.

Drucker, P. (1996) 'In the Tropics there is No Sin: Sexuality and Gay–Lesbian Movements in the Third World', *New Left Review* 218: 75–101.

McKenna, N. (1996) *On The Margins*, London: Panos.

Manalansan, M. (1995) 'In the Shadows of Stonewall', *GLQ: A Journal of Lesbian and Gay Studies* 2: 425–38.

Morris, M. (1995) *The Pink Triangle: Struggle for Gay Law Reform in Tasmania*, Sydney: University of New South Wales Press.

Parker, R. (1998) *Beneath the Equator*, New York: Routledge.

Polsky, N. (1995) *Then We Take Berlin*, Toronto: Knopf.

Tan, M. (1995) 'Tita Aida and Emerging Communities of Gay Men', *Journal of Gay & Lesbian Social Services* 3: 3.

Wells, P. (1994) *The Duration of a Kiss*, Auckland: Secker & Warburg.

Woods, G. (1998) *A History of Gay Literature*, New Haven, Conn., and London: Yale University Press.

Wotherspoon, G. (1991) *City of the Plain*, Sydney: Hale & Iremonger.

# 3

# REGION, RELIGION AND SEXUALITY

## Pilgrim through this barren land

*Kate Chedgzoy*

Guide me, O thou great Jehovah,
Pilgrim through this barren land;
I am weak, but thou art mighty;
Hold me with thy powerful hand.
   Bread of heaven,
   Feed me 'til I want no more.

Open now the crystal fountain
Whence the healing streams do flow;
Let the fiery, cloudy pillar
Lead me all my journey through:
   Strong deliverer,
   Ever be my strength and shield.

When I tread the verge of Jordan,
Bid my anxious fears subside;
Death of death, and hell's destruction,
Land me safe on Canaan's side:
   Songs of praises
   I will ever give to thee.
(William Williams Pantycelyn, 1764)

This is an essay about the quest for love and transcendence, tracking two quite different versions of that strange pilgrimage: my own past, written out in the mode of confessional criticism, and the recent British independent film *Butterfly Kiss*, a controversial fiction that depicts lesbian eroticism and religious obsession as painfully intertwined. What these two disparate 'texts' share is a commitment to investigating some of the strange congruences of queer desire and religious longing, as well as the painful tensions that pull at queer subjects and religious cultures. In each case, this investigation is carried out within a highly localized, regionally distinctive setting in provincial Britain. The central metaphor of the pilgrimage as a journey through space and time which enables a new creation of the self is thus contained within a specific, geographically and culturally marginal frame.

This topic matters to me because I grew up an intensely religious child, eagerly embracing the passion and empowerment that the practice of a particular kind of nonconformist Christianity then offered me. I spent my childhood in a small Welsh town, an odd mixture of working-class seaside resort and crumbling monument to the heyday of coal. A queer child, in my nana's phrase, dreamy, contrary, at odds with my world, I sought something that place did not offer me, something I did not know how to name. But there were some things there that helped me to glimpse the sublime, to perceive the emotional borderlands at the limit of what could be experienced and articulated. As I began in my late teens to formulate a sense of my lesbian identity I came – like many, though by no means all, queer Christians – to experience a conflict between the social world of the Welsh Baptist community I'd been raised in, and my emergent sense of my sexual self. Nonconformity is the religious mainstream in Wales, and the Welsh public sphere is saturated with its traditions and world-view. This gives religion a place in social life which is quite different from the role of the Anglican Church in England. Nevertheless, Wales shares with many other countries in the industrialized North a context of growing secularization and generally falling attendance at mainstream places of worship, punctuated by surges of involvement in groups which have a more charismatic, enthusiastic approach to Christianity. As a teenager, I was frustrated by what I perceived as the rather sedate and tepid culture of the chapel I had been raised in, and sought out a more radical group which encouraged an intense personal engagement with the spiritual life, and nurtured the flashes of emotional exaltation which I understood as moments of mystical experience – direct contact with the divine. For me, there was no necessary conflict between sexual desire and religious faith, though; it would be more accurate to say that the two were intimately and pleasurably interrelated.

I am not, now, a Christian: my religious desire faded away, in a process that was, one might say, a little like falling out of love, in the years immediately after I left home and moved to England. My actual journey away from the distinctive religious and social culture of South Wales seems to have derailed the spiritual pilgrimage to which I had been so intensely committed as an adolescent: my desires did not seem to mean quite the same in England as in Wales. Richard Crowe has spoken of how Welsh literary representations of male homosexuality expel it beyond the boundaries of Wales (Crowe 1997), and I could certainly construct a conventional narrative in which I had to leave Wales in order to become a dyke. But I do not want to use my history with religious desire and sexual desire as a way of telling an escape story, of how I fled the gloom and oppression of a Christian childhood in Wales for the heavenly light of adult life in the lesbian nation of Hackney. Setting aside my ingrained suspicion of progress narratives, such a linear tale would not do justice to the false starts, returns, and strayings from the path (what path?), that characterize my hesitant, dubious pilgrimage through several barren lands. This is not, then, a story about how I once was lost but now am found, was blind but now can see. Nor is it a version of the testimonies of religious experience I used to offer eagerly to my chapel youth group as a teenager, although in terms of narrative structure and collective function those were effectively identical to coming-out stories. The process of giving your testimonial – also known as witnessing – entails the narrating of a selfhood acceptable to the community that constitutes the immediate audience for the narration. Biddy Martin has written about the personal and political usefulness within lesbian feminism of the telling of coming-out stories as just such a form of witnessing: 'Self-worth, identity, and a sense of community have fundamentally depended on the production of a shared narrative or life history and on the assimilation of individuals' life histories into the history of the group' (Martin 1996: 143).

But there is clearly a key difference between these two ways of bearing witness. A testimonial of religious conversion is incited and endorsed by a powerful cultural and social institution, whereas the lesbian coming-out story is, as Martin emphasizes, a narrative of discontinuity and resistance, foregrounding those aspects of personal life that fail to fit or make sense within the terms of the culturally dominant ways of shaping narratives of subjectivity and sexuality. She suggests, therefore, that 'Lesbian autobiographical narratives are about remembering differently, outside the controls and narrative constraints of conventional models' (Martin 1996: 143). Discussing the collection of autobiographical writings by women of colour, *This Bridge Called My Back*, Martin shows how in these texts 'lesbianism is politicized less as an identity than as a desire that transgresses the boundaries imposed by structures of race, class, ethnicity, nationality; it figures not as a desire that can efface or ignore the effects of those boundaries but as a provocation to take responsibility for them' (Martin 1996: 152). In writings like these, the question of how relationships and priorities are to be adjudicated between the multiple facets of one's identity is often addressed by evoking particular locations, overwritten with associations drawn from the writer's personal history, 'concrete sites that evoke memories of home even as they suggest a kind of homelessness … spaces with permeable boundaries and heterogeneous collectivities and communities' (Martin 1996: 153). For the white reader of such texts, particularly a reader who is looking for help in shaping and situating her own autobiographical narratives, there is a risk that such vivid and concrete particularity can serve to re-locate the black autobiographer as the desirably exotic other, fortunate to be endowed with a home that can be recalled by way of pungent smells, bright colours, fertile social networks, and clamouring sounds. The exotic sensual plenitude of otherness licenses a sense of whiteness as drab and vacant, a kind of cultural deprivation, occluding the power relations which actually shape the experience of racialized differences (Dyer 1997). Writing about the places and times of my childhood, I fall too easily into a mode of elegy, plangently evoking the pearly emptiness of a winter beach traversed by a lonely child in a way which reinstates the production of whiteness as vacancy critiqued by Dyer. Conversely, when I describe my religious life to my secular friends, I am aware that it permits a pleasurable kind of self-exoticizing; my life can retrospectively take on the colour, vividness, strangeness of alterity. That this is achieved at the cost of making my past life other to myself is perhaps intrinsic to writing autobiographically, and need not be seen as entailing loss. For an awareness of the over-determination of the tropes through which I write my life can serve as a politicizing reminder of the need to take responsibility, as Biddy Martin demands, for the relation between the destabilizations of desire and the social and psychic infrastructures of 'race, class, ethnicity, nationality' (Martin 1996: 152) – not to mention gender, sexuality, religion.

## 'Songs of praises / I will ever give to thee'

Familiar – perhaps disablingly over-familiar – with critiques of autobiographical writing, looking for ways to narrate and theorize my own story which did not entail the performance, one more time, of either version of my testimonial/coming-out story, I sought, in drafting this essay, for different ways of writing. Hence my somewhat oblique approach, by way of a piece of music which connects my own experience to wider Welsh cultural contexts. But I am acutely aware that rather than providing a resolution to the hesitation and ambivalence with which I approach this writing, this choice serves to entangle me problematically in the complexities of identification and appropriation outlined by Dyer and Martin. Singing 'Guide me, O Thou Great Jehovah' stirs in me some of the most complex and profound emotions that still bind me to my Welsh childhood. But hearing it sung by a male voice choir or a rugby crowd provokes differently mixed feelings, about the great strengths and marked limitations of the almost exclusively masculine public culture of industrial South Wales. Literally the land of my fathers (the men of my father's family were miners in the Cynon Valley), this is a culture which has, for economic and political reasons, been annihilated in my lifetime. And it is a source of shame to me that I was too enmeshed in my own ambivalence about my relation to that world to play a part in its defence alongside the other lesbians and gay men who did support the miners' strike in 1984–5.

The hymn 'Guide me, O Thou Great Jehovah', quoted at the beginning of this essay, has the status of an alternative national anthem in Wales, affirming communal identity and pride when it is sung at national events, weddings, and funerals. Written in Welsh by the pre-eminent hymnologist William Williams Pantycelyn in 1764 and almost immediately translated into English, 'Guide me, O Thou Great Jehovah' was quickly absorbed into the culture of Methodism that flourished in eighteenth-century Wales. But another set of Welsh lyrics is sometimes sung to the same celebrated tune, 'Cwm Rhondda'; written by Ann Griffiths a couple of decades after Williams Pantycelyn's version, they resonate with very different implications:

> Wele'n sefyll rhwng y myrtwydd
> Wrthrych teilwng o fy mryd
> Er o'r braidd yr wy'n adnabod
> Ei fod uwchlaw gwrthrychau'r byd
> Henffych fore
> Caf ei weled fel y mae.

> See standing among the myrtles / An object worthy of my devotion / Though barely do I recognize / That he is above worldly objects / Hail to that morning / When I shall see him as he is.
> [My translation] (Davies 1865: 115)

Drawing on the language and imagery of the biblical Song of Songs, the woman poet here takes up the position of the desiring subject, eroticizing Christ as the object of her adoration. Jane Aaron has recently argued that Ann Griffiths' poetry expresses the combination of sensual and spiritual joy characteristic of the mystical tradition, and suggests that the intensity of her religious experience, and the confidence with which she expresses it, may flow directly from her involvement with Calvinistic Methodism (Aaron 1992: 35). Despite the limited opportunities for female leadership in the social world of early Methodism, Aaron convincingly argues that the distinctive structure of its spirituality opened up the possibility of experiencing female subjectivity in ways not available elsewhere in the culture. In particular, the ecstatic experience of conversion demanded by Calvinistic Methodism subverts many of the canons of gendered behaviour which prevailed in eighteenth-century Wales. Conversion, Aaron says, entailed

> a shattering of the human ego, a passivity in the face of the divine will, and an opening up of the heart to receive lightning flashes of grace … the experience was more likely to find expression through groans, cries and physical demonstrations rather than through conceptual utterance.
> (Aaron 1992: 36)

That these inarticulate human noises are also the sounds of sexual pleasure is by no means coincidental, and Aaron goes on to offer a persuasive account of the sensuality and 'blissful physicality' of much of Ann Griffiths's poetry (Aaron 1992: 38).

Within the terms of the eighteenth-century Welsh religious culture that produced these two hymns, then, Ann Griffiths's version proves to have a surprisingly radical political charge. From the millennial moment in which I write, though, what is most striking is the difference between the static, passive, individual erotic responsiveness of Griffiths, and the dynamic, collective movement narrated in William Williams Pantycelyn's version. His hymn is a condensed, poetic retelling of the journey of the children of Israel from slavery in Egypt, through the desert to the Promised Land, narrated in the Old Testament book of Exodus which is a cherished text of Welsh Nonconformity. It is the story of a departure, a journey, that is also a return home. The Exodus story is one that speaks of transcendent longing, for a home that has never been and perhaps never can be; for an end to desire that may only come with death. Pantycelyn's words speak of wanting, of desire satisfied or left unsatisfied. I address you, the object of my desire: I am asking you to assuage my hunger by feeding me on the bread of heaven 'til I want no more. I will turn away from the world as it is, joining an exodus community on a pilgrimage through a barren land in search of satisfaction elsewhere. This kind of imagery may seem fatalistic, relegating the assuaging of desire and the meeting of needs to the hereafter. But this need not be the case: the exodus story has often been used and appropriated by oppressed groups in profoundly political ways. For example, there is an extensive body of scholarship on the use of these kinds of tropes in African-American slave culture which stresses its political potential, as a way of imaging a place somewhere in this world where it is possible to say: I will change the world, I will demand that it accept the assertion of my selfhood and the legitimacy of my desires (Genovese 1972: 252–3). Exodus was thus originally a collective movement in search of a people's liberation, and the notion of an exodus community still has political resonance. This politicized understanding of tropes of pilgrimage and exodus can thus serve as a kind of hinge between the private desire for spiritual gratification and the public culture of nonconformity, a space where individual and communal journeys of desire can be mapped in relation to each other, opening up one way of understanding how the concern with personal transcendence, spiritual or sexual, can come to have any political effectivity. Movements for liberation and social justice, like feminism and the lesbian and gay movement, are similarly motivated by that sense of lacking, wanting, needing: motivated above all, perhaps, by the contradictions which make these hymns so powerful. The assertion of desire, of lack, of need, may itself be a gesture of considerable power. Articulating the nature of the exclusions to which you are subject and the desire for what you don't have can be a vital first step for a radical movement.

Hymns, like other kinds of subcultural anthems have a crucial performative function: when you belt out 'Cwm Rhondda', you constitute yourself, just for a moment, as a member of a community, and by doing so you reshape your relation to the world beyond that community. But singing hymns like 'Guide me, O Thou Great Jehovah', much loved and incessantly sung in South Wales, also offered me, as a teenager, one of the moments in life where I could glimpse the sublime, and for reasons which the chapel did not necessarily design: the sheer delight of music, the marriage of flesh and air in the human voice singing, those sensual physical pleasures which are, by definition, hard to put into words, are vividly embodied in the great Nonconformist hymns. As a child, one of my favourite hymns was 'Amazing Love', a song about how breathtaking, how wonderful, how astonishing it is to be loved, to be chosen. To the extent that Christian hymnography elaborates a sustained and various discourse of love, it may have something distinctive and as yet unheard to say to queer audiences. Love has largely been occluded from our academic musings on sexuality, its relation to more fashionable terms like desire, pleasure, and transgression scarcely addressed. A growing body of scholarly and personal writing on religion, gender and sexuality is informed by the assumption that religious practice and sexual practice offer different – and perhaps competing, irreconcilable – means to self-affirmation and self-realization, in a community and in the wider world (Webster 1995). This functionalist understanding of the relation between spirituality and sexuality only tells part of the story: it omits the sublime pleasures of self-annihilation and self-dissolution, which are harder to account for but not to be underestimated. For me, what has been most powerful about my involvement with organized religion and my life in the queer community is the interplay of self-assertion and self-abandonment for which both create distinct, but I would argue sometimes surprisingly similar, cultural spaces.

## 'I am weak, but thou art mighty'

To produce an autobiographical account which understands sexual and religious desire as mutually informing is not the same as reducing them to each other, or seeing one as standing in for the other. Enthusiastic religion has long been understood as sexual excess, and theorists like Lacan and Bataille have, as Michael Warner says, 'regarded all religion as an unrecognized form of sexuality'. But I agree with Warner, himself raised in a Pentecostal community, in thinking that you 'can reduce religion to sex only if you don't especially believe in either one' (Warner 1996: 43). Seeking a way of understanding the emotional congruence of sexual and spiritual desire without being reductive, Warner argues that 'ecstatic religions can legitimate self-transgression, providing a meaningful framework for the sublime play of self-realization and self-dissolution' (Warner 1996: 43). Precisely these psychic and embodied experiences are also central to sexual desire and erotic pleasure, in Warner's account. The question of self-realization in the world preoccupies most studies of homosexuality and religion, which seek to determine whether these two things are mutually complementary or contradictory in an individual's project to achieve it. The religious sublime, in contrast – that is, the sublime annihilation and reconstitution of subjectivity required by a certain kind of Protestantism – is seen as marginal, embarrassing, a curious cultural phenomenon ripe for symptomatic analysis. Thomas Weiskel comments that 'we have long since been too ironic for the capacious gestures of the Romantic sublime. ... To please us, the sublime must now be abridged, reduced, and parodied as the grotesque. ... The infinite spaces are no longer astonishing; still less do they terrify' (Weiskel 1976: 14). This is surely also true of the Western attitude to religion; that culturally specific secular rationalism which finds ecstatic religion simultaneously threatening and ridiculous also holds no place for the sublime. Like Warner, though, I believe we impoverish the range of ways we have to make sense of our desires when we resist attending to the sublime dialectic in which the self flickers between affirmation and dissolution; a flickering of subjectivity which can be located in experiences of both religious and sexual ecstasy.

The sublime is an elusive and complex notion; as Lee Edelman has ruefully remarked, attempts to define and analyse it are nearly always marked by a 'quality of excess, this metamorphic capacity by which the sublime always escapes our efforts to define it, [which] raises to the level of the sublime itself the attempt to wrest comprehensibility from its protean manifestations' (Edelman 1989: 213). In my thinking about lesbian sexuality and religious experience as aspects of the sublime, I have been influenced by Barbara Claire Freeman's important account of the feminine sublime, which she describes as 'a domain of experience that resists categorization, in which the subject enters into relation with an otherness – social, aesthetic, political, erotic – that is excessive and unrepresentable' (Freeman 1995: 2). Lee Edelman essays a definition of the sublime as a dynamic phenomenon, 'a relational mode that stages its paradigmatic confrontations at the bounds of (self-)definition, at the threshold or limen marking the highly charged division of self and other' (Edelman 1989: 214). This use of spatial metaphor to depict the sublime as taking place at the limits of experience and at the borders of the self suggests the concept's pertinence to the organization of religious and sexual experience through the metaphors of pilgrimage, journeying, and border crossing central to the texts discussed in this essay. Within Edelman's model, the flows of power between self and other are both highly charged and highly mobile: the empowerment of the subject that can result from the shattering encounter with the other need not take the form of an exercise of power over the other. And conversely, in both sexual and spiritual contexts the sublime can involve a submission to the other which, though ostensibly masochistic, opens up the possibility of a transcendence of self which cracks open the paradoxes of these binary categories.

This death to self and rebirth in Christ is required in Protestant conversion, and is dramatized most vividly in the denomination I grew up in by means of the ritual of adult baptism by total immersion, a momentary drowning I experienced in adolescence, and which enabled a rebirth into the adult community of the chapel by way of a subjective experience of sublimity I have only otherwise known in sex. This is no paradox. As the chapel community understands it, baptism by full immersion is a condensed, individualized rehearsal of the Christian subject's pilgrimage through life, and a metaphorical re-enactment of the journey across the Jordan to the promised land – a border-crossing that is also symbolized in death. It is also an act that requires you to perform in public the intimacy, self-abandonment, and trust in the other characteristic of a sexual encounter. Barefoot and clad in white, you step into the water and give yourself into the hands of the man or woman performing the baptism. They hold you firmly, go part way on the journey with you, but cannot join you fully on your descent beneath the waters and resurgence, although they must themselves have undertaken this crossing of the waters at some point in their past. You resurface, drenched, cleansed, to hallelujahs and embraces, the joyful greetings of a community welcoming you to itself. Though she is writing there not of religion but of sex, a passage in Lynda Hart's extraordinary recent book *Between the Body and the Flesh* brilliantly, uncannily, captures for me the world-dissolving and world-creating qualities of this experience:

> Brief, precious, infinitely worth waiting for, and endlessly repeatable ... it is in this moment that she is neither surface nor depth. Her body still partially submerged but her head breaking through the pool of tears, [she] inhabits the borderline for a split second. This breaking of the waters is the breach in language, where one catches a glimpse of full speech.
>
> (Hart 1998: 165)

Though it is by no means the only thing that is distinctive about the Baptist denomination, the symbolic significance with which the choice to be baptized as an adult is endowed is clearly underlined in its name. I use, here, the community's own preferred formula in speaking of adult baptism, but I was not myself quite an adult when I chose to be baptized. Precocious, gauche, and uncertain of myself, I sought baptism in my early teens: I can't quite recollect now the longings that motivated me to make an exception of myself in this way, but I imagine them as having comprised a queasy mixture of spiritual pride, an incipient tendency to mysticism, and a genuine desire for transformation, making new, crossing the border. For this explicitly adult act seemed to me to encode a ritual of transition from childhood to maturity, an opportunity to quit the jostling adolescent world where I had no bearings and accede prematurely to adulthood, to join a social world where names for my desires might be found. I walked through the waters of Jordan to land safe on Canaan's shore; momentarily I was transfigured, purified, shattered and remade.

## 'Death of death, and hell's destruction'

I now turn away from autobiography to a reading of the 1995 film *Butterfly Kiss*, a film which centres on a queer pilgrimage, a violent quest for transcendence and self-annihilation and closes with an impromptu baptism that transfigures but cannot redeem. Described as '[a]n often breathtakingly original meld of road movie, lesbian love story, psychodrama and black comedy ... [a] realistic fairy tale of murder and romantic obsession' (Aaron 1999: 77), *Butterfly Kiss* is an idiosyncratically English take on the genre of the road movie which roams the motorways and service stations of Lancashire. Its regional location was emphasized for British viewers by the casting of actors familiar from other Northern dramas – casting that was given a distinctively queer twist by the appearance in a supporting role of Emily Aston who had shortly before played the child Jess in the TV version of Jeanette Winterson's *Oranges Are Not the Only Fruit*, also set in Lancashire. The heroine's quest is imaged in Winterson's novel by means of a rewriting of fairy tales and Arthurian romances, a non-realist dimension of the book which in the TV version was conveyed by slow-motion title scenes set in a lurid, dreamlike fairground; *Butterfly Kiss* conflates these two fantastic scenarios by routeing the journey of its doubled protagonists via the Camelot theme park, where Arthurian metaphors are commodified in the service of a day out for a strange, *ad hoc* family.

Michele Aaron's discussion of *Butterfly Kiss* places it as one of a group of four movies concerned with female couples who kill: the other films, all released in 1994, are *Heavenly Creatures*, *Fun*, and *Sister My Sister*. Aaron traces the complex play of resemblance and difference among this group of films, arguing that they all 'share a cultural and geographical specificity in their settings', a characteristic which they deploy in the service of a claim to authenticity and authority in their representation of queer desire (Aaron 1999: 70). The narrative of *Butterfly Kiss*, for example, is framed as a series of flashbacks illustrating Miriam's account of her ultimately fatal involvement with Eunice. The sequences that depict Miriam offering up this autobiographical account to a silent, invisible interlocutor are shot in grainy black and white, drawing on the aesthetics of documentary in order to achieve this 'authenticity effect'. Yet the film is not located on the terrain I have been mapping in this essay, where autobiography, culture and politics intersect: its aesthetic of authenticity is located within the frame of a fictional drama, scripted by Frank Cottrell Boyce and directed by Michael Winterbottom. For me, one of the most fascinating aspects of *Butterfly Kiss* was its use of Christian iconography in Eunice's creation of a solipsistic queer cosmography. Clare Whatling's brief account of the film prefigures my interest in its use of religious discourses and images, as she describes the fascination and repulsion provoked by the film's display of 'the wounded body of the strange martyr Eunice' (Whatling 1997: 100), and cites Bea Campbell's perceptive comment that the film's plot moves 'inexorably towards an intimate apocalypse' (Whatling 1997: 101). Eunice is an essentially solitary figure, who puts the language and iconography of the Judaeo-Christian tradition to private use, as both punishment and therapy for her personal traumas. Religion in this film functions as the site of an individual psychic drama, and there is no sense of Christianity as either a social institution or a site of communitarian aspirations and pressures. As Miriam, one half of the lesbian couple at the centre of the film understands, Eunice's murders and the quest of which they formed part were not essentially other-directed, but self-involved: 'there was something missing for her ... someone ... something missing in herself'. Like Eunice, the film itself is bizarrely asocial: set in a part of the North of England that visibly bears the scars of economic decline and social exclusion, it nevertheless ignores the material world it sketches in and decontextualizes the lives of its central characters, maintaining a tight focus on the obsessive love between Eunice and Miriam. Any sense that the metaphor of a journey can be a way of mapping individual desires at the level of the social and political, as I argued earlier, is absent. The queer pilgrimage undertaken by Eunice and Miriam does not imply a journey beyond the boundaries of the self to connect with the other, but a wholly solipsistic drive to self-annihilation.

Eunice is propelled up and down the motorways of the North-west by her search for a woman called Judith: whether this Judith is an ex-lover, a purely symbolic figure, or an *alter ego* for Eunice herself never becomes clear. Eunice identifies her as a belated manifestation of the Judith who features in the biblical Apocrypha, and who with her woman companion slaughters the Assyrian leader Holofernes in order to defend the children of Israel when all seems lost. The invocation of the biblical Judith forms part of a network of references in the script which construct acts of shocking violence in terms of purification, sacrifice, and salvation. This is signalled most powerfully early on, when Miriam takes Eunice home to meet her housebound grandmother. We see Eunice from behind, silhouetted against a window in the tower-block flat, chanting in nursery-rhyme tones of the sacrificial violence that is the cornerstone of Christianity: 'Jesus died on the cross for you and he died on the cross for me ... Sticks and stones will break your bones, and you will be left to despair, but he will sing in his honeyed tones and take away all your care.' As Miriam's bewildered grandmother assents with a heartfelt 'Amen', Eunice turns round, displaying the chains, piercings, bruises and tattoos that mortify her flesh, in a postmodern version of the masochistic agonies self-inflicted by the saints of the early Church. Later, Miriam will emphasize that each of Eunice's seventeen tattoos has a meaning. In general, though, the movie construes Eunice's self-mortification not as a meaningful part of a spiritual practice which connects her to a collective social project but as an aspect of her pathology, tied to her repeated insistence that she is wicked, deserving to be hurt and punished. The potentially serious significance of Eunice's religious obsessions is further undermined because they are often played out in the mode of black comedy, as in her fatal sexual encounter with the hapless Brummie vaccuum-cleaner salesman, Mr McDermott. Eunice is drawn to him because he sells a product which offers the purification she yearns for, and because he is willing to join her in consensual sadomasochistic sex. Stripping off his clothes, she finds the scar of a kidney operation and declares with surreally comic relish, 'I love wounds. Deep in thy wounds Lord hide and shelter me. I love the bit where St Thomas puts his hand in Jesus's wound.'

Mr McDermott's consensual participation in s/m is important to Eunice because what she desires most urgently is to be known and acknowledged by an other who repeatedly eludes her, and who sometimes seems to be represented for her by Judith. A key scene in the movie takes place just after Eunice has killed the latest in a series of women who failed to incarnate Judith for her. Eunice and Miriam confront each other on a glassed-in walkway above the road, isolated from the streams of people bound on their own journeys below them. Eunice implies that when she kills people, she is seeking to be fully seen and acknowledged by them in a way that constantly eludes her: 'It's like I don't exist. ... I was going to kill her and she still wouldn't look at me. ... God's forgotten me,' she cries repeatedly. Perhaps what Eunice is doing on her murderous pilgrimage through the North of England is arrogating the powers of God over life and death to herself in a desperate struggle to get him to recognize and acknowledge her; she seeks her other so that she can exist to herself. In her sacrificial identification with the martyred Christ, an identification which is turned inside out and projected onto her victims, Eunice is trying to catch the attention of the awe-ful, jealous God of the Old Testament. Thus Eunice's assertion to Miriam that she intended to sacrifice Judith is the other side of the coin to her claim that once Miriam has killed her she will be assured of a place in heaven because she too will be a sacrificial victim. What Eunice seeks is a place where she will not be required to labour so agonizingly to maintain the boundaries of a subjectivity which is nothing but torture to her. For most of the film, torturing others is what enables her, momentarily, to enter such a space; finally, it is Miriam's sacrificial love that gives Eunice a more permanent way out.

Miriam too is co-opted into undertaking a desiring quest of her own, as she seeks by passing a series of trials to demonstrate her love for Eunice. These ordeals culminate in Eunice's demand that Miriam prove her willingness to witness to Eunice's existence by killing her. The last scene of the movie recapitulates its narrative structure, as the two women go on an exalted journey across a vast, desolate beach at dawn, a location as socially and spatially marginal as it is possible to devise. Incantatory call and response chants, drawing their rhetoric and metaphors from the prophetic books of the Old Testament, make Miriam a participant in the elaboration of Eunice's private theology and create a ritual which gives legitimizing meaning to their shared task. The divine has long been closely associated with the oceanic: Thomas Weiskel traces the eighteenth-century emergence of the natural sublime in which the emotions traditionally associated with the Deity are withdrawn from him and associated with the immensity of space and the natural phenomena – oceans, mountains – which seem to approach that immensity (Weiskel 1976: 14). Though Weiskel laments the disappearance of the sublime from the modern imagination, the oceanic remains a powerful metaphor of transcendence and otherness – for example, one of the women whose personal narratives of sexuality and spirituality are quoted in Alison Webster's *Found Wanting* finds that the erotic and the divine are interrelated, and that either may be 'nourished by windy mountain tops, deserted cliffs, rough seas, open expanses of countryside, being buffeted by the weather while out walking'. The 'loss of body boundaries and ego boundaries' she finds in sex is also a spiritual experience for this woman (Webster 1995: 175). In the liminal space of the Lancashire sea strand, these boundaries are dissolved for Eunice too when she submits at Miriam's hands to a drowning which is also a baptism. I have already spoken of adult baptism as a symbolic realization of the death to the self and rebirth in Christ, the sublime annihilation and reconstitution of subjectivity required by a certain kind of Protestantism. The symbolics of death entailed in baptism are literalized by the final scenes of *Butterfly Kiss*. To be baptized is to be washed in the blood of the lamb – violent and sacrificial imagery for an act of purification and liberation. Eunice wore her chains and piercings as the signs of a masochistic identification with Christ's self-sacrifice: freed from them and rendered 'Defenceless. Helpless. Sinless,' by Miriam's love, she is baptized into a new, painless death, and the end of *Butterfly Kiss* allows Eunice to find peace in the oceanic sublime, clasped to Miriam's breast in a final, blasphemously beautiful *pietà*.

## Safe on Canaan's side

In conclusion, I return briefly to Lynda Hart's *Between the Body and the Flesh*. What is particularly striking about this remarkable book is Hart's understanding of the desire for salvation that historically has most often been embedded in the languages and institutions of religion, and her recognition of the many other forms this desire can take. For instance, she finds a rhetoric of redemption and an essentially theological world-view in both the language of s/m writing and in the founding attitudes of radical feminism, mutually hostile though these two discourses are usually considered to be. Here, for instance, she is speaking of s/m testimonials, yet her words are equally relevant to much feminist autobiography: 'Redemption figures in these accounts not as parodic distance from the normative order of things but as accessing a "whole" or "real" self that has been fractured or damaged by the imposition of normalizing conventions' (Hart 1998: 81). She traces the use in s/m testimonials of metaphors drawn from Christianity, and a language of revelation, pilgrimage, and healing, 'partaking in the discourses of sacrifice, amendment, atonement. Not, however, in the service of those who have "sinned", but as compensation for those who have been sinned against' (Hart 1998: 81). This desire for salvation, coupled with a perverse reluctance to accept the terms on which it is offered, is beautifully articulated in Hart's discussion of Dorothy Allison's work, where the redemptive possibilities supposedly offered by both Christianity and feminism are found hopelessly wanting. In Allison's *Bastard out of Carolina* her protagonist, Bone, turns to

Christianity as the discourse of salvation most readily available to her, seeking healing for the bodily and psychic scars left by a sexually abused childhood, and troubled by sexual fantasies that repeatedly re-stage her experience of pain and helplessness. In the light of my earlier discussion of my own experiences as a Baptist, it seems important here to acknowledge the cultural specificity of the Baptist tradition in the American South, which provides the institutional framework for Bone's encounters with religion, and is quite different from the Welsh version. Bone goes to Baptist services, is stirred by the hymns, and longs to be able to join those who go forward and witness to their own salvation. But, as Lynda Hart says,

> Bone is ambivalent about being saved. . . . Her desire for community draws her toward the church; but the need to hold onto her singularity and the "secret" she keeps of her differences from those who can be saved makes this kind of witnessing impossible.
>
> (Hart 1998: 183)

Bone is baptized beneath a painting of Jesus undergoing the same ritual of death to the self and rebirth; she spends hours reading the Bible, especially the apocalyptic, prophetic Book of Revelation. But ultimately she does not want to be saved; her integrity requires her to work out her own salvation, outside the institutions that, in her world, promise to organize it for her. As Allison's text has it,

> I could not have explained, but it was not actually baptism I wanted, or welcome to the congregation, or even the breathless concentration of the preacher. It was that moment of sitting on the line between salvation and damnation with the preacher and the old women pulling bodily at my poor darkened soul. I wanted that moment to go on forever . . . . I wanted the way I felt to mean something, and for everything in my life to change because of it.
>
> (Allison 1993: 152–3)

Bone wants to dwell in the sublime moment of the undoing and reassertion of self, and to find in that moment the motor of change in her life and her world. But the very existence of Allison's novel, which has an intimate intertextual relation to her more overtly autobiographical text *Two or Three Things I Know for Sure* and exists on the borders of autobiography and fiction, testifies to the importance of understanding and using the dialectical relation between the seductions of dissolution, and the responsibility of reconstituting the self in the world – and, ultimately, remaking the terms of the relations between self and world. Perhaps it is this desire for transcendence and transformation that drives the difficult intimacy of religious and sexual desire, as ways of giving social meaning to that longing for a better world which is encoded in a set of richly resonant metaphors I have explored in this essay; metaphors which both hold open the dream of transcendence and stave off the pain of acknowledging its elusiveness.

## Acknowledgements

Thanks to Michele Aaron, Debbie Epstein, Di Paton and Deborah Steinberg.

## References

Aaron, Jane (1992) 'Daughters of Dissent: Women's Poetry and Welsh Methodism, 1780–1830', *Planet* 94: 33–43.

Aaron, Michele (1999) ' 'Til Death do us Part: Cinema's Queer Couples who Kill', in M. Aaron (ed.) *The Body's Perilous Pleasures: Dangerous Desires and Contemporary Culture*, Edinburgh: Edinburgh University Press: 67–84.

Allison, Dorothy (1993) *Bastard out of Carolina*, London: Flamingo.

—— (1995) *Two or Three Things I Know for Sure*, London: Flamingo.

Crowe, Richard (1997) 'Y Cysylltiad Seisnig: Cynrychioli Dynion Hoyw yn Llenyddiaeth y Gymraeg' [Foreign Bodies: The Representation of Gay Men in Welsh-language Literature], Paper given at the Non-Metropolitan Sexualities Conference, University of Wales, Aberystwyth, July.

Davies, Morris (1865) *Cofiant Ann Griffiths*, Dinbych: Thomas Gee.

Dyer, Richard (1997) *White*, London: Routledge.

Edelman, Lee (1989) 'At Risk in the Sublime: The Politics of Gender and Theory', in Linda Kauffman (ed.) *Gender and Theory: Dialogues on Feminist Criticism*, Oxford: Basil Blackwell: 213–24.

Freeman, Barbara Claire (1995) *The Feminine Sublime: Gender and Excess in Women's Fiction*, Berkeley: University of California Press.

Genovese, Eugene D. (1972) *Roll, Jordan, Roll: The World the Slaves Made*, New York: Pantheon.

Hart, Lynda (1998) *Between the Body and the Flesh: Performing Sadomasochism*, New York: Columbia University Press.

Martin, Biddy (1996) 'Lesbian Identity and Autobiographical Differences', in *Femininity Played Straight: The Significance of Being Lesbian*, London: Routledge: 137–61.

Warner, Michael (1996) 'Tongues Untied: Memoirs of a Pentecostal Boyhood', in Donald Morton (ed.) *The Material Queer: A LesBiGay Cultural Studies Reader*, Boulder, Colo. and Oxford: Westview Press: 39–45.

Webster, Alison (1995) *Found Wanting: Women, Christianity and Sexuality*, London: Cassell.

Weiskel, Thomas (1976) *The Romantic Sublime: Studies in the Structure and Psychology of Transcendence*, Baltimore, Md.: Johns Hopkins University Press.

Whatling, Clare (1997) *Screen Dreams: Fantasising Lesbians in Film*, Manchester: Manchester University Press.

# 4

# MARGINS OF THE CITY

## Towards a dialectic of suburban desire

*Barry Langford*

'Very English: paraquat parties behind the privet hedges, the pebble-dash prisons that keep the occupants *in* just as much as they keep the outside world out. English emotional and physical isolation turning ever inwards into psychosis, unnameable perversions in deep closets': this is rock critic Jon Savage's characterization of the imaginative geography of Siouxsie and the Banshees' 'Suburban Relapse', released in 1977 (quoted in Lebeau 1997: 283). What an instantly familiar vision of suburban spaces and sexualities: spaces defensively, neurotically huddled, outward convention (the pebble-dash) masking private perversion. This punk vision stands in a long tradition depicting suburban life as unfreedom and dissimulation, a picture easily duplicated across innumerable treatments of suburbia both in the social sciences and in fictional treatments in literature, film and television.

Should we be surprised that this widespread, sometimes unreflective deprecation of suburbia seems if anything only to have intensified as the suburban way of life has become increasingly the social norm? Every survey and census for decades has shown the centre of demographic, social and political gravity tilting irreversibly towards suburbia. It is now quiet suburban avenues, not teeming city streets, where one finds the key political battlegrounds in national politics. The decline of the local high street in the face of out-of-town superstores and malls is a much-remarked (and lamented) fact of commercial life. Soap operas, those barometers of changes in the cultural weather, have with *Brookside* and its adolescent counterpart *Hollyoaks* moved decisively away from the traditional inner-city community to the closes and culs-de-sac of the urban hinterland. Quite simply, the suburbs are our contemporary cultural dominant — in which case, perhaps their generally negative portrayal should be regarded simply as a backhanded tribute to their success and a testimony to their centrality.

Yet the suburbs are also, it is easy to forget, marginal spaces. This forgetting is in fact a crucial element in the negative depiction of suburbia: the suburbs are seen as marginal only in the most literal (physical) sense, the ragged fringes of great cities to which they stand in a purely negative relation. The interesting properties and the potentially critical perspectives of marginality that have attracted cultural critics to study (and celebrate) *demi-mondes*, itinerants, subcultures and subaltern groupings have been for the most part denied to the suburbs.

Over the past four decades, it has been the project above all of cultural studies to fill in the lacunae and ellipses of the normative social text, supplying its suppressed and denied content of contradiction and contestation. Yet where it has dealt with the suburbs at all, cultural studies has for the most part been surprisingly ready to endorse a normative reading of the suburban 'text'. Numerous other places and spaces in contemporary society and their associated practices have been interrogated and often critically recuperated for an oppositional perspective – especially those ignored or despised by a previous mandarin tradition of cultural criticism. But 'Metroland' has remained for the most part synonymous with the vices traditionally ascribed to it: petty snobbery, conformity, sexual repression, Rotarian philistinism, Little Englandism, and xenophobia – the familiar list goes on. Why this blind spot? In the first place, a number of the subcultural practices contemporary cultural studies is concerned to explore, excavate and, frequently enough, to validate – particularly youth subcultures such as punk and latterly dance culture, and social groups articulating non-conventional practices or codes of gender and sexuality – are understood and valued precisely as negations of miseries portrayed as integrally suburban. Although many such subcultures originate and even play themselves out within the physical and cognitive topography of the suburbs (sometimes, as latterly with the peripatetic rave culture organized around London's orbital motorway, quite literally), their principal value consists in their subversion of suburban domestic *anomie*. Sometimes, indeed, as canonically with punk, self-styled 'sound of the suburbs,' they may be construed as a self-generated negation, suburbia's own actualized immanent critique. (Later in this chapter, however, we will have cause to remind ourselves that punk was really less unproblematically oppositional than this construction attests.)

Continuing to address cultural studies' suburban blinkers, one ought to recall the vexed disciplinary genealogy of the culturalist critical turn itself. Inasmuch as cultural studies' professed textual politics aim to combat conformity and oppressive monovocalism at the level of the artefact or cultural practice – as a textual corollary to or adjunct of the more concrete political struggle against hierarchy and centralism – the suburb itself is inscribed on a topography of bland conformity and (to the extent that the suburban imaginary appears principally a white, middle- or aspirationally middle-class one) bourgeois essentialism. That is, if a prevailing (say, a Leavisite) prior tradition in literary and cultural criticism itself virtually demands to be read sociohistorically as the achieved academic hegemony of certain bourgeois/*petit bourgeois* positions, then for the critique of that critical tradition beginning in the early 1960s its own physical *habitus* becomes at least metonymically and perhaps also substantively part of the contested terrain. For some of the pioneers of emergent cultural studies, in fact – most notably Richard Hoggart – the synthetic, jerry-built material and cultural fabric alike of New Towns, ribbon developments and soulless speculative council housing estates could be polemically contrasted with the vibrant, bonding and responsive working-class culture they were everywhere displacing.[1] In any event, the paradoxical upshot of this complicated relationship is that cultural studies' disciplinary dispossession of the suburbs has effectively reintroduced to suburbia the very critical marginality its denial disguises as absence.

This chapter unpacks such general problems of the critical and theoretical construction of suburban space through a discussion of the cultural and especially the sexual geography of Hanif Kureishi's 1990 novel *The Buddha of Suburbia*. My concern in my encounter with Kureishi's text has been less to generate a coherent 'reading' as an end in itself than via this 'reading', coherent or otherwise, to pose certain questions relating both to the stability of the standard categories of suburban representation, and to suburbia's own constitutively deconstructive (so to speak) relationship to categorization's own ground. Coherence itself therefore is actually a crux, not a goal. For my intention has been not simply to rehabilitate suburbia as a positive pole, a site of resistance in its turn, with a flourish of the interpretative cape. In fact, one of the productive potentials I discern in Kureishi's text and his version of what I will call 'the suburban subject', is the recognition of the reactive and ultimately bankrupt nature of such turn-and-turnabout critical logic – a logic which remains present in, and has had its own problematic consequences for, cultural studies itself. In what follows, I will argue that the exemplary story of Karim Amir, Kureishi's protagonist, productively complicates the zero-sum, either/or game of identity demarcation by mobilizing in specific regions of behaviour and the practice of the self an irreducible ambiguity that itself draws on the indeterminacies of suburban subjecthood. As we shall see, as suburban desiring subject Karim on the one hand positively invites metropolitan interpellation; on the other, his suburban ambiguities tend to combat if not defeat this prospective definition or instantiation. Such ambiguities centre on the sexual politics of suburbia, resisting the imposition of simply dichotomous forms and moving onto a more uncertain and labile terrain of shifting sexual identity/identities.

In the opening sentence of *The Buddha of Suburbia* – 'My name is Karim Amir' – in the guise of a declaration of identity Kureishi gives us rather a set of questions and ambiguities concerning that identity: his narrator, protagonist, and *alter ego* Karim tells the reader not 'who I am'/who he is, but what it is he is *called*, how he is *known* to the world (Kureishi 1990: 3). His 'I' is not an avatar of Cartesian self-sufficiency, but a product of a self-assertion necessarily relational, dependent, hence only as stable as the contract of recognition and denomination itself. Karim's second sentence – 'I am an Englishman born and bred, almost' – again starts out by proffering an unequivocal self-definition, only to withdraw it in the same breath by that tacked-on qualification – an afterthought, '*almost*' – that simultaneously revives and subverts a category and a formulation that have alike long since ossified into cliché. Karim both reintroduces the contradictions that 'being English' works to reconcile or recuperate and by the uncertain parsing of the sentence also renovates and radically individualizes a usage which promotes group identity and convention. Who or what, after all, *is* Karim, '*almost*'? '*Almost*' born? Bred? '*Almost*' English? Or '*almost*' a man? And, for that matter, '*almost*' as in 'not fully' and/or as in 'not yet'? Packed with imagery of journeying, of youthful desire, adolescent *angst* and readiness for change, Kureishi's opening paragraphs place *The Buddha of Suburbia* firmly within the generic frame of the *Bildungsroman*. Such a frame suggests to the reader the second, evolutionary sense of 'almost'. But if *Bildungsroman* it is, it proves a perfectly postmodern one, explicitly invoking the educative paradigm only repeatedly and delightedly to throw into profound question the tenability of the identity to which by generic convention its narrator is intended to accede. Indeed, *The Buddha of Suburbia*, like much of Kureishi's work (including the screenplays *My Beautiful Laundrette* (1986) and *Sammy and Rosie Get Laid* (1988), and his second novel *The Black Album* (1994)), owes far less to the politics of identity than to those of insistent plurality. And the questions he poses echo those asked by Eve Kosofsky Sedgwick, and like hers they aim to challenge the epistemology of the closet: 'how certain categorizations work, what enactments they are performing and what relations they are creating rather than what they essentially *mean*' (Sedgwick 1990: 27 [original emphasis]). It is a matter of constellations of significance, not layers of meaning; of performance rather than revelation. So we need to look quite closely at the model of subject formation – or perhaps, given his scrupulous anatomization of the ephemera of youth styles, especially music and dress, we should say subject *fashioning* – Kureishi proposes for his protagonist, and the rather specific set of temporal, subcultural and geographic categories within which that process is enacted: respectively, that is, the mid-to-late 1970s, the pop revolution that covers the arc from glam to punk and beyond, and above all the white-collar suburbs of outer London.

*The Buddha of Suburbia* clearly invites its readers to place it in an extensive fictional tradition documenting the desperate social conformity, the spiritual and intellectual barrenness, the sheer bloody *absence* of suburbia, and the concomitant lure of the Real City; this seems indeed Karim's own predominant attitude, and he is not for the most part an unreliable narrator: 'how much I loathed the suburbs … I had to continue my journey into London and a new life, ensuring I got away from people and streets like this' (Kureishi 1990: 101). Sure enough, the novel is structured with perfect clarity as a binary of repression and release: 'In the Suburbs' prefaces 'In the City'. On such a reading, the novel's first section might be enrolled in a tradition that begins, perhaps, with the Grossmiths' *Diary of a Nobody* and develops with Chesterton and Betjeman: a fondly contemptuous (at best) catalogue of the cosy desperation of Metroland, set against either the timeless verities of the 'authentic' countryside or (as in Kureishi) the energizing tumult of the city proper.[2] And Karim does eventually leave the 'slow, heavy' world of suburban routine in Bromley for

London, 'so bright, fast and brilliant': a move which fulfils his desire for change, movement, direction, and action, and which enables his own self-reinvention from schoolboy to cosmopolitan actor. But if the novel proffers this familiar trope of an exhausted, sterile suburbia and concomitantly invites us to celebrate Karim's escape, it undermines this deceptively easy reading at the same time. Rather than rehearse the novel's manifest and over-familiar anti-suburbanism, I have preferred in this chapter to consider the ways in which, even as he sheds suburban constraints of routine and respectability, Karim nevertheless continues to exploit in the interests of his own self-fashioning elements of ambiguity and marginality pervasively present in suburban life but which typically go disregarded and for that matter disavowed. Karim's desire moreover goes beyond simply remaking himself as metropolitan – a desire he never realizes, and which Kureishi suggests may actually be on those bald terms unrealizable. Rather, his self-fashioning evolves under the gaze of an Other *constituted as* urban, certainly, but whose own integrity is hardly unproblematic. Shortly before the start of the Second World War, hence at the very end of the between-the-wars suburban explosion, the architect Robert Sinclair claimed a constitutive psychic mastery for the city over its hinterlands: 'London contrives to rule him [the suburbanite] in his most intimate moments' (Sinclair 1937: 106). Focusing in particular on the intimacies experienced by the sexed body and the body of colour, *The Buddha of Suburbia* encourages a second look at the structure of dialectical dominance attributed to the metropolis by a normative account like Sinclair's. The novel in the end suggests that Karim's pursuit of the confirmatory approbation of that metropolitan Other not only enacts a distinctively suburban drama of misrecognition but takes the suburban, however paradoxically, as a model for the desiring subject more 'cosmopolitan' than the metropolitan itself.

## Suburban dissimulations

To speak of suburbia instantly invites a certain jargon of authenticity – authenticity, that is, being what the lonely crowd of the suburbs, construed as secondhand, retentive, hypocritical, conformist, soulless, definitively lack.[3] And there are two distinct but equally key anti-suburban traditions in particular at work in *The Buddha of Suburbia*. We should note first that, by setting his narrative firmly in the lower-middle-class environs of London's south-east fringes, Kureishi stipulates the suburbia of the novel as the world of the between-the-wars semi-detached homestead and the ribbon development (rather than either of the principal post-war suburban landmarks, the sprawling out-of-town council estates that replaced the old inner-city working-class areas erased by heavy wartime bombing and subsequent slum clearance, or the planned New Towns such as Stevenage, whose establishment coincided with the dramatic expansion of existing New Towns in the immediate post-war years).[4]

These Edwardian and between-the-wars middle- and lower-middle-class suburbs, which in the years before 1939 grew in both population and geographical area at an unprecedented and spectacular rate, extending 'metropolitan London' deep into the Home Counties, are the canonical focus of high-cultural anxieties about the suburbs, and the classical targets of metropolitan anti-suburban derision. While synergistically dependent on the evolution and extension of local infrastructure (notably transport, and especially commuter railways and the Underground), these districts were in large part the product of an unparalleled speculative private-sector building boom, which attracted the scorn and condescension of the emergent design and architecture establishment in an assault that unfolded as part of the mid-century mass culture debates. As jazz was to Theodor Adorno, so the mock-Tudor semi was to the Bauhaus and the International Style: an excrescence, an intolerable affront, glaring testimony to the debasement and bastardization of popular taste. We encounter the most enduring testimony to this deprecation in the pages of high literary modernism: it was the suburbs whence the teeming hordes of clerks and secretaries in Eliot's *The Waste Land* would have commuted to jostle and herd like the nameless damned on London Bridge; and it was suburban Oakland that inspired Gertrude Stein's famous aphorism that 'when you get "there," there's no "there" there'. (Such examples can be multiplied almost indefinitely: see Carey (1992) for a comprehensive sampling.) Yet however paradoxically, modernists were just as likely to pillory the conformist suburbs for a certain *excess* of (albeit illegitimate) personality: the vision of mile after monotonous mile of suburban semi-detached estates, laid out in cookie-cutter uniformity, competes in the bestiary of modernist design orthodoxy with their contradictory flipsides, the stubborn resistance to system manifested by the functionally superfluous additions and flourishes, such as mock-Tudor fake half-timbering and excessively ebullient gables, that drove advocates of the International Style to distraction. Design historians have likewise noted the manifold possibilities for idiosyncratic symbolic self-expression in such quintessential suburban domestic items as birdbaths, garden gates, crazy paving, twee housenames like Bideawee or Dunroamin, and so on. The peculiar offence of the suburbs, then, was to be sites of *ambiguity*: specifically, the ambiguity that arises from the problem of personal style.

On the rigorously modernist, Flaubertian model, of course, style can – indeed must – be the painstakingly acquired and maintained expression of a distinctive and consistent personality; but since the Modern Movement regarded the stunted forms of selfhood begotten by suburbia as by definition incapable of such a project, and their expressions consequently aesthetically and spiritually bankrupt, suburban 'style' is therefore guaranteed to be superficial, contentless, perhaps even deceptive. In fact, it is less the reliable samenesses of suburbia that infuriate modernists after all, but on the contrary the suspicious *fluidity* that superficial uniformity masked, the potential polyvalency evidenced in semi-detached style: after all, the neo-Georgian terrace was the preferred model for new developments between the wars on the part of both professional architects and local authority planners not merely for its neoclassicism but more precisely for the capacity to streamline and organize vouchsafed by such classicism. By contrast, the suburban semi displayed a space that was mass-produced on the one hand, shockingly undisciplined and unreliably personalized on the other: the worst of both worlds indeed. Ambiguity and indeterminacy flowed from the 'complex, additive spatial vocabulary of bays and nooks' (Bentley 1981: 126) one met with in the suburban semi into the very vocabulary that described suburbia – *half*-timbered walls, *semi*-detached homes, alloying town *and* country, and so on. The personal style of the suburbs is thus revealed as hybrid and heterodox, and the presumptively monotone suburban self as iterative and changeable; certainly anything but the coherent form valorized by conservative and progressive modernists alike as, respectively, organic or smoothly functional.[5]

Such ambiguity must in turn inevitably complicate the apparently straightforward gender politics of anti-suburbanism. The Bauhaus/our house opposition is evidently strongly inflected by the sort of unspoken but inescapable gender categories that Andreas Huyssen and others have described at work elsewhere in the modernist mass culture critique: so, the firm, straight, hard, definite, virile lines of the Corbusier cube and the attendant certainties in social organization and behaviour it confidently promised, confront the rounded, cosy, comfortable, accommodating, permeable boundaries of the suburbs.[6] So to live in the suburbs was to be weak, passive, pacified: to be feminized. But the ambiguities of suburbia communicate themselves to this simple dichotomy too, diverting the sexual politics of the suburbs away from the relatively simple threat of emasculation and feminization onto a more treacherous footing, a shifting terrain of sexual indeterminacy. And this threat/promise of suburban perversity (for which the modernist critique perhaps lacked an adequate vocabulary) was in fact central to the second, later anti-suburban tradition that Kureishi invokes in *The Buddha of Suburbia* – a popular rather than a mandarin cultural front, and emerging to some degree at least out of suburbia itself. This was punk, proverbially 'the sound of the suburbs'.[7]

The first punks' most famously extreme, confrontational and visible style statements – their appropriation of fetish and bondage gear for daily wear – were intended as both deeply suburban and a clear rebuke to a suburban sexuality they excoriated as hypocritical, dissimulating, and coercive. Pioneer punk Jordan recalled the responses her apparel provoked when forced briefly to commute from Seaford on the Sussex coast to work at Malcolm McLaren and Vivienne Westwood's King's Road boutique *Sex*: 'Sometimes I'd get on a train and all I had on was a stocking and suspenders and a rubber top, that was it. Some of the commuters used to go absolutely wild, and they loved it. Some of the men got rather hot under the collar, paper on the lap' (quoted in Savage 1992: 95). Jordan's account, like Savage's quoted at the start of this chapter, typifies the punk response to the outrage and titillation they provoked (or disclosed): trading heavily on the 1970s metropolitan mythology of wife-swapping parties behind the net curtains, punk both exposed 'respectable' suburban public style as a blind, and at the same time decried the deviant styles it exposed as themselves deeply corrupt: suburban sadomasochism and bondage being taken – this was of course long before the age of the designer dominatrix – to evidence the penetration of the cultural logic of domination and coercion into the most intimate realms of human relations. (Hence, in part, Poly Styrene's famous war-cry, 'Oh Bondage – Up Yours!') Punk's importance in *The Buddha of Suburbia* is that through it Kureishi can render the critique of suburbia both performative and explicitly enacted on and through the body. Unlike modernist anti-suburbanism, punk nihilism offers no positive alternative to suburban false consciousness beyond its own brutal veracity; but it none the less shares its predecessor's conviction of suburbia's pervasive inauthenticity. Like modernism, punk too can see in the contradictions of suburbia only disavowal and repression. Confronted by the rebuke of the strong metropolitan body, the response expected and for that matter required of the ambiguous, inauthentic suburban body/self might be either to shrink back defensively within its proper boundaries, or to dissolve itself altogether *as suburban* into the authenticity of the metropolis (the latter obviously much the more difficult operation given that, as can be testified by anyone who has made the move from a non-metropolitan to a metropolitan environment, the metropolis quite jealously guards its gates and its privileges of residency and belonging).

Elizabethan and Jacobean London provides a clear genealogical precursor for this suburban perversity and indeterminacy. The indeterminate extramural status of London's suburban 'liberties' – outside the jurisdiction of the Lord Mayor and as Roy Porter puts it 'in effect ungoverned' (Porter 1994: 54) – permitted the eruption, especially on Bankside across London Bridge, of a sometimes riotous, even carnivalesque culture where the sexual licence of the 'stews' (brothels) cohabited with popular performance in the theatres, described by Steven Mullaney as 'a liminal breed of cultural performance, a performance of the threshold' (Mullaney 1988: 45). As extensively discussed in recent Renaissance scholarship, the sexual licence of the brothels in fact in some ways infected the stage and even its audience, most visibly in the cross-dressing which was of course a convention of the all-male Renaissance theatre, but which was adopted also (and in reverse) by some of the female members of the audience, whose transvestism clearly managed to *épater la bourgeoisie* as effectively (and at significantly greater personal risk, violent assaults on Johnny Rotten notwithstanding) than their punk descendants. The distance in time and the utterly different social, topographical and juridical status of Renaissance and twentieth-century suburbia notwithstanding, the affinity of suburbia and certain forms of *theatricalized* subversion persists. We will shortly come to consider the suburbs' paradoxically formative effect on their apparently authorizing metropolitan centre: so it may be worth registering here that the canonical vision of Renaissance metropolitan culture for subsequent generations — the vision of *The Alchemist* and *The Roaring Girl* — originated not within the metropolis but on its peripheries.

## Suburban simulations

In *The Buddha of Suburbia*, Karim does, as already noted, occasionally voice the standard critique of suburbia; but when he encounters punk, shortly after his move to London, his response to the latter's violent anti-suburbanism productively problematizes the terms of his own. Still into crushed velvet and the Rolling Stones in late 1976, Karim experiences the 'pallid, vicious little council estate kids with hedgehog hair' as a direct, snarling repudiation of his own suburban belatedness from 'an alien race dressed with an abandonment and originality we'd never imagined possible' (Kureishi 1990: 129–30). (Kureishi withholds any reference to punk's bondage/fetish styles, holding the s/m motif — as we shall see — so to speak in reserve for a more telling deployment later in the novel.) But although this 'originality' would in traditional terms validate punk, Karim in fact refuses to allow the punk rebuke to impose a regulatory standard from where he might be judged, preferring instead simply to register its difference, accountable in terms of its own specific origins and cultural trajectory. Karim is not motivated to become a punk himself, knowing that his own experience prohibits him imitating them: '"It would be artificial. ... We're not like them. We don't hate the way they do. We've got no reason to. We're not from the estates. We haven't been through what they have"' (Kureishi 1990: 132). This altogether characteristic sidestepping of the logic of exclusion engendered by the dichotomous engines of truth and falsity in turn points up Karim's most notable attribute, an accommodation to the difference of others enabled by a significant under-investment on his part in the notion of a coherent self.

That Karim becomes an actor is the conceit whereby the novel most obviously foregrounds the idea of a performative, public, rather than a reflective, inner self. If acting, as the Mephistophelian director Matthew Pyke explains, entails embodying another by being more fully oneself — 'to be someone else successfully you must be yourself' — then the obvious potential corollary for offstage identity is that the true self is always another. Kureishi stages Karim's progress in a way that deflects the depth-model trope of appearance and reality traditionally invoked by novelistic treatments of the theatre, and here underpinned by the suburban *mise-en-scène* with its own inbuilt discourse of authenticity, preferring to expand on a notion of the self as always already constituted in contingent relation to others, and not necessarily diminished by such a relationship. The novel is filled with *performances* of the real such as the Buddha of Suburbia himself, Karim's civil servant father Haroon, who plays the part of the Eastern mystic neither in full bad faith nor quite in all good conscience, but in a much more indeterminate and sceptical relationship to the very notion of a 'true' self; or Karim's stepbrother Charlie, who draws a very different lesson from punk, swiftly refashioning himself as punk sensation Charlie Hero, his mission 'to explain the despair of the young'. Karim goes to see Charlie's band, The Condemned, and finds him 'magnificent in his venom, his manufactured rage, his anger ... It was a wonderful trick and disguise' (Kureishi 1990: 153–4). If the novel has a presiding genius, in fact, it is perhaps less Buddha than Bowie – an old boy, Karim relates in passing, of his Bromley comprehensive[8] – and in particular *Hunky Dory*'s androgynous bard of transformation and self-reinvention who sings to Andy Warhol over the opening titles of the television adaptation (co-scripted by Kureishi). Kureishi declines to condemn, deplore, or cast in a tragic light Karim's suburban malleability but rather celebrates ambiguity and hybridity, arguing here as later in *The Black Album* for a wry agnosticism with which to face down the constraints of militant certainty, whether political, religious, familial or sexual.

Karim has two principal options for stabilizing his own identity: both ask him to situate himself in a determinate and fixed relation to the authorizing metropolitan centre, and in the end he takes up neither. The most obviously available is his race: but as his first stage role, blacked up to play Mowgli in *The Jungle Book*, ironically establishes, ethnicity is no source of self-definition for Karim, with his aristocratic Indian father and his English working-class mother. On the contrary, Karim's ethnic hybridity further encourages and enables his metamorphic culture-surfing. Karim is the predictable object of condescension and sympathy from those gifted with a stronger sense of racial authenticity, their own or that of others: for instance, his friend and sometime lover Jamila, self-educated and militantly race-conscious, or the fringe theatre director Shadwell, who patronizes Karim on the basis of his own cultural tourism in the Indian subcontinent: '"Everyone looks at you, I'm sure, and thinks: an Indian boy, how exotic, how interesting, what stories of aunties and elephants we'll hear now from him. And you're from Orpington"' (Kureishi 1990: 141). Shadwell's invocation of the suburbs here marks a doubled inauthenticity: their own, and the compounded lie they give to Karim's exotic Otherness. Karim's response is the typically pragmatic reflection that 'if I wanted the additional personality bonus of an Indian past, I would have to create it'. Unlike other Kureishi protagonists, moreover, Karim's family are not Pakistani but Muslim Indians: which is to say, always already a minority culture, internal exiles, literally 'unhoused' – in German, *unheimlich*, or as we would usually say 'uncanny,' that category which above all destabilizes, defamiliarizes and dislocates psychic and sexual orderliness.

It may be that Karim can so readily disclaim or ignore his ethnicity because, if anything, the dismissal of that identity is precisely part of the appeal of the metropolis for him: when he fantasizes a vision of London before moving there, the multicultural city is a negative rather than a positive value, a shield from harm rather than a source of empowerment – 'there were thousands of black people everywhere, so I wouldn't feel exposed' (Kureishi 1990: 121). It's also apparent from the comic business of the light-skinned Karim's ethnic 'authentication' by blacking-up that the body itself offers no unproblematic discourse of truth, being in no sense pre-social or external to social, discursive currents. Far from being stable or uncontested terrain on which to anchor a self, bodies are rather, as Judith Butler (1990) has said, 'performances of being'.

One might imagine that the metamorphic Karim would have no difficulty with this, and that similarly when we consider the presentation of his sexuality, this innate polymorphousness should translate quite readily into a deliciously polymorphous perversity. But in fact Karim seems to want to use sex and sexuality as an avenue towards the possibility of a self, only for the insufficiency and ambivalence of the desiring body as a ground for identity to be in its turn made clear to him. The complications here, though, do not centre as one might imagine on Karim's indeterminate sexual orientation. There is in that sense in fact little ambiguity to Karim's frank and even-handed bisexuality:

> I liked strong bodies and the backs of boys' necks. I liked being handled by them, their fists pulling me; and I liked objects – the ends of brushes, pens, fingers – up my arse. But I liked cunts and breasts, all of women's softness, long smooth legs and the way women dressed. I felt it would be heart-breaking to have to choose one or the other, like having to decide between the Beatles and the Rolling Stones.
>
> (Kureishi 1990: 55)

(We should register here the anticipatory note characterizing sexuality as consumer choice.) Ambiguity intrudes rather into the *act* of sex itself – an intentional pun, since Karim is compelled to recognize that the relational construction even of physical intimacy extends beyond the couple, that it too is simply another performance carried out beneath the gaze of a (metropolitan) Other. It is specifically at the point that he has to confront most directly the implications of his dialectic of suburban desire.

Put simply, the principal objects of Karim's sexual desire in the novel are signifiers of the metropolitan identity he fantasizes and craves for himself. Although Karim has numerous different sexual partners in the course of the novel, his two most important relationships are those with Charlie and with Eleanor, another member of Pyke's theatre company. Eleanor is upper class, cosmopolitan and bohemian: their relationship, Karim's first full-blown adult affair, importantly both symbolizes and mediates his initiation into the culture of the metropolis. Charlie meanwhile is an elusive figure flitting in and out of the action of the novel, whose very absence at each stage of Karim's progress into the metropolis – from Bromley to Baron's Court, and from London to Manhattan – denotes Karim's necessary supersession of that stage and the path ahead of him. To possess Charlie, and be possessed by him, thus becomes for Karim a confirmation of the imminence of his own longed-for urbanization. All of this is however expressed principally less through actual physical contact (Karim and Charlie never actually fuck: Karim jerks Charlie off in his bedroom at the start of the novel and it is after this that, as noted, Charlie becomes an extremely elusive, fugitive object of desire). Rather, desire is mediated by a specular compact: Charlie is so desirable because he is the possessor of a particular *look*, or gaze. Watching Charlie onstage, Karim is above all aware of his ability to fix upon himself the gaze of others: 'what admiration he extorted, what looks there were in girls' eyes' (Kureishi 1990: 154). As the cynosure of all eyes, what Charlie is of course provoking is the desire that he return that look. This is in fact Charlie's keynote: his first entrance in the novel is as, precisely, a gaze – Karim feels Charlie's eyes upon him before he sees him – and his miraculous charisma throughout the novel, its range progressively expanding from Bromley until it reaches positively global dimensions, is accountable in terms of his ability to cast and confirm the spectator through his own return of the proffered gaze. 'The attention he gave you, when he gave you attention, was absolute. He knew how to look at you as if you were the only person who'd ever interested him' (Kureishi 1990: 119). As Karim indicates, this responsiveness is hardly guaranteed; but withholding in turn only provokes a strongly resurgent desire Karim himself describes as 'neurotic'. To round off this impeccably Lacanian aspect, Charlie shares with all such objects of desire an ultimate ungraspability: 'he extorted, not only sex, but love and loyalty, before moving on' (Kureishi 1990: 119).

Karim's desire for both Charlie and Eleanor revolves around the idea of fulfilling *his* need to be desired by them by making himself into the indispensable satisfaction of *their* own desire. It is therefore a desire necessarily performative and narcissistic; and in both cases the particular intensity of his desire to render himself a worthy object of their desire, which will in effect enforce the compliment to and confirmation of his own selfhood, springs from his overriding desire for the same interpellation by the metropolis. With both of these love objects, however, the directness and intimacy Karim seeks is thrown into question at the very moment he seems on the verge of realizing it, by the unwelcome return of the performative principle Karim has made the basis for his own self-fashioning. When Karim and Eleanor are cajoled into group sex with Pyke and his wife, Eleanor both becomes in effect Karim's sexual dramaturge – instructing and arranging him in various combinations with herself and Pyke – and abstracts their own previous intimacy by inscribing her desire under the gaze of a more powerful Other, in this case Pyke: 'As he frigged her she spoke to him in incantatory fashion. I strained to hear, and heard for my pains Eleanor whisper how much she wanted to fuck him, how she'd always wanted it since she first admired him and then spotted him in the foyer of a theatre' (Kureishi 1990: 203). Similarly, when Karim finally catches up with Charlie in New York he becomes part of a sexual performance – a bit more than an audience and a bit less than a full participant. Here, under the instruction of a professional dominatrix Charlie resituates himself in relation to Karim's desiring gaze:

> I looked at Charlie, recalling the night in Beckenham I tried to kiss him and he turned his face away. How he wanted me – he let me touch him – but refused to acknowledge it, as if he could remove himself from the act while remaining there. ... Tonight Charlie's face was open, warm; there was no rejection in it, only enthusiasm. ... I never thought he would look at me like this.
>
> (Kureishi 1990: 253)

But with this apparent fulfilment of his desire Karim of course ceases to desire: 'I realized I didn't love Charlie any more. I didn't care either for or about him. ... He seemed merely foolish to me' (Kureishi 1990: 255).

This seems on the face of it slightly paradoxical: isn't Charlie giving Karim what he's wanted all along? In which case, why the disappointment and anticlimax? In the first place, the staged aspect of Charlie's acquiescence effectively disallows it: Charlie's 'open, warm' look is instigated by the hired dominatrix Frankie, who invites him and Karim to 'get into one another'. The whole scene is in fact shot through with a pervasive inauthenticity, of which the s/m ritual itself becomes a privileged signifier. Recalling that earlier Kureishi surprisingly suppressed the bondage styles of punk, here we find that style returning to Charlie – whom we already know to be a 'fake' punk, that is merely imitating or affecting disaffection and deprivation – as a sort of repressed index of his own self-alienation. S/m signifies for Kureishi what it did for the punks – the internalization of domination. (Kureishi has no real interest in the erotics of dominance and submission: the entire scene with Frankie is played out as comic grotesque, and concludes rather brutally when '[Charlie] gave her money and got rid of her', as if to underline the [mutually] exploitative nature of the whole transaction.) As a specifically *suburban* perversion, moreover – at least in the punk lexicon – s/m exposes Charlie's metropolitan pretensions, no matter that he cites so quintessentially modernist and urban a trope as self-degradation *à la* Rimbaud as his justification. (To do so, or to need to, of course, is to situate himself *outside* of that metropolitan discourse, to reveal his purely superficial relationship to it.) Charlie is in a word re-suburbanized: or perhaps the suburban is even revealed at the very heart of the metropolitan itself.

The performative element in these sexual situations both distances desire by formalizing and staging it and disables the desired object's ability to confer and confirm identity by the return of the gaze by exploding the imaginary duality of the encounter and revealing the triangulating presence of another – that is, another Other: the Other of the Other's own desire. The proximate object of the desiring subject is in Lacanian terms exposed as the *objet petit 'a'*, 'the other with a little O' rather than *Objet 'A'*, the Other itself. We could perhaps map the terms of the Lacanian dialectic onto Kureishi's geography as the objects 'L' and 'little "L"': 'L' here, obviously, for London. For it is the city itself, surely, from whose recognition Karim seeks confirmation; and it is the ultimate unknowability of the vast, indifferent city that makes its mediation by Eleanor and Charlie so urgent. In the words of another surprising proto-Lacanian text, Thomas Sharp's 1940 study *Town Planning*, 'the inhabitants of suburbia continually thwart themselves … the more they strive to embrace the object of their desire the more it escapes them' (quoted in Oliver *et al.* 1981: 48). As the fugitive object of Karim's desire, whose own desire is, precisely, what Karim desires from him, Charlie appears to stand in this tantalizing relation to the suburban desiring subject. But what Karim desires in Charlie is not Charlie himself, but rather the metropolis he fantasizes reaching through him and for which he can metonymically stand, but which neither he nor Eleanor nor any one love object can fully incarnate. (Another Kureishi project, the misconceived film *London Kills Me*, makes this drama of desire and disappointment clearer still, revolving around a goal more fugitive still, an object 'even littler "L"': a missing pair of shoes.)

What makes Karim's story more than a rehearsal of this familiar Lacanian psychosocial dynamic, however, is his own growing awareness of the inevitably phantasmic nature of the metropolitan Real for which he is grasping. Karim's last night in the suburbs is spent fantasizing about London 'and what I'd do there when the city belonged to me'. This is a quintessentially suburban fiction, the possessed's fantasy of taking possession. And just as Charlie seems to be conferring upon Karim the restorative or constitutive gaze Karim craves, so in the last chapter of the novel Karim is tantalized by the prospect of acquiring a metropolitan self: his theatrical success an obvious device for imaging him as the bearer rather than the seeker of the gaze – hence scattered references to his being noticed onstage, 'recognized' by strangers in the street, etc., and in the final pages the prospect of household recognition as the lead in a TV soap. Yet Karim in the end chooses not fully to accept that metropolitan personality: as if the scene with Charlie, by which Charlie's excessive self-interpellation by the metropolitan figures him as, precisely, irredeemably suburban (literally and figuratively), has in some sense bodied forth Karim to himself and exposed the viciously circular and futile nature of the compact. Here it might be useful to recall Lacan's derivation of his mirror stage model and its subsequent convoluted consequences for the subject from Alexandre Kojève's lectures on the master–slave encounter in Hegel's *Phenomenology of Spirit*. In Lacan's famous account of the 'mirror stage', the infant perceives in its own reflected image a unity and integrity unattainable in its uncoordinated, stumbling actuality. In many ways, this image which is both of oneself and apart from oneself, and whose idealized aspect simultaneously invites emulation and frustration, provides the template for Lacan's account of adult human social being as an always-already doomed pursuit of unrealizable desire. Out there – somewhere – if we could only grasp it, is that Other, that one that can satisfy our insatiable desire, which ultimately is no more than the desire to be confirmed in the identity we believe ourselves to possess. Lacan adds to this the Hegelian/Kojèvian notion of a 'struggle for mastery' between the subject of desire and its object: both striving for an absolute self-assertion, yet resentfully conscious of the ways in which each is dependent on the other, that the quest to be oneself relies on the confirmation of that selfhood by another.

As Karim grows, he starts to realize that as dependent as the suburbanite is on London, establishing his own identity against the (prior, more readily ascertained, socially and aesthetically canonical) Other, the relationality goes both ways. What seems to happen rather in the closing section of the novel is that Karim disinvests from the bankrupt quest for a fixed relation in or to the metropolitan, and in its place volunteers the wholesale ambiguities of the suburbs once again. Quite unlike the traditional closing chapters of the classic realist text, the last stages of *The Buddha of Suburbia* are full of loose ends, new characters being introduced, personal and professional possibilities being opened up. Moreover, there is a striking pattern of the 'suburban' characters acquiring metropolitan traits, and vice versa, to the extent that by the novel's conclusion these categories have been thoroughly destabilized. The tone of these final pages is of definite, imminent, but from the reader's point of view almost wilfully indeterminate change.

In *The Buddha of Suburbia*, it is London that functions as simultaneously the specular image in which the suburban subject jubilantly (mis)recognizes himself, the necessary but always elusive object of Karim's desire — '*Objet "L"*' — and as a no-longer-sufficient-unto-itself Other whose sexual and political energies are destabilized and challenged by the burgeoning suburbs as least as much as they inspire them. The danger of Karim's path — and this is a charge that has been levelled at Kureishi himself — is that his desire ultimately constructs itself under the guise of pure consumption. The novel after all concludes on the eve of the 1979 General Election: ahead stretches the 1980s and the culture of consumption and narcissism triumphant. And there is perhaps a suggestion that in his resistant indeterminacy, his sly repudiation of the metropolitan-structured categories of ethnicity and sexuality, Karim may end up figuring the triumph in the decade to come of that most suburban subject of all: the consumer. In a sense, Kureishi's novel — and my account of it — ends where Vincent Quinn's essay in this collection begins: at the point where the collective identity-groupings around ethnicity and sexuality that had evolved during the 1970s began to erode in the face of an unexpected challenge by the name of the 'free market'. Even as its moral agenda stigmatized and disempowered, Thatcherism held out another disingenuous yet insidiously appealing invitation: the opportunity to submerge the vexatious problems of identity altogether in the depthless, disconnected flux of consumer appetite. The subversive possibilities of a destabilized identity are discounted: the lure of the commodity dissolves all identities into air and evacuates the contested terrain of sexual and gender identities into the value-neutral non-place of consumer choice. I have tried to suggest that at the end of his distinctively suburban dialectic of desire Karim ends up, however paradoxically, taking the suburban as a model for the desiring subject more 'cosmopolitan' than the metropolis itself. But the novel leaves it open whether he will end up anywhere other than a marketplace of desire and identity alike – a subjecthood constituted that is under the auspices of a purely consumerist anti-essentialism, whose consequences we know only too well, having lived through the locust years on whose threshold Kureishi ambivalently leaves us.

## Notes

1 Needless to say, a sketch like this omits multiple complexities and ironies: for instance, that while the Leavises were themselves impeccably suburban in their own lifestyles and indeed in some of their more reactionary prejudices, especially in later life, 'the suburbs' themselves in general nevertheless formed part of the broad swathe of cultural debasement against which 'minority culture' must needs set its face; while equally Hoggart's valorization of a dying proletarian way of life in *The Uses of Literacy* is itself avowedly influenced by Leavis's own invocation of 'organic communities', etc. For a barely coded fictional sketch of the prevailing attitudes towards (other people's) suburbia amongst mid-century academics, one could do worse than review the closing chapters of J.R.R. Tolkien's *The Lord of the Rings* (1948), which (following the defeat of Sauron's cosmic threat) resolves itself into a bloody struggle against the more insidious threat posed by housing developments for the artisanal classes (Tolkien's own educational, regional and social profile parallels that of Leavis's quite closely).

2 Its transparent political agenda (and its elastic, Paul Johnson-esque application of the term 'intellectual') notwithstanding, John Carey's *The Intellectuals and the Masses* remains the best overview of literary treatments of the white-collar suburbs, especially chapter 3 (Carey 1992).

3 This paradigmatic psychological portrait of the suburbs owes a great deal to such influential American sociological studies of the 1950s as David Riesman, *The Lonely Crowd* (1950), William Whyte, *The Organization Man* (1956), etc.

4 For the factual detail regarding the expansion of the suburbs in the inter-war years and the evolution of their characteristic design contradictions, these paragraphs are principally dependent on the following: Oliver *et al.* (1981); Jackson (1991); Burnett (1980); Williams (1975).

5 For copious examples, see Barrett and Phillips (1987). Minus the design element, this preoccupation with the ambiguity that the suburban edges of the city 'proper', as by definition liminal spaces, can be seen throughout the recording of metropolitan expansion: for instance, in Dickens's famous description of the coming of the railway (later, of course, the arterial focus or indeed the *raison d'être* of the suburbs) in *Dombey and Son* (1848).

6 See Huyssen (1986), especially chapter 1, 'Mass Culture as Woman'. On the feminizing stigmatization of suburbia, see Wilson (1990). Alison Light (1991) discusses representations of suburbia as a focal trope of interwar masculinist anxieties.

7 Punk's aspect as suburban symptom is rehearsed in a fairly unexamined way in Savage (1992). For a more sceptical picture, see Lebeau (1997).

8 Although the suburbanization of Bromley was already well under way by the turn of the century, it remains the canonical suburb of choice for cultural and especially pop historians,

having begotten a unique cross-generational suburban response: from the Kinks to Bowie to punk (Siouxsie Sioux and the 'Bromley Contingent', the earliest and most notorious punk camp followers, of whom Billy Idol – an obvious model for Charlie in *The Buddha of Suburbia* – was also a sometime member) and most recently Suede (themselves of course in large part *Diamond Dogs*-era Bowie revivalists). Silverstone (1990: 4) describes it as 'exemplary' of suburbia generally, and for Andy Medhurst (1997: 271) Bromley is 'the most significant suburb in British pop history'. Certainly, Kureishi's choice of location for his novel is amply overdetermined.

# References

Barrett, H. and Phillips, J. (1987) *Suburban Style: The British Home 1840–1960*, London: Macdonald.

Butler, J. (1990) *Gender Trouble*, London: Routledge.

Burnett, J. (1980) *A Social History of Housing, 1815–1970*, London: Methuen.

Carey, J. (1992) *The Intellectuals and the Masses*, London: Faber & Faber.

Huyssen, A. (1986) *After the Great Divide: Modernism, Mass Culture, Postmodernism*, Bloomington: Indiana University Press.

Jackson, A. (1991) *Semi-Detached London*, Oxford: Wild Swan.

Kureishi, H. (1990) *The Buddha of Suburbia*, London: Faber & Faber.

Lebeau, V. (1997) 'The Worst of All Possible Worlds', in R. Silverstone (ed.) *Visions of Suburbia*, London: Routledge: 280–97.

Light, A. (1991) *Forever England: Femininity, Literature and Conservatism Between the Wars*, London: Routledge.

Medhurst, A. (1997) 'Negotiating the Gnome Zone: Versions of Suburbia in British Popular Culture', in R. Silverstone (ed.) *Visions of Suburbia*, London: Routledge: 240–68.

Mullaney, S. (1988) *The Place of the Stage*, Chicago: University of Chicago Press.

Oliver, P., Davis, I. and Bentley, I. (1981) *Dunroamin: The Suburban Semi and its Enemies*, London: Barrie & Jenkins.

Porter, R. (1994) *London: A Social History*, London: Hamish Hamilton.

Savage, J. (1992) *England's Dreaming: Anarchy, Sex Pistols, Punk Rock and Beyond*, New York: St Martin's Press.

Sedgwick, E.K. (1990) *Epistemology of the Closet*, Berkeley: University of California Press.

Silverstone, R. (1990) (ed.) *Visions of Suburbia*, London: Routledge.

Sinclair, R. (1937) *Metropolitan Man*, London: Allen & Unwin.

Williams, G.R. (1975) *London in the Country*, London: Hamish Hamilton.

Wilson, E. (1990) *The Sphinx and the City: Urban Life, Disorder, and Woman*, Berkeley: University of California Press.

# Part II

# BEYOND THE METROPOLIS

# 5

# EROTICIZING THE RURAL

*David Bell*

One day in 1867, a farm hand from the village of Lapcourt, who was somewhat simple-minded, employed here then there, depending on the season, living hand-to-mouth from a little charity or in exchange for the worst sort of labor, sleeping in barns and stables, was turned in to the authorities. At the border of a field, he had obtained a few caresses from a little girl, just as he had done before and seen done by the village urchins round about him; for, at the edge of the wood, or in the ditch by the road leading to Saint-Nicholas, they would play the familiar game called 'curdled milk'. So he was pointed out by the girl's parents to the mayor, led by the gendarmes to the judge, who indicted him and turned him over first to a doctor, then to two other experts who not only wrote their report but also had it published. What is the significance of this story? The pettiness of it all; the fact that this everyday occurrence in the life of village sexuality, these inconsequential bucolic pleasures, could become, from a certain time, the object not only of a collective intolerance but of a judicial action, a medical intervention, a careful clinical examination, and an entire theoretical elaboration.

(Foucault 1979: 31)

In 'Recognizing rusticity', Gerald Creed and Barbara Ching (1997) propose an archaeology that digs around in 'places that are culturally remote: in the sticks, in the middle of nowhere, in the backwaters of this country and many others, in a word, in the countryside' (Creed and Ching 1997: 1) in order to think about the role of the rural/urban distinction in structuring cultural hierarchies in contemporary society. They go on to argue that contemporary theorizations of identity politics have largely disregarded the social and cultural identifications made around this binary – a neglect that is only beginning to be addressed from within what we might call 'rural cultural studies'. Of course, as with all of the other structuring binaries of identification, the rural/urban distinction is loaded: the rural is marginalized while the urban is centred (and the metropolitan doubly so).

As other chapters in this volume make clear, constructions and theorizations of sexual identity have not been innocent in this respect. Metropolitan queer culture, for example, restates the links between urban life and homosexual identity and community, as Spurlin shows (Chapter 10, this volume; see also Bech 1997). At the same time, however, the rural and the rustic figure as particular symbolic sites in discourses of the erotic. This chapter is concerned primarily with thinking about some of the constructions of what Foucault refers to as 'village sexuality' as a way of considering the role of the rural/urban binary in the cultural construction of sexualities. Specifically, I hope to explore the role of representation in constructing popular notions of 'village sexuality' which trade on the rural/urban distinction in particular ways. As I hope to show, Foucault's 'inconsequential bucolic pleasures' still resonate with representations of the erotic rural – paradoxically, either to emphasize a rustic *naïveté* far removed from sophisticated 'metrosexuality' (rural negatively invested) or to romanticize the rural as a site free from the tainting traces of either urban depravity or urban regulation and surveillance (rural positively invested, in the way, I think, that Foucault is – not unproblematically – intimating). What this suggests, I want to argue, is that the rural occupies a very particular, but very complex, location in the wider sociospatial economy of desire (a similar point is made in Alan Sinfield's consideration of centre/margin distinctions in Chapter 1 of this volume). My own archaeology of sex in 'the middle of nowhere', then, aims to think about some popular representations and performances of the erotic rural – of the links made in the popular imagination between nature, rural life, and forms of sexual activity and identity – as a way of contributing to our understanding of the functions of the rural/urban distinction in processes of identification, and in cultural practices; not as an 'entire theoretical elaboration' (and certainly not a 'clinical examination'), but as some modest thoughts on the rural and the erotic.

## Representing the rural

There has emerged within rural studies an interesting and diverse body of work exploring the ways in which the countryside is represented in realms of popular culture, including children's literature (Jones 1997), toys (Houlton and Short 1995), advertising (Brandth 1995), other forms of literary and artistic production (Matless 1994), and popular film (Williamson 1995). Within this body of work exist many specialized focuses – Brandth's (1995) work on advertising, for example, is concerned with the articulation of masculinity in relation to ads for farm technology. There is also a strong trend of assessing the construction of particular countrysides within popular culture – most notably the rural idyll (Bunce 1994; Marsh 1982; Mingay 1989; Short 1991), and the ways in which this constructed countryside is mediated through expert, popular and lay discourses, all of which offer their own inflections (Jones 1995; Little and Austin 1996). Simultaneously, there is emerging in the literature on sexuality – especially in lesbian and gay studies – work on the rural, in part counterbalancing the previous focus on the urban as prime site for dissident sexual identity and community formation (Bell and Valentine 1995; Kramer 1995; Valentine 1997; Weston 1995); included in this work are studies of the rural as a symbolic resource within queer cultures (Abelove 1993; Bech 1997; Fone 1983; Sandell 1997; Woods 1987). My focus here is squarely with some particular inflections of the rural, as they intersect with sexuality – I want to explore some ways in which rusticity is eroticized or sexualized in popular culture, drawing on a range of historical and contemporary sources, both factual and fictional.

## Curdled milk: the erotic rural

There are countless ways in which rural erotics are articulated within popular culture, and I don't propose to review them all here. Indeed, as David Matless (1994: 40) notes: 'sexual themes are of course common in the literature of [the] pastoral and rurality … There is a wide variation in this, though, from the erotic to the boisterous.' The same is true of other popular cultural forms; the sex lives of country folk make for interesting subject-matter, especially when the sex itself takes on a noticeably 'rural character', as it does in the examples I explore below.

I've chosen to focus on three particular forms of rural erotics, all of which are powerfully symbolic in constructing forms of mythic rural sexualization: (a) what I'll call *white trash erotics*, (b) *bestiality*, and (c) *naturism*. Obviously, each has a very different way of sexualizing the country – and each has a very different role to play in constructing notions of the rural and of the erotic. There are clear linkages in the ways each is constructed within popular culture, but also clear distinctions: while white trash erotics and bestiality co-exist within a general popular-cultural trope of rural life (summed up neatly in Barbara Ching's (1997: 232) essay on country music as 'either impossibly degraded or impossibly innocent'), I'm using naturism to think about constructions of Nature, human nature, naturalness, the body and the rural idyll. White trash erotics and bestiality, on the other hand, might be seen as producing what Matless (1994: 40) calls 'idyll disturbance', showing the countryside's underbelly; a site of unwholesome – maybe even *unnatural* – existences and activities. Further, many commentaries on nudism – including discourses emerging from within naturist movements themselves – stress the decoupling of nudity from sexuality, emphasizing a spiritual, chaste purity instead (Mosse 1985). However, I hope to argue that naturism is profoundly about the erotic, a claim backed up by one of the few in-depth studies of modern naturism; Douglas, Rasmussen and Flanagan's (1977) *The Nude Beach*.

Of course, none of my three case-studies functions purely in the realm of the rural – white trash, as a US construct of an underclass, is centred more on socioeconomic marginalization than necessary rural location, but, I would like to argue, there is a particular construction of 'rural white trash' that can usefully be explored in this context (see also Creed and Ching 1997); similarly, bestiality is not a uniquely rural phenomenon, as Kinsey *et al.* (1948, 1953) found out; but again, there are distinct ways in which certain zoophilic acts are associated with the countryside (and especially with animal husbandry). Naturism, too, has both urban and rural manifestations, with a fully developed 'scene' ranging from naked towns to nudist resorts to naturist house-meetings and nude hillwalking. In this case, what I want to focus on are the linkages made in some contexts between nakedness, idyllic nature (especially wilderness) and forms of 'spirituality' – as expressed in, for example, Edward Carpenter's work, life and legacy, early twentieth-century nudist movements in Europe, elements of the so-called mythopoetic men's movement plus US 'radical fairies' and their counterparts, some feminist (and perhaps especially lesbian-feminist) ideas and practices, and, indeed, in parts of the contemporary naturist scene across Europe and America. I'll try to unravel these issues more fully in the detailed discussions that follow; the first of which is concerned with thinking about the sexualization of rural white trash.

## Sodomy and the judds

The first construction of rural erotics I want to explore, then, is that of so-called white trash: of (in this instance) mainly Southern US-based, poor rural white folk – those marginalized people labelled, in popular terms, as 'crackers, rubes, hayseeds, hicks, hillbillies, bumpkins, peasants, rednecks, yokels and white trash' (Creed and Ching 1997: 17). While I have chosen here to focus on rural USA, we could equally trace representations of what might be called 'rural rough trade' as a common trope in British popular culture – *Lady Chatterley's Lover* comes straight to mind – where there is a similar class-based construction of country folks' erotics (see Cavaliero 1977). There are, of course, obvious differences between the two, just as there are very different ways of imagining the rural in the UK and USA (Bunce 1994). That being the case, I'll confine my subsequent discussion to white trash in an American context.

There has been a recent surge of interest in the subject of white trash among US academics, with books like Jerry Williamson's (1995) *Hillbillyland* (on filmic representations of 'mountain folk'), Richard King and Helen Taylor's (1996) collection *Dixie Debates*, on 'Southern cultures', and most recently Matt Wray and Annalee Newitz's (1997) *White Trash*. Each of these concerns itself, in part, with questions of popular representations of white trash, and the first and last, at least, have quite a lot to say about the *erotics* of these representations, which is what interests me here. In addition, some interesting work on what I've previously called 'hillbilly horror' (Bell 1997) talks about the sexualization of country characters within the horror genre – Carol Clover's (1992) *Men, Women and Chainsaws* especially.

First off, though, a word about this section's title, which comes from the screenplay for Quentin Tarantino's *Pulp Fiction* (1994). Midway through the film, two characters from one of the movie's three interlocking stories, Butch Coolidge and

Marsellus Wallace, are engaged in a fierce street gun-battle. Butch runs into a store to try to get cover, and is followed by Marsellus, 'hot on his ass with a cockeyed wobbly run', as Tarantino (1994: 121) puts it. The store they stumble into is called the Mason-Dixon Pawnshop.[1] The store's owner, Maynard ('a hillbilly-lookin' boy'), floors them both with the butt of a rifle, ties them up in the back room, then phones his brother, Zed, who soon turns up at the store. They then bring out The Gimp – a man in full bondage gear housed under the floor 'in a hole big enough for a large dog' (125). The brothers take Marsellus off to another room, the dungeon; when Butch escapes his ties (he is being ineffectually guarded by The Gimp), he decides he can't just up and run, but must first save Marsellus from his fate. As he sneaks down to the dungeon, Samurai sword in hand, Tarantino writes: 'Sodomy and the Judds can still be heard going strong behind the door.'

This scene is, of course, a clear homage to John Boorman's *Deliverance* – the Mason–Dixon reference (and Country and Western stars the Judds) fixing Maynard and Zed to white trash hillbillyland, the sodomy replaying Bobby's rape by the Georgian mountain men in Boorman's movie, who added a bestial twist by making Bobby squeal like a pig. Both films mobilize a certain construction of poor white country folk – and particularly their sexualization; as Creed and Ching (1997: 23) note, 'rustic sexual expression often takes the form of homosexual rape' in American movies (the other example they cite is *Falling Down*). *Deliverance* carries further signifiers, too – of in-breeding, for example (with the deformed, imbecilic figure of Lonnie, the boy who plays 'Duellin' Banjoes' with Drew; see Bell 1997), also potent in many other depictions of rural white trash.

In fact, 'hillbilly horror' is a genre particularly crowded with characters whose sexualities resonate with popular constructions of rural erotics – of in-breeding, animalistic passions, and polymorphous perversions. Writing about *Deliverance* alongside the rape-revenge nasty *I Spit on Your Grave* and the *Deliverance* copy *Hunter's Blood*, for example, Carol Clover explores the ways in which the sex/gender system is coded in these horror narratives:

> Viewed as a group, these three films present a universe in which men are sodomizable in much the same way that women are rapable and with much the same meaning and consequences. They suggest a universe, that is, in which vagina and anus are indeed for all practical purposes the same thing and a universe in which that thing has no specific relation to male or female bodies.
>
> (Clover 1992: 158)

This quotation immediately brings to my mind one of my favourites from Kinsey *et al.*'s (1948) *Sexual Behavior in the Human Male*, from the section on 'Rural–urban background and sexual outlet'; during a discussion of same-sex activity among 'ranchmen, cattle men, prospectors, lumbermen, and farming groups in general', Kinsey et al. write:

> These are men who have faced the rigors of nature in the wild. They live on realities and on a minimum of theory. Such a background breeds the attitude that sex is sex, irrespective of the nature of the partner with whom the relation is had ... Such a group of hard-riding, hard-hitting assertive males would not tolerate the affectations of some city groups that are involved in the homosexual [sic]; but this, as far as they can see, has little to do with the question of having sexual relations with other men.
> (Kinsey et al. 1948: 457, 459)[2]

The notion of the affectations of city homosexuals also resonates with hillbilly horror — with the split between acts and identities; for while country men see 'sex as sex', it is urban men who are constructed in these movies as feminized and effeminate, as 'appearance-concerned, trinket-laden, physically weak, ... queasy about the hard facts of rural life ... and even, under duress, given to tears' (Clover 1992: 160). In a similar vein, Annalee Newitz's (1997) brief survey of white trash serial killer movies remarks on (class-based) gendered codings of victim and villain within this related genre, reading them in part as 'class revenge' pictures in much the same way as Clover reads hillbilly horror as the country's revenge on the city.

It's not just in the horror genre, however, that depictions of white trash erotics feature. John Hartigan, Jnr's (1997) discussion of constructions of white trash in popular culture generally, makes frequent allusion to sexualization, describing images of white trash as mobilizing 'a carnivalesque aesthetic, a transgressive celebration of the "grotesque" body (with its illicit sexuality and propensity for cathartic emotions)' (Hartigan 1997: 326); in books, in films, on TV and in music, he finds examples of 'the sexual charge carried in degraded objects' (p. 329), quoting, among others, country band Confederate Railroad's song 'Trashy Women':

> I like my women a little on the trashy side
> When they wear their clothes too tight and their hair is dyed
> Too much lipstick and too much rouge
> Gets me excited leaves me feeling confused
> I like my women just a little on the trashy side
> (quoted in Hartigan 1997: 329)[3]

Such a construction of 'trashy women', of course, emerged in the Bill Clinton 'Zippergate' scandal, with one White House strategist labelling Paula Jones 'trailer trash' — a remark that provoked complaint from trailer-park residents across the States (Reed 1998).

In his exhaustive survey of hillbilly film, Jerry Williamson (1995) echoes Hartigan's talk of the carnivalesque in a section on 'The Hillbilly as Priapus'. Films such as *Li'l Abner*, *Preacherman*, Russ Meyer's Ozarks-set *Mudhoney*, and soft-porn features such as *Shotgun Wedding* and *Scum of the Earth* all centre on the 'erotic tom-foolery' of rural 'priapic fools', full of 'unbridled lust' and 'burlesque leer' (Williamson 1995: 61–2). And, in *White Trash*, both Laura Kipnis and Constance Penley discuss similar manifestations of 'lumpen bawdiness' in popular cultural forms (Penley 1997: 94).

Kipnis (1997) recounts an interview with performance artist Jennifer Reeder who, in her created persona as superhero White Trash Girl, is simultaneously the girl of Confederate Railroad's dreams, and of their nightmares:

> White Trash Girl slunk into my office wearing a short, striped polyester miniskirt I'm positive I myself owned in junior high, a clashing paisley button-down shirt of some petroleum-based miracle fiber, topped off by a too-tight, powder-blue vest of tired, stained faux-suede. Bleached white-blonde hair peeked out from beneath some sort of go-go cap.
> (Kipnis 1997: 113)

Deploying the 'power in being trashy' (p. 119), Reeder enacts White Trash Girl's body as 'oozing and out of control' (p. 124), as an 'inbred biological disaster turned superhero' (p. 118). Her body has become a weapon, oozing toxic secretions (toxic puke, toxic menstrual blood clots).

Reeder's performances as White Trash Girl tie in with other popular cultural depictions of white trash women as brazen, sexually charged, assertive. Discussing *Thelma and Louise*, Jerry Williamson (1995: 226) describes their 'hillbilly gal defiance' as another aspect of this construction, tracking their attitude back to one of the earliest hillbilly movies, *The Moonshiner* (1904), on through a whole series of 'uppity women' pictures (including *Calamity Jane* and *Raising Arizona*) as well as a parallel stream of burlesque-inspired movies, and finally to 'our fullest embodiment of hillbilly gal as cultural devil' (p. 258) – Dolly Parton.[4] In a lot of these movies, it is either the country that 'hardens' the women (*Thelma and Louise*, *I Spit on Your Grave*) or the city and its ways that feminizes them (*Calamity Jane*), reversing the motif in hillbilly horror of urban men feminized by the rural.

Penley's (1997) 'Crackers and Whackers', meanwhile, examines a rather different trajectory – that of pornography's enduring fascination with white trash, borrowing from Kipnis's earlier essay on *Hustler* (Kipnis 1992) to talk about 'smutty folklore', bawdy humour, stag films, porn videos such as *John Wayne Bobbitt: Uncut* and *Tanya Hardon*, and trash-mags like *Outlaw Biker*; all of which, she argues, differ from other (non-trashy) forms of heterosexual porn in their relation to the male subject, who is ridiculed and humiliated as much as titillated, and in their use of transgression as cultural critique (however problematic this may be). One of the stag films she discusses, *On the Beach* (also known as *Getting His Goat*), made in 1923, vividly evokes the priapic fool of Williamson's discussion. A man stands leaning over a fence at 'Idylwild Beach', when he spies three women skinny-dipping. He steals their clothes, offering to return them only in exchange for sex. The women agree – but only if he pays them, and has sex through a hole in the fence. They then back a goat up to the fence, which the man happily fucks, gladly handing over all his money in return to "the best girl I've ever had" (Penley 1997: 95). One of the women later feigns pregnancy, fleecing the man once more. In this and the other forms of bawdy humour Penley discusses, men are naive, priapic idiots, women mischievous and canny. It was pointed out to me that a similar trope appears in John Dahl's neo-noir masterpiece *The Last Seduction*: urban femme fatale Bridget Gregory meets simple country boy Mike Swale (in Beston, near Buffalo), seduces and uses him – tormenting him with her discovery that Trish, the 'wife' he left behind in the city, is, in fact, a male cross-dresser. In all these narratives, country men's sexual *naïveté* offers a different take on Kinsey's 'sex is sex' addage for the rural male – vagina and anus, male and female, human and animal, are, as Clover says, 'for all practical purposes much the same thing' for the priapic fool who is sexually driven but clueless.

*Hustler* itself, of course, may well be the best contemporary example of the troubling transgression Penley finds in stag humour, with its uncommonly broad range of atypical models, its inclusion of 'hefty erect-appearing' penises absent from most other top-shelf magazines (Kipnis 1992: 375), and its unromanticized construction of the vulgar, embarrassing, Rabelaisian body. Particularly interesting in this context is Kipnis's account of *Hustler* owner Larry Flynt's background and upbringing, which he himself commemorated by building a replica of the Appalachian cabin he was raised in, 'replete with chickenwire and hay, and a three-foot lifelike statue of the chicken he claims to have lost his virginity to at age eight' (Kipnis 1992: 385). Larry Flynt's chicken-fucking – and the narrative of *Getting His Goat* – bring me neatly on to the next form of rural erotics I want to discuss: bestiality.

## Animal lovers

One of the most frequent ways in which rural erotics are portrayed in popular culture – and especially in popular humour – is through reference to acts of bestiality, with slang terms like 'sheep shagger' and 'tail lifter' being used to name-call country folk. The small literature on bestiality suggests more than a grain of truth in the comic stereotype. As we have seen, the country fool may be fucking animals out of *naïveté*; but other alternative explanations are offered, again chiming with Kinsey's comment that for country boys 'sex is sex, irrespective of the nature of the partner'. In most of these, opportunity and certain nuances of morality play central roles. Constant proximity to farm animals affords a suitable outlet for libidinal urges in the country, the argument goes, while moral codes might be elastic enough to accommodate a little horse-play – which could be seen as preferable to pre-marital sex between young farmers. As Midas Dekkers notes – commenting on Kinsey – in his amazing overview of zoophilia, *Dearest Pet*:

> Certainly, in the 1940s, in the American countryside animals were readily available for physical games, girls were not. Many farmers preferred to see their unmarried farm lads diving into the stall with their donkey than with their daughter.
>
> (Dekkers 1994: 133)

As Dekkers points out, Kinsey (as ever) provides a remarkably thorough statistical account of 'animal contacts' (Kinsey *et al.* 1948, 1953). Much of the discussion in *The Human Male* focuses on what is referred to as the 'farm boy', who differs most notably from his city cousin in the amount of animal-sex engaged in: an estimated 17 per cent of farm boys reached climax with four-legged friends (or, in cases like Larry Flynt, with two-winged friends), while a full 50 per cent had had some sexual contact with farm stock. Farm girls, on the other hand, reported less frequent animal interests to Kinsey's researchers. While the sights and sounds of the mating season aroused the boys' own basic instincts, 'farm-bred females had been oblivious to the coital activities which went on around them' (Kinsey *et al.* 1953: 504).[5] Kinsey's stress on 'boys' and 'girls' places animal-sex as fundamentally an adolescent activity, although some interviewees confessed that animals remained their 'major outlet' into their twenties and beyond.

Dekkers confirms the Kinsey findings' broader applicability: 'this has been the case in many different country areas, wherever and whenever marital morality is strict and contact with animals intimate' (Dekkers 1994: 133). He quotes writer Ivar Lo-Johansson's memories of early twentieth-century Swedish rural life:

> My grandfather had told me that in earlier days they had employed only women as shepherds. Now I myself have reached the age to understand why. The rancid smell of the sheeps' wool and their inviting behaviour aroused you. The soft coats of the young heifers, the way they climbed on top of each other in the woods and fields, the open way in which they showed their sex and lust, were even more seductive.
>
> (quoted in Dekkers 1994: 134)

In tracking evidence of bestial acts outside the USA, Dekkers refers to a slim body of work, much of which has used court records to trace cases where criminal proceedings ensued. Among these is work by Ronald Grassberger (1968), on Austrian court records from 1923 to 1965. Grassberger found around fifty cases per annum – almost all of these from country men. Grassberger paid as much analytical attention to his data as Kinsey's crowd, looking for seasonal variations, patterns in the sites for animal sex, and even a species breakdown. As Dekkers recounts:

> Vaginal copulation with cows and calves appeared to be by far the most popular. Mares and foals were mounted less often by human beings, approximately as often as goats, which in turn were five times more popular than sheep or pigs. ... [T]he number of copulations with horses in Austria was proportionately remarkably high, especially if one considers that a horse is actually far too tall for a human being.
> (Dekkers 1994: 135)

It is tempting to read some form of hierarchy into Grassberger's listing; what does it tell us about different animals' places in the hearts and minds of farm folk? Is it merely a reflection of opportunity, or is there some semblance of a 'petting order' here? Because these data were drawn by Grassberger from court proceedings, they may reflect no more than the *reporting* of bestiality, rather than its total incidence; the uneven distribution between stock may reflect their value, or other cultural norms prevailing about different animals – perhaps explaining the high number of cases concerning horses, who are working farm animals rather than walking food factories.[6] But – remembering Larry Flynt – where does Grassberger's hierarchy leave the chickens? Dekkers suggests that chicken-fancying is so normalized in some rural parts that it is only noticed when things go awry – he notes the Spanish case of a man crushed to death in 1990 by a boulder dislodged by his chicken-fucking movements (the chicken died also).

The popular construction, then, of bestial country folk is to some extent borne out by the scattered evidence from work by Kinsey, Dekkers and Grassberger; the erotics of animals are not unnoticed in the city (as Dekkers 1994: 138–9 writes: 'what meadows are for country children, the zoo is for city children: the place where they first see live sex ... The zoo is a paradise for voyeurs'), but the myth (and the actuality) of animal-sex is used to construct a peculiar and distinct form of rural erotics. The final form of rural erotics I now want to turn to is, as previously noted, very distinct from both white trash and bestial 'idyll disturbances', trading much more on idyllic, 'natural' constructions of the countryside – as a backdrop for human existence and pleasures in their unclothed, 'natural' state.

## Nude and natural

Sex is our allotment – in the heart of the city, our little square of heath. To make love, we fling off our clothes, abandoning the signs which mark us as civilised: law, art and language ... Sex, then, has been appointed to the domain ... within which we can experience ourselves as at once natural and human: that is, as beings continuous with the world beyond culture's indiscernible edge.

(Ward 1987: 161)

What I want to do in this section is not only to think about naturism in itself, but also to use the idea(l)s of naturism to begin thinking about the relationships constructed between sex and nature. For while naturism makes explicit links between the body and nature (though it is ambivalent towards sex, as I'll talk about later), there are other ways in which ideas about nature cojoin with ideas about sex and sexuality. An important springboard for my approach here has been Greta Gaard's recent essay 'Toward a Queer Ecofeminism' (1997), which makes some very interesting observations about the sexing of nature and the naturing of sex. Her task in the essay is to 'examine the ways queers are feminized, animalized, eroticized and naturalized in a culture that devalues women, animals, nature and sexuality [and to] ... explore how nature is feminized, eroticized, even queered' (Gaard 1997: 119). Arguing that 'queer sexualities [are constructed] as both "closer to nature" [i.e. primitive, uncivilized, animalistic] and "crimes against nature"' [where 'natural sex' equals procreative heterosexuality] (p. 119), Gaard draws on a wide range of material — from histories of witchcraft and of colonialism to studies of other species' sexual habits — to think about creating an ecopolitical culture which works at 'liberating the erotic [and] ... reconceptualizing humans as equal participants in culture and in nature' (p. 132).

As Jon Ward (1987) also argues, procreative heterosexuality has come to be constructed as *the* natural form of sex, and this conception of what's 'natural' serves, of course, to render other sexual expressions and activities 'unnatural'. In sex — as a 'natural' act — Ward says, culture is cast off; this argument functions in the same way, I want to argue, in discourses around naturism, where clothes (as culture) are cast off to free the natural body. As Ralph Rugoff (1995: 177) writes, in the context of American naturism, '[o]nly in nakedness can we find the unadorned truth of experience; only by stripping away civilization's false veneers can we move closer to Nature and her eternal verities'. Two contradictions then emerge from these twin castings-off. First, naturism is constructed as *nonsexual* — as if, perhaps, sex is not a natural act at all, but part of the culture stripped away. The body becomes essentialized or naturalized, also, rather than being seen as itself part of culture (although the rich ethnography of Douglas, Rasmussen and Flanagan's (1977) study reveals the great many ways in which the nude body is invested with cultural signification on the naturist beach — ways of walking, of lying, the stress on fitness, the all-over tan, attitudes to the display of genitals (especially male erections), non-clothed adornment, etc., all mark the body as a cultural product). Second, the casting-off of culture does not extend to the casting-off of (culturally constructed) moral codes: while we might expect the freeing of the natural body to release animalistic passions, the stress of naturism as nonsexual serves to naturalize these forms of morality while placing sex as part of the culture left behind in the wardrobe. I want to hold on to these ideas a while longer, as I discuss some formations of naturism which either concur with or dispute this (de)sexualization of nature.

One prominent desexualized rendering of idyllic, undressed nature is to be found in early twentieth-century nudist movements in Europe, which drew on Ancient Greece to construct an imagining of anti-modernist 'nature'. Athleticism, nudity and nature were combined, for example, in the German youth and 'life reform' movements (Mosse 1985), which sought to 'elevate nudity into a spiritual principle', in part by placing it in its rightful context – 'nudity was acceptable only ... when seen in an unspoilt natural setting: meadows, gardens, or against the background of the sea' (Mosse 1985: 51). In other (urban) settings, the naked body became lewd, pornographic, sexual. Natural nudity was thus invested with a 'moral purpose' (p. 54), transcending sensuousness and lustfulness, to create a chaste, spiritual *Nacktkultur* (nude culture), as one of its proponents, Heinrich Pudor, termed it in 1908. Tied in with other expressions of nationalism (such as the fetish of 'native plants'; see Wolschke-Bulmahn 1996), the nude body in natural landscape settings became a powerful national symbol in Germany at that time.

Some similar motifs run through the contemporary nudist scene. The Naturist Society's website, for example, emphasizes 'family-oriented, non-sexual nude recreation', illustrated by pictures of happy naked bodies set against 'natural' backdrops. The society's magazine, *Nude and Natural*, calls for 'body acceptance in a clothing-compulsive world', and reiterates that naturism is not erotic, while the 'family' orientation ties it clearly to procreative heterosexuality: '[n]udists don't fuck, they breed' (Rugoff 1995: 181). However, Douglas, Rasmussen and Flanagan's (1977) detailed study of a Californian nude beach shows the ways in which the public profile of naturism is *projected* as non-sexual while the practices of naturists at the beach suggest that, in the words of one informant, 'it's really sexy, no matter what people tell you' (p. 21). Later they list the motivations for skinny-dipping and outdoors sex – activities which predate and, they argue, help us understand nudism: 'Freedom, the sense of naturalness, of being one with nature, of being open, of a tingling feeling on skin caressed by the air, of romance, of natural beauty, of a certain delightful sense of naughtiness and abandon' (p. 32), while their in-depth account includes lengthy sections on casual (hetero and homo) sex, swinging, voyeurism and exhibitionism as fairly commonplace 'bareass beach' practices. Evidently, as countless respondents in their study reiterate, the nude beach is certainly about nature, about being 'natural' – but it is also rooted in the erotic in all kinds of ways: *naughty nature*, if you like.

The dream of a sexy Arcadia or Eden where nature rules has a long tradition in erotic literature and popular culture (Bech 1997; Fone 1983; Woods 1995) – as a (pre-cultural) site for 'free love', a place to 'cast off the yoke of civilization' and to be 'naked and in contact with nature' (Bech 1997: 148). In the lesbian and gay imaginary, such a mythic place-construction frees up sex from social norms (*contra* the discourses of naturism as nonsexual), marking same-sex desire as 'natural' (Bell and Valentine 1995; Fone 1983).

As Mosse notes, there existed a similar current of eroticism – especially of homoeroticism – in the early twentieth-century German naturist movement, but this was always stringently disavowed and exorcised. In England at that time, however, such erotics of naturism were more centrally located within the thoughts of life reformers such as Edward Carpenter, where nudity tapped into a 'back to nature' movement with many different agendas (Grieg 1984; Marsh 1982; Tsuzuki 1980; Weeks 1977). Here homoeroticism was neither disavowed nor exorcised – in fact, the linkages were made quite explicit as a thread through literary, artistic and reform materials emanating from the movement (and indeed outside it). As Carpenter wrote in *Love's Coming of Age* (1896): 'sexual embraces themselves seldom receive the benison of Dame Nature, in whose presence alone, under the burning sun or the high canopy of the stars and surrounded by the fragrant atmosphere, their meanings can be fully understood' (quoted in Marsh 1982: 22) – a philosophy he and his friends made flesh in their communal smallholding at Millthorpe, near Sheffield.

Carpenter's lived philosophies have had an enduring impact on queer culture, informing, amongst others, the US Fairie movement formed in the 1970s, and giving name to a gay men's rural retreat in Scotland, the Edward Carpenter Community (Woolaston 1991). In 'This Gay Tribe: A Brief History of Fairies', Mark Thompson (1987) charts the development of a rural, separatist gay men's movement in the USA, outflowing from the Gay Liberation Front – and particularly with some men's dissatisfaction with the urban-based gay political and social scene. Echoing the better known lesbian-separatist movement of the time (Cheney 1985; Valentine 1997), the fairies sought to reject urban life – including (indeed, perhaps especially) urban gay life – and seek spiritual and corporeal renewal through 'self-reliance and contact with raw nature' (Thompson 1987: 263). The fairies take at least part of their inspiration from Carpenter (plus Walt Whitman, who had himself both inspired and corresponded with Carpenter (see Katz 1976), and Thoreau, for *Walden* (Abelove 1993)), as well as drawing on neopaganism and Wicca. Thompson recalls an early fairie gathering in the Arizona desert, quoting from the local newssheet the sheriff's outraged commentary:

> A series of 'strange doings' were reported by the local sheriff, Waldo Pruitt, at a site about ten miles west of this small desert community [Benson, Arizona] ... Pruitt first became aware of the event through reports about

cattle displaying unusual behavior in the vicinity ... Informants also claimed that large groups of men there were engaging in orgiastic rituals.

'They said that all the animals in the area started to act real strange', the sheriff explained. 'I guess I don't mind what you do as long as you don't do it in public. But when you start in on plants and animals, well, then you've gone too far.'

(*Farmers' Arizonan Gazette*, 5 September 1979, quoted in Thompson 1987: 269–70)[7]

The shedding of clothes was always an important component of the men's rites, which included a 'mud ritual' in a dry riverbed, circle dancing, music and chanting. Similar activities continue to be offered by the Edward Carpenter Collective – such as its *Alchemy: Tyger Tyger!* week in Scotland, the publicity for which also continues the fairies' rejection of urban gay culture:

> We will discover an honourable and sustainable way to live intelligent and blissful lives as gay men and to be able to detach from a commercial and predatory gay culture whose deathwish mantra is *Live Fast, Die Young, Be A Beautiful Corpse*.

As noted, this separatism-in-nature is also paralleled in lesbian communes in the USA and beyond, where similar practices evoked similar linkages between nature, sexuality, spiritualism and, in this case, the feminine (Cheney 1985; Faderman 1991; Valentine 1997). There are further clear parallels, of course, with the so-called mythopoetic men's movement, where masculinity is renewed through returning to nature and through purification rituals – nudity, drumming, chanting, shamanism – and 'modern (metropolitan) man' is constructed as having been feminized by the impact of, among other things, the women's movement and male guilt. However, many men's groups rigorously (and phobically) police the homosocial/homosexual divide among members and activities, maintaining the security of a homosocial heterosexual profile which could be effectively shattered by the presence of homo-sexuality (Bonnett 1996; Pfeil 1995). Getting back to nature for the mythopoetic men's movement, then, means 'reclaiming' and (re)naturalizing heterosexual mas-culinity. In a notion not too far removed from the narratives of hillbilly horror, the country is the site of forms of 'unreconstructed' masculinity; while city men are feminized by the rural in films like *Deliverance*, for the men's movement this natural, feral, rural masculinity is a regenerative resource, provoking 'soft' city men to go wild in the country. (As far as I know, no one has so far plotted a movie around hillbillies meeting Iron Johns drumming in the woods; I'm sure it'd make for an interesting picture.) Here we find something missing from naturism's discreet and civilized engagement with nature – what Bonnett (1996) calls 'modern primitivism', which unleashes sublimated, instinctual, *animal* urges in men (hence, perhaps, the men's movement's special squeamishness for homosex).

## Contrary places: the natural and the unnatural

What has emerged through discussing my three forms of rural erotics, finally, is something about the relationship between nature, the rural and masculinity. Kinsey's 'sex is sex' construction – whether hypermasculinized (in hillbilly horror) or produced out of either (lack of) opportunity or *naïveté* (the priapic fool we first met with in Foucault) – circulates in representations of both white trash erotics and of bestiality. In the mythopoetic men's movement, the country offers masculinization for city men, although for both the men's and naturist movements, the association of nature with sex – or at least with anything other than procreative heterosex – is denied (though the 'radical Fairies' (homo)sexualize nature at the same time as masculinizing it).[8] Looking back at Greta Gaard's essay, we see here counters to her notion that 'nature is feminized, eroticized, even queered' (Gaard 1997: 119), for in these articulations of the rural, nature is masculinized, and ambivalently eroticized and queered. Each of the three rural erotics makes use of certain constructions of sexuality as *closer to nature* (and this may be either positively or negatively charged) and others as *crimes against nature*, again echoing Gaard. What joins them all is making visible a set of linkages between the rural and the erotic which help us understand cultural constructions of both. As Mark Lawrence (1997: 3) says, the rural can be seen as 'simultaneously a site of vestiginal wildness and the forward edge of a civilizing force, or again simultaneously a zone of historical recidivism but also of rustic retreat': it can be seen as naive and innocent or depraved and wild, straight or queer. *The erotic*, as a 'given "sign" of the rural', can be 'used in many different ways', with a 'metalanguage of nature' giving rise to a 'constellation of made, unmade and remade constructions' of the erotic rural (Lawrence 1997: 5, 14, 15). At the same time, *the rural*, as a given sign of the erotic, also evokes a constellation of meanings; I have only begun to scratch the surface of these constellations here. Other chapters in this book add much more to the theorization of the rural and the marginal within sociospatial economies of desire.

There remain, of course, questions left unanswered, loose-ends untied. If we are to talk of representations of the erotic rural, for example, we should be thinking about who is doing the representing, and for whom. While I don't intend to attend to that question with any detail or precision, it is worth thinking about the construction and performance of rural erotics from an urban perspective, for an urban audience (obviously in the filmic constructions I have talked about, but no less in Kinsey *et al.*'s surveys – which echo with Foucault's (1979: 32) experts 'speechifying, analyzing, and investigating' the 'furtive pleasures' of a 'village halfwit' in nineteenth-century rural France – or in the fetishizing of idyllic wilderness among Radical Fairies). Images of the country and of country life, therefore, tell us things about the city, too – and, in particular, about the working of the rural/urban, margin/centre, natural/unnatural hierarchy as a device which marks both, in the words of Creed and Ching (1997: 17), as 'contrary places'.

## Acknowledgements

Special thanks to Ruth Holliday and Richard Phillips for reading and commenting very helpfully on drafts of this chapter. Thanks also to Tim Edensor and Jon Binnie, and to the organizers and participants of the Nonmetropolitan Sexualities conference, Aberystwyth, July 1997.

## Notes

1 The Mason–Dixon line divides the northern and southern states of the USA, powerfully symbolizing the cultural specificities of the divided nation, by marking out the cartography of the urban/rural hierarchy.
2 See Katz (1976) for other material on cowboys, miners, etc.
3 There is an excellent essay on white trash and country music – particularly on the ways in which country stars perform (and some resist) 'rustic authenticity' – by Barbara Ching (1997) in Wray and Newitz's collection.
4 Williamson (1995: 258) discusses Dolly Parton as 'cultural devil' in some detail, talking about her own brand of 'hillbilly gal defiance', which relies on using her 'trashiness' to confront 'urban good taste' – like Roseanne famously once said (and I'm paraphrasing), everyone's worst nightmare is white trash with money.
5 This does not mean, of course, that bestiality is an exclusively male practice. As Dekkers recounts, both sexes enjoy their 'animal contacts'; in fact, as Diane Watt pointed out to me, there exists a strong current of erotica depicting women having sex with animals, including those found down on the farm.
6 There's some very interesting material on horses in Elspeth Probyn's (1996) *Outside Belongings*. She tracks the construction of the 'equestrienne lesbienne' in Colette's *The Pure and the Impure* and in Radclyffe Hall's *The Well of Loneliness*; in both cases, lesbian desire is mediated through horses. She also discusses the relationships between 'girls and girls and horses' in contemporary Western cultures, and talks about Quebecois TV drama *Les filles de Caleb*, where scenes of horse mating segue into the ecstasies of the principal characters, Emilie and Oliva, serving to naturalize their union. What's especially interesting is a spoof of the scene Probyn also reports: on an end-of-the-year satirical show called *Bye, Bye 91*, 'Emilie begs Oliva to "do like the horses". At which Oliva, played as the village fool, stands up and whinnies and prances' (Probyn 1996: 83) – here the male rural naïf misunderstands the schoolma'am's proposition, casting him not as priapic but as hopelessly innocent (as *Les filles de Caleb* unfolds, he is shown not just as incompetent but also as impotent).
7 The sheriff's complaint that the Fairies' activities scared the animals (and the plants!) chimes with one of the famous comments made at the time of the Wolfenden Report on public displays of homosexuality frightening horses. It makes me wonder why same-sex desire is constructed as animal-scaring – and how this might be related to my discussion of 'natural' and 'unnatural' acts.

8 I am aware that this argument would've taken a radically different tack if I'd have focused on lesbian separatism rather than the men's movement; my defence is that I am particularly interested here in constructions of erotic masculinity in the rural.

## References

Abelove, Henry (1993) 'From Thoreau to Queer Politics', *Yale Journal of Criticism* 6: 17–27.

Bech, Henning (1997) *When Men Meet: Homosexuality and Modernity*, Cambridge: Polity Press.

Bell, David (1997) 'Anti-idyll: Rural Horror', in Paul Cloke and Jo Little (eds) *Contested Countryside Cultures: Otherness, Marginalisation and Rurality*, London: Routledge: 94–108.

Bell, David and Valentine, Gill (1995) 'Queer Country: Rural Lesbian and Gay Lives', *Journal of Rural Studies* 11: 113–22.

Bonnett, Alastair (1996) 'The New Primitives: Identity, Landscape and Cultural Appropriation in the Mythopoetic Men's Movement', *Antipode* 28: 273–91.

Brandth, Berit (1995) 'Rural Masculinity in Transition: Gender Images in Tractor Advertisements', *Journal of Rural Studies* 11: 123–33.

Bunce, Michael (1994) *The Countryside Ideal: Anglo-American Images of Landscape*, London: Routledge.

Cavaliero, G. (1977) *The Rural Tradition in the English Novel 1900–1939*, London: Macmillan.

Cheney, Joyce (1985) *Lesbian Land*, Minneapolis: Word Weavers.

Ching, Barbara (1997) 'Acting Naturally: Cultural Distinction and Critiques of Pure Country', in Matt Wray and Annalee Newitz (eds) *White Trash: Race and Class in America*, New York: Routledge: 231–48.

Clover, Carol (1992) *Men, Women and Chainsaws: Gender in the Modern Horror Film*, London: BFI.

Creed, Gerald and Ching, Barbara (1997) 'Recognizing Rusticity: Identity and the Power of Place', in Barbara Ching and Gerald Creed (eds) *Knowing Your Place: Rural Identity and Cultural Hierarchy*, New York: Routledge: 1–38.

Dekkers, Midas (1994) *Dearest Pet: On Bestiality*, London: Verso.

Douglas, Jack, Rasmussen, Paul and Flanagan, Carol (1977) *The Nude Beach*, Beverly Hills, Calif.: Sage.

Faderman, Lillian (1991) *Odd Girls and Twilight Lovers: a History of Lesbian Life in Twentieth-century America*, Harmondsworth: Penguin.

Fone, Byrne (1983) 'This other Eden: Arcadia and the Homosexual Imagination', *Journal of Homosexuality* 8: 13–34.

Foucault, Michel (1979) *The History of Sexuality. Volume 1: An Introduction*, London: Allen Lane.

Gaard, Greta (1997) 'Toward a Queer Ecofeminism', *Hypatia* 12: 114–37.

Grassberger, Ronald (1968) *Die Unzucht mit Tieren*, Vienna: Springer.

Grieg, Noel (ed.) (1983) *Edward Carpenter: Selected Writings. Volume 1: Sex*, London: Gay Men's Press.

Hartigan, John Jnr. (1997) 'Unpopular Culture: the Case of "White Trash"', *Cultural Studies* 11: 316–43.

Houlton, Delphine and Short, Brian (1995) 'Sylvanian Families: the Production and Consumption of a Rural Community', *Journal of Rural Studies* 11: 367–85.

Jones, Owain (1995) 'Lay Discourses of the Rural: Developments and Implications for Rural Studies', *Journal of Rural Studies* 11: 35–49.

—— (1997) 'Little Figures, Big Shadows: Country Childhood Stories', in Paul Cloke and Jo Little (eds) *Contested Countryside Cultures: Otherness, Marginalisation and Rurality*, London: Routledge: 158–79.

Katz, Jonathan (1976) *Gay American History: Lesbians and Gay Men in the U.S.A.*, New York: Thomas Y. Crowell.

King, Richard and Taylor, Helen (eds) (1996) *Dixie Debates: Perspectives on Southern Cultures*, London: Pluto Press.

Kinsey, Alfred, Pomeroy, Wardell and Martin, Clyde (1948) *Sexual Behavior in the Human Male*, Philadelphia, Pa.: W.B. Saunders.

Kinsey, Alfred, Pomeroy, Wardell, Martin, Clyde and Gebhard, Paul (1953) *Sexual Behavior in the Human Female*, Philadelphia, Pa.: W.B. Saunders.

Kipnis, Laura (1992) '(Male) Desire and (Female) Disgust: Reading *Hustler*', in Lawrence Grossberg, Cary Nelson and Paula Treichler (eds) *Cultural Studies*, New York: Routledge: 373–91.

Kipnis, Laura with Reeder, Jennifer (1997) 'White Trash Girl: the Interview', in Matt Wray and Annalee Newitz (eds) *White Trash: Race and Class in America*, New York: Routledge: 113–30.

Kramer, Jerry Lee (1995) 'Bachelor Farmers and Spinsters: Gay and Lesbian Identities and Communities in Rural North Dakota', in David Bell and Gill Valentine (eds) *Mapping Desire: Geographies of Sexualities*, London: Routledge: 200–13.

Lawrence, Mark (1997) 'Heartlands or Neglected Geographies? Liminality, Power, and the Hyperreal Rural', *Journal of Rural Studies* 13: 1–17.

Little, Jo and Austin, Patricia (1996) 'Women and the Rural Idyll', *Journal of Rural Studies* 12: 101–11.

Marsh, Jan (1982) *Back to the Land: the Pastoral Impulse in England, from 1880 to 1914*, London: Quartet.

Matless, David (1994) 'Doing the English Village, 1945–90: an Essay in Imaginative Geography', in Paul Cloke, Marcus Doel, David Matless, Martin Phillips and Nigel Thrift, *Writing the Rural: Five Cultural Geographies*, London: Paul Chapman: 7–88.

Mingay, George (ed.) (1989) *The Rural Idyll*, London: Routledge.

Mosse, George (1985) *Nationalism and Sexuality: Middle-class Morality and Sexual Norms in Modern Europe*, Madison: University of Wisconsin Press.

Newitz, Annalee (1997) 'White Savagery and Humiliation, or a New Racial Consciousness in the Media', in Matt Wray and Annalee Newitz (eds) *White Trash: Race and Class in America*, New York: Routledge: 131–54.

Penley, Constance (1997) 'Crackers and Whackers: the White Trashing of Porn', in Matt Wray and Annalee Newitz (eds) *White Trash: Race and Class in America*, New York: Routledge: 89–112.

Pfeil, Fred (1995) *White Guys: Studies in Postmodern Domination and Difference*, London: Verso.

Probyn, Elspeth (1996) *Outside Belongings*, New York: Routledge.
Reed, Julia (1998) 'Trailer Trash Tactics and Ivy League Spite', *Observer*, 1 February: 12–13.
Rugoff, Ralph (1995) *Circus Americanus*, London: Verso.
Sandell, Jillian (1997) 'Telling Stories of "Queer White Trash": Race, Class, And Sexuality in the Work of Dorothy Allison', in Matt Wray and Annalee Newitz (eds) *White Trash: Race and Class in America*, New York: Routledge: 211–30.
Short, Brian (ed.) (1991) *The English Rural Community: Image and Analysis*, Cambridge: Cambridge University Press.
Tarantino, Quentin (1994) *Pulp Fiction*, London: Faber & Faber.
Thompson, Mark (1987) 'This Gay Tribe: A Brief History of Fairies', in Mark Thompson (ed.) *Gay Spirit: Myth and Meaning*, New York: St Martin's Press: 260–78.
Tsuzuki, Chushichi (1980) *Edward Carpenter 1844–1929: Prophet of Human Fellowship*, Cambridge: Cambridge University Press.
Valentine, Gill (1997) 'Making Space: Lesbian Separatist Communities in the United States', in Paul Cloke and Jo Little (eds) *Contested Countryside Cultures: Otherness, Marginalisation and Rurality*, London: Routledge: 109–22.
Ward, Jon (1987) 'The Nature of Heterosexuality', in Gillian Hanscombe and Martin Humphries (eds) *Heterosexuality*, London: Gay Men's Press: 145–69.
Weeks, Jeffrey (1977) *Coming Out: Homosexual Politics in Britain, from the Nineteenth Century to the Present*, London: Quartet.
Weston, Kath (1995) 'Get Thee to a Big City: Sexual Imaginary and the Great Gay Migration', *GLQ* 2: 253–77.
Williamson, Jerry (1995) *Hillbillyland: What the Movies Did to the Mountains and what the Mountains did to the Movies*, Chapel Hill: University of North Carolina Press.
Wolschke-Bulmahn, Joachim (1996) 'The Mania for Native Plants in Nazi Germany', in Mark Dion and Alexis Rockman (eds) *Concrete Jungle*, New York: Juno Books: 65–9.
Woods, Gregory (1987) *Articulate Flesh: Male Homoeroticism and Modern Poetry*, New Haven, Conn.: Yale University Press.
—— (1995) 'Fantasy Islands: Popular Topographies of Marooned Masculinity', in David Bell and Gill Valentine (eds) *Mapping Desire: Geographies of Sexualities*, London: Routledge: 126–48.
Woolaston, Graeme (1991) 'The Good Life', *Gay Times*, May: 39–40.
Wray, Matt and Newitz, Annalee (eds) (1997) *White Trash: Race and Class in America*, New York: Routledge.

# 6

# IMAGINED GEOGRAPHIES AND SEXUALITY POLITICS

## The city, the country and the age of consent

*Richard Phillips*

The contributors to this volume, and to the wider study of sexualities, move quite freely between histories and geographies of sex and sexuality on the one hand, and literary and cultural representations on the other. Some contributors concentrate on the former, others on the latter. In their studies of non-metropolitan America, for example, Angelia Wilson (Chapter 11) concentrates on experiences, William Spurlin (Chapter 10) on representations. More generally, writers on this subject display a tendency to privilege one or the other. Foucault has inspired many to privilege what may be called discursive constructions of sexuality – to treat literary representations of sexuality as if they mapped directly onto bodies and identities, in other words as if they *were* sexualities. Historian Michael Mason argues, conversely, that sexuality – encompassing forms of activity, demeanour, professed belief, private belief and more – is not reducible to discourse (Mason 1995: 40, 172–3). Other empirically minded historians and geographers point to differences between image and 'reality', with regards to sexualities and sexual spaces (e.g. Davies 1996). If image is not the same as 'reality' and neither is privileged, there follows the question of how the two spheres co-exist and interact. This means tracing an interplay between what one geographer has called metaphorical and material spaces of sexuality (Brown 1996). In this chapter I explore this kind of interplay, specifically between imagined geographies and concrete sexuality politics.

I begin with the kind of imagined geography that Davies interrogates – that of non-metropolitan (rural, provincial) purity and metropolitan impurity. As Raymond Williams has shown, big cities have often (if not always) been associated with sexual impurity or 'worldliness' (Williams 1985:1), as well as with other broadly negative characteristics like alienation, poverty, rootlessness, immorality and ill health; meanwhile rural and provincial places have been associated with 'innocence, and simple virtue' (Williams 1985:1), with positive qualities like stability, morality, healthfulness, contentment and beauty. Williams acknowledges counter currents to all this, images of the city as a place of 'light', the country as one of 'backwardness' and 'ignorance' (Williams 1985: 1); in this book, David Bell (Chapter 5) expands upon the sexual dimensions of these counter currents. But, as geographer John Short (1991) points out, negative images of the city and positive images of the country predominate. Usually, as Davies acknowledged, the city is associated with vice, the country with purity.

Metropolitan and non-metropolitan sexual geographies are constructed in relation to each other, in spatial/sexual dialectics, which often take the form of travel between the two spheres – between purity and perversity, naivety and urbanity, security and temptation, innocence and sin, and so on. In the classic Engiish pornographic tale Fanny Hill [*Memoirs of a Woman of Pleasure*] (Cleland 1748–9), the journey to the city brings all sorts of sexual temptation and pleasure to its heroine – and titillation to its readers. Likewise, but with emphasis on morality rather than pleasure, William Hogarth's *Harlot's Progress* (1733) (a series of six prints, echoed by storytellers and playwrights such as Theophilus Cibber), portrays the downfall of an innocent country girl, an easy victim of London vice. To cite a recent example, the Czech film *Mandragora* shows boys (including 14-year-old Marek), runaways from small towns and villages, being sexually exploited in Prague, and falling into lives of poverty and drug abuse. Sexual journeys of this type are vehicles for a wide range of morality and sexuality politics. Though they draw upon transhistorical geographical and moral images (which Williams traces to Classical times), and though they address moral and sexual politics of equal historical and geographical breadth, the contents and political references of these narratives are also historically specific. In *The Country and the City*, Williams (1985) shows that positive images of country and negative images of the city have changed over time, adapting for example to industrialization and urban growth. As the form and detail of the stereotypically sexual city and pure country have changed over time, so have their specific references. Hogarth's *Harlot's Progress*, for example, used stereotypical images of city and country to address broad moral questions, but it also brought specific detail (for example, reference to contemporary figures including Mother Needham and Colonel Francis Chartres, procuress and client respectively), to name and shame individuals and to address the moral climate of the day (Jarrett 1976). Similarly, *Mandragora* addressed broad moral questions, and more specifically attacked the exploitation of Czech boys by Western men. The release of the film in the Czech Republic (1997) also coincided with a number of high profile trials, in which foreign men were tried in Prague for sexual offences against minors (the trial of British radio celebrity, Christopher Denning, helped ensure international media coverage of the episode).[1] Sexual journeys, like those of Fanny Hill, Moll Hackabout and Marek, have been adapted in a variety of contexts to address a variety of sexuality politics. Concerned as they are with the loss of sexual innocence, these journeys are particularly adaptable for addressing age of consent politics.

In this chapter, I examine two sexual journey narratives that addressed contemporary age of consent politics. In both stories young people travel to London, where they lose their sexual innocence. The first, an 1885 newspaper story entitled 'The Maiden Tribute of Modern Babylon', explicitly argued the case for raising the female age of consent. The second, a 1975 television documentary entitled *Johnny Go Home*, implicitly argued the case for maintaining a higher age of consent for gay men. In each story, young people – portrayed as child-like, small, innocent, naive, uncorrupted, vulnerable, pre-sexual – leave non-metropolitan (rural and/or provincial) homes and travel to London, where they are exposed to sexual dangers, and where sooner or later they are corrupted. Each story is based loosely on fact, highlighting but misrepresenting real sexual danger and exploitation. Each story illustrates the need to pass or maintain legislation to 'protect' young people – age of consent legislation. Though it is difficult to assess its impact precisely, it is possible to say that the first – by W.T. Stead in the *Pall Mall Gazette* – helped force Parliament to raise the female age of consent to 16, while the latter – by John Willis for Yorkshire Television – set back campaigns by gay rights activists, who sought to equalize heterosexual and homosexual ages of consent. Stead's media campaign is well documented, partly through the work of cultural historians and biographers such as Judith Walkowitz ([1992] 1994), Edward Bristow (1977) and Raymond Schults (1972). *Johnny Go Home* will be less familiar to many readers, partly because it is overshadowed in the annals of television documentary drama and campaign journalism by an earlier programme, *Cathy Come Home* (1966), which addressed some similar themes (homelessness, but not sexuality). Re-reading 'The Maiden Tribute' and *Johnny Go Home*, my angle is critical and comparative, focused on *rhetorical spaces*, particularly the metropolitan and non-metropolitan, and relationships between these, and the significance of these spaces for politics of sexuality, specifically relating to ages of consent.

## Falling towards London: the age of consent for 'girls'

'The Maiden Tribute of Modern Babylon', a serialized newspaper report published in the *Pall Mall Gazette* in July 1885, brought issues of sexuality and sexual exploitation to the attention of British newspaper readers, and onto their national political agenda. 'The Maiden Tribute' exposés made a cultural and political splash: outside the *Pall Mall Gazette* offices, riots broke out among people trying to buy copies; newspapers around the country and as far away as India and America reported and commented on the scandal; spurred on by public opinion and by a wave of purity movements, the British Parliament passed draconian new sexual legislation (Bland 1995; Bristow 1977).

'The Maiden Tribute' centres around the story of a 13-year-old girl procured and sold into prostitution. Stead staged the act (illegally, as it turned out), in order to produce a shocking 'true story'. He also established a 'Secret Commission', which explored the sexual life of the metropolis. 'The Maiden Tribute' articles tell the story of a girl sold into slavery, while presenting a more general picture of vice in the metropolis and 'white slavery' on the Continent. He reported 'The Violation of Virgins', explained 'How Girls are Bought and Ruined', and described 'The International Slave Trade in Girls'. 'The Maiden Tribute' is both pornographic and melodramatic, covering such titillating ground as 'Confessions of a Brothel Keeper' and 'Strapping Girls Down', while telling the pathetic stories of vulnerable girls, sold or abducted into lives of prostitution (see Walkowitz [1992] 1994). Stead's title refers to a myth, explained at the outset:

> In ancient times, if we may believe the myths of Hellas, Athens, after a disastrous campaign, was compelled by her conqueror to send once, every nine years a tribute to Crete of seven youths and seven maidens. The doomed fourteen, who were selected by lot and amid the lamentations of the citizens, returned no more. The vessel that bore them to Crete unfurled black sails as the symbol of despair, and on arrival her passengers were flung into the famous Labyrinth of Daedalus, there to wander about blindly until such time as they were devoured by the Minotaur, a frightful monster, half man, half bull, the foul product of an unnatural lust.[2]

In Stead's version, non-metropolitan England sends young female virgins to a metropolitan sexual labyrinth, which violates and consumes them. Stead leaves the 'youths' out of his story, though they remain between the lines, and the political outcome has implications for them too — for boys (and men) as well as girls (and women) — as we shall see.[3]

Stead made his political objectives very clear, partly to avoid being labelled a pornographer, mainly to focus public attention on an issue that was slipping off the political agenda. The Criminal Law Amendment Bill, designed to raise the female age of consent and otherwise 'protect' children and women from sexual exploitation and violence, had been passed by the Lords but dropped in the Commons in both 1883 and 1884, and there was no reason to assume it would do any better in 1885. Benjamin Scott, a purity campaigner and reformer, visited Stead and won his support. Stead was known as a pioneer of what Matthew Arnold was to call the 'New Journalism' and a veteran of newspaper campaigns, notably the 'Bitter Cry'[4] campaign (1883–4), which addressed the state of working-class urban housing and resulted (or at least ended, in February 1884) with the formation of a Royal Commission on slum housing (Schults 1972). Journalistically progressive, focused and politically effective, Stead had demonstrated an ability to run a media campaign — something he did once again in 'The Maiden Tribute' articles. 'The Maiden Tribute' illustrated the need for, and explicitly agitated for the passing of, a Criminal Law Amendment Bill that would raise the female age of consent from its current level of

13 to 18 or 21 (Bristow 1977: 111). Stead argued that the discrepancy between British and Continental ages of consent led to the export of young girls to the Continent (British 13-year-olds could legally have sex, while their Continental counterparts could not). Stead laid out his concerns:

I. The sale and purchase and violation of children.
II. The procuration of virgins.
III. The entrapping and ruin of women.
IV. The international slave trade in girls.
V. Atrocities, brutalities, and unnatural crimes.[5]

An increase in the age of consent was presented, by Stead, as an important part of the solution to these problems.

Stead's political project (regarding the female age of consent) and his 'Maiden Tribute' articles both rest upon a well-known contemporary 'corruption theory' of femininity, which divided women into those who remained pure and those who had been corrupted or 'ruined' by pre- or extra-marital sex. As a warning and as an argument for greater 'protection' of girls and young women, Stead tells the stories of women who pass from one side of polarized femininity to the other, as they pass from one side of polarized geography to another: from non-metropolitan to metropolitan space.

'The Maiden Tribute' stories concentrated on the metropolis, on mapping London's vice. Judith Walkowitz provides a sustained and probably definitive reading of Stead's sexual geography of London. Her interest, in *City of Dreadful Delight: Narratives of Sexual Danger in Late-Victorian London* (Walkowitz [1992] 1994), is the sexual geography of the city *per se*. Mine, in contrast, is the sexual geography of the city and its position in a wider spatial and sexual framework, structured around metropolitan and non-metropolitan dynamics.

The metropolis is portrayed as a space of sexual danger to girls and young women – easy 'victims of the lust of London' – who are summarily corrupted.[6] There are many snares: in the East End, over-crowded conditions throw people together, and the result is often sexual, sometimes incestuous.[7] In the West End, rich men pay for sex, often with children or very young women. On the streets of the city, strewn as they are with drink and prostitution, immorality is contagious.[8] Once a girl or woman enters London, her fate is sealed. Like the labyrinth in Crete, which was large as a town, those who entered London 'could never find their way out again'[9] Victims 'could never retrace their steps, so inextricable were the paths, so blind the footsteps, so "innumerable" the ways of wrong-doing'.[10] To enter London is to descend into a dark, subterranean world. 'Stead determined to "drag this great evil to light" through his "investigations in this subterranean region".'[11] One of the *Pall Mall Gazette's* correspondents – a 'Christian lady' – compared Stead's London to the most subterranean place of all: '(Shelley's description of) hell'.[12] To descend is to fall, figuratively and morally, and London is a space of fallen girls and women, who lead (what used to be called) 'gay', amoral lives. Bad mothers, they sell their own daughters into prostitution.[13] Evil parodies of feminine virtue, they even pose as nuns[14] in order to trap innocent girls at railway stations, sending the latter to brothel keepers.'[15] As Walkowitz argues in more detail, London is a bad place populated by fallen women (Walkowitz [1992] 1994).

As a space of corrupted and fallen women, London must be placed in context, in relation to spaces of pure and virtuous women. Although these spaces and women are marginalized in Stead's report, they are ultimately its point, for the femininity they represent is at stake. Virgins in 'The Maiden Tribute' have come to London from non-metropolitan – rural, provincial and/or semi-colonial – homes. Their virginal identities are ascribed partly by association with this non-metropolitan geography. Clichés about rural purity and provincial simplicity are mapped onto rural and provincial women. The Secret Commission, which paid so much attention to metropolitan vice, ignored non-metropolitan vice. Though Stead described his revelations as 'a shuddering horror that will thrill throughout the world',[16] there was nothing very surprising about the idea of urban debauchery; readers would have been more surprised and horrified to find out about rural debauchery. Ellice Hopkins and other purity activists would later insist that rural areas and the provinces had nothing to be morally complacent about (in her undated pamphlets *Work in Villages* and *Smut in the Wheat*), but it did not suit Stead's purpose to do the same. In his account, a simplistically polarized moral geography mapped onto simplistically polarized femininity. Rural places and the women who lived there were constructed as natural, pure, innocent and healthy, but always vulnerable to corrupting influences from outside. In a section entitled 'WHERE MAIDS ARE PICKED UP', for example, Stead explains how 'Young girls from the country, fresh and rosy are soon picked up in the shops';[17] from the country and of the country, these girls sound like plums or apples, and apparently they are acquired as easily. Rural women are naive, easily tricked, lured to the city under false pretences. Stead explains that 'The simplest, and by far the commonest [method of procurement] is to engage a girl [from] the country by advertisement or otherwise to help in the housework.' The youthfulness of these 'Unwilling Recruits' (Stead's subheading) is emphasized: 'The child – she is seldom more than fifteen or sixteen – comes up from her country village with her box, and is installed in service.' Away from home, she is vulnerable:

> The girl is tempted to drink, and by degrees she is enlightened as to the nature of the house. It is a dreadful awakening. What is she to do? In all London she has no friend – no one to whom she can appeal.

Eventually she succumbs, loses her innocence, and 'Her character is gone.'[18]

The idea that rural girls and young women are lured to the city and corrupted is reinforced and embroidered with a series of similar case histories. In a section on 'RUINING COUNTRY GIRLS', Stead explains that 'The country girl offers an almost unresisting quarry. Term time, when young girls come up to town with their boxes to seek situations, is the great battle season of the procuresses.' For example:

> A country girl arrived by the Great Northern Railway at King's Cross. She put her boxes in the left luggage room and went out, as thousands have done before her to see what London looked like, and to inquire her way about.[19]

Like many before her, she is drugged, abducted and raped.

> It is pitiful to think of the number of young girls who have been tenderly trained and carefully educated at home and at school in our country villages who will come up to town in the course of the present year only to discover that the business on which their parents fondly built high hopes as to their future position in life is little better than an open doorway – a pathway leading to hell.[20]

Vulnerability is enhanced by youth; nascent femininity is at stake. Typically, one 'child was about fourteen, dark, with long black hair and dark eyes. She was not fully grown, and promised if well cared for to develop into a woman of somewhat striking appearance.'[21] Of course, if not 'well cared for' in youth, she could not develop into such a woman.

Stead's non-metropolitan geography and femininity, which is defined mainly by rurality, is also provincial and, in some instances, semi-colonial. Stead adapts the now-familiar story of entrapment for prostitution to the Irish. Among the Irish, many characteristics attributed to rurality – naivety, simplicity, child-like vulnerability – are multiplied. Similarly for provincial girls and young women. A 'Birmingham girl', for example, is said to have arrived in London with a 'rural bloom' in her cheeks.[22] While the 'modus operandi' of procurers 'was very simple', apparently it was not as simple as the non-metropolitan girls themselves.[23] 'The Irish girl, being innocent and inexperienced, setting foot for the first time in a foreign city, without friends and not knowing where to go', was easily trapped. 'When the girl is once within the brothel she is about as helpless as a sparrow when caught by the falling brick of the schoolboy's trap.'[24]

Illustrating the child-like vulnerability of girls and young women aged 13, 14 and more, Stead reinforced his explicit arguments for an increase in the age of consent. Stead exaggerated the youthfulness of women who were travelling to London, and of most prostitutes, in order to make this case. Emphasizing their lack of sexual desire and agency, casting them only as victims, Stead presented his demands for an increase in the age of consent as something that would protect rather than restrict young women. Demands for a higher age of consent were made plausible, to some extent, by a general deferral of economic and other aspects of adulthood, first among middle-class boys whose education was prolonged, eventually among working class boys, and girls.[25] The concerns and objectives published in the *Pall Mall Gazette* were reiterated and pursued in a highly organized campaign, in which Stead cooperated with purity activists including Benjamin Scott, William Coote and Ellice Hopkins. They organized a demonstration in Hyde Park, which took place on 22 August 1885, attended by up to a quarter of a million people, which formally launched the National Vigilance Association (NVA) (Anon. 1885; Bristow 1977: 112). Public opinion, or at least that of a group of vocal activists, demanded and obtained a change in the law. Central to the Criminal Law Amendment Act (1885) was an increase in the female age of consent.

The purity movements of the 1880s and 1890s, which produced the NVA and promoted the Criminal Law Amendment Act (1885), are often interpreted as repressive (e.g. by Hyam 1990). Josephine Butler's campaign for the defence of personal rights was eclipsed by a movement geared more towards policing the morality of others (Bland 1995). The Act itself combined a mixture of debatably repressive measures, some of which genuinely protected children and women from sexual abuse by legislating against sexual abuse by men. The NVA annual reports catalogue a selection of the cases, brought by a combination of the new legislation and ongoing efforts by NVA activists, which resulted in prosecutions. The cases, many involving offences against children and young women, underline the reality of the protection (not just the repression) afforded by the new legislation and demanded by NVA members and other purity campaigners. However, as Bland and other historians have pointed out, there was a repressive dimension to the new law, which afforded young women the kind of 'protection' that deprived them of sexual agency and, imposing an idealized innocence[26] and purity upon them, refused to acknowledge their sexuality (Lind 1999). But the most repressive measure of all in the Act related not to women but to men.

The myth at the heart of Stead's 'Maiden Tribute' revelations was, of course, a myth of the corruption not just of seven maidens but also seven youths. There was no need for the youths, if Stead was really only interested in maidens. He could have chosen a different myth, or he could have edited the myth to exclude the youths, but he did not. Once introduced, the youths were barely mentioned, but they remained as a hidden subtext, an obvious and suggestive silence. Stead had broken one tabooed region of sexual discourse, attacking what he not unreasonably called an 'absurd conspiracy of silence'[27] in his exposés of heterosexual vice; the controversy he aroused appears to confirm that his act was indeed transgressive. He stopped short of breaking another taboo, as he would have done had he printed detailed revelations of the corruption of youths.[28] Still, when MPs amended and finally passed the Criminal Law Amendment Act, male homosexuality emerged from the subtext of the 'Maiden Tribute' and the margins of purity campaigns. For whatever reason (the motivation of MPs is a matter of conjecture), the Act included an amendment (the Labouchere Amendment), which introduced draconian legislation against male homosexuality – making private, consensual acts punishable by two years in prison.[29] As one measured historian put it, 'Even more than prostitutes or child rapists, whom parliament voted against flogging, homosexuals were to suffer agony from the moral panic' (Bristow 1977: 115). This legislation remained in place for over eighty years. In 1967, male homosexuality was partially decriminalized in England and Wales, with a higher age of consent for male homosexuals (21) than heterosexuals (16) (the Sexual Offences Act, 1967, did not apply in Scotland or Northern Ireland, where it remained illegal for consenting male adults to have sex with each other, even in private). Once again, issues of youthful vulnerability and corruption were presented as arguments for and against higher and lower ages of consent. The kind of narrative that served Stead so well, in the *Pall Mall Gazette* campaign, was once again employed, though this time the 'youths' assumed centre stage.

## Falling towards London: ages of consent for 'boys'

Like 'The Maiden Tribute', *Johnny Go Home* tells a dramatic, ostensibly true story of children who leave homes in the country (the countryside or provinces, and suburbs) and travel to the city, where they are sexually vulnerable and easily corrupted. In the Victorian tale, pathetic stories of 'fallen girls' illustrate the case for raising the female age of consent. In its modern counterpart, equally pathetic boys illustrate the legitimacy of unequal ages of consent for homosexual and heterosexual men. The producer-director of *Johnny* explained that he was mainly concerned with youth homelessness; he portrayed vulnerable youths because he wanted to show that they should be housed (Willis 1978). Perhaps inadvertently, he also suggested that they should be protected, sexually. *Johnny's* portrayal of sexual vulnerability retold in contemporary form a myth of (vulnerability to) homosexual corruption and contagion, which was (and remains) a common argument for differential ages of consent. The 'sickness theory' portrayed homosexuality as a form of contagious disease 'from which young people, in particular, must be protected' (Sturgess 1975: 10). The 'corruption theory' asserted that early homosexual encounters would do severe psychological harm and/or turn a young man into a homosexual. The idea that male sexuality might still be undecided at 16, hence open to corruption, was formalized in the Wolfenden Report, upon which the Sexual Offences Act 1967 was based, which recommended a higher age of consent for homosexuals (Grey 1992; Wolfenden 1957). As gay rights activists were to point out, medical evidence contradicted this assumption, by showing 'that a person's sexual orientation is laid down in the early years of life- – long before 16' (CHE 1976: 1). Central to the contagion and corruption myths are older, stereotypically predatory homosexuals:

> It is still widely – but erroneously – supposed that a typical homosexual 'seduction' invariably involves an innocent young boy being sexually 'seduced' and 'corrupted' against his will by an older man in a dirty raincoat.
> (Sturgess 1975: 19)

*Johnny Go Home* is replete with such figures – caricatured paedophiles presented as homosexuals, shadowy *dramatis personae* chasing boys round London – walking arguments against equalizing the age of consent. The loneliness and otherness of these figures, and the world they inhabit, echoes an official argument for differential ages of consent, presented in the Wolfenden Report. Wolfenden recommended a higher age of consent for homosexuals because he felt they should make a 'mature judgement about actions of the kind which might have the effect of setting [them] apart from the rest of society' (Miller 1995: 284). The isolation of homosexuals, to which Wolfenden refers, is socially and historically produced, partly by material and legal systems, partly by myths that characterize homosexuals as victims and predators – myths reproduced in stories such as *Johnny Go Home*. In this manner, *Johnny* counteracted the efforts of contemporary gay rights activists, who made an equal age of consent, and an extension of legalization to Scotland and Northern Ireland, their top priorities (CHE 1976: 1; Sturgess 1975).

*Johnny Go Home*, a two-hour drama documentary made for Yorkshire Television (YTV) by John Willis (producer-director), Michael Deakin and John Fairley (executive producers), was broadcast on 22 July 1975.[30] It made an immediate splash, prompting widespread media attention and two debates in the House of Commons, and winning a BAFTA (British Academy of Film and Television Award) for best factual programme (1975). Media coverage ensured that many people who did not actually see the documentary heard or read about it, and those who did see it had their knowledge reinforced, perhaps altered. 'It was shocking. It was horrifying. It was appalling,' wrote one newspaper television critic. 'It must rank among the greatest documentaries ever to appear on British television.'[31] As MP Norman Fowler told the Commons on 31 July 1975, 'Public concern has been caused by the television programme *Johnny Go Home* and by the newspaper reports following the film, and rightly so.[32] The story was retold (with more detail and a wider cast of characters) in a book of the same title, published the following year (1976), co-written by Deakin and Willis. Like the programme (which defence lawyers in a paedophile trial attempted to ban[33]), the book was the subject of legal action (the authors were sued for criminal libel[34]), which only succeeded in attracting public attention to the documentary and the issues it raised. In this chapter I refer to both programme and book, but emphasize the former, the more significant of the two.

*Johnny* dramatizes a 'true' story, entertaining viewers while drawing their attention to a social issue. Drama documentary had been pioneered on British TV by the 1966 play *Cathy Come Home* (Kilborn 1997; MacMurraugh-Kavanagh 1997; Paget 1990). *Johnny* follows *Cathy*, both in its hybrid of 'fly-on-the-wall'[35] documentary and drama,[36] and its attention to homelessness. *Johnny* focuses specifically on homelessness among young people. Perhaps because it was government policy only to prioritize the housing needs of young single people if they were demonstrably 'vulnerable to sexual or financial exploitation', *Johnny* concentrates on embroidering the ways in which young homeless people may be vulnerable.[37] Their vulnerability to violence, substance abuse and sexual exploitation is portrayed, in each case biographically. Part one, 'The End of the Line: The true story of Annie and Tommy', tells the story of two young runaways, 16-year old Annie Malone who has been homeless since she was 12, and a recent runaway from Scotland, Tommy Wylie, whose age is not given but who is said to look about 12 (according to a policeman, who is overheard guessing). Part two, 'The Murder of Billy Two-Tone', portrays in graphic detail the murder of a homeless 19 year old. The book is also based on the stories of three runaways – Billy, Annie and Ronnie (a 13-year-old character based on Tommy), plus a wider cast of characters, mainly other runaways. In each version, Billy is the victim of violence, while Annie is vulnerable to drug and alcohol abuse, Tommy/Ronnie to sexual exploitation. Billy and Tommy/Ronnie fall victim to Roger Gleaves, a hostel keeper with a track record of violence and convictions for sex with under-age males (boys as young as 14). Gleaves personifies the danger that awaits young people when they arrive in the city. In *Johnny* the general pattern is that a child or young adult travels to London, where he or she is vulnerable, and is corrupted.

The runaways in *Johnny*, like their counterparts in 'The Maiden Tribute', leave homes in the country, though not the countryside, for the distant metropolis – London. Country, as Raymond Williams noted, is an ambivalent term, referring not only to a rural area, but to a 'whole society' (Williams 1985: 1). Though a 'whole society' must by definition include the capital city, Williams retains a basic distinction between *The Country and the City*, particularly between the whole society and the capital city. This distinction structures the geography of 'The Maiden Tribute', where country means rural, and that of *Johnny*, where country means broader non-metropolitan society. In *Johnny* the home of each runaway is sketched, before their journey to the city is described in detail. Accents, notably Tommy's thick Glaswegian, serve as a reminder that the young runaways are not at home. In both stories the non-metropolitan is the natural locale of home, and in both stories home is in danger of being corrupted. As in the 'Maiden Tribute', homes in the country are threatened partly by economic forces. In the 1880s an agricultural depression hit the countryside, while industrial towns and cities continued to grow. In the mid-1970s a manufacturing recession hit the regions, while relatively buoyant service industries protected London and the South East from the worst of the decline. While the 'Maiden Tribute' says little about the economic context of rural to urban migration, *Johnny* addresses the causes of migration from the regions to London – unemployment and poor housing, notably in Scotland, Ireland, the Midlands and the North. Deakin and Willis (1976: 181) conclude that 'It cannot be an accident that many of the kids [in London homeless shelters] came from the places where the unemployment is worse.' But *Johnny* is not economically reductionist. On the contrary, it examines all economic classes of homes – from the well-heeled London suburb of Finchley to the council estates of Glasgow – and concludes that push factors for young runaways are more cultural than economic.

*Johhny* interprets the actions of young runaways as reactions to failing homes. It does not present coherent arguments about how homes are failing, or about what constitutes a good home. Confusingly, *Johnny* criticizes homes for not living up to an ideal, though that ideal is not wholly endorsed. British homes are presented as the shabby descendant of an ideal: the locale of nuclear family, the sphere of women and children, where children are raised and nurtured. This idealized home is a minimally sexualized space; sexuality is limited to the reproductive heterosexuality of the parents, while the 'children' (though they may be as old as 15 or 16) are pre-sexual, innocent. *Johnny* reproduces this ideology of home, to an extent. It buys into the idea of childhood innocence, assuming that children are not corrupted (sexually or otherwise) until after they leave home. This ignores the realities of sexual danger in the home, and sexual reasons for leaving home (Dibblin 1991; Finkelhor 1986). *Johnny* also buys uncritically into the ideal of home as a space of nuclear family, a sphere of nurturing women and nurtured children. This attitude is revealed in a series of implied criticisms of women, who should be but are not at the centre of family and home. A tearful Annie tells how she grew up in a meticulously respectable house in Finchley, but how as a baby she was nearly killed by her mother, who was then committed to a mental hospital. She explains that her stepmother was distant and unloving, and attributes her descent into an underworld of drugs and begging to her 'bad family background' and 'broken home'. Similarly, for Johnny, mother is a 'distant memory of meals on time, and above all of affection and attention' (Deakin and Willis 1976: 53). Lucy (whose case history is told in the book, not the programme) is adopted; she has false parents, and somehow this accounts for their distance, their inability to understand her. Tommy/Ronnie is the son of respectable parents who run a 'comfortable and spotlessly clean home'. There is a suggestion, however, that his home is emotionally cold, that someone is failing to nurture the boy. Tommy's mother, interviewed (interrogated?) at length, appears to confirm this. She explains that her husband 'keeps everything to himself', including his feelings of love and perhaps despair for his son, and she admits that Tommy 'thinks we're too strict' – apparently, the household is governed more by rules than by love. The emotional coldness of homes is expressed also in descriptions of home towns such as Bannockburn and Castlemilk, Billy and Tommy/Ronnie's respective home towns. Billy leaves a place where 'One dim housing estate the colour of wet felt merges into another' (Deakin and Willis 1976: 131). Tommy (after five months in London) revisits an estate that appears dirty and dull, colourless and lacking in warmth. His respectable family, who occupy a respectable flat and work in nearby factories and shops, appear to be getting by – not much more. To many of their residents, Bannockburn and Castlemilk were home, but to the makers and perhaps the viewers of *Johnny*, they were anything but. From the perspective of Deakin and Willis's programme, these estates and dwellings did not seem like Tommy's home, or anyone's.

Despite its adherence to a conservative ideal of home, *Johnny* acknowledges that such an ideal is not always possible. Annie's mother will always be schizophrenic, Lucy will never have a biological mother, and Johnny's mother will not come back, for she is dead. Updating Annie's story, the programme hints that alternatives to the ideal are possible, that home need not consist of nuclear family, and that nurturing may be given by someone other than the mother. Annie has found home and family, for the first time in her life, in a street theatre commune. Alternative constructions of home and family are not developed in any depth, though, and if there is any coherence to the programme's approach to home, it is that the conventional ideal is best, but that alternatives should be sought where this is not possible. Conservative newspaper critics interpreted *Johnny* in this manner, emphasizing its general faith in what the *Daily Mail* called 'old fashioned' ideas of home and family.[38] It is from failing homes – homes not living up to this (ill-defined) ideal – that the young people in *Johnny* are running.

If the non-metropolitan is the sphere of home (however inadequate), the metropolitan is its other – the sphere of homelessness, both material (lacking an address) and ideological (lacking attributes associated with certain ideological constructions of home, such as stability, heterosexual order and maternal nurturing). London in the mid-1970s was a sphere of conspicuous homelessness, of people sleeping rough and squatting, regularly catching the eyes of passers by, journalists (including Jeremy Sandford, author of *Cathy Come Home*, who wrote about homelessness in the London *Evening Standard*), academics (notably Professor John Greve) and government (Greve was appointed to report on London's homeless, which he did in 1970) (Greve *et al.* 1971). But material homelessness was never so neatly confined to the metropolis; it was a national problem (Dibblin 1991: 13). In *Johnny*, London is portrayed as the quintessential space of homelessness, not just because it fails to provide material homes but also because it represents a broader, ideological void, a glaring absence of home. The void lurks beneath a veneer of bright lights, 'a fabulous cave of glitter and excitement' (Deakin and Willis 1976: 27). Like the candy-coated, fairy tale house in *Hansel and Gretel*, this glittery place lures young runaways, only to present them with a series of dangers and a cruel parody of home, which underlines what they are lacking. Annie leads the camera crew around her former 'home', a squat. She picks her way through smouldering debris, burnt out 'derelict and squatted houses'. She climbs a shaky staircase, stepping carefully to avoid syringes that are lying on the floor. Here, 'There were no beds, only a pile of indescribably squalid sheets and a mattress on the floor, and plates which had never been washed since the day they had been lifted from Woolworths in Oxford Street' (Deakin and Willis 1976: 46).

Home is not just falling short of an ideal, as it is in the provinces; it is thoroughly corrupted, and remnants of home remain only as reminders of what has been polluted and lost. The streets near one of Gleaves's hostels, for example, are littered with 'kids and mysterious pieces of rusted iron which may or may not have begun life as bedsteads', while 'here and there a garden is adorned with a soggy and obviously unwanted mattress' (Deakin and Willis 1976: 89). Children playing around rusted and rotten beds are an omen of the sexual corruption that is to come, in this space outside the law. Returning to London, after his short return trip to Scotland, Tommy is met by Gleaves and taken to one of his hostels. As he is driven off, a voice-over dramatizes his predicament: 'Tommy didn't know, and we had yet to discover, these hostels were a world apart – normality consisted of horror and violence'. Tommy enters a space where there are no parents or neighbours, where there is no morality, sexual order, rules, or stability – none of the qualities that make a place home.

London is a place of falling. Like 'The Maiden Tribute', *Johnny* is replete with images of descending into an underworld. One newspaper television critic suggested that 'You could regard your TV as a diving-bell anchored in the lower depths.'[39] In 'The Maiden Tribute' the journey downward led to the labyrinth explored and described by Stead, but also to a more generic underworld, mapped and visited by writers and activists, urban explorers and philanthropists. In *Johnny* the vertical journey leads to precisely the same place – as Deakin and Willis (1976: 178) put it, to an 'underworld … as sinister and as squalid as the London of Dickens or Dr Barnardo'. Annie is pictured huddling around a fire in the (then) derelict Covent Garden, in a city that the narrator says has hardly changed since Dickens's time. Like Stead, Willis investigates and describes particular issues and individuals, locating them in a generic metropolitan underworld. 'The situation the documentary uncovers is scarcely credible outside the 19th century'[40], wrote one critic. Thus *Johnny* and its critics invoked a popular geographical image – a stereotype of 'Victorian London' – and put it to use, to make a moral, political point.

A place of falling, London is a place of the 'fallen' (Deakin and Willis 1976: 81). The debt to Victorian moral and geographical imagination is once again clear, though the Victorian 'fallen woman' – 'ruined' by pre-marital sex or prostitution – had lost much of her currency by 1975.[41] The fallen woman had been replaced, notably by drug addicts and homosexuals, people corrupted into lives of debauchery. In *Johny*, sexual corruption is simplifed and gendered, reduced to the danger of boys being corrupted by men, and falling to homosexuality. According to this logic, girls and young women are not in any essentially sexual danger. Annie is raped, though drugs appear to be her main enemy, for the rapist is an 'addict' and Annie is 'too far gone to look after herself' (Deakin and Willis 1976: 46). Lucy has sex with older males, but she retains control over these transactions, exchanging sex for food and shelter, then leaving when her boyfriends have no money left. Sexual dangers faced by girls and young women are not acknowledged. In contrast, sustained interest is paid to essentially sexual dangers faced by boys and young men. The young male runaway (Tommy, on arrival at Euston) is portrayed as an 'innocent in the city'. Fresh from the barely sexualized space of home, he is pre-sexual and innocent, in danger of falling and being corrupted. Waiting at the station, and present throughout the city, are men waiting to corrupt him. *Johnny* showed, as one television critic put it, that children 'could plummet and be maimed, emotionally or physically, for life'.[42]

Boys are in danger of corruption from the moment they arrive in London. Tommy makes friends at the Playland amusement arcade, which despite its childish name is, the narrator explains, a 'meat rack' frequented by rent boys and their clients: 'every evening its frontage is lined with boys on the game'. Viewers are never told whether Tommy becomes directly involved in prostitution, or whether he is sexually abused. However, they do watch as he is driven away by Gleaves, and as he sits crying on one of Gleaves's hostel beds later on. Other boys, facing similar dangers, are easily and explicitly corrupted. Johnny, after whom the programme is named, makes only a fleeting appearance, before the final credits. A picture of child-like innocence, he is blond, angelic and very young-looking. He looks anxiously about as shadowy figures in raincoats pass him on either side. Johnny stands outside an amusement arcade (which viewers have been told is a pick-up area), eating food wrapped in paper (when presumably he should be fed, and otherwise nourished, in the home). The narrator explains that Johnny is 'only eleven, and already he's familiar with the streets of the West End'. The message is clear: in the words of researcher Di Burgess, 'we have this little 10-year-old runaway. He was found in Soho. He looks so beautiful and innocent. But you know how easily he may be corrupted.'[43] The book is explicit about how he may be – and is – corrupted. It explains how Johnny falls in with a man in his mid-twenties, who was himself corrupted as a youth. Ernie 'had once been rather a nice looking teenager. But now his face is a trifle lined and battered, as though from too many late nights and rough parties' (Deakin and Willis 1976: 55). He worked as a rent boy from age 15 to 20, but then found it difficult to attract the punters. Fallen morally as well as sexually, Ernie was given to stealing and even murder – killing a man who tried to 'get fresh with the boy with whom he had been mates' (Deakin and Willis 1976: 56). Clearly, Johnny is going the same way, and by the time Ernie is imprisoned for theft, 'Johnny has grown up for good' (Deakin and Willis 1976: 64).

Added to the myth of corruption was the assertion – partly accurate, partly self-fulfilling – that, once corrupted, homosexual men would face loneliness and social exclusion. This reiterated the old argument for differential ages of consent, which had been presented in the Wolfenden Report (1957). The story of corruption and fall is repeated, in this manner, in the story of a boy named as Nicholas Lawlor, who is picked up and interviewed in a police operation. Nicholas is a slight youth, whose height is given as 5′ 7″, and whose mop of hair and soft-looking skin give an impression of childishness. Nicholas explains how he fell into renting after a few nights on the streets of London. He went to Playland, where 'a guy came up to me and said, "do you want a coffee?"'. Nicholas went to the man's place. From there it was all downhill. Asked how he felt about his new career, Nicholas said that at first he 'was pretty horrified' but quickly found that 'it was an easy way to make money'. He had been corrupted, and his had become a 'boring and lonely' way of life; people would think 'he's one of them – keep away from him'. Nicholas, picked up by the police in a night club in Soho, inhabits a world apart, a sexualized space of loneliness and exclusion, which represents the kind of undesirable otherness cited by Wolfenden as a reason for setting differential ages of consent.

The myth of homosexual corruption and exclusion, reproduced in *Johnny*, rests upon a confusion of homosexuality and paedophilia. Paedophiles are represented as homosexuals. For example, a hostel warden (speaking on the programme) refers to Gleaves's 'homosexual' encounters with boys, and adds that 'most of the people who worked for [Gleaves] were homosexual'. In the book, Gleaves is explicitly labelled a 'homosexual' (Deakin and Willis 1976: 176). But the sexual encounters and sexual orientations of Gleaves and many of his employees were not homosexual but paedophile, for they involved children not other men. The same is true of Ernie, the man in his twenties who sleeps with 11-year-old Johnny; although he is attracted to children rather than men, 'everybody knows he is gay' (Deakin and Willis 1976: 56). This confusion of sexual categories had wider currency, extending to the more liberal media (the *Guardian* newspaper understood *Johnny* as a story 'about children lured into homosexuality and prostitution'[44]), and to courts of law (for example, a man charged with abusing 10 and 11 year olds was asked in court 'if he was a homosexual'[45]). In April 1998, when Gleaves was once again jailed, this time for the attempted rape and indecent assault of two 14-year-old boys, the language was very different. No longer a homosexual, Gleaves had become a 'sex abuser' and a 'paedophile'[46] In 1975, however, the language of paedophilia had less currency. The term 'paedophilia' had yet to enter the *Concise Oxford Dictionary* (which it did in 1976).[47] Child sexual abuse had yet to take its place on the agendas of mental health and child welfare professionals, as it did in the late 1970s (Finkelhor 1986: 10). Researchers had yet to examine child sex abuse in detail, to find that girls are two to three times more likely than boys to be sexually abused, and that most abusers are male relatives, step-fathers in particular (Finkelhor 1984: 3). As a portrayal of sexual danger faced by children, *Johnny* was not wrong (when boys are attacked it does tend to be by care givers such as those depicted in *Johnny*: Finkelhor 1984: 160) but it was both biased and partial. By overlooking abused girls and abusive fathers ('heterosexuals'), and emphasizing a comparatively rare but stereotyped form of abuse/abuser, and doing so at a time when paedophilia was poorly understood, *Johnny* was able to buy into a corruption myth that confused paedophilia with homosexuality, and legitimated a differential age of consent.

Tracing the impacts of *Johnny Go Home*, journalists and critics have asked whether it accomplished the 'good' things its producer-director intended, mainly with respect to youth homelessness. This is not the place for a detailed assessment of *Johnny's* impact, the potential breadth of which demands more systematic treatment. A Working Group on Homeless Young People, set up by the government in response to *Johnny* in September 1975, illustrates the breadth, or rather the malleability and diffuseness, of issues raised by the documentary. When newspaper journalists commented on *Johnny*, each adapted it to their own political agenda, and when MPs debated it in the House, they did much the same. 'I should like to extend the scope of the problem wider than just that displayed by the film', said one Member, as she both diluted and appropriated *Johnny*, returning to issues that were already on her party's agenda, specifically the proposed Housing (Homeless Persons) Bill.[48] The Working Group was to include representatives of many statutory and voluntary departments and agencies, ranging from the DHSS (Department of Health and Social Security), which chaired the Group, and CHAR (the Campaign for the Homeless and Rootless), to the Charity Commission and the Department of Prices and Consumer Protection. The Working Group's report, published in July 1976, was as broad as the interests of its participants. Its recommendations came under many headings, and covered much ground (DHSS 1976: 2). *Johnny* had become less focused than previous media campaigns on related issues, notably Ken Loach's *Cathy Come Home*, which contemporary observers credited with the successful launch of Shelter, the housing charity. Looking back, many critics suspect that the impact of *Cathy* may have been overstated (Kilborn 1997: 235; Paget 1990: 91; Shelter 1976: 4; Widdowson 1977: 3). It did not take so long to become pessimistic about *Johnny*. In April 1976, the London *Times* was already reporting that disillusion had set in, quoting a campaigner as saying 'We have achieved practically nothing and this is a damning indictment to society.'[49] Certainly, most of the Working Group's recommendations came to little. A pessimist might say that once the *Sun* had traced a few runaways for its front page,[50] and once a few thousand leaflets had been distributed to youth clubs, the fuss died down. A more optimistic observer might attribute to *Johnny* the appearance of a hostel here, a health centre there, and a slight modification to the Housing (Homeless

Persons) Act, 1977 (Willis 1978: 109). However, both pessimists and optimists have limited themselves, considering only whether *Johnny* achieved the good things its producer-director and some others intended, the changes they wanted to bring about.

By focusing on tangible effects rather than on the content of the programme, book and media coverage, hence on an agenda as wide and as narrow as the remit of the Working Group, observers have missed some of the importance of *Johnny*. They have been distracted from the cultural politics of sexuality, central to the documentary, which leads less to tangible good works than to negative effects, specifically to the reproduction of inequality between heterosexuals and homosexuals.

*Johnny* did not invent the idea of corrupted boy turned homosexual, but the producer did go out of his way to reproduce it, long after others – including makers of television documentaries – had attempted to challenge it (MacMurraugh-Kavanagh 1997). *Johnny* exaggerated the youth of the runaways, hence their adaptability as symbols of innocence and the plausibility of their asexuality. An MP told the Commons that *Johnny*, which he had watched, showed 'children and young people'.[51] Tommy was particularly young looking. Quoted in the media, he later said that 'The TV people implied I was a boy of 14. … The truth is I was 16 and knew exactly what I was doing'.[52] Closer scrutiny, notably by Under-Secretary of State for Health and Social Security Mr Michael Meacher,[53] and by the Working Group, revealed that most runaways, and all but one of those referred to Gleaves hostels, were 17 or older (DHSS 1976: 2) – they were neither children nor young people (according to contemporary legal definitions, a child was under 14, a young person under 17), and they were all above the heterosexual age of consent. Many runaways left home not as pre-sexual children vulnerable to corruption but as adolescents or young adults, some driven out by 'issues concerning sexuality' – some sexually abused in the home, some others facing problems of a gay or lesbian adolescence (McCluskey 1993: 5, 7). The programme misrepresents the gendering of sexual danger, overstating dangers faced by male runaways and understating those faced by their female counterparts (boys and young men are in less danger than girls and young women, not more) (Dibblin 1991: 9; McCluskey 1993: 7). Youth prostitution, too, was less common and less male-dominated than *Johnny* had suggested (DHSS 1976: 5). At the expense of distorting what was known about the sexualities of adolescents and young people, and about the sexual dangers they faced, *Johnny* twisted the story of young homeless people to fit a corruption myth, one of the effects of which was to legitimate a differential age of consent, thus singling out young gay men as adults who need to be treated as children for longer than their heterosexual counterparts. Meanwhile, the misleading gendering of sexual danger marginalized some of the difficulties (including sexual violence) faced by girls and young women, in the hands of heterosexual men.

## Conclusion

Stories of sexual journeys, from the purity of home and country to the corruption of the city, have made a difference within cultural politics of sexuality, notably in the production and reproduction of age of consent legislation. These stories illustrate an interplay between metaphorical and material sexual geographies, between imagined and real (lived and regulated) sexualities.

I have not tried to contradict images simply because they 'misrepresent', though I have brought together something of a case for demythologizing imagined sexual geographies. For these geographies, structured as they are around simplistic moral distinctions – between good and evil, pure and impure – are mapped onto people, who then appear to be (not just to represent) good and evil, purity and impurity, vulnerability and threat. In age of consent narratives, these distinctions legitimate the protection of pure (who are caricatured as vulnerable, young and innocent) people from their impure (predatory, old and experienced) counterparts. For the former, this means a loss of sexual agency, particularly if they are showing signs of interest in their own sex.[54] For the latter, it means marginalization and sometimes excessive regulation, a degree of scapegoating. These crude moral differences translate to power differences, notably between people who protect (heterosexual men) and others who are protected (girls and young men), or protected from (some heterosexual and all homosexual adult men). Space, brought into this discourse of sexuality politics, has facilitated a series of caricatured moral distinctions. This constitutes an argument for demythologizing imagined sexual geographies, and perhaps more generally for leaving space out of the discourse of sexuality politics.

But, as Raymond Williams pointed out, the broader rhetoric of the country and the city, a rhetoric with sexual dimensions, is almost transhistorical. This imagined geography (of country and city) is not easily demythologized, and these spatial metaphors (in morality and sexuality discourse) are not easily dismissed. It is important to reflect on why this is the case, to ask why imagined geographies and spatial metaphors are so resilient. Williams links the imagined geography of the country and the city back into material concerns, material relationships between country and city: 'the relations are not only of ideas, but of rent and interest, of situation and power; a wider system' (Williams 1985: 7). From this perspective, imagined geographies represent, and perhaps legitimate, a series of material inequalities between the city and the country. It would be over-simplistic to suggest that the metropolis is simply more powerful than the country, and that the imagined geography naturalizes and legitimates that arrangement. The reality is obviously much more complex. Still, a broad pattern of inequality between the city and the country did structure the stories I have described. Recall that 'The Maiden Tribute' and *Johnny Go Home* were both produced during times of heightened inequality between metropolitan London and non-metropolitan Britain and Ireland, associated respectively with agricultural depression in the countryside and industrial decline in the regions. Hardest hit were those on the margins not only of geography but also society – notably the young, the working classes and, particularly in the 1880s, girls and women. The sexual geographies in 'The Maiden Tribute' and *Johnny* each represent the vulnerability of people belonging to these doubly (spatially and socially) marginalized groups. They condense a range of power differentials into metropolitan/non-metropolitan geographical difference, and translate all this into sexual vulnerability. Structural social and economic problems, with the conspicuous inequalities and vulnerabilities they produce, are thus translated into *sexual* inequalities and vulnerabilities, defused as a matter of individual choice and morality. Social and economic tensions are therefore contained and controlled, through the regulation and repression of sexuality, specifically that of young people and homosexuals, familiar scapegoats. It follows that ages of consent should be seen not in isolation, as matters of sexuality politics *per se*, but instead as part of a broader material and political system. Likewise, sexualized imaginative geographies should be seen not as matters of sexuality and morality *per se*, but as constituents of a broader economy of power and difference.

## Notes

1  *Guardian* 17 December 1997, G2: 8.
2  *Pall Mall Gazette* 6 July 1885 XLII.6336: 1.
3  The language of girls and women, boys and men is problematic, and depends upon changing and contested constructions of childhood, adolescence and adulthood.
4  Stead reprinted Andrew Mearn's pamphlet *The Bitter Outcry of Outcast London*.
5  *Pall Mall Gazette* 6 July 1885 XLII.6336: 2.
6  *Pall Mall Gazette* 6 July 1885 XLII.6336: 3.
7  'There are children, many children, who are ruined before they are thirteen; but the crime is one phase of the incest which, as the Report of the Dwellings Commission shows, is inseparable from overcrowding.' (*Pall Mall Gazette* 8 July 1885 XLII. 6338: 1 ).
8  *Pall Mall Gazette* 7 July 1885 XLII.6337: 2.
9  *Pall Mall Gazette* 6 July 1885 XLII.6336: 1.
10  *Pall Mall Gazette* 6 July 1885 XLII.6336: 1.
11  *Pall Mall Gazette* 9 July 1885 XLII.6339: 2.
12  *Pall Mall Gazette* 9 July 1885 XLII.6339: 4.
13  *Pall Mall Gazette* 7 July 1885 XLII.6337: 2.
14  Though nuns were themselves commonly sexualized, portrayed by some post-Reformation writers as sexually corrupt and corrupting (e.g. Diderot 1797).
15  *Pall Mall Gazette* 8 July 1885 XLII.6338: 4.
16  *Pall Mall Gazette* 6 July 1885 XLII.6336: 1.
17  *Pall Mall Gazette* 7 July 1885 XLII.6337: 5.
18  *Pall Mall Gazette* 7 July 1885 XLII.6337: 2.
19  *Pall Mall Gazette* 8 July 1885 XLII.6338: 4.
20  *Pall Mall Gazette* 10 July 1885 XLII.6340: 4.
21  *Pall Mall Gazette* 7 July 1885 XLII.6337: 4.
22  *Pall Mall Gazette* 7 July 1885 XLII.6337: 4.
23  *Pall Mall Gazette* 8 July 1885 XLII.6338: 6.

24 *Pall Mall Gazette* 8 July 1885 XLII.6338: 4.
25 Some historians argue that adolescence was discovered in Britain and America in the Victorian period, particularly the 1880s and 1890s (Demos and Demos 1969; Kett 1977), although historians do sometimes speak of adolescence in earlier contexts.
26 Children's sexual innocence is more imagined than real (Moore and Rosenthal 1993).
27 *Pall Mall Gazette* 10 July 1885 XLII.6340: 1.
28 Homosexual themes were addressed in print, though rarely in such respectable and widely circulated publications as the *Pall Mall Gazette*. Taboos were, of course, context specific. A homosexual prototype for Stead's story had been told, in the relatively obscure *Sins of the Cities of the Plain or, Confessions of Mayyanne* (1881). In *Sins of the Cities*, a bootblack boy is seduced and sold into prostitution in Paris.
29 The mystery of Labouchere's motivations, and those of his fellow MPs, in drafting and passing the Amendment has been widely debated, not only by academics (such as Weeks 1977) but also by more creative writers (notably Stoppard 1997).
30 Since *Johnny Go Home* 'was the subject of a number of long-running legal actions following its broadcast', it has been 'placed under restriction' by the TV company that owns it (Chris Wissun, Granada Programme Lawyer, personal communication, 9 June 1998). However, the programme can be viewed at the British Film Institute, London.
31 J. Murray, 'Shame on You London', *Daily Express* 23 July 1975.
32 *Hansard* H.C. (Fifth Series) 1974–5 896.2359.
33 Jurors, trying four men accused of procuring boys at the Playland Arcade (featured in *Johnny*) were forbidden to watch the documentary, which was broadcast as advertised.
34 *Guardian* 28 February 1989.
35 'Yorkshire TV used unobtrusive microphones and cameras and film needing no scare-them-away artificial lights. One spied and eavesdropped' (*Dail Mail* 23 July 1975: 14).
36 TV critic Clive James pointed out, in the *Observer* (27 July 1975), that 'supposedly real-life characters were all role-playing like mad'.
37 Policy on youth homelessness was stated in Circular 18/74, issued in 1974, which some housing authorities followed but many others ignored. This circular was, however, the basis for the Housing (Homeless Persons) Act 1977, which was more systematically applied.
38 *Daily Mail* 30 July 1975: 7.
39 *Daily Mail* 23 July 1975: 14.
40 *TV Times* 19–25 July 1975 30.80: 8.
41 Hubbard (1997) shows, however, that the 'fallen woman' retains some currency.
42 *Daily Mail* 23 July 1975: 14, 23.
43 *TV Times* 19–25 July 1975 30.80: 10.
44 *Guardian* 23 July 1975: 1.
45 *Sun* 30 July 1975: 9. This is an irrelevant question, since there is no correlation between homosexuality and paedophilia. Though male homosexuality is sometimes age-structured, this form of homosexuality concerns older and younger men, not men and boys. Relationships between men and boys, like those between men and girls, are not homosexual but paedophile. Of these the latter, in which men abuse girls, is by far the most common (Finkelhor 1984). In other historical contexts, forms of male homosexuality (relationships between older and younger men) and paedophilia (between men and boys) had been grouped together, under the heading 'pederasty' (Greenberg 1988), and the confusion between homosexuality and paedophilia may have been a legacy of this archaic term.
46 *Guardian* 1 April 1998: 8.
47 *Understanding Paedophilia* June/July 1976 1.2: 8.

48 *Hansard* H.C. (Fifth Series) 1974–5 896.2364.
49 *Times* 9 April 1976: 3.
50 *Sun* 29 July 1975: 1.
51 *Hansard* H.C. (Fifth Series) 1974–5 896.2359.
52 'Tricked You, Says Runaway Tommy', Glasgow *Sunday Mail* 3 August 1975.
53 Meacher told the Commons that 'the focus of the programme may have misled us: there are considerable numbers of vulnerable young people living in this strange sub-world of the rootless – and seriously damaged by their experiences in it – who are older, being in their late teens or early 20s' (*Hansard* H.C. (Fifth Series) 1974–5 896.2373).
54 Lind concludes a critical survey of legal regulation of child sexualities as follows: 'That children are already taking on sexual identities … and that they are becoming politically active about those identities should serve as a warning that intolerant legal regulation is likely to' [harm children]. 'If we add to this an acknowledgement that many of these children are seriously harmed and that the aim of the construction of innocence in childhood is to protect them from harm, then we have established a clear case for the reform of law – affecting both childhood and adulthood – which constrains diverse sexualities' (Lind 1999: 15).

## References

Anon. (1885) "The Protection of Girls: Demonstration in Hyde Park", *South London Press* (August 29) XLV. 1 145: 3.

Bland, L. (1995) *Banishing the Beast. English Feminism and Sexual Morality 1885–1914*, London: Penguin.

Bristow, E.J. (1977) *Vice and Vigilance: Purity Movements in Britain Since 1700*, Dublin: Gill and Macmillan.

Brown, M. (1996), 'Closet Geography', *Environment and Planning D, Society and Space* 14: 762–9.

CHE (Campaign for Homosexual Equality), USFI (Union for Sexual Freedom in Ireland), SMG (Scottish Minorities Group) (1976) *The Case for Homosexual Law Reform*, London.

Cibber, T. (1733) *The Harlot's Progress*, London.

Cleland, J. (1748–9) *Memoirs of a Woman of Pleasure*, London: G. Fenton.

Davies, R. (1996) *Secret Sins. Sex, Violence and Society in Carmarthenshire 1870–1920*, Cardiff: University of Wales Press.

Deakin, M. and Willis, J. (1976) *Johnny Go Home. Based on the highly acclaimed YTV documentary*, London: Futura.

Demos, J. and Demos, J. (1969) 'Adolescence in Historical Perspective', *Journal of Marriage and the Family* 31: 632–8.

DHSS (Department of Health and Social Security) (1976) *Report of Working Group on Homeless Young People*, London (British Library 385/242).

Dibblin, J. (1991) *Wherever I Lay My Hat. Young Women and Homelessness*, London: Shelter.

Diderot, D. (1797) *The Nun*, trans. T. Robinson, London.

Finkelhor, D. (1984) *Child Sex Abuse*, New York: Free Press.

—— (1986) *A Sourcebook on Child Sexual Abuse*, Beverly Hills, Calif. and London: Sage.

Greenberg, D.F. (1988) *The Construction of Homosexuality*, Chicago: University of Chicago Press.

Greve, J., Greve S. and Page, D. (1971) *Homelessness in London*, Edinburgh: Scottish Academic Press.

Grey, A. (1992) *Quest for Justice: Towards Homosexual Emancipation*, London: Sinclair Stevenson.
Hopkins, E. (n.d.) *Work in Villages*, London: Church of England Purity Society.
—— (n.d.) *Smut in the Wheat*, London: Church of England Purity Society.
Hubbard, P. (1997) 'Red Light Districts and Toleration Zones', *Area* 29.2: 129–40.
Hyam, R. (1990) *Empire and Sexuality*, Manchester: Manchester University Press.
Jarrett, D. (1976) *The Ingenious Mr Hogarth*, London: Michael Joseph.
Kett, J. (1977) *Rites of Passage: Adolescence in America, 1790 to the Present*, New York: Basic Books.
Kilborn, R. (1997) *An Introduction to Television Documentary*, Manchester: Manchester University Press.
Lind, C. (1999) 'Law, Childhood Innocence and Sexuality', in L. Moran., S. Beresford and D. Monk (eds) *Legal Queeries*, London: Cassell.
McCluskey, J. (1993) *Reassessing Priorities: The Children Act 1989. A New Agenda for Young Homeless People?* London: CHAR.
MacMurraugh-Kavanagh, M.K. (1997) 'Drama into News: Strategies of Intervention in The Wednesday Play', *Screen* 38.3: 249–60.
Mason, M. (1995) *The Making of Victorian Sexuality*, Oxford: Oxford University Press.
Miller, N. (1995) *Out of the Past*, London: Vintage.
Moore S. and Rosenthal, D. (1993) *Sexuality in Adolescence*, London: Routledge.
National Vigilance Association (1885–1896) *Annual Reports* (Volumes 1–11), London.
Paget, D. (1990) *True Stories? Documentary Drama on Radio. Screen and Stage*, Manchester: Manchester University Press.
Sandford, J. (1976) *Cathy Come Home*, 2nd edn, with new preface by the author, London: Marion Boyers.
Schults, R.L. (1972) *Crusader in Babylon: W T Stead and the Pall Mall Gazette*, Lincoln: University of Nebraska Press.
Shelter (1976) *Ten Years On. A Progress Report*, London: Shelter.
Short, J. (1991) *Imagined Country*, London: Routledge.
Stead, W.T. (1885) *Pall Mall Gazette* XLII.6336–6367 (July 6-August 11).
Stoppard, T. (1997) *The Invention of Love*, London: Faber & Faber.
Sturgess, B. (1975) *No Offence. The Case for Homosexual Equality at Law*, London: CHE.
Walkowitz, J. ([1992] 1994) *City of Dreadful Delight: Narratives of Sexual Danger in Late-Victorian London*, London: Virago.
Weeks, J. (1977) *Coming Out: Homosexual Politics in Britain from the Nineteenth Century to the Present*, London: Quartet Books.
Widdowson, B. (1977) *Hostel for a Home. A Shelter Report on Hostels for Homeless Families*, London: Shelter.
Williams, R. (1985) *The Country and the City*, London: Hogarth Press.
Willis, J. (1978) 'Television and Social Problems: A Case History' *Educational Broadcasting International* 11.3: 108–12.
Wolfenden, J.F. (1957) *Report of the Committee on Homosexual Offences and Prostitution (Parliamentary Command Paper 247)*, London: Home Office.

# 7

# THE QUEER POLITICS OF GAY PASTORAL

*David Shuttleton*

This chapter presents a brief analysis of some of the ideologically diverse inflections of romantic pastoral conventions within the homosexual literary imaginary; a project with obvious connections with those of other essayists in this volume concerned with how sexual identities are shaped within rural/metropolitan dialectics. It has broad affinities with that area of recent cross-disciplinary critical studies concerned with cultural linkages between rurality and sexuality cited in the opening paragraphs of David Bell's contribution (Chapter 5), and to which his earlier collaborative work on lesbian and gay ruralist culture is itself a valuable contribution (Bell and Valentine 1995). Whilst Richard Phillips' not unrelated essay in the present volume (Chapter 6) examines two specific examples of the relations between social practice – specifically legislation – and cultural signification, like Bell, my concern is primarily with cultural signification, predominately in early twentieth-century literary texts, although a framing example from recent gay cinema in particular gestures towards related pastoral conventions in the visual arts.

I restrict my analysis to male same-sex love and desire; partly as a matter of expertise, but also to avoid, in a short essay, a conflation of two distinctive sex-gender politics. Nevertheless I write with an awareness of a related field of lesbian-feminist criticism concerned with the uses of pastoral conventions in female traditions of romantic friendship and eroticism; a cultural tradition to which Angelia Wilson alludes (Chapter 11) and to which Anira Rowanchild's account of Anne Lister (Chapter 8) belongs (Cheney 1985; Donoghue 1993).

My concern with male same-sex pastoral conventions is usefully prefaced by noting a brief pastoral sequence from the recent British gay 'feel-good' movie *Beautiful Thing* (Dir. Hettie Macdonald), which indicates the contemporary use of such codes within popular gay culture. *Beautiful Thing*, released in 1995 and since screened on British TV, is an essentially up-beat story of first-love between Jamie and Ste, two 16-year-old boys, neighbours on a landing of a low-rise block of flats on a council estate at Thamesmead in south-east London. Jonathan Harvey wrote the screenplay based upon his own very successful stageplay.

Ste is bullied into acting as a domestic servant by his elder brother and abusive single-father. He finds refuge with Jamie and his brusque, but basically kind-hearted single-mother, Sandra, and after several 'sleepovers' sharing Jamie's bed the two lads fall in love. After finding the address in *Gay Times* Jamie persuades Ste to go with him to 'The Gloucester', a gay pub by Greenwich Park Gates were they are targeted by a drag-act who teases them in front of all the regulars, clucking, 'I feel like chicken tonight.' Leaving the stage, 'she' flashes her eyelashes and pins the boys at the bar: 'I think I'll have two of you and ten of your mate.' Sexual flirtation is made through suggestive allusions to breast feeding and 'Mothercare'.[1] A jump-cut suddenly reveals the two lads chasing each other excitedly through a wood to Mamma Cass singing 'you've got to make your own kinda music'. This game of tag culminates in a passionate embrace against a tree; an open-air kiss which marks the full blossoming of this gay romance after earlier hesitant, erotic intimacies within the thin-walled confines of a council-flat, with Jamie's mother and lover in the next room, and Ste's brutal father just through the party-wall.

Within this rite-of-passage into gay self-consciousness, the woodland setting sentimentally signifies the 'naturalness' of same-sex desire; a liberated pastoral space where, as the Mama Cass lyrics used elsewhere remind us, 'holding you at night just seems kinda natural and right'. The fact that Ste and Jamie's greenwood is merely a suburban park, simply underscores the conventionality of this romantic suburban same-sex pastoral as ultimately theatrical artifice, in fact a floodlit film-location, and one which echoes many heterosexual romantic, pastoral sequences from mainstream classic Hollywood cinema. In *Beautiful Thing*'s sentimental gay revision, a pastoral *mise-en-scène* reinforces the film's endorsement of sexual authenticity. This could be read as being somewhat at odds with a visible, metropolitan gay subcultural socialization which, as represented by the drag-queen, is marked by the gender disturbance of transvestism, camp language codes and, albeit good humouredly, with the hints of predatory sexual commodification implicit in 'her' habitual recycling of advertising slogans. Somewhat equivocally, in *Beautiful Thing*, pastoral romance is energized, even enabled by an essentially metropolitan gay-subcultural sociality at the same moment as it appears to be presented as an escape and a retreat from it: tensions to which I shall return in my conclusion.

*Beautiful Thing*'s appropriation of a pastoral visual grammar familiar in the heterosexual romance of classic Hollywood cinema belongs to a queer film history which would include the similar woodland fantasy 'chase-me' sequence in Jean Genet's darker *Un Chant D'Amour* (1950). But it probably owes far more to Derek Jarman's queer appropriations of a distinctively literary, English pastoralism, as exemplified by his most lyrical film *Angelic Conversation* (1985), structured around Shakespeare's Sonnets. These cinematic precedents ultimately derive their pastoral iconographic language from a classically rooted tradition within Western literary and visual art which, whilst conventionally concerned with such primary binarisms as 'Nature' and 'Culture', 'Innocence' and 'Experience', has, since its Classical origins been intimately associated with male–male desire.

## Queering gay pastoral

For some time gay scholars have been reclaiming the neoclassical generic pastoral tradition as a homosexual genre (Norton [1974] 1997; Fone 1983). Rictor Norton prefaces an extensive survey of English Renaissance pastoral literature by asserting that 'if any particular genre can be called a homosexual genre, the evidence would point most convincingly to the pastoral tradition', which from its ancient Greek origins as lyric poetry depicting the life of shepherds or herdsmen has been concerned with homosexual love (Norton [1974] 1997: 1). This is in itself somewhat reductive, for *The Idylls* of the Greek poet Theocritus, active in the late third century BC, and the *Eclogues* composed between 42 and 39 BC by the Roman poet Virgil, portray a polymorphous range of desires, ranging from male–male love-elegy to heterosexual romance and bawdy bestiality. But whilst subsequent, homophobic Christian and humanist ethical prescriptions and later bourgeois codes of politeness have repeatedly sought to erase or veil pastoral's queer libidinal economies to produce hetero-normative Arcadias, this is not so much a seamless tradition of repression but rather suggests a Foucaldian mechanism of incitement to discourse, as the project to police the same-sex desire of the ancients effectively kept such desires troublingly visible for generations of translators, editors, and scholarly critics.

Back in 1983 in a groundbreaking essay on 'Arcadia and the Homosexual Imagination', Byrne R. S. Fone isolated several classically derived romantic scenarios – typically bathing scenes, parkland rendezvous, rural walks, and camping episodes – producing a useful formalist iconographic grammar of pastoral motifs evident across a wide range of English and American literature. Both Norton and Fone construct a 'gay' pastoral canon reaching

> from Theocritus's *Idylls* to the chapter entitled 'Bee and Orchid' in Marcel Proust's *Cities of the Plain*, from Walt Whitman's *Calamus Leaves* [sic] to A.E. Housman's *Shropshire Lad* ... from the Greek poets' praise of boys in the gymnasia to all the flashbacks to adolescent experience in Boy scout camps in American gay fiction in the 1960s.
>
> (Norton 1974: 1)

For Fone in particular, this canon reveals an 'Arcadian Ideal' which 'has been used in the homosexual literary tradition in a fashion that speaks directly to the gay sensibility' (Fone 1983: 13).

Both Norton and Fone thus assume an essentialist conception of a transhistorical and transcultural 'gay sensibility' and 'homosexual imagination'. The latter in particular tends towards the mythologization of his own 'Arcadian' references, producing a set of universal homosexual pastoral paradigms associated with Utopian spaces, coterie codifications, and rituals of initiation and gift-giving. In this idealist conception of a 'gay sensibility' each instantiation of queer pastoral offers a confirmation of certain eternal verities, but ignores the function of literature itself as cultural practice and as one of the multiple discourses which has served to construct or contest a variety of psycho-social sexual definitions (for this distinction see Sinfield 1998: 146–50). In Fone's case, a celebratory idealism isolates a specific ideological function for 'gay pastoral'; one largely restricted to an essentially aristocratic 'Greek' ideal, even though, in many of the modern texts he cites, this model is unevenly active alongside other more egalitarian constructions derived from a Whitmanite (American, democratic) or a Carpenterian (English socialist) politicized vision of 'comradely love' which eventually underpinned the Western gay liberation movement of the 1970s (Sedgwick [1985] 1992: Coda). The reduction of the queerness of pastoral to a timeless abstraction is to succumb to the escapist pull of pastoral's own dominant rhetoric, which seeks to evade time, history and material political realities through a retreat into a phantasmic ideal space which is pre-cultural, if not pre-social, and often, by implication, superior and preferable.

I do not intend offering my own personal survey of examples of queer pastoral from the literary tradition (they are numerous); rather, my concern is with the diverse and sometimes ambivalent ideological uses to which such conventions have been put by writers often working with differing models of the sex/gender system and necessarily producing differing same-sex-oriented identities. It is this politics of representation which is largely missing from earlier accounts of 'gay' pastoral which have been happy enough with having restored a high-cultural aesthetic to those deemed its rightful owners. This is not to ignore the value of fantasy for progressive sexual politics. Nor is it to deny the emancipatory value of recovering or indeed inventing traditions for subcultural solidarity when resisting the state sanctioned oppression which shaped the lives of most of the writers and artists whose work concerns me (for strategic constructions of a 'homosexual' literary canon see Woods 1998: Chapter 1). But there are costs incurred by crass canonization. To suggest that every homoerotic pastoral trope points us towards the good and the beautiful is to erase narrative and historio-cultural specificity. Pastoral conventions have been invoked at least as much in rejection of a minoritizing homosexual or gay identity as they have been employed for any coded endorsements or overt celebrations of same-sex desire.

To cite one particularly sobering example, the earliest homosexual emancipationist journal, Adolph Brand's *Der Eigene* (1896–1931), upheld a 'back-to-nature' aesthetic prevalent amongst the dissident, middle-class youth movements of late-Wilhemine and Weimar Germany, being typically illustrated with some now rather quaint photographs of athletic young men posing naked together in lakeside meadows and woodlands. But by the late 1920s much of the accompanying text in this 'high-brow' journal was distinctly anti-feminist and often supportive of a nationalistic masculinist, supremacism approaching Nazism (Oosterhuis and Kennedy: 1991; Sinfield 1994: 117). To produce a monologic 'gay pastoral' tradition not only sets limits on the potentialities of queer desire, but involves a wilful evasion of the sometimes unpalatable politics of queer culture and means losing the chance to learn anything from history.

Pastoral may be a homoerotic genre, but it nevertheless constructs identities within existing, often exploitative, hierarchies of social class, gender and ethnicity. For as Raymond Williams has shown in *The Country and the City* ([1973] 1993), pastoral is a mode which consistently serves to mythologize the actual relations of property, production and labour which prevail within and between 'town' and 'country', between the metropolitan and the rural, between the purportedly cultivated and the so-called primitive, between colonizer and colonized, be it in an ancient city-state, or in a later feudal or capitalist economy. Moreover pastoral passions – what Bell and Valentine usefully term 'rural erotics' – have predominantly, since their ancient literary inception, been represented by an urban literary elite for an urban literary elite. Although Theocritus placed his Arcadia in his native Sicily, he was writing for the metropolitan literary circle of Callimachus in the third century Hellenic colony of Alexandria. Similarly Virgil wrote his *Eclogues* for the Roman circle of Maecenas under the patronage of Octavian (later, Emperor Augustus) (Halperin 1983: 194–5). In the modern period, a queer pastoral imaginary has served both elitist and emancipatory, aesthetic and polemical, misogynist and separatist, nostalgic and, as already suggested, sometimes blatantly fascistic structures of feeling. I want to approach a few selected examples with a general theoretical consideration of how, as signifiers of 'the Natural', pastoral codes have played two distinctive polemical functions within a modern homosexual discourse which was largely forged in opposition to condemnatory orthodox scriptings of same-sex desire as fundamentally 'unnatural'.

## Urban pastoral/rural camp

Historians of sexuality are largely in agreement that a modern Western homosexual identity emerged as a metropolitan phenomenon enabled by the particular conditions of social mobility generated by capitalist industrialization and imperialism (Weeks 1981: chapter 6). By the close of the nineteenth century, conservative and reformist sexologists alike equated neurotic sexual perversion with the febrile life of the city. In *Berlins Drittes Geschlect* ('Berlin's Third Sex') (1904), Dr Magnus Hirschfeld, the liberal reformist German sexologist, even tried to use the association of homosexuality with city life to launch a counter-argument for its inherent respectability. Those who condemned and those who embraced Decadence were in mutual agreement that the natural home of unnatural vice was the metropolis, the heart of modernity. For the orthodox, the modern city with its restless, arbitrary mingling of known natives and repudiated outsiders, represented a jungle of Darwinian degeneration harbouring secret dens of perversion. In this context, George Mosse notes how reports of vice trials, including most famously that of Oscar Wilde in 1895, frequently allude to the biblical 'Cities of the Plain', Sodom and Gomorrah, whilst in contrast 'the village or small town close to nature ... symbolised those eternal values that stood outside the rush of time [where] the nation and manliness were at home; here one could still recall the healthy, happy past' (Mosse 1985: 32). As with Bell's populist sites of 'rural erotics', in figuring a return to a lost primitivism, or a reversion to a polymorphously perverse, pre-oedipal imaginary, queer pastoral can be read as personally ennobling and culturally restorative on the one hand, whilst on the other repudiated as 'rural idiocy', marking a Darwinian regression, and a disturbing erosion of the boundary between the human and the bestial.

As Alan Sinfield in particular has shown, the dominant, modern, particularly English conception of the homosexual has been of a dandified Wildean aesthete, an effete, effeminate, leisure-class queer (Sinfield 1994). Typically this cultivated metropolitan or cosmopolitan homosexual is an urban, indeed urbane, figure with an associated camp sensibility. Wildean Decadence deliberately celebrated metropolitan artificiality. Thus Vivian, in 'The Decay of Lying', Wilde's *fin de siècle* manifesto of an anti-bourgeois aesthetic of 'art-for-art's-sake', wilfully inverts the sentimental clichés of a popular Victorian cult of Wordsworthian nature worship:

> *Vivian.* But Nature is so uncomfortable. Grass is hard and lumpy and damp, and full of dreadful black insects ... If Nature had been comfortable, mankind would never have invented architecture, and I prefer houses to the open air. In a house we all feel of the proper proportions. Everything is subordinated to us, fashioned for our use and our pleasure. Egotism itself, which is so necessary to a proper sense of human dignity, is entirely the result of indoor life. Out of doors one becomes abstract and impersonal.
>
> (Wilde 1891: 3)

Throughout 'The Decay of Lying', Vivian wittily sets his 'Egotism' against 'Nature' as the sentimentalized signifier of all that liberal humanism had traditionally claimed as profound, permanent and universal; that 'abstract' ideal of 'human nature' which defined homosexuality as 'unnatural'. So whilst an Arnoldian muscular-Christian orthodoxy was recommending brisk and bracing cross-country walks to maintain the manly strength of the Empire, the Vivians of the *fin de siècle* defiantly preferred to cruise along in the footsteps of the father of urban dandies, Charles Baudelaire, whose 'leisurely descriptions' of the pavement culture and Arcades of Second Empire Paris epitomized for Walter Benjamin that quintessentially modern figure, 'the *flaneur*, who goes botanizing on the asphalt' (Benjamin [1936] 1973: 36).

When being *against nature* is central to Wilde's production of this 'transgressive aesthetic', which we now recognize as homosexual camp, the pastoral as an entrenched convention for the representation of Nature enters into a peculiarly conflicted, ironic position within what Jonathan Dollimore has usefully theorized (borrowing his subtitles) as 'The Perverts Revenge on Authenticity' within the 'Post/Modern Gay Sensibility' (1991: *passim*). For, as Susan Sontag observes in opening her 'Notes on "Camp"', 'it is not a natural mode of sensibility, if there be any such'. Indeed, 'the essence of Camp is its love of the unnatural: of artifice and exaggeration. And Camp is esoteric – something of a private code, a badge of identity even, among small urban cliques' (Sontag 1966: 275). In Wilde's own metropolitan, Bohemian social circle, this coded celebration of the unnatural was epitomized in that paradoxical symbol, a green carnation (an artificial botanical form which does not occur in 'nature'). Remarking on this paradoxical relationship between nature and camp, Sontag suggests that 'all camp objects, and persons, contain a large element of artifice. Nothing in nature can be campy ... Rural camp is still man-made, and most campy objects are urban. (Yet, they often have a serenity – or a naivety – which is the equivalent of pastoral. A great deal of Camp suggests Empson's phrase, "urban pastoral")' (Sontag 1966: 279, referring to Empson 1935).

Sontag's identification of a slippery urban(unnatural)/natural(rural) rhetorical dialectic usefully describes some of the ironic strategies of Wilde's disciples. A 'Rural Camp' aesthetic is found in the stylized fictions of the famously camp aesthete, Ronald Firbank (1886–1926), recently analysed by Joseph Bristow as self-conscious attempts at a 'queer modernism' (Bristow 1995: chapter 3). Firbank's *Valmouth* of 1919 suggests a post-impressionist, country-house 'artificial pastoral' in which an Anglo-Catholic English landscape stretches 'beneath the crepuscular, tinted sky' (Firbank, n.d.: 9). But Firbank's own queerness was often textually displaced onto lesbianism, and transgressive inter-class, inter-generational or inter-racial relations. Thus centenarian Lady Parvula de Panzoust, in a rare case of heterosexuality, has the hots for the farm-lad, David Tooke, a 'crazy Corydon',[2] whilst his love-lorn sister Thetis mopes for Captain Thoroughfare's return from Ceylon, at the very woodland spot where he had told her of 'his middy-chum, Jack Whorwood, who was not much over fifteen, and the youngest hand on board. "That little lad", he had said, with a peculiar smile that revealed his regular pointed teeth, "that little lad, upon a cruise, is, to me, what Patroclus was to Achilles, and even more"' (Firbank n.d.: 22). Rumours of the Captain's 'many-sided nature', are confirmed when he returns home secretly married to a 'native' girl, but tellingly preceded by his orchid collection (including the species 'Sodom'!), and accompanied by the vain Lieutenant Whorwood, who

> as he lagged along in the faint boreal light behind his friend ... resembled singularly some girl masquerading as a boy for reasons of romance. He

had a suit of summer mufti, and a broad-brimmed blue beaver hat looped with leaves broken from the hedgerows in the lanes, and a Leander scarf tucked full of flowers: loosestrife, meadowrue, orchis, ragged-robin.

(Firbank n.d.: 86)

This is a very queer pastoral, although Firbank's 'Rural Camp' aestheticism typically eschews any narrative or ethical closure.

Just as the orchidaceous image of the sissified, citified queer as a hybrid hot-house flower persists as a popular stereotype, these ironic inflections of an inauthenticating pastoral remain active within a postmodern, metropolitan Anglo-American queer art-culture for which Wilde still remains a figurehead; active, for example, in the subtle, camp resonances of Robert Mapplethorpe's exquisitely erotic flower photographs. It is perhaps in Jarman's crucially elegiac concern with gay gardening and 'Modern Nature' – an ironic phrase actually used in Wilde's 'The Decay of Lying' – exemplified in such late works as *The Garden* (1990), with its engagement with both AIDS and ecological crisis that we find an overtly polemical use of this 'rural camp' aesthetic (for Jarman's ironic pastoralism, see Chedgzoy 1995: 177–9).

## Pastoral authenticity

But, as Dollimore has shown, alongside Wilde's transgressive aesthetic of nature a prevalent modern homosexual/gay discourse has made the non-ironized counter-claim that homosexuality is 'natural', and as such, within a rights-based ethic, necessarily deserving of social equality (Dollimore 1991: 39–63). This claim for authenticity is usually made through a rhetorical strategy which Dollimore usefully terms 'transgressive reinscription', whereby an authorized discourse is appropriated for counter-hegemonic use (Dollimore 1996: 33–5). Such reinscription surfaces in the overtly homoerotic novel *Teleny: or the Reverse of the Medal*, ([1893] 1985) produced clandestinely by Wilde's circle in 1893, when the queer dandy Des Grieux declares to a friend that with Teleny as his new lover, he 'was far from being ashamed of my crime, [but] felt that I should like to proclaim it to the world'. He wants to inscribe this 'love' onto nature:

> 'For the first time in my life I understood that lovers could be so foolish as to entwine their initials together. I felt like carving his name on the bark of trees, that the birds seeing it might twitter it from morn till eventide: that the breeze might lisp it to the rustling leaves of the forest …'
>
> 'Still I had thought that on the morrow – the intoxication passed – you would have shuddered at the thought of having a man for a lover?'
>
> 'Why? Had I committed a crime against nature when my own nature found peace and happiness thereby? If I was thus, surely it was the fault of

my blood, not myself. Who had planted nettles in my garden? Not I. They had grown there unawares, from my very childhood ...'
(Wilde (?) and others [1893] 1985: 130)

Des Grieux appropriates the elements of heterosexual pastoral romance to reinforce the argument that since homosexuality is 'natural' it is not a cause for shame.

A very similar strategy underpins Gide's early homosexual polemic *Corydon: Four Socratic Dialogues* (France 1911; translated, US 1950), which in employing pastoral conventions to claim authenticity illustrates how, early in the century, a radically pursued essentialism can produce strategies of binary category inversion which are as potentially subversive as any celebrated by post-structuralism For example, in Dialogue III Gide's narrative persona, Corydon, invokes the same-sex loves of classical shepherds to suggest that heterosexuality is not necessarily instinctive:

> [Since] ... the untutored shepherds of Theocritus were very unsophisticated in their efforts [to make love to girls] ... this puzzle of the opposite sex cannot be solved always, or even often, by 'instinct' alone ... And that is why, in Virgil, we find Damoetas under the willows mourning the flight of Galatea, while Menalcus, lying beside Amyntas, already tastes the pleasures of love without let or hindrance.
> (Gide [1920] 1952: 93)

Corydon also subverts Longus' heterosexual late-Hellenic pastoral prose-romance *Daphnis and Chloe* (*c:* third century AD), by noting that Daphnis has to learn how to make love to Chloe. This is not 'a model of naturalism' but rather supports Corydon's counter-claims against the orthodoxy that heterosexuality is natural. To his adversary's response that 'if heterosexuality calls for some tuition' then nowadays there is obviously no shortage of pupils, 'either in town or country', Corydon concedes that nowadays 'in the country, [especially] homosexual diversions are fairly unusual and rather disreputable':

> Yes ... everything in our conventions and in our laws impels one sex towards the other. What a conspiracy there is, both furtive and frank, to induce the small boy, even before his desire has awoken, to believe that pleasure can be realised only with a woman; that apart from her there is no delight. What an exaggeration there is, even to the point of absurdity, of the attractions of the fair sex when compared with the systematic effacement, distortion and caricature of the male.
> (Gide [1920] 1952: 93–4)

Exploiting the apparent 'naturalness' of pastoral same-sex passion to suggest a cultural fall into heterosexuality, Gide launches the trangressively counter-intuitive argument that it is this compulsory heterosexuality which is constructed and inauthentic since it needs to be taught and culturally maintained; later developed for lesbian-feminism by Adrienne Rich ([1980] 1993). Gide almost anticipates subsequent post-structuralist strategies which argue for the constructedness of sex/gender labels and the trangressive reach of sex-gender performativity. But, as if to remind us that such binary inversion is not necessarily productive of a politically progressive discourse (see Dollimore 1991: 44–5), it is notable that *Corydon* merely overturns established notions of 'the Natural' to support a highly elitist notion of homosexual superiority and institutionalized pederastia; it is also grossly misogynist.

## Academic arcadias

At Harvard in 1839, Henry David Thoreau (1817–62), the future author of *Walden* (1854), the Bible of American backwoods escapism, pondered in his Journal why, since 'History tells us of Orestes and Pylades, Damon and Pythias why should not we put to shame those old reserved worthies by a community of such?' and caught 'glimpses of a serene friendship-land' of romantic friendship: 'What is this rural, this pastoral, this poetical life but its invention? ... Even Plato's republic is governed by Platonic Love (quoted in Katz 1976: 487).[3] But it is only gradually in the latter half of the nineteenth century, and often in direct response to Whitman, that homophile pastoralism transforms into a democratic sexual polemic. In England especially it emerges out of and alongside the neo-Hellenic academic movements promoting passionate friendship and chaste ideals of pederastic mentorship (Dellamora 1990; Dowling 1994).

As an undergraduate at Oxford in the 1850s, the classicist John Addington Symonds (1840–93) — now recognized as the founder of modern 'gay' literary scholarship — sought out fellow 'Arcadians', and retrospectively regarded his youthful absorption in pastoral poetry as instrumental to his understanding of his life-long desire to have sexual relations with manly peasants (Grosskurth 1964: 75, 109, 233; Bristow 1995). The shepherd-boy as metropolitan homoerotic fantasy is traceable back to at least the mid-eighteenth century. Given the long-term fascination with the Mediterranean littoral amongst classical educated homosexuals, the peasantry of Italy, Greece, and North Africa were often miscast as picturesque remnants of Arcadia; in some cases this rendered them vulnerable to crude sexual exploitation, whilst also producing genuinely transgressive bonds across class and ethnic difference (Aldrich 1993).

The homoerotic interest in rustics, real or imagined, native or exotic, belongs within a wider structure of feeling usefully traced by Williams: a 'rural-sexual metaphor', through which the rural labourer came to embody 'the virtues of the earth, in the new fertile sense [of] rough land, rough grappling with nature, rough feelings, rough honesty' (Williams [1973] 1993: 252). The rural rough was a somewhat specialized fetish for upper-class gents seeking a release from bourgeois inhibitions through sexual contact with labouring men (Sinfield 1994: chapter 6). Social historian Jeffrey Weeks describes rituals of turn-of-the-century homosexual prostitution as 'class and gender interactions', in which the ideas that 'working class equals masculine, equals "closeness-to-nature"' played 'important roles … affecting, for instance the stance adopted by the "prostitute" and the behaviours he was expected to tolerate' (Weeks 1981: 56–7). Noting the 'complex patterns' of such inter-class homoerotics, Weeks observes that they might be configured as forms of 'sexual colonialism' at the same time as being deemed genuine attempts at class reconciliation.

I shall shortly be addressing this enduring rural fantasy, particularly in relation to E.M. Forster's still influential *Maurice* (written 1914; published 1971). But it is easy to forget that for 55 years *Maurice* was only read in manuscript by a coterie of Forster's friends. Whilst it might now seem sentimental, *Maurice*'s influence has been as a 'period piece' for a gay-lib/post-gay readership, for whom its idealism has clearly played an emancipatory role, not least for pro-gay literary criticism. Forster's original investment in rural homoerotics is usefully read within the broader context of a queerly inflected contemporary neo-paganism.

## Stories of panic

Neo-Hellenic pastoral same-sex romanticism informs many Victorian and Edwardian novels of public school and Oxbridge life which betray an intense nostalgia for an uninterrupted male intimacy. With varying degrees of unconscious and coded homoeroticism, this literature employs the familiar conventions to explore the vicissitudes of 'Arcadian' passions in recurrent pastoral settings: bathing and boating scenes, intimate country walks, and on grassy banks by cricket pitches. But after the Wilde trials these often turgidly tragic fictions – rarely are both lovers allowed to live beyond the upper-sixth – become vulnerable to recognition as homosexual: this is just what the Belfast-born aesthete Forrest Reid (1875–1947) discovered when, as a somewhat naive mature student at Cambridge in 1905, he published his particularly florid Platonic romance *The Garden God: a Tale of Two Boys*.

*The Garden God* describes how, after a term of cricket-pitch yearnings, dormitory kisses and endless allusions to the predestined ideal love of Plato's *Phaedrus*, the 16-year-old schoolboy lovers Graham and Harold spend the Summer 'Vac' together. After innocently cavorting naked on the beach together, the besotted Graham poses Harold as classical statues, offering up pagan prayers of adoration to a beloved whom he believes to be the incarnation of his secret childhood dream of Dionysian Pan, the 'Garden God' of the title. But to ensure that such love cannot find physical fulfilment this side of the grave, Reid has Harold summarily killed by a runaway cart, leaving a bereft Graham to grow up into a reclusive bachelor aesthete who spends the rest of his days in rural retirement awaiting the moment when death will reunite him with his 'Friend'.

Reid's morbid tale caused him some social embarrassment. His literary hero and dedicatee Henry James gave him the 'cold shoulder', whilst survivors of Wilde's circle wrote him disturbingly confessional letters. Returning to suburban Belfast, Reid penned more pastoral novels of boyhood friendships enacted in secret 'Dream Gardens' presided over by magical statues of 'Garden Gods'. His sometimes prurient fixation upon the fragility of youthful innocence suggests a self-defeating, ultimately futile desire to sustain or return to a pre-oedipal, pre-social pastoral dream of pure, innocent boy–boy love. *The Garden God* appeared within a year of another tale of eternal youth, James Barry's *Peter Pan*. Both works belong within a neo-pagan aesthetic exemplified by what at the time were the academically respected paintings of Henry Scott Tuke (with whom Reid's work has been linked by his recent editors), paintings in which pastoral codes legitimate depictions of naked youths in 'Nature' (Cooper 1994: 40–1). But if now we are less inclined to read such works as being sexually innocent, this retrospective reading owes much to the impact of another work of 1905, Sigmund Freud's *Three Essays on Sexuality* through which the definitional reach of the sexual was taken backwards to before puberty and polymorphously haemorrhaged beyond the physical into the subterranean depths of the mental.

Thus, in keeping with Bell's related observations regarding the conflicted function of 'the natural' as sexualized signifier, pastoralism clearly has a far from unequivocal mimetic relationship with homoeroticism *per se*. Edwardian idylls encourage anachronistic assumptions regarding coded intent, but there is no reason to doubt Reid's sincere shock when his chaste, prose-lyric of a spiritualized 'Greek Nature' was associated with the beastly perversions being labelled by sexologists. In 1914, when his literary admirer Forster trusted him with the manuscript of *Maurice*, Reid was surprised, though not wholly unsympathetic, to discover that Forster was prepared to label himself 'homosexual' and sanction genitality. Reid exemplifies a continued faith in a chaste pastoral discourse amongst those who shunned, if not actually rejected, a minoritizing homosexuality and as a result, despite the fancy footwork of his recent 'gay' editors, his paedophile pastoralism cannot be unproblematically appropriated into a contemporary, dominant, assimilationist homosexual sensibility.

None the less, despite disavowals, neo-paganism did have a coded function. Forster's *Commonplace Book* shows that by 1926 he was aware that his own fictional use of neo-pagan leitmotifs had affinities with what he identified as a 'Pan school' of 'Satanic intimacy', traceable from the Hawthorne of *The Marble Faun* to Reid, and 'petering out in Hichens and E. F. Benson'. Forster clearly associates this tradition with homosexuality (the entry starts with a discussion of the homosexual subtext of *Billy*

*Budd*, and it concludes with the remark that 'H[enry] J[ames] in The Turn of the Screw, is merely declining to think about homosex') (Forster 1985: 17–18). Recent commentators have echoed Forster by noting the prevalence of homosexually coded uses of Pan in turn-of-the century literature and visual art (alongside Bacchus and Dionysius, the related nature gods of ecstatic revelry, and associated fauns and satyrs) (Hoare 1997: 80, footnote). Nijinsky's controversially erotic performance in the Russian ballet *L'après midi D'une Faun* (1910), became iconic of this distinctly queer, neo-pagan modernist aesthetic. Appropriately, Forster's first published fiction was 'The Story of a Panic' (1906), a short story in which Eustace, a polite, bookish, middle-class English boy holidaying in the Tuscan hills is thrown on his front by an odd supernatural force which 'panics' his family. This epiphany transforms Eustace into an anarchic free-spirit who proceeds to run wildly after goats and other farmyard creatures. He is last seen one moonlit night, jumping over the garden wall accompanied by Gennaro, a local peasant boy, the apparent source of the supernatural disruption, who is depicted suggestively as Pan incarnate.

Citing this tale in their 'Introduction' to their recent collection of essays on *Queer Forster*, Robert Martin and George Piggford note its reliance upon two connotations of 'panic'. On the one hand as 'Pan-ic' generated by 'Eustace's apparent fear, which becomes his triumphant loss of identity in his metamorphosis, and the more conventional form felt by the proper English for whom decorum, like identity, must be maintained at any price, on the other hand Pan 'also points to the Pan-sexuality that Eustace adopts, discovering polymorphous pleasure that can communicate at least the suggestion of bestiality' (Martin and Piggford 1997: 4–5). In a telling illustration of the intentional fallacy, in the 1920s Forster admitted in a paper read to his Bloomsbury intimates that back in 1906 he had been unconscious that 'The Story of a Panic' was basically about 'buggery' until, upon publication, Charles Sayle, the Cambridge librarian, blurted this interpretation out to Maynard Keynes at a party (Furbank 1977–8: 113). It was this maturer Forster who, by 1926, is wanting to 'out' what he could now read as the 'homosex[ual]' subtexts of fellow neo-pantheists. Forster might now be charged with setting boundaries to a queerness which, as Martin and Piggford suggest, insists 'on the peculiarities of passion [and] a constantly baffling eros that can strike at any moment, touching anyone, and that is not gentle and loving but powerful and disruptive' (Martin and Piggford 1997: 4), but at the time Forster wanted to liberate homophile writing from a self-oppressively tragic or satanically phobic strait-jacket.

## Garden gods to gamekeepers

Forster had gained some self-confidence in part through his personal contact with the a 'back-to-nature' cultist Edward Carpenter (1844–1929), a poet, romantic socialist and homosexual polemicist who worshipped a very different type of 'Garden God' to the largely bloodless beings who were the obsession of Reid (Tsuzuki 1980). *Maurice* was famously inspired by Forster's personal contact with Carpenter; or more precisely with the latter's working-class lover, George Merrill. In the revealing 'Terminal Note' of 1960, Forster recorded how he had originally been inspired to write *Maurice* by a touch 'just above the buttocks' from Merrill when a guest at their Ruskin-inspired, socially experimental market-garden at Millthorpe near Sheffield (Forster 1971: 'Terminal Note'; Fletcher 1992). In particular, Forster notes that the character of the fictional gamekeeper Alec Scudder 'starts as an emanation from Milthorpe [*sic*], he is the touch on the backside'. In the same place he winsomely recollects how Carpenter had hoped for 'the generous recognition of an emotion and the reintegration of something primitive into the common stock' (Forster 1971: 221).

For all its surface naturalism *Maurice* has its poetic roots in a queer neo-pagan, primitivist mythos. The gamekeeper, Alec Scudder, responds to Maurice's invocation at the bedroom window by appearing as if by magic, Pan-like, out of the night-woods. Forster's fictions put social flesh onto the neo-pagan dreams of his contemporaries as garden gods turn into gamekeepers and 'nonedescripts' into garden boys:

> Where all is obscure and unrealised the best similitude is a dream. Maurice had two dreams at school; they will interpret him. In the first dream he felt very cross. He was playing football against a nonedescript whose existence he resented. He made an effort and the nonedescript turned into George, the garden boy.
> (Forster 1971: 25–6)

He later emphasized that a happy ending had been 'imperative': 'I was determined that in fiction anyway two men should fall in love and remain in it for ever and ever that fiction allows, and in this sense Maurice and Alec still roam the greenwood.' This must be read against the tragic tone of late-Victorian homophile romance (Woods 1998: chapter 18).

Historically, as Robert Martin has argued, *Maurice* is better read as being not so much 'a plea for homosexuality but rather a dramatised conflict between competing models of same-sex desire' (Martin and Piggford 1997: 6). The novel is positioned between two contemporary discourses concerning sexual identity which Martin associates with Symonds and Carpenter; the one idealist, Platonic and elitist (Clive), the other romantic, socialist and feminist (Alec). This is also registered as the inadequacy of a chaste, academic, pastoral mythos (Clive's uninspired trip to Greece), and the embracing of Carpenter's vision of an English pastoral modelled upon the homoeroticized backwoods landscape evoked in Whitman's 'Calamus' poems. Eve Sedgwick in particular has articulated Carpenter's crucial role as a translator of

Whitman's 'manly love' of yankee roughs into a more class-marked, English-socialist ethos (Sedgwick [1985] 1992: Coda). Thus in Carpenter's influential long poem *Towards Democracy* (1881; expanded until 1905), written in imitation of Whitman's *Leaves of Grass* (1852, and expanded), he sings a "Hymn to Pan", invoking 'Democracy' to arrive for 'the shame-less lusty unpresentable pal', who is equated with a homoerotic goat-god, alongside celebrating 'the gloried face of him I love: the long days out alone together in the woods, the nights superb of comradeship and love' (Canto XIII).

Forster subscribed to this liberal investment in the socially healing value of contact with the rural rough's purportedly untamed, elemental virility, which offered the effeminized intellectual an antidote to febrility and mechanization. But he remained anxious about the sustainability of such attachments, suppressing an epilogue to *Maurice* depicting an encounter with 'two woodcutters some years later' which 'gave universal dissatisfaction'. His associate Lytton Strachey (the model for the Wildean Risley), 'said that the relationship of the two rested upon curiosity and lust and would not last six weeks' (Forster 1971: 219; Furbank 1977–8, II: 15). In practice such relationships took various forms – prostitution, educative mentorship, companionable employment, domestic 'marriage' – and involved complex negotiations around inherent disparities of economic and social power. Certainly the roughs were by definition cast in the role of muse, represented objects of desire, rarely as representing subjects. Such aestheticism risked reducing the rural labourer to a mere body of honed muscle; a noble savage or elemental transhistorical force, without subjective depth or genuine social context (Williams [1973] 1993: 252).

The appropriation of manliness by this generation of homosexuals was largely class-bound, as middle-class Englishmen, already predisposed to distance themselves from an effete leisure-class, supported a virilizing counter-discourse to the morbid model of the 'Invert' as an *effeminatus* (Sinfield 1994: chapter 6; Bristow 1995: *passim*). As Sinfield summarizes, 'in this [manly] model neither partner is to be effeminate; in fact, it seems to be to eliminate everything to do with women' (Sinfield 1994: 111). Although Whitman and Carpenter both gesture towards 'Democracy' arriving for women (the latter in particular actively supported women's suffrage), their primary concern is with the recovery of an Ur-masculinity. Their masculine, backwoods landscapes contrast not so much with urban public space – which is maligned – but more tellingly with a claustrophobic domestic space of a demonized, oppressive middle-class femininity, reinforcing Victorian orthodoxies of 'masculine' and 'feminine' spheres. But such Lawrentian links between hypervirility and a native ruralism can easily lead to a disturbingly masculinist supremacism, as witnessed in the Nazi 'Volk cult' in which a worship of the heroic body of the male labourer harnessed to a right-wing 'Back-to-the-Land' nationalist polemic remained catastrophically wedded to some incipient Darwinian and eugenicist agendas (Mosse 1985: chapter 3; Steakley [1975] 1993).

## Other countries: pastoral dreams and lonely bars

Pastoral authenticates an apparently purer homosexuality in later novels which no longer tried to sustain homosexual chastity. Anxieties regarding manliness dominated post-war American fiction, and Gore Vidal's *The City and the Pillar* (1948), now reprinted as 'America's first serious homosexual novel', strongly reifies familiar dichotomies between rural manliness and a relentlessly demonized, abject metropolitan, sea-board effete queerness. The mawkish romanticism of Vidal's pessimistic tale of migration to the city as a falling away from an Eden-like, pastoral scene of same-sex bonding into betrayal and self-hatred belongs to a particularly homophobic post-war climate. But its specific pastoral setting seems subtly predictive: a derelict river-hut once occupied by an ex-slave which, in contrast with Forster's private boathouse, hints at parallels with another specific history of oppression with which a subsequent, predominantly white, North American gay-lib movement was soon to make productive, if problematic, identifications.

The pastoral lovers, the athletic Bob Ford and clean-cut Jim Willard, are near-social equals, boys-next-door in a small Virginia town. After Bob's high-school graduation, on the eve of his departure to the navy in search of sexually accessible girls, they take a final camping trip on the wildwood banks of the Potomac where they discuss their dreams for the future and eventually indulge in some manly love-making (it starts as wrestling). In a direct reversal of *Maurice*, this pastoral romance comes very early in a circular narrative, providing the naively besotted Jim with an authenticating, emotional reference point; a sustaining romantic dream throughout his subsequent, unsuccessful quest for Bob which takes him away from his Virginia roots. After a spell in the Navy, Jim drifts into alienating metropolitan subcultures, initially as a mercenary kept-houseboy to a Hollywood actor and subsequently amongst 'queer' artist-intellectuals in New York. In these coastal enclaves Jim is 'repelled by the queens'. As Dollimore has usefully theorized, such scenes of 'internal discrimination', in which 'camp becomes a quintessential expression of an alienated inauthenticity', are common in mid-century novels.[4] If Vidal's aim was to show that even all-American boys can be queers, or that, for Bob at least, homosexuality is an act rather than a subjecthood, he does so at the expense of reinforcing effemaphobia.

But, in contrast to *Maurice*'s open-ended fantasy of greenwood romance, Vidal's novel ultimately fractures any self-delusive dreams of a place beyond the reach of social catagorization, closing with Jim's failed attempt at returning home to re-live his pastoral romance with the now married Bob. After a subsequent failed reunion in New York, Jim makes a final move on Bob in their shared hotel bed but is met with rejection: 'Let go of me, you queer.' Enraged, he beats-up and rapes Bob: '[Jim] left the hotel, not caring where he went. For a long time he walked aimlessly, until at last he came to one of the many bars where men looked for men. He entered, prepared to drink until the dream was completely over' (Vidal [1948]

1994: 183). Jim's final, violent acceptance of his own queerness is presented as some sort of defeat; a defeat measured through the loss of pastoral dream-romance, since, in this circular plot, the closing scene provides the explanation for the opening chapter depicting a dejected Jim getting drunk in a queer bar. In the closing paragraph, he draws rivers and islands on a wet bar-table:

> He wondered for a moment where he was. He looked about him but there were no clues, only a bar in a city. What City? ... But the top of the table was no longer home. ... Rivers, lakes, islands were unfamiliar; he was lost in a new country. There was nothing for him to do except turn his attention to the other people in the barroom. Now that he had lost his private world, he wanted to see what, if anything, the others had found.
> (Vidal [1948] 1994: 213–14)

Not untypically, here pastoral idealism represents and sustains a private, unselfconscious, non-socially identified and manly notion of homosexuality against which subculturally socialized, gender-trangressive, metropolitan identities are found wanting. This polarization productively brings us full-circle to the related but structurally reversed juxtapositioning of the gay scene and pastoral in *Beautiful Thing*.

## Queer pastoral/gay heritage

Historically, *Beautiful Thing* belongs as far forward of the political watershed of Stonewall as Vidal's novel lies behind it, but it is perhaps the intervening trauma of AIDS which has encouraged a deep thread of pastoral nostalgia within an Anglo-American 'gay heritage' culture industry as it has emerged over the last fifteeen years. In my opening account of *Beautiful Thing* I refrained from noting that both the pastoral sequence and the scene in 'The Gloucester' were both added in the filming: in the play-script the action is restricted to the balcony and Jamie's bedroom. This intrusion of a pastoral *mise-en-scène* surely owes something to Merchant-Ivory's 1987 film adaptation of Forster's quintessentially English Edwardian homosexual pastoral romance *Maurice*, and that other, equally nostalgic stage-to-film adaptation, Marek Kanievska's *Another Country* (1984). Released at the height of the wave of homophobia intially generated by the AIDS crisis, Merchant-Ivory's adaptation of *Maurice* in particular seemed to appeal to liberal audiences, offering a melodramatic fantasy of eventually finding 'true', as in one-to-one, romance in a socially less complicated age. Ironically, back in 1960 Forster already feared that *Maurice* was dated. Whilst he would not go so far as to agree with a 'friend who said it *only* had a period interest', the elderly novelist thought that his manuscript was already bathed in the deep glow of nostalgic regret for 'an England where it was still possible to get lost':

> It belongs to the last moment of the Greenwood ... Our Greenwood ended catastrophically and inevitably. Two great wars demanded and bequeathed regimentation ... science lent her aid, and the wildness of our island, never extensive, was stamped upon and built over and patrolled in time. There is no forest or fell landscape to escape to today [ ... ] no deserted valley for those who wish neither to reform nor corrupt society but be left alone. People do still escape, one can see them any night at it in the films. But they are gangsters not outlaws, they can dodge civilisation because they are part of it.
>
> (Forster 1971: 221)

This liberal humanist lament for a beleaguered authenticity threatened by modern conformities has been sounded again and again (Williams terms it a 'backwards escalator' effect), and had already been fully recycled when Forster joined the reactionary chorus. Ironically, by the 1980s many not-so-vulgar cinema audiences on both sides of the Atlantic where eagerly consuming carefully a crafted version of a 'civilized' pre-First World War England of athletic public-school boys, ancient quads, strawberries and cream, and 'timeless' village greens in Merchant-Ivory's 'Forster Cycle'. As Finch and Kwietniowski remark, when suitably distanced within this nostalgic vision of a still imperial England, homosexuality could also become 'Heritage', 'like a rather ungainly grand piano around which character actors and vintage cars would gather' (Finch and Kwietniowski 1988: 73). The distribution poster for *Maurice* was a still of Maurice (James Wilby) and Clive (Hugh Grant) lying in a chaste embrace in a field.

Whilst affecting, *Maurice* came late in the Forster cycle, its release coinciding with Thatcher's homophobic legislation, 'Clause 28', which continues to inhibit British teachers from providing social support and essential health-care education to the likes of Ste and Jamie. In a note on the play-script of *Beautiful Thing*, Jonathan Harvey remarks that 'the age of consent is an issue close to my heart', one instrumental in his writing a play about teenage gay-love. Just as tellingly in the present context, he was also conscious of class. With this 1980s heritage film-cycle in mind, he writes,

> Growing up gay in Liverpool in the eighties, the only role models I had on T.V. and film were very middle or upper class ones. Two public schoolboys punting through Cambridge in cricket whites might have been exciting to watch, but it had very little to do with my personal experience. I suppose I wanted to redress this imbalance. I also wanted to redress the idea that if you are working class and gay that you end up getting kicked out onto the streets and sell your body for two Woodbines and a bar of Caramac.
>
> (Harvey 1994: 210)

The film-adaptation of *Beautiful Thing* suggests, therefore, a perhaps deliberate attempt to produce an innovative *déclassé*, suburban homoerotic gay pastoral for 1990s England. It is notable that both play and film end, not with the lads lost in a wood but with Sandra accepting Ste in a reconfigured post-nuclear family which replaces the greenwood as the sustaining place for same-sex love. But the urban gay-scene also has a role to play when at the close of the play/film Sandra agrees to go out with the boys to see a male stripper: now you go to the gay-pub with your real mum (not a drag-substitute?).[5] In the play, as they wait for her on the balcony, Jamie and Ste start to dance together having ensured that Ste's dad and brother are not at home. The *film* ends with the pleasantly Utopian image of Ste and Jamie dancing more openly in each other's arms, in the sunshine, in the public space between the blocks of flats where they are joined by Jamie's mother and Leah who has come out as a lesbian.

'Queer space is virtual space', suggests Jean-Ulrick Desert (Ingram *et al.* 1997: 105). Wondering whether 'such identified space explicitly exists', he asks rhetorically 'is such space preconceived and designed?' and, questioning the notion of a coherent gay or queer 'culture', he adds, 'is it really a cultured space?' '"Culture" as it is reinvented today', he adds, 'may indeed be a garden path to a virtual utopia, an escape from a dominant culture that benefits from a minorities' self-imposed exile.' This apt controlling metaphor reminds us of the sometimes regressive meanings of queer pastoral. If we are to celebrate a homosexual pastoral tradition we need to be alert to how, in uncritically invoking past representations, we also run the risk of remaining trapped within other repressive technologies of privilege, privatization and exclusion.

## Notes

1  A British retail-chain for maternity products.
2  *Valmouth*'s satire on this particular inter-class miscegenation, familiar from D.H. Lawrence's *Lady Chatterley's Lover*, can be traced to Firbank's apprenticeship tale, 'Lady Appledore's Mésalliance: an Artificial Pastoral' (Firbank 1991), in which the eponymous heroine falls in love with her young cousin Wildred, who, strapped for cash, has posed as a gardener at her country house and rescued her orchids from wilt!
3  Thoreau, famed for his solitary hut-life by Walden Pond (1845–7), had lived very briefly with his Harvard friend Charles Stearns Wheeler in a small hut near Flint's Pond, Lincoln, New Hampshire, in what Jonathan Katz implies may have been an attempt to live out this homophile pastoral dream of a community of loving friendship (Katz [1976] 1992: 481f.).
4  He cites Radclyffe Hall's *The Well of Loneliness* (1928), James Baldwin's *Giovanni's Room* (1956), and Angus Wilson's H*emlock and After* (1952) (Dollimore 1991: 55–8). I would add Mary Renault's *The Charioteer* (1953); also in Baldwin's *Another Country* (1962), the most romantic relationship is notably a gay pastoral interlude set, at a distance from the queer bars of New York, in France.
5  The potentially threatening – at least for the socially uncertain – depiction of the gay-pub in the film only has justification in one line in the play-text from a later, rather witty exchange

when Ste is very upset because Jamie has come-out to his own mother and fearing that she will tell his father (Act II, scene ii): when Sandra mentions that 'you found the Gloucester', and tries to reassure Ste that he will find other places were people will not want to 'kill' him, he petulantly replies 'I hate it' (Harvey 1994: 204).

## References

Aldrich, Robert (1993) *The Seduction of the Mediterranean: Writing, Art and Homosexual Fantasy*, London and New York: Routledge.

Bell, David and Valentine, Gill (1995) 'Queer Country: Rural Lesbian and Gay Lives', *Journal of Rural Studies* 11: 113–22.

Benjamin, Walter ([1936] 1973) 'The Paris of the Second Empire', in *Charles Baudelaire: a Lyric Poet in the Era of High Capitalism*, trans. by Harry Zohn, London: NLB.

Bristow, Joseph (1995) *Effeminate England: Homoerotic Writing after 1885*, Buckingham: Open University Press.

Chedgzoy, Kate (1995) *Shakespeare's Queer Children: Sexual Politics and Contemporary Culture*, Manchester: Manchester University Press.

Cheney, Joyce (1985) *Lesbian Land*, Minneapolis: Word Weavers.

Cooper, Emmanuel (1994) *The Sexual Perspective: Homosexuality and Art in the Last 10 Years in the West*, London and New York: Routledge.

Dellamora, Richard (1990) *Masculine Desire: The Sexual Politics of Victorian Aestheticism*, Chapel Hill and London: University of North Carolina Press.

Dollimore, Jonathan (1991) *Sexual Dissidence: Augustine to Wilde, Freud to Foucault*, Oxford: Clarendon Press.

Donoghue, Emma (1993) *Passions Between Women: British Lesbian Culture 1668–1801*, London: Scarlet Press.

Dowling, Linda (1994) *Hellenism and Homosexuality in Victorian Oxford*, Ithaca and London: Cornell University Press.

Empson, William (1935, and reprinted) *Some Versions of Pastoral*, London.

Finch, Mark and Kwietniowski, Richard (1988) 'Melodrama and "Maurice": Homo is where the Het is', in *Screen* 29: 3: 72-80.

Firbank, Ronald (n.d.) *Valmouth and other Novels*, Harmondsworth: Penguin.

Firbank, Ronald (1991) *The Early Firbank*, edited by Steven Moore, London and New York: Quartet Books.

Fletcher, John (1992) 'Forster's Self-erasure: "Maurice" and the Scene of Masculine Love', in Joseph Bristow (ed.) *Sexual Sameness: Textual Differences in Lesbian and Gay Writing*, London and New York: Routledge.

Fone, Byrne R.S. (1983) 'This Other Eden: Arcadia and the Homosexual Imagination', in Stuart Kellog (ed.) *Literary Visions of Homosexuality*, New York: The Haworth Press: 13–34 (also printed in *The Journal of Homosexuality* 8 (3/4) Spring–Summer 1983).

Forster, E.M. (1948) *Collected Short Stories*, London: Sidgwick and Jackson.

Forster, E.M. (1971) *Maurice*, Harmondsworth: Penguin.

Forster, E.M. (1985) *Commonplace Book*, edited by Philip Gardiner, Stanford: Stanford University Press.

Furbank, P.N. (1977–8) (vol. 1) *E.M. Forster: a Life*, Oxford: Oxford University Press.
Gide, André ([1920] 1952) *Corydon: Four Socratic Dialogues*, London: Secker & Warburg.
Grosskurth, Phyllis (1964) *John Addington Symonds: a Biography*, London: Longmans.
Grosskurth, Phyllis (ed.) (1984) *The Memoirs of John Addington Symonds: the Secret Life of a Leading Nineteenth-Century Man of Letters*, London and New York: Huchinson and Random House.
Halperin, David M. (1983) *Before Pastoral: Theocritus and the Ancient Tradition of Bucolic Poetry*, New Haven and London: Yale University Press.
Harvey, Jonathan (1994) *Beautiful Thing*, in Michael Wilcox (ed.) *Gay Plays 5*, London: Methuen.
Hoare, Philip (1997) *Wilde's Last Stand: Decadence, Conspiracy & the First World War*, London: Duckworth.
Ingram, G.B., Bouthillette, A.-M. and Retter, Y. (eds) (1997) *Queers in Space: Communities|Public Places|Sites of Resistance*, Seattle: Bay Press.
Katz, Jonathan Ned ([1976] 1992) *Gay American History: Lesbians and Gay Men in the U.S.A.*, New York: Crowell.
Martin, Robert K. and Piggford, George (eds) (1997) *Queer Forster*, Chicago and London: University of Chicago Press.
Mosse, George L. (1985) *Nationalism and Sexuality: Middle-Class Morality and Sexual Norms in Modern Europe*, Wisconsin: University of Wisconsin Press.
Norton, Rictor ([1974] 1997) 'The Pastoral Homosexual Tradition', essay available on the World Wide Web at www.infopt.demon.lit.text.co.uk
Oosterhuis, Harry and Kennedy, Hubert (1991) *Homosexuality and Male Bonding in pre-Nazi Germany* (for *Der Eigene*), Binghamton, N.Y.: Harrington Park Press.
Reid, Forrest ([1905] 1986) *The Garden God: a Tale of Two Boys*, London: Brilliance Books.
Renault, Mary ([1953] 1959) *The Charioteer*, London: Four Square.
Rich, Adrienne ([1980] 1993) 'Compulsory Heterosexuality and Lesbian Existence', in Abelove, Borde and Halperin, David M. (eds) *The Lesbian and Gay Studies Reader*, London and New York: Routledge: 227–54.
Sedgwick, Eve Kosofsky ([1985] 1992) *Between Men: English Literature and Male Homosocial Desire*, New York: Columbia University Press.
Sinfield, Alan (1994) *The Wilde Century*, London: Cassell.
Sinfield, Alan (1998) *Gay and After*, London: Serpent's Tale.
Sontag, Susan (1966) 'Notes on "Camp"' in *Against Interpretation and other Essays*, New York and London: Farrar, Strauss & Gironx.
Steakley, James D. ([1975] 1993) *The Homosexual Emancipation Movement in Germany*, Salem, N.H.: Ayer Company Publishers, Inc.
Tsuzuki, Chushichi (1980) *Edward Carpenter 1844–1929: Prophet of Human Fellowship*, Cambridge: Cambridge University Press.
Vidal, Gore ([1948] 1994) *The City and the Pillar*, London: Abacus Books.
Weeks, Jeffrey (1981) *Sex, Politics and Society: the Regulation of Sexuality Since 1800*, London: Longman.
Weeks, Jeffrey (1985) *Against Nature: Essays on History, Sexuality and Identity*, London: Rivers Oram Press.

Williams, Raymond ([1973] 1993) *The Country and the City*, London: The Hogarth Press.

Wilde, Oscar (1891) 'The Decay of Lying', in *Intentions*, London and Leipzig: Heinemann and Balestier: 3–45.

Wilde, Oscar (?) (and others) ([1893] 1985) *Teleny: or the Reverse of the Medal*, London: Gay Men's Press.

Woods, Gregory (1998) *A History of Gay Literature: the Male Tradition*, New Haven, Conn. and London: Yale University Press.

# 8

# SKIRTING THE MARGINS

Anne Lister, self-representation and lesbian identity in early nineteenth-century Yorkshire

*Anira Rowanchild*

Lesbian history has characteristically been represented as one of silence, discontinuity and absence. This chapter examines the significance of a study of Anne Lister, an early nineteenth-century Yorkshire woman, in articulating aspects of that elusive history. In 1975, Adrienne Rich drew attention to the 'silence and lies' by which 'women's love for women' has been suppressed (Rich 1980: 190). Recent lesbian scholarship has gone a long way towards revealing some of those hidden connections and secrets. Lillian Faderman transformed notions of romantic friendship in her 1981 survey of love between women, *Surpassing the Love of Men*, arguing that the eighteenth-century fashion 'dictated that women may fall in love with each other' (Faderman 1991: 74). She concluded, however, that 'most love relationships between women during previous eras ... were less physical than they are in our times' (Faderman 1991: 19). She had not had the benefit of reading the first published transcription of Anne Lister's coded diary, Helena Whitbread's, *I Know My Own Heart* (1988), which Emma Donoghue, Ros Ballaster and Martha Vicinus draw on in their later studies. In *Passions Between Women* (1993), Donoghue notes an occasional tendency among historians of lesbian history to mythologize and thus perhaps reinforce the silence identified by Rich (Donoghue 1993: 3), while Ballaster suggests that Lister's 'understanding of her own lesbian sexuality ... indicates a continuing "underground" tradition for women who desired other women' (Ballaster 1995: 28). Martha Vicinus, observing that 'conceptual confusion is perhaps inevitable in regard to lesbians, given the historical suppression of female sexuality in general', echoes Rich's earlier warning that lesbian history consists largely of 'nuances, masks, secrecy, and the unspoken' (Vicinus 1996: 235).

What is most remarkable about Anne Lister, according to Jill Liddington, who has carefully researched her life and times, is that she 'lived her life on the sexual margins, yet largely managed to retain her social respectability within the heart of Halifax Tory-Anglican gentry' (Liddington 1998: xviii). In this chapter, I examine Lister's negotiations to maintain that delicate balance. I shall also address the problematic question of the existence in Lister's time of a discourse encompassing woman-to-woman sexual relations. Evidence from Lister's diary and letters can, I believe, help to dispel and displace some of the myths and silences surrounding the presentation of and discourse on lesbian identity in the early nineteenth century.

My primary area of interest, however, is one raised by other chapters in this volume. How does a rural location (albeit an early nineteenth-century one) impact on the presentation and performance of lesbian identity? Paul Cloke and Jo Little have remarked on 'the devices of exclusion and marginalization by which mainstream "self" serves to "other" the positioning of all kinds of people in socio-spatial relations of different countrysides' (Cloke and Little 1997: 1). The understandable concentration of many commentators on locating Lister's lesbian identity within her literary production has often obscured those socio-spatial relations, but, as Jill Liddington has argued, Lister's diary 'overflows the neat categories convenient to historians' (Liddington 1994: 9). Liddington has herself addressed the complexities and contradictions of Lister's social and sexual affiliations. Here I try to extend the available categories by situating the development of Lister's lesbian identity within the geographical, political and economic context of the early nineteenth-century West Riding.

## Whipped every day

Anne Lister was born in a small village in the East Riding of Yorkshire in 1791 into a family of poor gentry. Her father was a gambler; her mother, according to Lister's diary and correspondence, was an alcoholic. Her three brothers died young, leaving Lister and her younger sister as survivors of a family in social decline. Her early childhood was wild and unmanaged, 'a great pickle', as she called it (Whitbread 1988: 2). At 7 years old she was expelled from her dame school in Ripon, where she later recalled being 'whipped every day', but in 1805 she was sent to a smart girls' boarding-school in York for two years (Whitbread 1988: 227). This proved to be a turning point in her life for there she mixed with girls from wealthy and aristocratic family backgrounds, began to explore her sexual and emotional attachment to her own sex, and to write a diary that eventually extended to approximately four million words, of which around a sixth are in code, explicitly documenting the conduct of her life, the progress of her social ambitions, and her desire for women. In 1815, she moved away from her parents to live permanently with an unmarried uncle and his sister at Shibden Hall, a large country estate on a hill a mile or so above Halifax, West Yorkshire, which she inherited on his death in 1826. She died in 1840 of a fever contracted while travelling in Russia.

Lister's diary and letters declare the existence of sexual activity, relationships, and networks between women that challenge assumptions about both the isolation of romantic friendship in the early nineteenth century, typified by Elizabeth Mavor's study of Eleanor Ponsonby and Sarah Butler, the Ladies of Llangollen (1971), and the metropolitan stereotype of swashbuckling sapphism epitomized by the character of Mrs Harriot Freke in Maria Edgeworth's novel, *Belinda* (1801). Her inheritance of Shibden Hall established Lister within her desired class, offering her the economic and social power of the minor landed gentry, while allowing her a privileged space in which to explore her lesbian identity. Her diary and its elaborate code, I propose, were vital to the maintenance of both her sexuality and her social position. Her 'crypt-hand' was based on the Greek alphabet, but later incorporated other idiosyncratic symbols (Whitbread 1988: 142). Its ostensible purpose was to conceal intimate diary entries, but although unlike many early nineteenth-century diaries, Dorothy Wordsworth's or Fanny Burney's, for example, Lister's journal was a private rather than a family document, she gave out copies of the key to the code to lovers, thus allowing the possibility of a readership. In her physical environment at Shibden Hall, Lister created secret places parallel to those provided by her diary. The grounds of the hall were surrounded by walls within which Lister laid winding paths and built a little rustic hut. Only those invited entered the grounds or house at Shibden, and Lister policed the wider estate, personally supervising agricultural operations, and any alterations to cottages or field boundaries. I shall later explore the part these textual and physical productions played in the reconciliations and mediations Anne Lister employed in order to reconcile her marginal sexual identity with her central social position.

Halifax was described in Defoe's *A Tour through the Whole Island of Great Britain 1724–6* as 'healthy as any part of England' being provided 'by the bounty of nature' with the means of full employment, 'I mean coals and running water' (Clayre 1977: 1–3). Its reputation was constructed then on the idea of the cultivation of natural abundance. The town doubled in population during Lister's lifetime, and its manufacturing industries grew immensely. Like many local landowners, Lister was not involved in the textile manufactures, but a good deal of her income was derived from the extractive and transport industries, coal-mining and stone quarrying, for example, that supported the mills and factories, and from land leased or sold for use by industry. However, she saw herself and her life as rooted in the traditions of the rural gentry. Indeed, as a child she prepared herself for the life she subsequently led by reading books on agricultural practices, studying accounting and following her uncle's guidance on matters of estate management. In a letter written to her Shibden aunt when she was 12, she describes herself as 'always fond of farming & I think I have a little taste that way' (Green 1992: 28). The rural West Riding of Yorkshire supported several houses of the minor gentry and the great estates of absentee aristocrat landlords like Earl Fitzwilliam and Lord Wharncliffe. Lister subscribed vigorously to the proprietorial traditions of her class. For example, she referred to her tenants and servants as 'my' people (Liddington 1994: 40). Over her people, Lister had the power to hire and fire and she would ruthlessly dismiss servants for minor offences and evict tenants as she pleased. After the 1832 Reform Act, she could call on the political allegiance of over fifty enfranchised male tenants, and she relates a firm '1/4 of an hour's talk' she had to have with a tenant who showed an inclination to vote against the Tory candidate (Liddington 1994: 39). While Lister was happy to reap the profits of local industrialization, the idea of the countryside as a place given in trust to the ancient families was strong in her. She wrote to her brother in 1813, shortly before he died, using the language and imagery of the caring cultivator to evoke her fervour for the traditional values of the rural gentry: 'You my dear Sam, are the last remaining hope and stay of an old, but lately drooping family. Seize it in its fall. Renovate its languid energies; rear it with a tender hand, and let it once more bloom upon the spray' (Green 1992: 38).

As I shall show, the wildness of the surrounding moorland appealed to Lister's erotic imagination and featured in her flirtations and fantasies, while in her fashionable garden and landscaping schemes she tried to combine cultivation with isolation or retreat. Her gender might have been expected to compromise her active participation in the rural economy, for by the 1830s 'the negative effects on women who openly operated in the market' of 'the construction of domestic ideology and the lure of new patterns of consumption' were beginning to be felt (Davidoff and Hall 1994: 272). Lister was fortunate in that there were a number of other independent unmarried women landowners in the particular locality, including Caroline Walker of Walterclough Hall and Elizabeth Wadsworth of Holdsworth House, who had both attended the same school as Lister in York. They, like Lister, engaged in occupations that crossed gender boundaries, estate management and supervision of agricultural activities, for example. In addition, there were networks of culturally and socially active women in the environs of Halifax, formally instituted in Female Friendly Societies, or more often informally through acquaintance and interest. Lister profited both from the relative flexibility of social discourse in relation to class and gender in this rapidly expanding provincial town, and from the status gained from her membership of an old country family. All these important aspects of Lister's biography, wealth, family, political and economic power, an interest in contemporary fashions, and a vast middle-class and aristocratic acquaintance, gave her a central role in the locality.

Lister's sexual identity, however, distinguished her as in some respects marginal. During her time at the York school, she began to examine her sexual nature, concluding that she 'love[d] and only love[d] the fairer sex and thus, beloved by them in turn, my heart revolts from any other love than theirs' (Whitbread 1988:145). Several of her fellow pupils became her lovers. One, Eliza Raine, was most useful in providing Anne with an entrée into York society, and into aristocratic circles, through her cousin, Lady Crawford. Very early on, then, Lister's lesbian affairs were entangled with her desire to raise her social standing above the sunken fortunes of her parents. Lister had no independent fortune of her own at this time and her attachment to her well-off women lovers was, and remained, both amorous and financial, as her diary amply demonstrates. Despite her power as a landowner, she was, as I shall discuss, subject to harassment and hostility as a result of her sexual identity.

## Too fond of women

Lesbian identity as a conceptual possibility in earlier centuries has been problematized notably by Michel Foucault's famous declaration that

> we must not forget that the psychological, psychiatric, medical category of homosexuality was constituted from the moment it was characterized – [Carl] Westphal's famous article of 1870 [*Archiv für Neurologie*] on 'contrary sexual sensations' can stand as its date of birth – less by a type of sexual relations than by a certain quality of sexual sensibility.
> 
> (Foucault 1990: 43)

However, the apparent absence of discourse on lesbian sexual experience and identity in the early nineteenth century is belied by Lister's diary. Lister not only recorded her intimate sexual activity, but also explored and interpreted her sexual feelings and actions and their origins, concluding at one point that, 'my conduct & feelings [are] natural to me inasmuch as they were not taught, not fictitious, but instinctive … I had met with those who could feel in unison with me' (Whitbread 1988: 297). In her 1824 diary she relates a conversation that clearly indicates shared assumptions about a condition of being 'too fond of women':

> [Mrs Barlow] began talking *of that* one of the things of which Marie Antoinette was accused of was being too fond of women. I, with perfect mastery of countenance, said I had never heard of it before and could not understand or believe it … I said I believed that when reduced to the last extremity – I was going to mention the use of phalli but luckily Mrs Barlow [interrupted] … I said I had read of women being too fond of each other in the Latin parts of the works of Sir William Jones.
> 
> (Whitbread 1992: 32)

Lister's attempt to disguise knowledge of the condition of being 'too fond of women' acknowledges the dangers of an open declaration of such experience. Her humorous reference to the 'use of phalli' overturns what Terry Castle has called 'the kind of depressingly chaste female–female bonding' emblematized by the Ladies of Llangollen (Castle 1993: 93). Lister was herself doubtful of the Ladies' vaunted celibacy, remarking after visiting them, 'I hesitate to pronounce such attachments uncemented by something more tender still than friendship' (Whitbread 1988: 210).

Ros Ballaster has described the disappointments experienced by contemporary lesbians and feminists when heroines like Ponsonby and Butler, and Anne Lister, are 'revealed to have espoused far from progressive politics in other aspects of their lives' (Ballaster 1995: 16). The Ladies of Llangollen consciously contrived the image of simple pastoral seclusion in their Welsh cottage, and while Lister made no attempt at an appearance of artlessness, she was unambiguous about her role as Tory country landowner. But a carefully cultivated central social role and deep conservatism did not always protect these women from inimical attentions directed at their sexuality. Indeed, Castle attributes the popular conception of the Ladies' relationship as purely platonic to a 'back-and-fill operation' they conducted in order to disguise the true nature of their relationship which had been the subject of a prurient newspaper article (Castle 1993: 106).

Lister too was not safe from verbal or even physical abuse. On 28 June 1818, for instance, she was accosted on her walk home from Halifax by some passers-by, identified as townsfolk in her diary by the term, 'the people' (Whitbread 1988: 90). She wrote later:

> The people generally remark, as I pass along, how much I am like a man I think they did it more than usual this evening. At the top of Cunnery lane, as I went, three men said, as usual, 'That's a man' & one axed [sic] 'Does your cock stand'. I know not how it is but I feel low this evening.
> (Whitbread 1988: 48–9)

This was not a unique occurrence. Lister recorded other instances of harassment in her diary. On a visit to York, she noted that she 'preferred going alone ... tho' at this early hour (about 8), one could not walk about unobserved. Some men & woman declared I was a man' (Liddington 1994: 64). When she went to board the Whitby mail coach 'there were several bad women standing about ... They would have it that I was a man & one of them gave me a familiar knock on the left breast & would have persisted in following me but for James [the footman]' (Whitbread 1988: 65). She did not always have the energy to respond as assertively as on the occasion when 'a tipsyish-looking young man' accosted her on her way into town. She wrote, 'fancying I was going to strike him with my umbrella, ... [he] stepped back, saying, "If you do, I'll drop you"'. Lister boldly replied, '"I should like to see you"' (Whitbread 1988: 50). The landowning class still had considerable local influence, but Lister did not have the seigniorial relations with the mill and factory workers that she had with the cottagers and farm hands on her estate, and these hostile responses reveal some complex negotiations of power. While they may have been defiant gestures aimed at a member of the landowning class, the language used shows that Lister is most vulnerable in relation to her female sex and her sexuality.

Lister was a woman of striking appearance. Early in life, she had vowed always to wear black, and had adopted the riding-habit favoured by the Ladies of Llangollen as her customary attire. She was an active countrywoman and spent many hours each day riding, driving or walking her estate, but this outfit, though acceptable on the farm and the hunting-field, was considered strange wear for a concert or a ball, or a walk round town. Lillian Faderman observes of this period that 'if a woman dressed like a man, it was assumed she behaved as a man sexually', but goes on to propose that the real root of the antagonism 'was not the sexual aspect of lesbianism as much as the attempted usurpation of male prerogative' (Faderman 1991: 17). However, in the privacy of her home at Shibden, Lister could wear 'my drawers put on with gentleman's braces … & my old black waistcoat & dressing-gown' with impunity (Whitbread 1988: 1). Her immediate household was fully acquainted with her sexual nature and the other occupants of the hall, relations, servants and workpeople, did not apparently hinder Lister's exercise of authority, although, as I shall shortly consider, she was not entirely freed from adverse criticism. Emma Donoghue has nominated women cross-dressers of the seventeenth and eighteenth centuries as 'female outlaws', and although Lister confined the circumstances in which she adopted overtly masculine dress to the privacy of home, these safe occasions may have allowed her, in Donoghue's words, to 'act out [her] rebellion in the tiniest details of clothes and manner as well as in the important choice of who to love' (Donoghue 1993: 103).

## Country matters and fondling circumstances

If Lister's social status as country landowner could not protect her from the openly inimical attentions of working people, the hostility she encountered from her own class was much more covert and she seemed to have the measure of it, although it cost her much diligent observation and manoeuvring. For example, in 1816, Lister heard of rumours, apparently circulated by two female acquaintances, that she was 'not fit society for young people', having been seen being too fond with one of her female friends. She defended herself vigorously in a letter to the sister of one of her accusers. She had taken great care, she wrote, to avoid being seen in any 'fondling circumstances' whatsoever, and she could call witnesses to the fact. If anyone should accuse her of lying over this matter they should remember that 'Want of candour is not a trait which peculiarly marks my disposition – My head may be in fault often – I pray to God my heart never' (SH: 7/ML/76/2). This is an interesting defence, for Lister assumes the moral high ground in the letter, rebuking its recipient for any latent mistrust. She does not deny 'the fondling circumstances', but rather that she has not been seen in such circumstances. This was the year after she took up residence at Shibden and Lister's prospects of wealth, and position may have aided her cause. Indeed, as Lister consolidated her social status, she came to expect genteel society to acknowledge her unconventional lifestyle. The culmination of this came in 1832, when she at last found her ideal life-companion. Lister was 41 when she successfully wooed Anne Walker, a wealthy young heiress from an estate adjacent to Shibden. Even in love Lister observed her equal passion for rank and wealth, for during their early meetings she remarked in her diary that 'Miss W & I got on very well ... If she was fond of me & manageable, I think I could be comfortable enough with her' (Liddington 1994: 41). Already, in her fantasies, Anne Walker excited her: 'incurred a cross [orgasm] last night thinking of Miss Walker' (Liddington 1994: 41). Walker was no doubt a thrilling companion as she had the ability to fulfil Lister's most burning desires, for more money, status, companionship and sex, and Lister determined that their relationship should be treated in all respects as a marriage. Following a brief courtship, the couple lived together until Lister's death in 1840 when Walker inherited the entire Shibden Hall estate on condition that she did not subsequently marry. Had she done so her claim to the estate would 'thenceforth cease ... as if the said Anne Walker should have then departed this life' (Liddington 1994:10).

Lister was eventually so confident that the relationship was accepted by society that in 1836, when Lady Stuart of Richmond neglected to invite Walker to accompany Lister on a visit, Lister took great offence and wrote insisting that she would not stay without her partner. She received a surprisingly ingratiating reply from Lady Stuart:

> My house *is now entirely at your service* for yourself and Miss Walker ... I have had my own Bedroom pulled to piece[s] to have it *washed* & *glazed* ... [I will sleep] in the Dressing room. Your friend can occupy what was ... [my niece] *Vere's room.*
>
> (SH: 7/ML/966)

This exchange is a good example of how Lister achieved an equilibrium between central and marginal identities. Lady Stuart could certainly have damaged Lister's standing and reputation had she chosen, but Lister was intimate with Lady Stuart's niece, Vere Hobart, so could perhaps have made interesting counter revelations. Indeed, Lister was not ashamed to use her lesbian lovers to gain entry into fashionable society, and to help finance useful projects, and she engaged in many affairs and flirtations among her local female acquaintances, many of whom were wives and daughters from neighbouring estates. There was scarcely any time before 1832, when she plighted her troth to Anne Walker, that she did not have at least two serious sexual relationships and a number of casual flirtations on the go. Lister's provocative appearance and manner seemed to act like tinder on the young women living in the manors. A summary of her Christmas 1825 diary reads:

| | | |
|---|---|---|
| Christmas Eve | flirting w. | Isabella Norcliffe |
| Christmas Day | do. | Mrs Milne |
| Boxing day | do. | Miss Duffin |

(Liddington 1994: 19)

The readiness of the female population of the West Riding to get into bed with Lister is accountable, I suggest, not only to her personal charisma, but to the power acquired from her social networking and her solid, if impecunious, landowning background. Her attentions were flattering and among the rural landowners and middle-class her patronage was important to those who wished her to donate to their good causes, like the museum, the new village school, or the reading club, and to those who wished to enter into commercial partnerships with her, or to recruit her political allegiance. Although her income was not great and the expense of her ambitious house and garden improvements and her travels abroad soon outstripped her modest £1,500 a year, she had a huge network of social acquaintance, accrued through her participation in the social life of the area, and reinforced by her lesbian relationships. Her marginal desires seemed to aid her movement to the centre of society.

## The crypt-hand alphabet

An examination of Lister's use of code, what she called her 'crypt hand alphabet', in her diary illuminates the interrelationship between Lister's sexual identity and her status among the rural gentry (Whitbread 1988: 142). As she extended the scope and length of her diary, she employed the code increasingly. Its obvious presence in the text signposted to casual observer and privileged reader alike the existence of a secret, and constructed its contents as a treasure to be recovered by the knowledgeable, or lucky, seeker. This secret central core radiated its influence outwards, reaching first those privileged few, Lister's lovers, who held their own keys to the crypt hand. Next were the friends to whom she allowed glimpses through her own reading of edited extracts. Then it touched those casual social acquaintances on the fringes of Lister's attention, who learned by hearsay of the existence and contents of the diary. Finally, there were those unfortunates who suspected themselves to be the objects of Lister's opprobrium and lived on the outer circle in fear of disclosure. The diary's time-consuming place in her daily schedule must have been common knowledge among servants and callers, and neighbours and acquaintances were known to worry about the possibility of appearing unfavourably in it, presumably because there was an underlying threat that this personal document could, in certain circumstances, be made public.

The diary, and the apprehension of the diary, allowed Lister to expand the territory of her authority and influence, while, at the same time, it helped create special relations within the favoured group of her female lovers. The key to the code that she bestowed upon them enabled them to communicate in a secret language and even to decipher each other's diaries. Lister was not incautious in the freedoms she offered, however, for while the key gave members of that group a way into the diary, their access to it was dependent upon entry to Shibden Hall, where Lister kept the individual volumes, and Lister was not liberal with invitations. The rural seclusion of the hall and its walled boundary discouraged casual callers and made the presence of strangers an occasion for remark. Even the uncoded sections of the diary were written in a difficult abbreviated hand, which got smaller and less legible as time went on. Further security was provided by the assurance that, should any of her lovers get a sight of diary entries without Lister's permission, it was clearly against their interests to make its contents widely known for they might thus draw attention to their own sexual interests.

## Love-making in the hut: landscape and lesbian identity

The same mixture of secrecy and privilege may be found in her landscaping and building plans. Here again she moved freely between her central identity and its margins. The existing environment at Shibden Hall with its boundary walls, dark interiors and acquiescent workforce, already offered a degree of privacy and protection from the harassment and hostility of townspeople, for Lister, as I have shown, was most vulnerable to attack when she was away from her home territory. However ancient Shibden Hall might be, its buildings and garden did not equal those elaborate productions at the recently built homes of mill owners and industrialists. In 1832, as she began her courtship of Anne Walker, Lister entered into a fever of landscape and building projects which would not only improve the status of Shibden by exhibiting her wealth and fashionable taste but would also extend her areas of security by constructing secret walks, hiding-places, and lookouts. Garden improvements, together with description and analysis of the state of play with Anne Walker, are the predominant topics in the later part of the 1832 diary, as Lister employed and supervised labourers to move soil, plant trees in the grounds of Shibden Hall and lay out a new garden walk with a rustic seat, and, significantly for her love life, a thatched garden hut. These landscaping activities were the physical equivalents of her diary, their meaning and function tending both to reinforce Lister's social position and to aid the exploration of her sexual identity.

Lister's clearest indulgence of her marginal desires occurs in the fantasies she constructs in her coded diary. These are sometimes located in the particular qualities of the physical environment of Shibden and the West Riding, as this diary entry for 1821 demonstrates:

> Foolish fancying about Caroline Greenwood, meeting her on Skircoat Moor, taking her into a shed there is there [sic] & being connected with her. Supposing myself in men's clothes & having a penis, tho' nothing more. All this is very bad.
>
> (Whitbread 1988: 151)

This imaginary scenario enacted a dangerous situation, for while Skircoat Moor was on the one hand isolated and unpopulated moorland, on the other it was surrounded by roads bearing traffic to and fro between Halifax and neighbouring villages. Her erotic encounter might have been hidden within the shed, but the risk of discovery and exposure was high. Jay Appleton in *The Experience of Landscape* suggests that human beings favour a rather different environment to that imagined here by Lister, one in which they can see without being seen, or discovered. Appleton asserts that 'there is much evidence to show that at both human and sub-human level the ability to see and the ability to hide are both important in calculating a creature's survival prospects'. Landscape is classified according to this principle by designating its components thus: 'Where [the observer] has an unimpeded opportunity to see we can call it a *prospect*. Where he has the opportunity to hide, a *refuge*' (Appleton 1996: 66). Lister sacrificed the strategic value of prospect to the sexual excitement to be drawn from the dangers of refuge in her fantasy of the shed on Skircoat Moor.

Lister attempted to reproduce a version of this fantasy, and to combine the sexual freedom and excitement it offered with a bid for social recognition, when, in the course of her garden improvements, she built the little hut inside the grounds of Shibden Hall. Gaston Bachelard discusses the significance of huts to the perception of intimate spaces, in *The Poetics of Space* (1994). He suggests that it is the hut's 'centralized solitude' that is attractive. Indeed, Lister seems to construct her hut in just the way he describes, as 'a dreamer of refuges dreams of a hut, of a nest, or of nooks and corners in which [s]he would like to hide away, like an animal in its hole' (Bachelard 1994: 30). But for Lister, as I have shown, the shed or hut is imbued with additional erotic meaning that combines cosiness with risk. The hut, or shed, in her Skircoat Moor fantasy may have offered her privacy for her illicit liaison, but in an oddly public and exposed location. Her control of a wider geographical location allowed her to experiment with the realization of her fantasies, for the garden hut was protected by the Shibden boundaries from the hostile eyes of Halifax town and the wild moor beyond. The garden hut, therefore, gave symbolic rather than actual refuge, for Lister already had an established area of safety. In other words, even though the hut was not essential to Lister's physical survival in Appleton's urgent terms, it was necessary to the fulfilment of her sexual and social self. Like her diary, Lister's hut, built during the time that she began to pay attentions to Walker, had several practical, symbolic, social and amatory functions. It helped establish her as a leader of fashion, as well as giving her a space in which to hide. It was almost a physical equivalent to the code, crypt-like in its ability to conceal and to isolate. It offered a semblance of that secluded but thrillingly public location on Skircoat Moor that Lister fantasized about, but in a safer managed setting. It provided privacy out of sight and earshot of casual curiosity and a controllable space that could not be entered uninvited. Those within it were thrown into an intimacy created as much by its reproduction of a 'centralized solitude' as by its tiny physical dimensions. While one person alone inside the hut might have experienced herself at the 'centre of concentrated solitude', two people would have felt the force of their mutual isolation, and furthermore been obliged to sit very close (Bachelard 1994: 32). Jacqueline M. Labbe points out that in conduct manuals of the late eighteenth and early nineteenth centuries 'the garden illustrates the very precepts those conduct books seek to inculcate: domestic retirement, decoration, the promise of (properly-confined) fertility, quiet, soothing pleasure, even ... utility' (Labbe 1997: 46). Those conservative precepts were endorsed by Lister, and although she did not have to observe them herself, she liked to find them in other women. She objected to women (beside herself) behaving in an unfeminine fashion: 'Miss Ann Paley seems a nice enough woman (girl) but lolls her arm over the chair back or sticks her elbow out with her hand akimbo in rather too masculine a manner' (Whitbread 1988: 100). There is, therefore, a self-conscious irony in her construction of a garden walk and rustic retreat whose initial purpose, besides its nod to fashion, was to place the docile and decorative Anne Walker within her power. For Lister, the landscaped garden, combining the management of nature with erotic and economic power, was an ideal sphere in which to gain both relational control and self-control and to encompass both central and marginal aspects of her identity.

The hut played a crucial part in Lister at last securing Walker's acquiescence to her life-plans. These last-minute negotiations reveal a curious meeting of rural landscape, class ambition, sexual desire and social mores. On 27 September 1832, Lister arranged to meet Walker at her Lightcliffe home and to walk with her back to Shibden across the moor. Once within Lister's territory, the couple 'sauntered ... in my walk – then on returning rested in the hut & must have sat there a couple of hours'. The next day Walker paid a formal visit to Shibden Hall. Lister again took her to the hut where they sat for three-quarters of an hour 'Bordering on lovemaking in the hut ... Our liaison is now established.' Significantly, Lister concludes, 'I am reprovided [for] & the object of my choice have perhaps three thousand a year or near it – probably two-thirds at her own disposal' (Liddington 1994: 42). That 'three thousand a year' clearly excited her quite as much as Walker's physical presence. During the next week or two, Walker began to show signs of apprehension and, as Lister recounts, 'then got into the old story of [how] she felt she was not doing right morally, could not consent, had determined to say no'. Lister 'laughed it all off' so successfully that she received an apology from Walker, who then 'let me grubble [grope] her this morning gladly enough' (Liddington 1994: 43–4). Later the same day, Lister pressed Walker for a promise, even suggesting that 'our present intercourse without any tie between us must be as wrong as any other transient connection'. At last, Walker gave her answer:

> Miss W- told me in the hut if she said 'yes' again it should be binding. It should be the same as a marriage & she would give me no cause to be jealous. [She] made no objection to what I proposed, that is, her de[c]laring it on the Bible & taking the sa[c]rament with me at Shibden or Lightcliffe church.
>
> (Liddington 1994: 44)

## Conclusion: they are accustomed to my oddities

Lister's attitude to marriage is consistent with her attempts to construct safe spaces in which to develop her sexual identity, while staying within the bounds defined by her conservative values. The concept of marriage enclosed Lister within a conformist tradition of which she approved and provided her with an intimate relationship from within which she could look out at and command, but, at the same time, hide from her peers, superiors and subordinates. While Lister's enthusiasm for the institution may seem to be a case of wilful self-deception, for she could not in reality be married to Walker, it also reflects the complexity of the social and sexual tightrope she walked and arose from a clear understanding of its symbolic properties, while acknowledging the disparity between its apparent potential and the actual experience. Marriage with Anne Walker, then, was quite consistent with Lister's practice of combining the sexual and amatory and she and Walker lived together as a married couple until Lister's death. It is a measure of the success of Lister's negotiations that this was a balancing trick achieved only during her lifetime. After that Walker's grasp on the supporting structures created by Lister faltered and when she inherited a life interest in Shibden Hall, her sister, together with the Lister family solicitor, hatched a plan to have Walker declared of unsound mind. In 1843 they recruited a constable to remove her by force. Walker was found shut up inside Lister's old room and taken to an asylum, where she remained there for the rest of her life. A similar fate befell Eliza Raine, the lover from Lister's schooldays. Raine, like Walker, was an heiress, but shortly after she came into her inheritance she was committed to an insane asylum. It is perhaps reasonable to conclude that Lister's careful construction of a lesbian identity within the context of her provincial location and traditional rural heritage was significant in protecting her from outright condemnation and even from loss of liberty. Her judicious juggling of her economic, social and political power with her marginal sexual identity preserved her from the vulnerability and opprobrium experienced by Raine and Walker. Lister's life-narrative, rather than being full of contradictions, irrationalities and irreconcilable differences, was consistent and rational to a remarkable degree. Her landscape and literary productions, I would argue, demonstrably share meaning and function with her social and emotional activities. Their function was to produce a safe social, physical and textual environment in which to construct a lesbian identity, while reinforcing her power and position among the rural gentry.

Lister lived in a period of great change in the rural economy of her locality, and in her business dealings and social relationships she showed herself able to adapt to the shift from old to new centralities. While adhering to the conventions of the countryside as settled and secluded, lauding the traditional values of the rural gentry, she drew her income from industry and rents that supported the rapidly expanding manufactures and competed in displays of wealth and fashion with the new middle class thus created. Her marginal sexual identity she managed with equal aplomb. She was discreet when necessary, but when she had secured her central position with the inheritance of Shibden Hall she was not afraid to demand recognition for her lesbian relationships from her peers. The greatest threat to her sexual identity came from those townspeople who were themselves marginal. The mill and factory workers, essential to the growing economy of this provincial northern town, were to a large extent disfranchised by the still powerful hold of local landowners in the borough, whose tenants voted *en masse* for the squirearchy's favoured candidates. Their verbal and physical harassment wobbled Lister's confidence more than the disapproval of her social equals. However, Lister's success in reconciling her own circle, which, as I have shown, was covertly unsympathetic to her sexuality, may be ascribed principally to her skilful deployment of her textual and physical productions to shape and discipline her public and private self, to monitor and predict local opinion, and to create spaces where her central and marginal identities could co-exist and mutually reinforce each other. No wonder then that she wrote in 1832:

> The thought of exile from poor Shibden always makes me melancholy. Come what may, I have been happier here than anywhere else ... I am perfectly contented ... I am attached to my own people – they are accustomed to my oddities, are kind, are civilised to me.
>
> (Liddington 1994: 40)

## References

Appleton, J. (1996) *The Experience of Landscape*, Chichester: Wiley & Sons.
Bachelard, G. (1994) *The Poetics of Space*, Boston, Mass.: Beacon Press.
Ballaster, R. (1995) '"The Vices of Old Rome Revived": Representations of Female Same-

sex Desire in Seventeenth and Eighteenth-century England', in S. Raitt (ed.) *Volcanoes and Pearl Divers: Essays in Lesbian Feminist Studies*, London: Onlywomen Press: 13–56.

Castle, T. (1993) *The Apparitional Lesbian: Female Homosexuality and Modern Culture*, New York: Columbia University.

Clayre, A. (ed.) (1977) *Nature and Industrialisation*, Oxford: Oxford University Press.

Cloke, P. and Little, J. (1997) *Contested Countryside Cultures: Otherness, Marginalisation and Rurality*, London: Routledge.

Davidoff, L. and Hall, C. (1994) *Family Fortunes: Men and Women of the English Middle Class 1780–1850*, London: Routledge.

Donoghue, E. (1993) *Passions Between Women: British Lesbian Culture 1668–1801*, London: Scarlet Press.

Faderman, L. (1991) *Surpassing the Love of Men*, London: The Women's Press.

Foucault, M. (1990) *The History of Sexuality, Volume 1*, Harmondsworth: Penguin.

Green, M. (1992) *Miss Lister of Shibden Hall: Selected Letters 1800–1840*, Lewes: The Book Guild.

Labbe, J.M. (1997) 'Cultivating One's Understanding: the Female Romantic Garden', in *Women's Writing* 4(1): 39–56.

Liddington, J. (1998) *Female Fortune: Land, Gender and Authority: The Anne Lister Diaries and Other Writings, 1833–36*, London: Rivers Oram.

Liddington, J. (1994) *Presenting the Past: Anne Lister of Halifax 1791–1840*, Hebden Bridge: Pennine Pens.

Rich, A. (1980) 'Women and Honour: Some Notes on Lying', in *On Lies, Secrets and Silence: Selected Prose, 1966–1978*, London: Virago: 185–94.

SH: Shibden Hall Muniments (Calderdale Archives).

Vicinus, M. (1996) '"They Wonder to Which Sex I Belong": The Historical Roots of the Modern Lesbian Identity', in *Lesbian Subjects: A Feminist Studies Reader*, Indiana: Indiana University Press: 233–59.

Whitbread, H. (1988) *I Know My Own Heart: The Diaries of Anne Lister 1791–1840*, London: Virago.

Whitbread, H. (1992) *No Priest But Love: The Journals of Anne Lister from 1824–1826*, Otley: Smith Settle.

# Part III

# DECONSTRUCTING METROPOLITAN MODELS

# 9

# MARGINALIZATION AND RESISTANCE

## Lesbians in Mexico

*Sue Willman*

> Ella se encontraba en la calle con su pareja, se depidieron de beso y en ese momento los policias las rodearon, parece que las venian siguiendo desde hace rato y estaban esperando a que hicieran 'algo' para abordarlas, las acusaron de 'Faltas a la moral', es un articulo del codigo penal donde calquier persona que hago algo publico que perjudique a la 'moral' de otras personas puede ser culpada y encarcelada, es una ley ambigua y represora, porque no esta claro cual es el delito.

One evening in 1998, Maria de Jesus Corona met her girlfriend in Mexico City where they live. I have translated Mariana Pérez Ocaña's account of the incident. (The other quotations appearing in this chapter, most of which originated in Spanish, are reproduced in translated form only.)

> She met her partner in the street, they kissed goodnight, and at that moment they were surrounded by police. It seemed the police had been following them for a while in the hope that they would 'do something' so that they could accost them and charge them with 'Lack of morals'. This is an article of the [Mexican] penal code under which anyone who does something in public which is 'damaging to public morals' can be convicted and imprisoned. It is an ambiguous and repressive law because it is not clear what the crime is.

Maria's experience of public morality as interpreted by the police, backed by the legal system, demonstrates one aspect of how lesbians in Mexico have been marginalized. Whilst the causes of this marginalization are generally traditional ones such as repressive laws, religion and machismo, progressive modern movements like feminism and the left have also played a part. This chapter examines these contradictory sources of marginalization and then moves on to look at how Mexican lesbians have survived, working from an autonomous position on the margins. It looks at how these lesbians relate to the US/European centres and

Western metropolitan models of a lesbian and gay movement. It considers the ways in which the Western centres have been a source of support, moving on to assess to what extent they may have dictated the development of the movement in Mexico and even resulted in further marginalization.

I began my research into the lives of lesbians in Mexico in January 1998 in cyberspace with conversations through the Mexican lesbian and gay community chat forum *Aqui Estamos* and the Centro Documentacion y Archivo Histórico Lésbico de México, America Latina y El Caribe (CDAHL), the Latin American Lesbian Archive, based in Mexico City. I then spent two months travelling in central America, mostly in Mexico interviewing politically active lesbians and feminists. My first visit was to the Archive. There I interviewed its founder, lesbian academic Norma Mogrovejo, on 29 March and began the process of discovering Mexican lesbian writing. I travelled north and south through the provinces. In San Cristobal de las Casas in the Chiapas I met Zapatista sympathizers and visited Colectivo de Encuentro entre Mujeres (COLEM), a women's collective, where I interviewed Brenda Vellasz on 19th April. The journey culminated in my attending El Foro sobre Diversidad Sexual y Derechos Humanos the first Conference on Sexual Diversity and Human Rights held in Mexico City in 1998 from 12–14 May 1998 (under the aegis of the centre-left Revolutionary Democratic Party (PRD), which controlled local government in Mexico City. Amongst the lesbian speakers, I heard Mariana Pérez Ocaña, editor of *LeS VOZ*, the national lesbian magazine, deliver a series of radical demands for social and legislative change. At a more grass-roots level, Maria de Jesus Corona of the lesbian Zapatista Commitee gave personal testimony of her arrest and detention referred to in the opening quotation. On my return to Britain I interviewed both women in a series of E-mail exchanges in September and October 1998 and continued my dialogue with Mogrovejo, who had completed her doctorate on the lesbian struggle in Latin America by September 1998. Both the dialogue and my research are a continuing process which involves a mutual exchange of material, ideas and information. The invisibility of lesbians in Mexico has been a persistent obstacle. In what follows I describe the results of my attempts to find written or physical evidence of their lives.

## Contexts of marginalization

### *Looking for lesbians*

'In the majority of Latin American countries, the lesbian movement is comprised of one or two small groups of lesbians in which there are scarcely more than one or two women "publicly out"' (Mogrovejo 1996: 49). The lack of 'out' lesbians makes it difficult to trace lesbian existence in Mexico and this is compounded by the scarcity of published material in either Spanish or English, the first indicators of their marginalization. When interviewed at the Archive, Mogrovejo referred to the thirty or so lesbian groups which have existed in Mexico as evidence that lesbians have moved further out of the margins than in many other Latin American countries, but was concerned about the absence of any record of this. She repeatedly described the process of simply uncovering past and present lesbian life as 'archaeology'.

The modern history of the Mexican lesbian and gay movement begins with poet and activist Nancy Cardenas, who famously came out on national TV in 1973 in front of a record number of viewers. When she died twenty years later, Mogrovejo recalled

> there was a fear amongst lesbians that as well as losing their public face they were losing their history ... At the Fourth Lesbian Feminist *Encuentro* in 1994, I described lesbian activity as semi-clandestine in Latin America and called for the creation of a lesbian historical archive to preserve the history of Latin American lesbian movement.

As a result the archive was established — from a series of boxes in Norma's flat. It is now part of *Enlace Lésbico*, a network of lesbian organizations which vigorously promote lesbian visibility. It is also part of Norma's own project to promote the visibility of lesbians in Mexico and in Latin America, which she sees as a political priority.

There is a substantial body of work documenting the feminist movement in Latin America and Mexico in particular, but it is mostly silent on the lesbian contribution to the movement (e.g. Chinchilla 1997: 214–26). Lesbian analysis by academics and activists based in Mexico such as Gloria Carega, Claudia Hinjosa, Yan Maria Castro, Norma Mogrovejo and Mariana Pérez Ocaña is published in shortened form as magazine articles (e.g. Castro 1997), or remains unpublished academic work. A notable exception is Mogrovejo's *El Amor es bXh* (Mogrovejo 1996). Then there is work in English, usually articles in US based academic journals (e.g. Luibheid 1998). I questioned Mogrovejo and Mariana Pérez Ocaña about the limited availability of lesbian writing, in particular theoretical work. Pérez Ocaña referred to Mexico's economic problems, and the extent to which lesbians were involved in a struggle for food, housing and basic services. 'Those lesbians who write theory almost always do it at the level of reports ... to write theory you need to have the basic necessities, that's why there is little published theory.' Apart from poverty, she blamed the influence of machismo on the shortage of lesbian material originating in Mexico: 'To avoid being sacked from their jobs, marked-out, stigmatized, lesbians prefer not to publicize their sexual orientation, and that is reflected in the minimal intellectual and artistic lesbian output.' Women's video collective Telemanita has recently begun to make short lesbian documentaries in an attempt to increase visibility. Mogrovejo said that the lack of writing in Spanish made it harder for lesbians in Mexico and Latin America as a whole to move out of the margins. 'Our community doesn't have the opportunity to develop lesbian theory because most of the material is in English and not accessible to us.' The archive has attempted to address this problem by publishing translations. It has also published two home-grown works, *No Me Alcanza*, María Amparo Jiménez's erotic poetry (Jiménez 1996), and Mogrovejo's lesbian theory (Mogrovejo, 1996).

Mexican lesbian literature in Mexico is represented by respected novelist Rosamaria Roffiel, the only widely published writer of novels by and for lesbians, best known for *Amora*. Roffiel is also responsible for an occasional lesbian section in the national feminist magazine *Fem*, and works of poetry. Aside from Roffiel's prolific work, Mexican literature consists of the self-published *Con Fugitivo Paso* (Enríquez, 1996) which is currently distributed by *LeS VOZ*, and a novella by Sarah Levi-Calderon. Poetry has proved a more popular medium – from the early 1970s with the work of Mexican lesbian and gay movement pioneer, Nancy Cardenas, and more recently with Sabina Berman and María Amparo Jiménez (1996). As with theory, lesbians who do publish tend to use their own resources, which limits the available finance.

There is a body of material available on the movements of gay men in Mexico reflecting their higher levels of visibility (e.g. Carrier 1989; Sanchez-Crispin and Lopez-Lopez 1997). This visibility arises perhaps from a degree of social tolerance of male homosexuality, at least in relation to the 'active agent', (see Carrier 1989: 227), which is not extended to lesbians. As the recent study, 'Gay Male Places of Mexico City' (Sanchez-Crispin and Lopez-Lopez 1997: 212) indicates, 'gay spaces' are either commercial venues, public areas such as metro stations, or areas associated with sex-workers. There are no lesbian and gay centres/bookstores in the capital which could serve as meeting places. According to Pérez Ocaña the poorer economic position of women excludes the majority of them from the few commercial venues which have high entry costs. Public 'cruising areas' are not usually frequented by women and the risk of arrest makes them unattractive.

In my search for lesbian activity, I considered the sales of Mexico's only lesbian magazine, *LeS VOZ*. It is sold publicly in Mexico City, Guadalajara and Tijuana. Elsewhere in Mexico it is only available by subscription, due to the lack of lesbian-friendly outlets outside these centres. Pérez Ocaña insisted that this indicated the lack of women/lesbian-friendly spaces rather than a lack of lesbians. Although it is easier to sell the magazine publicly outside Mexico, to Latinas in San Francisco, Canada and Costa Rica, most of its readers live in Mexican provincial towns. There is a gay men's scene in most of Mexico's large towns, but an absence of exclusively lesbian activity. The women I interviewed agreed that lesbians were a token presence at gay venues, many of which were exclusively male or mixed. They also confirmed that Mexico's lesbian and gay community has followed the pattern of 'metropolitan bias', migrating to Mexico City or to Guadalajara. Mexico City is one of the largest cities in the world with an estimated 10–15 per cent of its population gay/lesbian/bisexual/transgendered. Guadalajara, the second city, has had an active gay community since 1981 (Carrier 1989: 226). Neither city has an established permanent lesbian meeting place.

The further one travels south from the US border and the further from Mexico City, the more marginal the lesbian community becomes. The town of San Cristobal de las Casas in the Chiapas presents a clear example of this. The Chiapas is a remote, mountainous region, as far as you can get from the US border. The region is the focus for the current struggle for autonomy by the indigenous people with the support of the Zapatistas and there is a visible, macho presence of the occupying government forces. San Cristobal is the base of human rights and political organizations. It is popular with travellers and has an active women's collective, COLEM which campaigns effectively against sexual and domestic violence, but is silent on sexuality. At the feminist bookshop/cultural centre, la Casa de la Luna Cresciente there are no lesbian books for sale. Amongst the books for borrowing there was an edition of Pat Califia's *Macho Sluts*, in English and therefore inaccessible to most of the centre's users. There are a number of radical bookshops well stocked with revolutionary publications as well as *Fem*, but no sign of *LeS VOZ*. The gay men's scene is evident in a café society, but there is little evidence of lesbian activity anywhere in the town. San Cristobal is a base for the Zapatista movement but its lesbian committee is based in the Mexico City. Asked why there was no sign of lesbian life in San Cristobal, Pérez Ocaña explained:

> The case of the provinces is very serious from my point of view. Although there are very many lesbians everywhere in Mexico … lesbians and gay men live isolated lives in the provinces and resort to marriages of social convenience or gradually emigrate to the cities to improve their life. In a big city, it is easier to be anonymous. Even in cities lesbians prefer anonymity; this is harder to achieve in the provinces.

She suggested that lesbians living in small towns and rural areas were more likely to be suffering from poverty or unemployment than those in cities and were therefore more dependent on hiding their lesbianism to maintain employment or family support. After poverty, she cited machismo as the main cause of repression in the provinces. The *machismo* she referred to is the male dominance of women by the *macho* male. It was no surprise then, that when asked about the women's collective she explained, 'lesbians working in the feminist movement are not visible and don't want to be seen as lesbians'. It has been easier to introduce *LeS VOZ* to countries outside Mexico than to the provinces. Pérez Ocaña attributed this to the lack of spaces for women, and for lesbians in particular. 'It doesn't mean there are no lesbians – most of our subscribers live in small towns or in the provinces.' Moving on from locating lesbians on the margins of Mexican society, I will examine their responses to the factors which have driven them there, starting with fear of physical violence and the police.

## Surviving the sources of marginalization

### *Resisting institutionalized and individual male violence*

Mexico shares with Brazil the highest rate of lesbian and gay murders in the world. The International Lesbian and Gay Association (ILGA) has petitioned the European Union claiming that the Mexican police have failed to investigate the 125 homophobic murders of the past three years or bring any charges. Between 1991 and 1994, twelve transvestites were murdered in Tuxtla Gutierrez the provincial capital of the Chiapas, allegedly with direct or indirect police involvement. When local lesbian, gay and transvestite groups took to the streets in 1993 to protest, one of the organizers, a transvestite called 'Vanessa' (Neftali Ruiz Ramirez), was shot dead, reportedly by the Chiapas State Judicial Police. Ramirez was vice-president of Tuxtla Gutierrez Gay and Transvestite Group (Amnesty International 1997: 14–16). Homosexuality is not a criminal offence for either men or women under Mexico's democratic constitution. Instead the police use morality laws, designed to control prostitution, to arrest and harass lesbians, gay men, transvestites in the street and other public places. The morality laws are also widely used by *operativos de seguridad* during periodic raids on gay bars and clubs. In the early 1990s gay magazines stopped printing listings of gay venues because of fear of police raids and attacks by homophobic groups (Sanchez-Crispin and Lopez-Lopez 1997: 200).

Despite fears of homophobic or police violence, lesbians have continued to work from the margins. This chapter opened with a description of Maria de Jesus Corona's arrest. After four hours she bribed the police to secure her release: 'because I wasn't just risking my own safety, but that of my partner'. Despite this experience and her belief that she had been targeted by the police, she has continued her political work as one of few 'public' lesbian figures. She decided to use the experience to speak publicly about the treatment of lesbians in Mexican society, most recently at the national conference on sexual diversity. When asked about her work in the Zapatista lesbian committee, she emphasized the parallels between her own struggle for autonomy as a lesbian and that of the indigenous people she supports through this work. Indigenous women in the Chiapas have publicized their experiences of rape and physical violence by the police and army as part of an effective strategy to generate public support for the Zapatista cause. In 1977 Luz Maria Medina founded the lesbian group Lesbos when she was tear-gassed out of a gay bar. I repeatedly found evidence that lesbians in Mexico had responded to physical repression with an increase in political and public activity, rather than a retreat into the margins, a theme which also pervades their response to the Catholic Church.

### *Subverting marginalization by the religious right*

Mogrovejo ends her analysis of the lesbian movement in Latin America with the statement, 'We cannot forget the characteristics of our Latin American society, eminently traditional, trapped in the narrow conceptions of Catholicism' (Mogrovejo1996: 55). Despite the separation of the state from the church in Mexico, the Catholic Church has retained its pervasive influence reflected in the slogan of the lesbian and gay movement during the 1970s and 1980s: "Homosexuality is not a sin". Before examining the treatment of lesbians, it must be acknowledged that feminists in Mexico have been a target of the religious right for many of the same reasons. During and after the 1987 Latin American Feminist *Encuentro* in Mexico the Catholic Church maintained that 'women were destined to be "guardians of family and public morality". Feminism, they argued, pointed women in the direction of materialism, individualism, and egotism and, thus, was inherently opposed to church doctrine'. (Chinchilla 1997: 214). In such a climate it is hardly surprising that feminists distanced themselves from lesbians. When Costa Rica hosted the second Latin American Lesbian Feminist *Encuentro* in 1990, the Catholic Church joined with extreme right wing groups in launching an attack on the event in the tabloid press. A national newspaper, *El Expreso*, reported 'Apart from the moral issues, as well as the damage to the country's image and the upbringing of young people, the congress will begin on Good Friday, which shows disrespect for the religious customs of Costa Rica ...' The government responded by banning women from travelling unaccompanied by men at the time of the conference. Not surprisingly, numbers were reduced, but for those who remained 'it only reinforced our conviction of the need to organise as lesbians' (Madden Arias 1996: 136). Similar tactics were used in Mexico City in 1998, by Pro-Vida, Mexico's Pro-Life Committee and La Asociacion Nacional Civica Feminina which mobilized against the conference on sexual diversity. Media reports of the event were dominated by accounts of the family values response, and an emphasis on gay marriage which Pro-Vida condemned as 'a gross caricature of marriage and the family' (*el Universal*, 15 May 1998: 2). Pro-Vida chairman Jorge Serrano Limon was widely reported making statements such as 'Homosexual and lesbian groups are made up of aggressive people who seek to legalise pretend marriages and adoption of children ... homosexual sex is sterile and lacking in purpose' (*el Norte*, 14 May 1998). TV Aztec focused on pro-life demonstrations outside the conference before moving swiftly onto a report on drug-trafficking.

One of the lesbian responses to the Catholic Church has been to subvert it, using it as a rich source of lesbian and feminist icons, from the madonna to the black Virgin of Guadalupe (a manifestation of the Virgin Mary who appeared to an indigenous

Mexican in 1531). The early feminist writings of a ninteenth-century nun, Sor Juana Ines de la Cruz, inspired the contemporary lesbian group El Closet de Sor Juana to take her name. The religious right has marginalized women both as lesbians and as feminist. To what extent have hetero-feminists themselves marginalized lesbians?

### *Resisting marginalization by the Women's Movement*

The marginalization of lesbian interests by the feminist movement is a recurrent international theme even as we reach the millennium. I examine the manifestations of this in Mexico and consider how they have been shaped by circumstances peculiar to Latin America.

When lesbian members of the Coalition of Feminist Women wanted lesbian demands incorporated into those of the Coalition in 1977, heterosexual feminists refused, because they regarded it as a threat to Mexico's nascent women's movement. The lesbian-feminists responded by joining forces with bar-dykes politicized by police raids to form the first autonomous lesbian group Lesbos. It was followed by Oikabeth, which defined itself as socialist feminist, attempting to make alliances with men in left-wing parties, unions and revolutionary movements, as well as with the left of the gay movement. In 1979 when Oikabeth joined the Frente National Por la Liberacion y los Derechos de las Mujeres, (FNALIDEM) – National Front for the Liberation of Women's Rights – with women from trade unions, feminist groups and with links to the communist party, the communist women left, saying: 'if these women are allowed in then alcoholics, prostitutes and criminals will follow'. So early marginalization by the women's movement forced lesbians to organize autonomously to survive but also moved them to form new alliances, campaigning about issues such as the treatment of lesbians and gay men in Cuba in 1980.

It has been difficult for lesbians to organize without feminist support. The *Encuentro* (variously translated as conference, encounter, happening, meeting) has been an important focus for bringing together feminists and lesbians across race and class lines, unique to Latin America. An understanding of the *Encuentro*'s role assists analysis of the lesbian movement in Mexico. At the first Latin American feminist *Encuentro* held in Columbia in 1981, the main debate was about whether/how feminism and socialism should be integrated, but lesbians were already agitating from the margins. They called for 'the right to free sexual preference' to be included amongst the demands of the feminist movement. The proposal has still not been accepted, but this has not prevented lesbians from voicing it. At the 1987 Feminist *Encuentro* in Mexico, Trinidad Gutierrez made one of the most direct attacks on the feminist movement's marginalization of lesbians:

> She said that in spite of the active participation of lesbians in the struggles of the Feminist Movement in Mexico, it had been a long and difficult task

for lesbians to be recognized within the movement. She accused the Feminist Movement of "heterosexual blindness" in seeing lesbianism as a separate struggle, to be dealt with solely in the context of sexuality. As a result lesbianism had remained "in the closet" of feminist analysis, reduced to leading a marginal and invisible existence within feminism.

(Mogrovejo 1998: 29)

Mogrovejo is not convinced that feminists are ready to end their marginalization of lesbians. She recalled that in 1990 at a national *Encuentro*, Mexican feminists finally agreed to accept the lesbian 'sexual preference' demand. However, she cited her own struggle to secure funding for the archive, 'a space for lesbian existence', as an example of continuing marginalization. It is situated in Mogrovejo's apartment in a high-rise block on a downtown Mexico City housing estate. 'This weekend we have a lesbian mothers' conference – ten women, my flat will be full. Feminist organizations are afraid that if they give us space they will lose their funding.'

One advantage of this form of marginalization is that it has enabled lesbians to develop outside of the institutional government/party framework. Pérez Ocaña said there was no state funding for their lesbian organizations because 'To attract funds you need to belong to a certain political and social elite; in Mexico everything is institutional.' This is echoed by Corona when discussing her participation in the organization of the 20th Gay Pride march as a member of the Zapatatista lesbian committee: 'our position was clear, in favour of the autonomy of the movement and against the *oficializacion* [government take-over] of the march. We voted against a PRD deputy [local government politician] being a speaker because we have always said there are no lesbians or Zapatistas *oficiales*.' How has the experience of marginalization by the left led lesbians to this insistence on protecting their position of autonomy on the margins?

### *The struggle against machismo and marginalization by the Homosexual Movement and the left*

Pérez Ocaña suggested that machismo was the most significant factor in forcing Mexican lesbians, especially those in the provinces, to choose between leaving their families or remaining invisible. She continued: 'In a country in which everything is based on family privilege, it is difficult to survive without a family.' Machismo is a recurring theme in the writing of Latina lesbians. But Gloria Anzaldúa, Chicana writer (of Mexican origin, born on what is now US territory), believes this concept of machismo is 'an Anglo invention', the response of the Mexican man to colonial oppression and poverty.

> For men like my father, being macho meant being strong enough to protect and support my mother and us, yet being able to show love. Today's

macho has doubts about his ability to feed and protect his family. His "machismo" is an adaptation to oppression ... Only gay men have had the courage to expose themselves to the woman inside them and to challenge the current masculinity.

(Anzaldúa, 1987: 83)

Anzaldúa's optimism about gay men's attitudes towards women does not reflect the experience of Mexican lesbians, pushed onto the margins when they attempted to participate in the 'homosexual movement'. In 1971 when Mexico's first gay organization appeared (the Homosexual Liberation Front, FHAR) its spokesperson was a lesbian, Nancy Cardenas, but it was primarily male and based on the patriarchal organizational models of the left. Oikabeth joined it as an autonomous lesbian group in 1978. By 1979 the lesbians had left FHAR 'because of the aggression of a male member of one of the collectives' (Castro 1997: 12). The final relationship breakdown took place at the 1984 Gay Pride march. There was a conflict between male 'radicals' led by ex-militants from FHAR and 'reformists' represented by a coalition between Lambda and Oikabeth. 'The presence of women in the Lesbian–Homosexual Movement, particularly in the group Lambda was another cause of tension. The reformists decided the march would have a mournful character and a coffin would be carried representing the deaths of lesbians and gay men as a result of violence and repression.' The 'radicals' arrived with big phalluses 'to portray a controversial image'. The lesbians interpreted the phalluses as direct aggression against women. 'The radicals, accompanied by a group of gangs ... prevented the reformists from holding their planned meeting, broke the coffins they were carrying, pushed, shouted abuse and even resorted to physical violence to force a retreat by Lambda and its allies' (Mogrovejo 1998: 12). This led to the lesbians splitting from the men, rejecting their phallocentric attitude. 'Some returned closer to the feminist movement and others set up autonomous lesbian groups' (ibid.). Lesbians survived the political divisions and Mexico's economic collapse of the 1980s by directing their energies away from institutional politics into self-help groups and non-governmental organizations. More recently there has been some form of *rapprochement* with the left of centre PRD, but this seems to demonstrate a new approach, shaped by past experience of the left.

### *Speaking from the margins: lesbians and the left today*

The PRD conference on sexual diversity and human rights was the most significant political development of 1998 for the lesbians I interviewed. Pérez Ocaña explained the historic and symbolic importance of the conference to lesbians, despite their marginalization within its organizational structures. She outlined the political background as 'a grave economic crisis combined with a moral repression in which conservative and church groups exercise their influence over a growing population'. For decades the PRI (Institutional Revolutionary Party) have dominated Mexico's government and institutions. In 1997 an opportunity for change appeared in the form of a bid to take over local government in Mexico City by the PRD, which supported minority groups. There was a tacit understanding that the PRD would get the queer vote in exchange for legal reforms. Pérez Ocaña was as critical about the PRD as she was about the other political parties

> Every time there are elections the parties turn to the gay and lesbian movement to get votes. During the sexual diversity conference this was hotly debated because the way that politics works in this country has always been one of 'expediency'. For example, article 21 of the penal code which relates to the law against perversion of minors states 'anyone who induces a minor to take part in prostitution, crime, drug-taking, homosexuality or alcoholism will be sentenced to imprisonment'. This law was approved by all the political parties in 1993 or 1994 and then during the 1997 elections they promised support to lesbians and gay men … a total contradiction.

Soon after coming to power in Mexico City, PRD leader Cuahtemoc Cardenas met with the lesbian network Enlace Lésbico which presented proposals for legislative reform, including protection against discrimination on grounds of sexuality. A more limited, but relatively radical set of demands were agreed at the PRD conference to the delight of the lesbian community. Six months later, when the first of these demands was placed before the legislative chamber, Pérez Ocaña told me 'there was a resounding "no" to the recognition of adoption by same-sex couples. The same groups who defended the PRD during the conference kept quiet in the chamber even though the PRD has a majority.'

Disillusionment with the political parties has attracted lesbians and other disaffected minorities to the Zapatistas who distinguish themselves from conventional party politics of either the left or the right, making it clear that they do not aspire to govern. The Committee of Lesbian Zapatistas was founded in 1997, at the same time as the Frente Zapatista de Liberacion Nacional (FZLN), the Zapatistas' political wing. Maria de Jesus Corona's involvement with the lesbian Zapatistas is her response to the marginalization of lesbians by the other political movements. She is optimistic about the role of lesbians as an autonomous group within the Lesbian Committee of the FZLN when compared with past struggles with the parties of the left.

> Until today we could not work with any party on the left … We have criticized the myopia of the left in relation to women's and lesbian issues

and we did not believe that it was just a class struggle, or that it would be solved by a change of the political party in power.

The Zapatistas have established themselves as a new voice in radical politics both in Mexico and internationally. Their rejection of the traditional vanguard politics of the left, which depended on a leader within a hierarchical structure and involved a bid for political power, has offered an alternative to lesbians interested in political activity. The Zapatistas central tenet is autonomy. They have profited from their ability to acknowledge the parallels between their struggle for autonomy for the indigenous peoples and that of other marginalized groups in society, such as women, lesbians and gay men. During peace negotiations with the Mexican government, the Zapatistas' most detailed demand was 'the indigenous women's petition' detailing the specific demands of women, including the right to have 'the partner of their choice'. The apparent difference between the FZLN and other leftist movements is that these struggles are not marginalized or subordinated to the class struggle but are seen as part of an overall project of political autonomy. A further distinction is their approach to globalization. The Zapatistas have identified globalization as a primary source of their oppression and have responded by using global communication channels such as the internet to promote the cause of the indigenous people, seeking international support for their struggle. How have lesbians approached globalization?

## Mexican lesbians in the global context

### *The relationship to the US*

The influence of gay tourism from the US, and neighbouring California in particular, has been a factor in the development of visible lesbian and gay communities which is specific to Mexico, and almost as significant as the 'metropolitan' bias to cities. It has led to Pacific beach resorts like Acapulco and Puerto Vallarta becoming a mecca for gay men, and generated a thriving gay scene in towns close to the US border like Monterrey. Both Mexican and American gay men are visible in these places. American/European lesbians have a more marginal presence but have tended to favour the state of Tijuana, a popular destination for organized lesbian holidays from California, again close to the border. The ability of a Mexican or Chicana lesbian to participate in the bordertown scene, as compared with a gay man or white American lesbian, is diminished by the various forms of marginalization discussed above. Take the experience of crossing the US border by a Mexican/Chicana lesbian, carefully documented in 'Looking Like a Lesbian' (Luibheid 1998). Sara Harb Quiroz was born in Mexico in 1934, naturalized as American in 1954 and prevented by the immigration service from re-entering the US in 1960 after a trip home because she 'looked like a lesbian'. Until as recently as 1990 lesbian immigrants were excludable and deportable from the US, deemed as falling within a provision directed at 'aliens' with a 'psychopathic personality' or 'mental defect'. It is not clear whether Quiroz, who had short hair and wore a shirt and trousers to work actually was a lesbian, which she denied. As Luibheid points out, 'these sexual categorizations themselves substantially derive their meanings from metropolitan centers, which are materially and ideologically implicated in the production of women as racial or ethnic minorities'. It may be that culturally based assumptions about what a lesbian looks like have prevented or assisted other Mexicans and Chicana women passing through US immigration control. Luibheid refers to four other case-studies. However, the case exemplifies the marginalization of Mexican women with lesbian identities in relation to other Mexicans (faced with strict immigration monitoring on grounds of race, enough in itself) and white American lesbians (whose sexuality would not be used to exclude them). It also demonstrates the role of marginalization in forcing lesbians into a position of invisibility. This invisibility is perpetuated by the Latin American media.

### *US/European models of metropolitan gay life and media bias*

Shortly before the 1993 Latin American Feminist *Encuentro* in El Salvador, a right-wing magazine, *Gente*, featured the headline 'Are the lesbians coming?' *Gente* orchestrated a hate-campaign, implying that hundreds of lesbians and gay men, possibly infected with AIDS, would be arriving from the US (Stephen 1997: 17–19). The press in Mexico, and more generally in Latin America, has fastened upon a Western metropolitan model of lesbian and gay life, treating 'homosexuality' as a US import. They have attempted to keep lesbians on the margins either by suggesting that all lesbians are Western or by focusing on a Western gay lifestyle, ignoring the reality of the lives of Mexican lesbians. In 1973 when Nancy Cardenas became the first lesbian to be interviewed on national television, the subject matter was the dismissal of a gay man from the US civil service. The media have continued to avoid issues which really affect Mexican lesbians, such as police harassment. Their response to the PRD sexual diversity conference in 1998 was to limit coverage almost entirely to the issue of gay marriage. Pérez Ocaña was critical of media coverage of the conference 'ignoring valid and serious demands … we should have the right to marry, but the issue is not our political priority'.

Same-sex marriage is a clear illustration of an imported Western model of sexuality. In Mexico it has been introduced from the US by the Metropolitan Community Church. The church records an average of one lesbian or gay marriage each month during the past nine years, mostly in the parts of Mexico near to the US border where it is most active. The practice appears non-existent in the southern provinces and insignificant even in Mexico City. As discussed, the prominence given to the marriage issue has provided the religious right with fertile ground on which to organize opposition to the lesbian and gay movement. To what extent has the same-sex marriage movement benefited lesbians in the context of a country where religion, tradition and family values have so clearly been a source of their marginalization and where economic dependence on men remains a reality for the majority of women? Can the fact that this demand has been taken up by sectors of the lesbian and gay community be related to the lack of published Latin American lesbian and gay political analysis?

### *Cultural marginalization: another aspect of the US/colonial influence*

Pérez Ocaña explained that her magazine *LeS VOZ* publishes lesbian theory from US/European sources because there is so little Mexican material. 'I don't believe that the influence of other countries is negative, on the contrary we are nourished by the thinking of other women like ourselves who can develop theory because they have the necessities covered.' Pérez Ocaña has published translations of lesbian theory by Marilyn French and a brief history of Radclyffe Hall in *LeS VOZ*, but when I asked her opinion of Gloria Anzaldúa, Chicana lesbian-feminist theorist, replied that she did not know her work. Anzaldúa is of Mexican ancestry, raised in Texas, and English is her first language. She challenges the imperialism of English language by writing in a mixture of English, Spanish and Tejana (the language of the hispanic Texans). She was editor (with another Chicana lesbian, Cherrie Moraga) of the first widely read anthology of black women's writing, *This Bridge Called my Back* (1981). The lack of 'women-of-colour' anthologies forced her to repeat the exercise with *Making Face, Making Soul, Haciendo Caras*. In her introduction she states:

> Theorists-of-color are in the process of trying to formulate "marginal" theories that are partially outside and partially inside the Western frame of reference (if that is possible), theories that overlap many "worlds" ... In our literature, social issues such as race, class and sexual difference are intertwined with the narrative and poetic elements of a text, elements in which theory is embedded. In our *mestizaje* theories we create new categories for those left out or pushed out of existing ones.
> 
> (Anzaldúa 1990: 25)

Clearly Anzaldúa's theories and experience can speak to Mexican lesbians in a way that Marilyn French's cannot. Pérez Ocaña is interested in the connections between Mexican and Chicana lesbians and interviewed Ramona Ortega, a Chicana lesbian who visited the *LeS VOZ* collective (Pérez Ocaña 1997: 24). Why is it the case that she is familiar with white feminist theory, originally written in English, but not with Anzaldúa? It can partly be attributed to the marginalization of Latina women and their writings, particularly lesbian writings, in the US. In 'Breaking the Silence: Putting Latina Lesbian History at the Center', Yolanda Chavez Leyva discusses how although clearly present in the US, Latina lesbians were historically marginalized and unrepresented in official records (Chavez Leyva 1996: 145–52). It was not until 1995 that a major New York publishing house issued an anthology of Latina women's writing (Milligan *et al*. 1995: 1). As yet there is no similar volume of work by lesbians based in Mexico, although Mogrovejo is seeking a publisher for her thesis on the history of lesbians in Latin America.

For Mogrovejo the (lack of) finance for lesbian existence is central to their marginalization. The limited funding which the Archive and groups like the magazine *LeS VOZ* have secured originates in Europe and the US. Does this have an influence on the movement? Pérez Ocaña believes it doesn't, insisting that where there are strings attached funds would be refused. But perhaps the influence is more subliminal. A year before the first Latin American Lesbian Feminist *Encuentro* in Mexico, nine Latin American lesbians were invited by the International Lesbian Information Service (ILIS), based in Amsterdam, to participate in their conference in Geneva. The conference decided to establish a Latin American lesbian network based on the separatist model which was fashionable in Europe at the time. This met with fierce resistance at the *Encuentro* because many organizations did not fit the separatist criteria:

> Separatism in Latin America and the Third World is a reactionary philosophy ... With the conditions imposed by the Network almost all lesbian organizations in Latin America were excluded, as they almost all worked with gay or heterosexual feminist groups. This is because the Latin American reality is different to that in Holland.
> (Mogrovejo 1998: 26)

The separatism question diverted the debate from issues which were more fundamental to the Latin American participants. Veteran Mexican lesbian activist Yan Maria Castro recorded her frustration:

> We were unable to carry out any discussions on activities which lesbians living under dictatorships and totalitarian regimes could organize ... It had been our objective to find a stance that lesbians could take in the face of public debt, inflation and unemployment; to find a way of forming part of the national reality. All of this was not discusssed ... There was a bloody self-defence workshop given by some Europeans ...
> (Mogrovejo 1998: 27)

The lesbians I interviewed in Mexico were keenly aware of the political, economic and social influence of the US and Europe. Yet they were in favour of sharing resources within the international lesbian community as a means of organizing more effectively in the face of globalization. Has there been a movement away from a colonialist imposition of Western metropolitan models towards a situation in which the benefits are more mutual? In the Zapatista context, financial and political support from the West is reciprocated in the form of the inspiration which the Zapatista movement provides. Similarly Mogrovejo has worked from an internationalist perspective in Latin America and the West, attempting to share her knowledge and experience, speaking most recently at the Gay Games in Amsterdam.

## Conclusion

The experiences of lesbians in Mexico speak for themselves, demonstrating an impressive ability to survive expected and unexpected forms of marginalization. I have scarcely touched upon the costs of this struggle or questioned what lesbian life in Mexico would look like if they had not faced marginalization from such a multitude of sources. Yet just as they have resisted and adapted to marginalization by sources such as the religious right, the lesbians I encountered have attempted to adapt Western metropolitan models to their advantage, choosing increased visibility as a political priority around which they can unite. They work within Enlace Lésbico, aiming to increase the visibility and strength of the lesbian movement in Mexico from a position of autonomy. They also work in coalitions addressing other issues such as the Zapatista struggle and AIDS education. Their own economic position and the absence of any secure funding for even the most mainstream lesbian projects distinguishes them from lesbians in Western metropolitan centres. Here then are lesbians working from within apparently insurmountable margins, pushing back those margins as they pursue struggles for visibility, autonomy, equal rights and survival!

## References

Amnesty International (1997) *Breaking the Silence: Human Rights Violations Based on Sexual Orientation*, London: Amnesty International.

Anzaldúa, Gloria (1987) *Borderlands/La Frontera: the new Mestiza*, San Francisco: Spinsters/Aunt Lute Book Company.

—— (ed.) (1990) *Making Face, Making Soul = Haciendo Caras: Creative and Critical Perspectives by Women of Color*, San Francisco: Aunt Lute Foundation Books.

Carrier, Joseph M. (1989) 'Gay Liberation and Coming Out in Mexico', *Journal of Homosexuality* 17 (3–4): 225–52.

Castro, Yan Maria (1997) 'Apuntes sobre la historia de los grupos lésbicos en México, años 70, Linea Autonomista', *Les Voz*, no. 4: 11–12.

Chavez Leyva, Yolanda (1996) 'Breaking the Silence: Putting Latina Lesbian History at the Center', in *The New Lesbian Studies: Toward the Twenty-First Century*, Bonnie Zimmerman and Toni McNaron (eds) New York.

Chinchilla, Norma (1997) Marxism, Feminism and the Struggle for Democracy in Latin America' in Rosemary Hennessy and Chrys Ingraham (eds) *Materialist Feminism, A Reader in Class, Difference and Women's Lives*, London: Routledge.

Enríquez, Victoria (1996) *Con Fugitivo Paso*, Mexico: LeS VOZ.

Gutierrez, Trinidad (1987) 'En el feminismo desde el closet o acerca del trabajo de las mujeres feministas lesbianas en el movimiento feminista'. Paper presented at the Fourth Latin American Feminist Conference, Taxco, Mexico.

Jiménez, María Amparo (1996) *No Me Alcanza, It Is Not Enough*, Centro de Documentacion y Archivo Histórico Lésbico, Mexico.

Luibheid, Eithne (1998) 'Looking Like a Lesbian: The Organization of Sexual Monitoring at the United States–Mexican Border', *Journal of the History of Sexuality* 8 (3): 477–506.

Madden Arias, Rose Mary (1996) 'outraging public morality, the experience of the lesbian feminist group in costa rica', in Monika Reinfelder (ed.) *Amazon to Zami: Towards a Global Lesbian Feminism*, London: Cassell.

Milligan, Bryce, Milligan, Mary Guerrero and de Hoyos, Angela (1995) *Daughters of the Fifth Sun, A Collection of Latina Fiction and Poetry*, New York: Riverhead Books.

Mogrovejo, Norma (1996) *El Amor es bXh – 2, Una Propuesta de Analisis Historico-Metodologica del Movimiento Lesbico y Sus Amores Con los Movimientos Homosexual y Feminista en America Latina* (Love is bXh -2, A Historical and Methodological Proposal for Analysis of the Lesbian Movement and its Love Affairs with the Homosexual and Feminist Movements in Latin America), Centro de Documentacion y Archivo Histórico Lésbico, Mexico.

—— (1998) 'Un amor se atrevio a decir su nombre: La lucha de las lesbianas y su relacion con los movimientos feminsta y homosexual en Latinoamerica', Unpublished doctoral thesis, UNAM, Mexico.

Moraga, Cherríe and Anzaldúa, Gloria (eds) (1981) *This Bridge Called My Back: Writings by Radical Women of Color*, Watertown, MA: Persephone Press.

Pérez Ocaña, Mariana (1997) 'Dentro del movimiento: Ramona Ortega', *Les Voz*, no. 4: 24–5.

Sanchez-Crispin, Alvaro and Lopez-Lopez, Alvaro (1997) 'Gay Male Places of Mexico City', in G.B. Ingram, A.-M. Bouthillette and Y. Retter (eds) *Queers in Space: Communities | Public Spaces | Sites of Resistance*, SeattleBay Press, 1997

Stephen, Lynn (1997) *Women and Social Movemements in Latin America: Power From Below*, Austin: University of Texas Press.

Vargas, Virginia (1991) 'El movimiento feminista latinamericano: entre la esperanza y el desencanto (apuntes para el debate), *El cielo por asalto*, no. 2 (Autumn).

# 10

# REMAPPING SAME-SEX DESIRE

Queer writing and culture in the American heartland

*William J. Spurlin*

Despite the focus of academic queer studies on a broad critique of normalizing ideologies across the social terrain (which include those of race, gender, national identity and culture, and class, *in addition to* sexuality) as opposed to narrow theorizations of homophobia and heterosexism apart from other oppressive regimes, the discipline has yet to self-reflexively engage its own normalizing gestures. For instance, queer scholars and activists in the US have decried the politics of privatization taking place in many American cities, most recently in New York, that aim, largely through re-zoning laws, to 'clean up' public sexual spaces, such as pornographic shops, adult book stores, and sex clubs. As Lauren Berlant and Michael Warner have noted, queer commentary has emerged at a time when United States culture increasingly fetishizes the normal (Berlant and Warner 1995: 345), and this is particularly so in legislative efforts to keep the sexual private by prohibiting or making otherwise less accessible public sexual spaces, including, but not limited to, those of lesbians, gay men, and other sexual dissidents. Yet a common rhetorical strategy used by queer activists and scholars to gain the support of lesbian and gay assimilationists who may support legislation to clean up city 'sleaze' is an appeal to the myth of the queer child. What effect, they ask, will re-zoning laws that sanitize and desexualize the city have on queer youth who migrate to urban areas from other parts of the country? Without diminishing the importance of resisting a politics of sexual privatization and other normalizing ideologies of sexuality, it is the myth, especially the problematic assumptions behind it, that I wish to engage, largely because it also operates in other contexts of queer identity politics and queer scholarship, and relies heavily on a romanticized prototype of the queer child who saves money and gets on a train bound for New York or some other coastal city in search of a new life more compatible with his or her emerging sexual identity.

Or so we fantasize. ... The myth of the queer child also presumes another myth prevalent in contemporary queer studies – that of the metropolitan centre as a mecca for queer community, self-servingly constructed by urban queers, where lesbians, gay men, bisexuals, transsexuals, and transgendered people from the non-metropolitan peripheries, such as the rural South and the Midwest in the United

States, can gather to escape oppressive familial and social relations back home. Indeed, from the recent surge of books in the growing field of lesbian and gay literature, in scanning advertisements for queer cultural and political events, and in looking at both 'mainstream' and independent lesbian and gay films, it sometimes appears as if the only places to truly self-identify as 'queer' are in large metropolitan centres in the West – New York, London, San Francisco, Amsterdam – where one cannot only experience, but supposedly articulate a more 'authentic' queer identity and fully participate in the various cultural, social, and political networks inhabited by other queers.[1] Yet the field of academic queer studies has undertheorized geopolitical spatialization as a significant axis of analysis and its role in constructing queer identity, and queer inquiry has shown little interest in cross-cultural variations of the expression and representation of same-sex desire. Consequently, with its narrow Eurocentric, and therefore imperialistic gaze, queer studies has not seriously engaged how queer identities and cultural formations have taken shape and operate outside of large metropolitan locations.

In contemporary American queer studies, not only is there a metropolitan bias in thinking about queer location but a coastal one as well, and we have yet to address the limitations of narrowly ascribing queer culture(s) to concentrated geographic areas and political spheres. Specifically, in the US, we have not yet begun to challenge popular assumptions that the seaboard cities are the only centres of queer culture and the primary locations from which queers can speak, when, in fact, many lesbians and gay men in the American Midwest, and in other non-urban parts of the country, often express dissatisfaction with queer communities in large urban areas on the coasts because queers in coastal cities often have a rather narrow image of what constitutes a queer identity and simultaneously exclude or marginalize those who do not fit their image of 'queer'.[2] Moreover, in terms of textual and cultural production, the focus of this chapter, for many lesbians and gay men living and writing in Michigan, Ohio, Wisconsin, Minnesota, Missouri, Illinois, Indiana, Nebraska, and Kansas, the Midwest – the heartland – is a significant vantage point from which to create as authors, poets, and cultural workers.

Similar to other work in queer studies, it remains crucial to question an essential queer identity, reduced to sexual difference alone and defined *a priori* by discrete markers, and to carry these ideas further as we more radically theorize geopolitical spatialization as a viable location from which to be positioned in the world. As we have already come to understand, queer identity, like other identities, takes multiple, contingent, and fluid forms in a variety of contexts, and is not only organized around 'sexual orientation', but is always already mediated by race, gender, social class, and other subjectivizing factors. Queer theorists, such as Eve Sedgwick, Diana Fuss, David Halperin, and others influenced by Foucault, have helped us to understand sexual identities not as fixed or stable but as socially situated, eliciting otherness, and breaking down the hetero/homo opposition by which we have traditionally categorized sexual identity. Diana Fuss, for example, succinctly argues the case in pointing out that 'borders are notoriously unstable, and sexual identities rarely secure'. 'Heterosexuality', she continues, 'can never fully ignore the close psychical proximity of its terrifying (homo)sexual other, any more than homosexuality can entirely escape the equally insistent social pressures of (hetero)sexual conformity' (Fuss 1991: 3). But rupturing the hetero/homo binary, while important, does not seem to go far enough, and lesbians and gay men of colour have made the case for even more complex theorizations of 'queer'. Philip Brian Harper, for instance, has argued that 'the great promise of queerness' lies in its potential to mobilize modes of social subjectivity not accounted for in advance by the structures of ideological narratives through consciously deploying the public arena as a constitutive element within subjective identification itself. But, in citing Lauren Berlant and Elizabeth Freeman's essay 'Queer Nationality', he rightfully laments the lack of participation of economic, social, ethnic, and non-American cultures in queer-inflected uses of public space and points out that such work is 'queer' only if it takes into account 'this whole constellation of factors in addition to and in their imbrication with sexual object-choice' (Harper 1997: 25).

These are very important distinctions; yet very often queer studies focuses its attention on queer public space in large metropolitan centres as if queer activism is absent or non-existent in non-urban locations, where in fact, it is often needed most and is practised with considerably more risk. Jacqui Alexander has spoken of the self-serving ideology in queer studies and queer social practices in speaking of lesbian and gay resistance in the Bahamas and other post-colonial contexts which I think applies to non-urban locations in the West as well, in so far as the imperial tendencies of queer studies and queer activism are coming from queer collective ideologies and discursive practices in metropolitan locations, largely in the US. She writes that the absence of visible lesbian/gay movements outside of urbanized, Euroamerican locations is often seen as a defect in political consciousness and maturity, using the presence of publicly organized lesbian and gay movements in (metropolitan areas of) the United States as evidence of their originary status and their superior political maturity (Alexander 1997: 69). Not only does the kind of thinking that she identifies relegate lesbians and gay men in the midwestern US to the peripheries of queer politics, it simultaneously marginalizes queers in nearly all non-metropolitan regions, including those in post-colonial locations. We still need to ask about the formation of new hierarchies (and therefore new margins) in our interpretations and representations of queer identities that privilege urban American coastal cities as sites of queer power, cultural capital, and solidarity over other geographic locations in the US (and elsewhere). Queer studies needs to begin to address the difficulty of identifying and isolating a set of 'common' attributes and experiences that supposedly unite queer people. How do we define that 'common' ground? Who has a voice in defining it?

## QUEER WRITING AND CULTURE IN AMERICA

Besides complementing present work in contemporary American queer studies, then, this chapter also extends it in an attempt to further destabilize representations of queer identity by calling into question the coastal/mid-continent opposition which often divides American queers. Michael Warner, Steven Seidman, and others have questioned seriously the notion of queer community altogether since we are differently sexualized and politicized and because our history has much more to do with noncommunity, dispersal, and resistance to disciplinary normalizing social forces rather than with localization and coherence (Warner 1993: xxv; Seidman 1993: 133). It is important, therefore, to consider how the specificity of queer midwestern location, as *localized* and as *dispersed*, may operate not only as a site of resistance to heteronormativity and homophobia, but as a mode of critique for (re)reading other queer identities and queer cultural practices and for broadening queer ways of looking at and understanding the world. At the same time, we need to address the concomitant question as to how literary/cultural representations of the Midwest, or, more specifically, the cultural landscape of the Midwest as we stereotypically *imagine* it (pastoral, innocent, 'wholesome', conventional, etc.), may be affected and revised by the intervention of queer cultural production.

What do we think of when we imagine the American Midwest? What are some of the cultural myths about the Midwest that prohibit us from imagining it as a possible site of queer cultural production? From a historical perspective, much American literature of the first half of the nineteenth century, perhaps influenced to some extent by Emerson's and Thoreau's musings on nature, as well as a concerted effort by many writers of the time to embody in fiction a quintessential American experience, romanticized small town and farm life. Many literary texts of this period celebrated the beauty of natural settings where people could live in harmony with nature and avoid the so-called moral temptations of large cities. Later in that century and early in the next, writers such as Edward Eggleston, Frank Norris, Sinclair Lewis, and Sherwood Anderson would challenge this agrarian myth, showing in their novels that there is more to the Midwest than Eden-like innocence and the rustic pleasures of small town and rural life. As Ray Lewis White and other critics of midwestern literature point out, such works as Eggleston's *The Hoosier Schoolmaster*, Twain's *Adventures of Huckleberry Finn*, Hamlin Garland's stories in *Main-Travelled Roads*, Edgar Lee Masters's *Spoon River Anthology*, Anderson's *Winesburg, Ohio*, and Sinclair Lewis's *Main Street* debunked the idyllic, pastoral image of midwestern small towns. White argues that these works helped shape a new image of such small towns as being 'replete with loneliness, repression, restriction, and only occasional rebellion and liberation' (White 1990: 25).

However, the agrarian myth and the subsequent refigured image of the Midwest as repressive have not only helped to influence current constructions of the Midwest in general, which do not seem to make it an attractive place for sexual minorities, but have been reinforced by the axes of contemporary queer power on the American East and West coasts, as well as by other gay narratives written specifically about the non-urban Midwest. Edmund White, for instance (who spent part of his childhood in Cincinnati, Ohio), in a chapter on the Midwest in his book *States of Desire: Travels in Gay America*, casually observes that gay men and women in Kansas City and other parts of the Midwest 'untouched by gay liberation' seem to equate gay identity and gay life with either being in gay bars or being in bed. White goes on to say that after emerging from either of these enclosed, private spaces, one lives one's public life in the world of heterosexuality, living by the beliefs of the dominant culture; he offers that 'the notion that affectional preference, sexual appetite, shared oppression might color all of one's experience' eludes gay people in the Midwest (White 1991:156). White does acknowledge that the heartland is what one makes of it, that the 'stability' of the Midwest can be felt as 'irredeemable despair', a cultural trope inherited from late nineteenth- and early twentieth-century American fiction, or as 'wholesomeness', in that many gays, especially gay couples, are able to adapt to 'the work-centered, down-to-earth, conservative Midwest with ease and satisfaction' (White 1991: 193).

More recent, though not quite as pessimistic as White, Will Fellows's 1996 book *Farm Boys*, a collection of memoirs by gay men who grew up on rural farms in the Midwest roughly between the post-war years and the mid-1970s, addresses the specificity of midwestern location and the ways in which it affects and is affected by perceptions of landscape, desire, and the de-centring of subjectivity. Indeed, many of the memoirs collected seem to be directly influenced by Willa Cather's own reflections on writing her novel *O Pioneers!* (1913) and the landscape of her native Nebraska which she often visited after leaving it in 1896. In an interview with the *Sunday World-Herald* in Omaha in 1921, Cather recalls:

> Whenever I crossed the Missouri River coming into Nebraska the very smell of the soil tore me to pieces. I could not decide which was the real and which the fake me. I almost decided to settle down on a quarter section of land and let my writing go. ... I knew every farm, every tree, every field in the region around my home and they all called out to me. ... I had searched for books telling about the beauty of the country I loved, its romance, the heroism and strength and courage of its people that had been plowed into the very furrows of its soil and I did not find them. And so I wrote *O Pioneers!*
>
> (quoted in Bennett 1961: 138–9)

Yet the essays in *Farm Boys*, transcribed by the editor from taped interviews with each of the men and later sent to each subject interviewed for editing, as well as Fellows's own introduction and afterword that contextualize the interviews, still seem disturbingly informed by dominant cultural readings of the Midwest and cultural stereotypes of gay men. In his lengthy introduction, Fellows remarks that:

with few exceptions, the boys whose stories are presented here ... generally sought to avoid fieldwork and the repair and maintenance of farm machinery and vehicles. This was typically attributed to an *inherent* 'mechanical disability' and to the dusty, dirty, boring nature of driving machinery back and forth in the fields.

(Fellows 1996: 11; emphasis added)

He goes on to say that when 'these boys' were attracted to farm work, 'it was generally the care, feeding, and breeding of livestock and the cleaning and maintenance of these animals' shelters that they found most appealing and satisfying'; that is, 'the "housework" of the farm' (Fellows 1996: 11). Fellows also points out that most of the subjects he interviewed had richer and more satisfying relationships with their mothers and other females than with their fathers or other males; therefore, he says, they had stronger inclinations to work in the house and garden than to do farmwork (Fellows 1996: 12). Is a pattern emerging here? Have we suddenly reverted to pre-*DSM-III* medical/psychiatric constructions of the queer child defined by gender abjection and the 'failure' in boys to reach the 'masculine ideal'?[3] While it is certainly true that most of the boys interviewed grew up during the most homophobic height of American psychiatry (from the Kinsey Report of 1948 through the debates in the late 1960s that eventually led to the 1973 decision to delete homosexuality as a diagnostic category from the *DSM*), it is surely conceivable, at the same time, that gender-conforming boys who enjoyed the manual labour of farm life could also have become gay adults and did not feel like 'misfits' who had to escape it, just as it may equally be the case that some heterosexual men who grew up on midwestern farms found the discipline and labour of farm life intolerable as boys and left it for more urban areas as adults.[4] Fellows, in his readings of the gay men he interviewed, his transcription of the interviews, his selection of which narratives and which parts of selected narratives would be published, in addition to his reification of stereotypes of gay men as weak, effeminate, and generally unsuited for the physical demands of manual labour on the farm, relies heavily on monolithic images of midwestern farm life, which he describes as isolated, prudish, religiously conservative, and conventional, all of which restricted sexual activity (Fellows 1996: 20). This, as well as an assumed, but not thoroughly analysed, rural-to-urban migration among the gay men he interviewed, which may relate to such other factors as educational, economic, and career opportunities, leads me to question whether the representations of the Midwest in the book come from the actual narratives supplied by the gay men he interviewed or were established *a priori*.

The problem here, as in Edmund White, is that gay men and lesbians are merely included, that is, minoritized, in the Midwest in languages that name sexual identities in ways that reproduce heterosexist ideologies with dominant cultural constructions of the Midwest, including queer oppression, left intact. As Warner reminds us in his introduction to *Fear of a Queer Planet*, it is not enough to merely include lesbians and gay men in a theory or view of the world that otherwise remains unaltered (Warner 1993: xv–xvi). Linnea Johnson, who has written on Cather's work and life in Nebraska and on the island of Grand Manan in New Brunswick, reflects on how critics have 'off-read' Cather's life by their elision of the prominence of her lover, Edith Lewis, thereby missing the landscape of which Cather wrote. The question that needs to be asked, then, is not only how queers form part of the already socially constructed landscape of the Midwest, but how we may re-read and revise that landscape as a result of queer cultural intervention. Recent queer writing from the Midwest has begun to more radically contradict the rather dismal picture that White and Fellows portray. Indeed, what is most interesting is the pockets of resistance to queer oppression that White found in his travels through the heartland and Fellows in his interviews, not just resistance to the status quo but resistance to the cultural tropes of queers in the Midwest as lonely, conforming to dominant social practices, and internalizing homophobia, which neither White nor Fellows adequately develop as an alternative trajectory through which to read queer location in the Midwest. This is best evidenced in White's conversation with Evan, an activist in Kansas City, who speaks of entrapment and arrest for cruising ('soliciting' was the charge) in a gay bar there and was sentenced to see a psychiatrist:

> 'I got off lightly', Evan said, 'but my lover didn't. He had rheumatic fever. He also drank too much; he had never been able to accept his homosexuality. When he heard I had been arrested, he went to bed and drank himself to death. He was just forty-one. His relatives descended and stripped our house bare. When I removed my own things, they accused me of stealing them. They still call me at work to harass me. I have no legal rights. Though we'd been together for years, we weren't married. It was an illegal relationship. That's when I became an activist.'
>
> (White 1991: 161)

Of course, resistance can work in a variety of ways besides overt political activism, which is not limited to what White refers to as a few 'isolated incidents' in the Midwest as it is much more widespread than we may have otherwise assumed. The stereotypes of the Midwest and the coastal/mid-continent split in American queer culture are more easily dismantled through a focus on women's writing, as in the example of Cather I mentioned earlier, and through ensuring, as I will discuss later, that the axis of sexuality in queer inquiry does not obscure and over-exceed that of gender as argued by lesbian theorists such as Biddy Martin. It is also important, as in the case of the activist, Evan, quoted in White above, that we read critically around the superficiality of the heteronormative façade of midwestern life. Even though Fellows's book is about gay men who grew up in farm families in the midwestern

United States, this does not imply that one may easily erase the specificity of lesbian desire, and this is brilliantly captured in the description of one of Fellows's informants of an elderly neighbour woman whom he perceives at a young age to be an alternative role model for queer children. Despite his use of the sexist term 'old maid', he remembers her with affection:

> Minnie was an old maid, very manly in her dress, who lived her entire life on the farm where she was born. Whenever we went to her place to buy eggs, her house was as neat as a pin and her kitchen always had the smell of something freshly baked. She was very warm and had a distinctive, contagious laugh. She enjoyed chatting with my dad as much as with my mom. We sort of adopted Minnie as an aunt or grandmother. In one sense people probably thought, 'How strange, living all by herself', but she was well-liked and respected by the neighboring farmers. ... I really admired the respect that she commanded, and I sometimes thought that I would like to live like she did.
>
> (Fellows 1996: 13–14)

Interestingly, the insight of this informant, both as a child and as an adult recalling Minnie, hints at the possibility of non-heterosexual lives and experiences outside of heteronormativity in the Midwest which Fellows does not develop as a way of resistantly reading juridically-prescribed gender roles and the politically erected links, which heteronormative culture codes as natural and causal, between gender identification (as one sex) and desire (for the opposite sex). While the informant as a child did not specifically name Minnie as 'lesbian', most likely because he did not have the discourse available to him to name her as such, neither he nor his friends identify her abjectly, but 'adopt' her as part of their familial and affectional relations in opposition to child-rearing practices, still in existence today, that do not see lesbians or gay men, or, whatever their sexuality, those adults simply perceived to be queer through their nonconformity to gender norms, as 'appropriate' role models for children. In speaking of avuncular relations, whether linked by blood or by marriage, or simply as a way of naming relations to people older than ourselves who aren't related by blood or by marriage, Eve Sedgwick writes:

> Because aunts and uncles (in either narrow or extended meanings) are adults whose intimate access to children needn't depend on their own pairing or procreation, it's very common, of course, for some of them to have the office of representing nonconforming or nonreproductive sexualities to children. We are many, the queer women and men whose first sense of the possibility of alternative life trajectories came to us from our uncles and aunts [real or imagined] – even when the stories we were

allowed to hear about their lives were *almost* unrecognizably mangled, often in demeaning ways, by the heterosexist hygiene of childrearing.

(Sedgwick 1993: 63)

Much queer literary writing coming out of the Midwest reflects on or represents, in varying ways, midwestern childhood experiences of growing up. One often finds recurrent narratives about the ties between children and queer adults; Robert Rodi, for instance, author of such critically acclaimed novels as *Closet Case* (1993) and *Fag Hag* (1992), reflects on his midwestern upbringing in a suburb in northern Illinois in a memoir 'Mister Kenny', and on a gay neighbour he knew as a child from the perspective of the gay man he has himself become. Though Mister Kenny is not specifically named as an uncle, Rodi writes poignantly of the affection he and his friends shared for him, who, much to their delight, gardened wearing a lady's hat and sparked the discomfort of their parents. In writing about being first invited into Mister Kenny's apartment, Rodi recalls:

> we were fascinated by Mister Kenny's apartment because it was one of the few homes to which we had access that wasn't ruled by children. It was a strictly adult domain, and despite its tidiness and order Mister Kenny allowed us to root through it, to pull out photographs and knickknacks and say what's this and who's that and where did this come from. We were especially intrigued by any photographs from the Olden Days, as we called them. ... The snapshots from Mister Kenny's later, civilian life were mainly of him sitting in dark rooms squinting at the flash with other thin, pale men in skinny ties and white socks, which we found utterly hilarious. It was a special treat to find a photograph of a woman because she would invariably be wearing something even funnier, but pictures of women were few in Mister Kenny's albums. Mister Kenny had a record collection, too, which consisted mainly of boxed sets of operas. He would occasionally try to play us an aria from one of these, telling us to listen, children, just listen to the melody, but as soon as he set the needle on the vinyl and the trill of the soprano filled the room, we would clutch our necks and make choking sounds, and Mister Kenny would have to give it up. ... It was a wonderful afternoon, intimate and exciting and filled with awe and laughter, but I remember, too, that little Gordy Raddatz ... squeezed by me and settled into Mister Kenny's lap to watch the proceedings. Mister Kenny let him sit there for a few moments but appeared enormously uncomfortable – I remember to this day the contortions of his face – and eventually slid free of little Gordy and stood upright for the remainder of our visit.

(Rodi 1996: 40–1)

Similarly, from the point of view of a gay uncle, midwestern poet William Reichard considers what it means to have had a nephew named after him in his poem 'For Liam When He Grows Up'. Refusing the sentimentality of the gesture of his sister to give him a 'legacy' in heterosexist terms through her child who will carry on his name, Reichard contemplates what exactly that legacy might mean: 'William and Billy and Willy and Bill / faggot and cocksucker, homo and queer' (Reichard 1996: 33). He goes on to wonder how he might seem Other to this child, despite the bond that was intended to be created between them, when considering 'the heterosexist hygiene of child rearing' and the subtle, homophobic coding that primary caretakers, whether consciously or not, pass on to children, which they, in turn, may echo as

> in cards sent at Christmas to
> 'Dear Uncle Bill, *funny* uncle,
> I hope you are well.'
>     (Reichard 1996: 33;
>         emphasis added)

Much queer writing in the heartland, reflecting, then, on growing up in the Midwest, or in simply writing about queer desire, whether or not authors *intend* their work to be political, resists heteronormativity in its struggle to speak to and name the world queerly.

On the other hand, the prominence of such cities as New York, San Francisco, and Los Angeles in queer political and cultural achievements is certainly justified, though it is not the case that there is something *inherently* urban, cosmopolitan, and, in the case of the US, coastal, about queer experience. This becomes more evident when we look at the historical work of Lillian Faderman, Jonathan Ned Katz, Allan Bérubé, and others, which has noted, for example, how the Second World War, in ironic contrast to the antihomosexual stance of the military and its discharges of 'undesirable' lesbian and gay personnel after the war, contributed not only to the creation and development of queer communities in the seaboard cities but to the eventual emergence of a queer political movement as we know it today. Allan Bérubé, in *Coming Out Under Fire*, notes that mobilization for the war helped to loosen the constraints that locked many lesbians and gay men in silence, isolation, and self-contempt, and points out that the significance of homosexuality was intensified by the military as it built a bureaucratic apparatus to identify and manage homosexual personnel. Because it was disrupted and exposed by the war, gay life in the post-war years grew as lesbian and gay veterans identified with each other's struggles and formed communities as members of a homosexual minority (Bérubé 1990: 256–7). But, for the most part, these communities formed in large coastal cities. Specifically focusing on the difference of gender on this point, Lillian Faderman further elaborates that the war brought huge numbers of women together in these cities to participate in the civilian workforce where they were also able to appreciate other females as serious, self-sufficient human beings away from restrictive family relations, and where relatively large lesbian communities could be created where only an inchoate lesbian consciousness had been forming (Faderman 1992: 121). The military further contributed to the development of queer culture when it became even less lenient in its policies toward homosexuals once the war was over; Faderman speaks of how thousands of lesbian and gay personnel were loaded on to 'queer ships' and sent to the nearest US port – New York, Los Angeles, San Francisco, Boston, and others. Since many of those discharged for being homosexual believed they could not go home, or were too ashamed to do so, many stayed where they disembarked and their numbers helped to form large enclaves in port cities along both coasts (Faderman 1992: 126).

While certainly the large concentration of lesbians joining the workforce in metropolitan areas on the coasts during the war, in addition to the large numbers of discharged lesbians and gay men after the war, led to the development of queer communities in these areas, it is important to bear in mind that the reasons for the urban bicoastal prominence of queer communities in the US are *social* and *historical*. Queer identity and queer culture, because they are not monolithic and homogeneous, but subject to history and to social context (and are therefore variable and contingent), are not self-evidently bound to urban coastal areas. As I have been suggesting, this becomes more apparent when we examine the specificity of lesbian cultural practices. As Warner has pointed out that the predominance of white, middle-class men in gay organizing is not simply the result of evil intent or willed exclusion, the institutions of queer culture-building have none the less been market-mediated and dominated therefore by those with capital – typically middle-class white men (Warner 1993: xvi–xvii). We do need to account for, then, the slippery relation between oppression and privilege among middle-class gay white men and their hold on such gay businesses as bars, media, and resorts, in addition to commercial and residential real estate used for gay businesses and gay residential areas, which, I might add, are largely situated in metropolitan areas along both coasts of the US. This not only helps give credence to queer culture as restricted mainly to these locations, but reflects male privilege in both the dominant culture and among queers in so far as the 'signs' of queer culture, especially those made visible through capital and marketing and advertising practices in the queer media, reduce it, economically at least, to gay *male* culture. Looking specifically at the history of lesbians in the United States will help not only to foreground gender as an axis of analysis, not to be escaped or over-ridden by the greater mobility of queer desire (Martin 1994: 102), through, for instance, making a cross-gender identification, but will help shift questions of geopolitical spatialization and queer migration away from an exclusive focus on metropolitan spaces.

In the 1970s, for example, many lesbian-feminist communities sprang up in various parts of the American heartland, certainly in cosmopolitan cities like Chicago, Minneapolis, and Detroit, but in smaller university towns as well, such as Bloomington, Indiana; Ann Arbor, Michigan; Madison, Wisconsin; and Iowa City, Iowa. Women's music festivals attracted huge crowds, with self-affirming lyrics of lesbian politics, love, and unity, and the first National Women's Music Festival was held in Champaign, Illinois, in 1974 (Faderman 1992: 220, 222). Women's presses provided periodicals that spoke to lesbian-feminist issues and some, such as *Lesbian Connection*, which began in 1974 based in East Lansing, Michigan, kept down costs so poorer women could buy them at a reduced price or obtain them for free (Faderman 1992: 224). Looking at the Midwest through the lens of lesbian-feminist cultural practices helps to further dismantle the stereotype of the Midwest as a place for social conformity with little or no resistance. Faderman notes that in the 1980s, such cultural events as the Michigan Womyn's Music Festival and the Midwest Women's Festival became sites of intense political differences and disagreements between lesbians who were cultural feminists, and tended to see pornography, public sex, and sadomasochism as connected to violence to and exploitation of women, thereby validating the system of patriarchy, and radical lesbians, who saw these as ways for lesbians to resist sexual politics that repressed women and to explore sexual feelings and sexual practices that had been marked as taboo for them (Faderman 1992: 250–1).

Queer communities in American coastal cities often play a role in helping to define, articulate, and sustain queer identity elsewhere and it is here that academic queer studies must examine its hegemonic impulses and acknowledge that in the Midwest (and in other locations outside of the axes of queer power), where the concentration of lesbians and gay men is smaller, the construction of queer identity, the social positioning of oneself as 'queer', is much more contentious. It becomes a more rigorous struggle between assimilation to larger heterosexual worlds and resistance to heteronormative demands for invisibility through asserting difference. Much queer American midwestern writing illustrates, in varying degrees, this continuing struggle. In some work, the struggle toward assimilation plays a more prominent role, as in Gary Pool's short story 'Victims of Circumstance' where a gay male couple, who own and operate a French restaurant in Springfield, Missouri, and, in their legal case to jointly adopt an African-American son, present themselves as responsible people similar to other heterosexuals who wish to become parents. In the poem 'Christmas in the Midwest' by Maureen Seaton, a woman brings home her lesbian lover where they sleep in a double bed 'beneath handmade quilts' (Seaton 1991: 71) hoping for acceptance and validation from her parents. Another example is the letter Rachel writes to her lover, Hannah. In Claudia Allen's play *Hannah Free*, Rachel describes how much she loves and misses Hannah (who has gone to New Mexico as part of her military service during the Second World War), but how she cannot leave the midwestern town where she lives.

The Canada geese are on the lake, taking a rest on their way south. I walk over and listen to them honk; I feed them cracked corn when I can get it. ... I miss you, Hannah. I wish you'd stay home, but at least this time I know you're doing war work: you're not just running away from me. New Mexico sounds beautiful, but I'd miss my mulberry tree out back and my lilac bushes hanging over the driveway. You've been having dinner with the same woman all the time. What's that mean, 'dinner'? I thought you were going to war; instead you're going to dinner. Well, I'm not knitting you any more warm socks, even if you are in the service. You're down there 'having dinner' while I'm up here alone, squirming in my sleep. Well, I know people read your mail, so I won't say any more.

(Allen 1992: 151)

In some cases, given the current political backlash against lesbians and gay men and the fetishization of the 'normal' in American culture, issues of assimilation and social and sexual conformity seem to mark contemporary lesbian and gay midwestern writing, but as soon as one attempts to fix these as categories, new areas of indeterminacy arise, further destabilizing our paradigms for representing sexual difference and region. Other queer writers in the Midwest write poignantly and unapologetically of the *difference* of queer desire, addressing the need to name and represent our sexual lives despite hetero culture's insistence that we remain silent, while at the same time calling into question tacit assumptions of normalcy, narrowly defined notions of familial and community life, and fixed ideas about race, gender, and class. Antler, for example, winner of the Walt Whitman Award for poetry and praised by the late Allen Ginsberg as one of the most important American poets writing today, combines the physicality of the landscape with gay longing and desire. In 'On My Way to the Lake Michigan Sunrise on the Milwaukee Lakefront Breakwater', he celebrates spring and the sunrise on Lake Michigan as well as the not yet fully conscious sexuality of 'sleeping boys with erections'. In other midwestern queer writing, the specificity of midwestern landscape takes a less prominent position, forming a backdrop to other meanings. African-American poet Terri Jewell, who lived in Michigan until her death in 1995, uses metaphors of landscape to rework images of soil and fertility in order to describe the orgasmic eroticism between two women in 'Agrology':

Your buttocks rained a moister substance
soaked fertile rows down to bedrock ...
as we lie spent and fallow ...

(Jewell 1996: 145)

In still other work, the specificity of the heartland as place is not as important as the Midwest being a nexus where queer desires, diasporic identities, and multiple languages and cultures intersect and converge; for beyond signifying a geographic space, the Midwest is also a perspective, a way of positioning oneself in the world. Along these lines, Chinese-American lesbian poet and fiction writer Kitty Tsui, who lives and writes in Indiana, tells unabashedly of her love for female body parts, leather, and food in 'A Femme in Butch Clothing':

> I like it that she's Chinese. We have a common language and culture, even though she was born in the Midwest and I was born in the Far East. And I speak Cantonese and she doesn't. Her second language is French. I like it that I don't always have to explain, educate, or entertain. We share the same love for learning and leather. For food. Food is a very esoteric thing. And we Chinese enjoy an esoteric farrago of food.
> 
> To name a few, there's *jook* for breakfast, *dim sum* for lunch, and tofu with liquid cane sugar for desert. Fermented black beans. Fermented bean curd. Squab. Squid. Conch. ...
> 
> My femme is as skilled in the kitchen as she is in the bedroom. She can handle a blade as well as a fist. She can stir-fry as well as she can kiss, beat cream as well as she can unroll a condom. ...
> 
> She is my femme in butch clothing. She wears 501s, leather chaps, work boots, and men's shirts on the street. Cashmere, silk, or satin to bed. She knows the fastest way to undo my pants and the fastest way to bring me to multiple orgasms with her mouth on my clitoris.
> 
> (Tsui 1996: 36–37)

One cannot assert, then, that there is an easily definable queer midwestern identity, sensibility, or style of writing in the US; to do so would essentialize both the Midwest and queer midwestern writing as well as maintain the coastal/heartland split. In much queer midwestern writing, one finds recurring images of snow, flatlands, cornfields, cows, farms, and prairie which form part of the Midwest landscape; yet the region geographically and socially is obviously not reducible to these agrarian images. Another problem is that, unlike New England and the South as sites for regional writing, the American Midwest is an expansive area, indeed the largest region of the US, and to attempt to reduce it to distinguishable criteria runs the risk of eliding differences within it. The Midwest is not antithetical to queer identities and cultural practices; in fact, reading American queer writing 'a-coastally' strongly suggests that the Midwest *enables* the production of queer culture. To assume otherwise, to disparage queer location and cultural production in the Midwest, dangerously serves and perpetuates homophobic ideologies that assert that there is no place for queers in 'Middle America'. Instead, in order to seriously engage sexual difference in its varied and multiple forms, queer studies needs to address more inclusive ways of being queer and analyse the production of queer culture in the different locations from which our voices can be heard.

## Acknowledgements

A few of the ideas in this chapter were formerly presented in my introduction '"What?!" Queers in the Midwest?' in *Reclaiming the Heartland: Lesbian and Gay Voices from the Midwest* (K.L. Osborne and W.J. Spurlin, eds, Minneapolis: University of Minnesota Press, 1996, pp. xi–xxv). I am grateful to the University of Minnesota Press for permission to use brief excerpts from that copyrighted material and to further develop the ideas in this chapter.

## Notes

1 I use the term 'queer' to refer not only to academic queer studies but to an oppositional political praxis that works against other normalizing ideologies in addition to those of (hetero)sexuality as already discussed. Occasionally, I use the term 'lesbian and gay', usually to speak of the specificity of sexual identities in the American Midwest or of representations of same-sex desire in midwestern writing by lesbians and gay men. I am reluctant, however, to read the Midwest solely under the slightly more conservative rubric of lesbian and gay liberation politics which once again reifies the coastal/mid-continent split so long as one assumes that queer politics in the US are predominately produced in cities, especially along the coasts, and that the logic of assimilation, toleration, and equal rights is the prominent, if not only, dimension of lesbian and gay politics and cultural work in the Midwest. I would argue instead that *both* political impulses operate in *both* locations, and that they are more a matter of back-and-forth movement determined by context and specific political needs and purposes rather than determined in advance. At the same time, it is important to remember that the social positioning of oneself as gay or lesbian in the Midwest is very often a *queer* position, and, as I shall argue later, one that is contentious and works against not only normalizing sexual ideologies but against the normative more generally. Hence, my usage of 'queer' in relation to the specificity of the Midwest is both deliberate and political. As David Eng reminds us, 'gay and lesbian' and 'queer' are not mutually exclusive terms (Eng 1997: 50n), and a focus on queer cultural practices in the Midwest may help further problematize impulses in queer studies to set up clear-cut dichotomies between these two terms and to reduce the political praxes they imply to specific geographic locations.

2 On this specific point, there has been some work in sexuality studies which contests the urban as a primary site for dissident sexualities, as David Bell discusses in more detail in Chapter 5 in this collection. Of particular note in gay studies is Mark Thompson's study of the US Radical Fairy movement in the 1970s which sought to reject urban gay life and to link sexuality with spiritual solace in nature. Lillian Faderman's work *Odd Girls and Twilight Lovers*, which I discuss later, similarly chronicles the lesbian-separatist movement in the 1970s where many separatists established communal farms on the grounds that the city 'was a man-made world where lesbians' energy was diverted in a struggle to survive and live true to their principles' (Faderman 1992: 238).

3 The *DSM* refers to the *Diagnostic and Statistical Manual* published by the American Psychiatric Association (APA) and used to diagnose psychiatric disorders. The third edition (*DSM-III*),

published in 1980, was the first to remove homosexuality as a category of psychopathology as a result of the APA's historic 1973 decision. The *DSM-III* retained 'ego-dystonic homosexuality', which was reserved for individuals who were distressed by homosexual arousal and desired to increase heterosexual arousal. The revised edition of the *DSM-III* (*DSM-III-R*), which was published in 1987, deleted ego-dystonic homosexuality as well. The category of Gender Identity Disorder in Children, however, first appeared in 1980 in the *DSM-III* and remains in the current *DSM-IV* published in 1994.

4 For a more detailed discussion of the ways in which psychoanalysis and psychiatry have conflated gender and sexuality by still prescribing that *identification* as one sex must necessarily result in the *desire* for the other sex (even though the *DSM* has depathologized atypical sexual object-choice, yet has (re)pathologized atypical gender identification evident in the new diagnostic category of Gender Identity Disorder, or GID, in Children), and for an argument of the ways in which gender atypical children rupture the heterosexual matrix and impair its efficient manageability, see my 1998 essay 'Sissies and Sisters: Gender, Sexuality and the Possibilities of Coalition' in *Coming Out of Feminism?*

# References

Alexander, M.J. (1997) 'Erotic Autonomy as a Politics of Decolonization: An Anatomy of Feminist and State Practice in the Bahamas Tourist Economy', in M.J. Alexander and C.T. Mohanty (eds) *Feminist Genealogies, Colonial Legacies, Democratic Futures*, London: Routledge.

Allen, C. (1992) *Hannah Free*, in C. Allen, *She's Always Liked the Girls Best*, Chicago: Third Side Press.

Bennett, M.R. (1961) *The World of Willa Cather*, Lincoln: University of Nebraska Press.

Berlant, L. and Freeman, E. (1993) 'Queer Nationality', in M. Warner (ed.) *Fear of a Queer Plant: Queer Politics and Social Theory*, Minneapolis: University of Minnesota Press.

Berlant, L. and Warner, M. (1995) 'What Does Queer Theory Teach Us About X?', *PMLA* 110 (3): 343–9.

Bérubé, A. (1990) *Coming Out Under Fire: The History of Gay Men and Women in World War Two*, New York: Penguin.

Eng, D.L. (1997) 'Out Here and Over There: Queerness and Diaspora in Asian American Studies', *Social Text* 15 (3–4): 31–52.

Faderman, L. (1992) *Odd Girls and Twilight Lovers: A History of Lesbian Life in Twentieth-Century America*, New York: Penguin.

Fellows, W. (ed.) (1996) *Farm Boys: Lives of Gay Men from the Rural Midwest*, Madison: University of Wisconsin Press.

Fuss, D. (1991) 'Inside/Out', in D. Fuss (ed.) *Inside/Out: Lesbian Theories, Gay Theories*, London: Routledge.

Harper, P.B. (1997) 'Gay Male Identities, Personal Privacy, and Relations of Public Exchange: Notes on Directions for Queer Critique', *Social Text* 15 (3–4): 5–29.

Jewell, T.L. (1996) 'Agrology', in K.L. Osborne and W.J. Spurlin (eds) *Reclaiming the Heartland: Lesbian and Gay Voices from the Midwest*, Minneapolis: University of Minnesota Press.

Katz, J.N. (1992) *Gay American History: Lesbians and Gay Men in the U.S.A.*, rev. edn, New York: Penguin.

Martin, B. (1994) 'Extraordinary Homosexuals and the Fear of Being Ordinary', *Differences: A Journal of Feminist Cultural Studies* 6 (2–3): 100–25.

Reichard, W. (1996) 'For Liam When He Grows Up', in K.L. Osborne and W.J. Spurlin (eds) *Reclaiming the Heartland: Lesbian and Gay Voices from the Midwest*, Minneapolis: University of Minnesota Press.

Rodi, R. (1996) 'Mister Kenny: A Memoir', in K.L. Osborne and W.J. Spurlin (eds) *Reclaiming the Heartland: Lesbian and Gay Voices from the Midwest*, Minneapolis: University of Minnesota Press.

Seaton, M. (1991) 'Christmas in the Midwest', in M. Seaton, *Fear of Subways*, Portland, OR: Eighth Mountain Press.

Sedgwick, E.K. (1993) 'Tales of the Avunculate: Queer Tutelage in *The Importance of Being Earnest*', in E.K. Sedgwick, *Tendencies*, Durham, NC: Duke University Press.

Seidman, S. (1993) 'Identity and Politics in a "Postmodern" Gay Culture: Some Historical and Conceptual Notes', in M. Warner (ed.) *Fear of a Queer Planet: Queer Politics and Social Theory*, Minneapolis: University of Minnesota Press.

Spurlin, W.J. (1998) 'Sissies and Sisters: Gender, Sexuality, and the Possibilities of Coalition', in M. Merck, N. Segal, and E. Wright (eds) *Coming Out of Feminism?*, Oxford: Blackwell Publishers.

Thompson, M. (1987) *Gay Spirit: Myth and Meaning*, New York: St Martin's Press.

Tsui, K. (1996) 'A Femme in Butch Clothing', in K. Tsui, *Breathless: Erotica*, Ithaca, NY: Firebrand Books.

Warner, M. (ed.) (1993) *Fear of a Queer Planet: Queer Politics and Social Theory*, Minneapolis: University of Minnesota Press.

White, E. (1991) *States of Desire: Travels in Gay America*, New York: Penguin.

White, R.L. (1990) *Winesburg, Ohio: An Exploration*, Boston, MA: Twayne Publishers.

# 11

# GETTING YOUR KICKS ON ROUTE 66!

Stories of gay and lesbian life in rural America
c. 1950–1970s

*Angelia R. Wilson*

> In a word, the modernist laments fragmentation while the postmodernist celebrates it.
>
> (Barry 1995: 84)

## Introduction

Undoubtedly the central issue of the modern 'gay and lesbian movement' which we locate from the Stonewall riots has been the need to create, express or even discover an identity which sets us apart from the heterosexual other. This need hurled us along the treacherous path of drawing boundaries between them and us; of making up lists of who we are, and are not; of solidifying acceptable political positions of those included under the gay and lesbian umbrella. The building of gay and lesbian 'community' then, or at least the political positing of a gay and lesbian identity, necessitated constructing a coherent story about our experience of marginalization. Expressions of collective identity are stories told to ensure sameness – of deviant desire and of social exclusion. They are, in the words of Jeffrey Weeks, "necessary fictions" (1995: 98–9).

And as the solitary listener, we hope to find elements in these collective fictions which resonate with our own experience. That is what we – the sexually excluded – listen for, a small particle with which we can identify; something, someone, telling our story. At least this is my own positioning to stories told of non-heterosexual desire. Growing up as an itinerant preacher's daughter in the small towns of the Texas panhandle, I was well acquainted with social exclusion. When puberty brought a flood of desire that was not reflected amongst my peers, my community or my limited knowledge of broader American culture I believed that exclusion would become my home. I remember as a teenager lying in my bed where I could hear the traffic on Route 66 only a block away and dreaming of life that waited down the road. Every peaceful country image was tainted for me by the knowledge of conservatism lurking beneath the surface, ready to isolate, if not annihilate, difference. I now live far away from my rural birthplace. And the road has taken me in search of stories of how others negotiated the parochial aspects of rural life which contextualized their sexual desire. Searching through accounts of the lives of gay men and lesbians in rural America, I found collective 'necessary fictions' of rural exclusion and isolation. I also found stories that reflected my own.

Stories of urban migration and of rural exclusion have been analysed in this collection by William Spurlin (Chapter 10) and were regularly a part of the archive ephemera where I began my research. Given the familiar construction of the homophobic countryside and the understandable response to it – 'I found myself here, and got the hell out' – I only briefly consider this type of story in the section entitled 'Social exclusion … help!'. It is worth noting however that our acquaintance with this story is reliant upon those who escaped – to a space in which, an audience to which, the tale could be told and retold. That does not make it fiction, it simply acknowledges its role in dividing the urban from the rural. It is also my story, or a part of it – 'Flight' in search of the familiar, escape from the threat of parochial damnation.

I also came across, both in this research and in my own academic coming of age, a different version of country life. As a student of feminism I heard my political sisters paint the pastoral countryside from a distinctively non-heterosexual perspective. In the separated rural space lesbians could commune with Mother Nature and rediscover the power of womanhood. In her informative discussion of lesbian separatism 'Making Space', Gill Valentine explains the impetus behind the lesbian land movement as it emerged in the 1970s:

> In order to avoid maintaining or perpetuating patriarchy in any way and to enable women to construct an ideal new society beyond the influence of men, some lesbian feminists adopted the spatial strategy of distancing themselves from mainstream society by establishing separatist communities that excluded all heterosexual and gay men … spatial isolation meant that it was easier for women to be self-sufficient and purer in their practices in the country than in the city, and because essential notions about women's closeness to nature meant that the countryside was identified as female space.
>
> (Valentine 1997: 111)

Lesbian feminists encouraged women to 'Find yourself in the country' – emphasizing self-discovery in the rural idyll, chosen isolation from the heterosexist world, creating a women-centred rural community. The familiarity of this story, which I consider in the section on 'social isolation', is reliant upon accounts of participants who had access to a community, an audience[1]. While I admire their ideals – 'Fight' to reclaim the strength of sisterhood; contest the claim of man to dominate property and space – this story reflects only a brief portion of my own.

Each of these versions presents two monolithic perspectives of 'the rural' – as hostile or idyllic – which I move away from in the final section. This redirection is due in part to the fact that neither of these stories reflect fully my experience of rural life. Almost every summer I migrate home for a few weeks to see the sun and visit my family. My parents have retired and have returned to the homeplace – a house my grandfather built in a small town populated mostly by kinfolk. I am no longer an outsider, a preacher's daughter. I am simply a Wilson. However, I am unmarried and over thirty in a place where girls become wives before they can legally drink alcohol. Yes, they all know that I am 'gay'. I am not run out of town, or even accosted on the street by someone concerned about my whereabouts in the afterlife. It would be easier, for them and me, if I were married with two kids. But that is about social embarrassment in the face of difference. It is not idyllic but neither is it hostile. Perhaps of more academic significance, this redirection attempts to voice some of the stories I came across which do not fit easily into the above categories. They are not stories of people looking to the city for comfort, or joining up with lesbian separatists. They are stories of non-heterosexuals living in rural communities and just getting on with life. People that reflect the complexity of identity or, as Weeks notes, whose identities 'tell us about multiple social belongings' (1995: 90). These stories, in turn, call us to revisit our (mis)conception of country life as necessarily hostile or idyllic if only enjoyed in lesbian isolation.

### Setting the scene

Before considering some of the more familiar narratives, it is important to locate this material in a historical and social context. The bulk of the written evidence considered in this chapter dates from the 1950s through the late 1970s. Recent interviews are with older lesbians recalling their experiences during this same time period. Thus they share a broadly similar cultural and historical timeframe: post-Second World War, the publication of Kinsey *et al.*'s *Sexual Behavior in the Human Male* (1948) and *Sexual Behavior in the Human Female* (1953), and the emergence of new social movements. For example, in his comprehensive account of gay and lesbian history Neil Miller notes the importance of the Second World War in cultivating American gay and lesbian identity (1995). 'The mobilization of millions of people', writes Miller, 'turned American society upside down, bringing young men and women from farms and small towns into sex-segregated environments, to port cities like New York and San Francisco, away from the structures provided by family, church, and hometown' (p. 231). Migration to the more anonymous urban centres perhaps reflected not only the desire to find a same-sex encounter but a desire to leave the all too familiar confines of rural and family life. It is perhaps then not surprising that the accounts of rural exclusion are often told by those who have found their contentment, their voice and their audience in the comfort of the urban collective.

Between the Second World War and the social revolution of the 1960s, Kinsey posited in the American consciousness scientific evidence of the range of sexual practices experienced by the 'average' citizen. His findings about the ubiquitous nature of homosexual experience may have given comfort to isolated individuals and to the embryonic homosexual political movement, but it scared the hell out of many Americans. Miller notes the reaction of evangelist Billy Graham: 'It is impossible to estimate the damage this book will do to the already deteriorating morals of America' (in Miller 1995: 251). Moral panic concerning widespread homosexuality was intensified in the McCarthy era as homosexuality became equated with communist espionage. Whatever normalizing effect Kinsey might have had on urban attitudes towards homosexuality, it would have been quickly dismissed in rural America by an outburst of patriotism, fear of communism and conservative Christian morality.

The social revolution led by the civil rights movement, signified by Rosa Parks in 1955 and followed by second wave (sub-urban) feminism declared by Friedan's *Feminine Mystique* in 1963, became fertile ground for the Stonewall Riots. Undoubtedly the gay and lesbian movement in all of its varied manifestations was urban led. 'Denny' the author of 'Now we are marching on' was portrayed in Stonewall, the movie, as a small town hick – a migrant to New York who joined the Mattachine Society[2] and then the Stonewall Riot. We 'remember' him for his revolutionary lyrics, but only because he sang them in the city rather than in the cornfield. The need to find others with similar experiences may have moved some to the city – a place in which stories of exclusion became a massive volume of narrative constructing an empowered gay identity. An identity which seemed so encompassing that lesbian feminists began to assert their voices, or weave their own narratives. In doing so, many of them actively sought power through separatism in the country. The road, in fact, did run in both directions.

## Social Exclusion ... Help!

The Mattachine Society of New York archives lodged in the New York Public Library include approximately a hundred letters of inquiry dated from the 1950s through the 1970s. My search through them found only ten letters from people in 'non-metropolitan' areas of populations of less than 100,000. Each of the ten letters were received between 1959 and 1966. While I will not identify these by name, I will assume that female names indicate women (2) and male names indicate that the writer is a man (8). Of course this may not be the case. Four of the ten *imply* they are homosexual – 'we' shouldn't put up with oppression. Only one correspondent revealed his age, 19, and this was an acknowledgement that he would be too young to become a member. Three correspondents noted their occupations – one female nurse and two male ministers counselling homosexuals. In general, the response from the Mattachine Society regardless of the correspondent's request/concern was to provide information concerning the purpose of the organization. When necessary, the response included rather pointed statements that they did not act as a pen-pal club or provide contacts in the correspondent's local area. This point was especially stressed when responding to requests for information about the Daughters of Bilitus (DOB).[3] The concerns of the correspondents I have categorized as follows:

- requests for more information about the Mattachine Society (9);
- requests for names of others in their area or pen pals (3);
- church ministers wanting information about homosexuality to aid them in counselling situations (2 – Methodist and Episcopalian);
- list of books on homosexuality and/or books which could be checked out from the Mattachine library (1, aged 19);
- complaint about local news article concerning sexual deviants, copy forwarded to Mattachine (1 – no request for further information);
- requests for information on the Daughters of Bilitus (2 women);
- adamant request for contact with female pen pals, including a request for information on Daughters of Bilitus (1 – male);
- specific questions concerning the intersection of identity and desire – e.g. why do homosexuals find effeminacy attractive? (1)

Perhaps unsurprisingly given the social invisibility of homosexuals during this time period, most correspondents wanted more information on the Mattachine Society and homosexuality in general. The additional requests are somewhat unsurprising as well. Requests reflect some of the primary concerns of those isolated in rural America: how can I make contact with others like myself?; how can I deal with the teachings of the church?; where can I find more information about my homosexuality?; why do you think homosexuals are this way? Even one man requesting, in more than one letter, contacts with women in the organization and an address for Daughters of Bilitus resonates with familiar male sexual fantasies about lesbians. Perhaps it was a woman writing under a male name. Either way the response from Mattachine was to provide the DOB address but clearly state that it was a women-only organization and that neither organization would provide him with individual women's addresses.

The concerns expressed in these letters are not dissimilar from the men's experiences of exclusion in rural America found in the chapter by Spurlin. In the 1970s and 1980s gay and lesbian publications frequently retold stories of exclusion and escape. For example, from rural Wisconsin:

> 'I grew up in a small town ... some young people were lucky enough to discover a cousin or friend with whom they could be openly, secretly sexual ... most often, the friend or relative has now turned straight ... Yet, for most of us, the longing for that special friend or the admired classmate was destined to remain platonic. We had to be satisfied with a glance in the shower room, a touch in the halls, a tackle on the football field ... Growing up in a small town, it is almost impossible to avoid learning the macho culture of the pool halls and barber shops ... we were macho with our macho friends, and, if we were lucky, we could be ourselves with our true friends ... growing up in a small town can be painful or happy depending on the person. The effeminate male may experience great humiliation at the hands of his classmates. And there are many instances of depression and even suicide among gays who cannot deal with their own feelings, or the society that represses them. But most of us just grew up gay, aware that we were different, adapting to our environment in order to hide our feelings. We were safe as long as nobody found out'.
>
> (*Among Friends*, 1986)

In a 1977 *Lesbian Connection* survey I discuss below, one respondent answers the question 'Have you ever been in the armed forces? ... If so, would you recommend them to other lesbians?': 'no but [it may be] ... the only way out of a small town – that's how I got into the WACs. But I don't know how healthy they are for your head. I was in 12 years ago ... doubt if they have changed' (1977b: 20). For those growing up gay in small towns across America the lack of information, the social exclusion, religious condemnation, and public and private humiliation triggers nothing less than a survival instinct: 'I found myself, my gay self, in a rural community, and I got the hell out.'

## Social isolation ... finding yourself in the country

John D'Emilio notes in 'Capitalism and Gay Identity' that in the second half of the nineteenth century, capitalism allowed men and women to earn a living outside the confines of the interdependent family unit (D'Emilio 1983b). He convincingly argues that economic mobility of post-war America enabled homosexual identity to emerge in social spaces created by those whose desire led them to the city. Migration to such urban social spaces is a familiar story of the 1950s and 1960s isolated homosexual. No doubt this is the story of many escaping from rural communities today. But this economic independence, along with the growing solidarity of sisterhood, moved others in the opposite direction in the 1970s. For example, radical feminists, charging that contact with men amounted to no less than conspiracy with the enemy, inspired some to attempt utopian collectives in the rural idyll. Information on lesbian land groups provided great insight to this country girl wondering why any 'deviant' would choose rural life.

Lesbian separatists migrating to the countryside had no less than idealistic expectations of rural life. It was to be the kind of women only, collectively organized, back to nature experience that everyone should have access to if not live in permanently. Valentine explains the 'urban/male rural/female' dichotomy which motivated the movement in this way:

> because spatial isolation meant that it was easier for women to be self-sufficient and purer in their practices in the country than in the city, and because essentialist notions about women's closeness to nature meant that the countryside was identified as a female space. In contrast, the 'man-made' city was blamed for draining women's energy. In this way women idealized the rural in a political way – imagining it as simple, peaceful, safe space untainted by patriarchy.
> 
> (Valentine 1997: 111)

Importantly, Valentine emphasizing that this draws 'upon stereotypical representations of the rural as a healthy, simple, peaceful, safe place to live ... like traditional visions of rural "community", many lesbian separatist imaginings of a common lifestyle also seem to have led to the marginalization and exclusion of "others"' (1997: 109–10).

For example, the *Ozark Women on Land* information leaflet from May of 1976 announced a 'secured' 80 acres of land in north-west Arkansas open to 'sisters who want to live/work collectively to create women's spaces in the country and to grow women's food'. While they had no house as yet they were clear of their political motivations:

> This experiment on 80 acres is for, by and with women identified women. No men will be on this land ... we wish to relate to female children, to help female kids grow as strong sisters. We do not feel that we or our younger sisters should be responsible for the potential sexism of male children, who no matter how hard we try to keep out sexist energy will still be a male in this society and able to oppress both our younger sisters and us.
> 
> (May, 1976)

Envisioning their relationship to others in the country they want 'to think of ways we can be self-sufficient in the country, e.g., growing herbs to "sell" or barter with sisters and/or allies; starting a feminist bookstore or an organic juice bar; changing our diet from meat, dairy products, and eggs to sprouts, fruit, and nuts; teaching nutritious healing, feminism, and skills in workshops for women in the community'. As far as the internal workings of the collective go:

> We believe in responsible magic, grouped processes where decisions are made by the women who are involved ... We discourage the philosophy of individualism or 'coupleism' where it interferes with the survival of us all or stifles the collective process ... [All women are invited] who want to relate to this land whether she wants to live here full-time, work for the summer, camp and work, spend the weekend or stay here on her way cross country ... work is being stressed.
>
> (ibid.)

While *Ozark Women on Land* 'sells' itself as a rural separatist collective, the leaflet is quick to point out that the farm has easy access to an urban social space 'only thirty miles from ... a university town with a women's center, a women's newspaper as well as a small "alternative" community'. In general then it seems to have everything: a women-only space; a collective politics; a plan to deal with others in the country; and if all else fails, connection to an urban alternative community.

Similar images appear in the *Lesbian Connection Directory of Land Groups*, invoking a range of interesting responses from readers. First, an urban reader notes that seeing these opportunities listed made her think she 'really could make the leap from this dirty city to a more peaceful environment' (p. 8). Another reader from Minneapolis writes about splitting up with her lover and the sacrifice of having to leave the farm which five women had purchased jointly:

> Returning to an urban environment, I envy the chores I left behind: the early rising to milk the goats, regardless of snowdrifts and sub-zero temperatures; rounding up livestock that slipped through fences; banking straw more securely around the foundations to enhance heat restoration; pitching ... and scraping stalls ... Here in the city, my farming has to be restricted to memories and cultivating a few vegetables on my balcony ... It's lonely here in the city; no one seems to know what I'm talking about when I mention how gentle or affectionate or clever goats can be; or that chickens come in dozens of colors besides white; and that buying vegetables at the co-op isn't as sustaining as growing them yourselves.
>
> (*Lesbian Connection* 1979: 4)

From a very different perspective, one woman challenges this notion of the rural idyll, pointing out the financial pressures of living on a lesbian farm:

> I have noticed recurring and unrealistic attitudes toward 'wimmin on land'

which range from idealizing our self-sufficiency to guilt-baiting our non-urban 'privileges' ... our desire to share the experience of the land is large and sincere ... but we are also thus more vulnerable to getting ripped off or imposed upon by bad attitudes ... it is important ... for the 'sisterhood' and the very survival of land groups to discuss and understand what can and often does go wrong.

(*Lesbian Connection* 1979: 8)

Cheney (1985) and Valentine (1997) note that what often went wrong was the social exclusion of 'undesirable' women.

Each lesbian land, by defining its own common ways of living and appropriate ways of behaving, constructed its own shared identity or groupness. These desires for mutual identification or homogeneity simultaneously appear to have generated boundaries and exclusions. ... Some refused to be controlled by the dominant identities of the communities they were living in and pushed against their boundaries by mobilising the performance of 'other' identities. Others chose to leave one community and join or set up another. In this way, the lesbian lands were not stable communities but were fluid, with new women coming and going as different identities were maximised and minimised.

(Valentine 1997: 119)

It is worth noting briefly the story of Wanda and Brenda Henson who established Camp Sister Spirit in Ovett Mississippi in 1993. The social exclusion, indeed life-threatening harassment, faced by this collection of women in backwater Mississippi has only been equalled by their sheer determination to provide a women-owned farm and retreat (for an example of their story see Chesler 1994). After hearing of the violence incurred by these women at the hands of the Ovett natives, Suzanne Pharr reflected upon her own experience on a women's farm in north-west Arkansas in the 1970s:

Our house was both isolated and exposed, and we could not survive there without strong relationships with our neighbors. ... We built those relationships slowly in numerous ways. The first was by introducing ourselves to our neighbors and to those who lived in the small town and by constantly asking for advice. We hung out where the local people did – at stores, the lumber mill, restaurants – and had long conversations about ourselves and about the area. We purchased goods and services from people who lived around us. When people drove by and stopped on the dirt road by our house to chat, we stopped whatever we were doing and talked.

> We went to community events such as basketball games and estate sales and church fund-raisers. People became interested in our successes and disasters and our stubborn hard work. They thought we were strange but good hearted and often amusing.
>
> (Pharr 1994: 14)

Setting up an isolated space in the country will undoubtedly invoke a hostile response. Unknown outsiders are never welcomed in small towns. So, as Pharr suggests, while rural life is often riddled with in/outsider social structures the best way to overcome such division is to recognize the premise of interaction established by the American pioneers: the key to survival in a rural community is interdependence.

The desire to provide space for women to find themselves in the country – in isolation from the oppressions of the world – is commendable as political statement. However, it is also utopian. Isolation of self or group, even chosen isolation, necessitates the exclusion of others. And difficulties do arise from rigid boundaries of who is and is not acceptable in a 'lesbian community'. In addition, isolation in a rural setting flies in the face of larger community interdependence. So while finding yourself in the country may be possible, it by no means ensures lesbian utopia.

## No place like home

Upon my emergence from the closet, the stories I heard were very similar to the two above narratives. The social exclusion, religious damnation and familial rejection moved countless sexual 'deviants' away from their country home toward the anonymity, and promised acceptance, of the city. In this narrative the response to such exclusion was escape. Not long after, in the company of 'sisters', I heard a more radical tale. Their response was to find strength in isolation. For only the (separated) sisterhood offered acceptance through the anonymity guaranteed in the collective identity. This tale of isolation, of distinguishing between us and them, was uncomfortably familiar to me, well versed in religious distinctions. For a time I believed these 'necessary fictions' were the only accounts of gay and lesbian rural life, or at least the only 'sane' accounts. Surely any gay man or lesbian finding themselves alone in the country should leave, only to return if accompanied by comrades in arms – maybe literally. But these options sat rather uncomfortably with my own story, and with the cacophony of voices testifying to the diverse lives of non-heterosexuals in rural America.

These voices began to be heard with the emergence of 'gay and lesbian' publications in the 1970s. Although these were inevitably produced in urban centres, many made their way to the countryside via pink underground railroads. One publication in particular, *Lesbian Connection*, attempted to address the difficulties of lesbian isolation. First published on 3 August 1974, its purpose was to establish a 'national lesbian communications network'. *L.C.* was created by the Ambitious Amazons out of the Lansing area – nine women ages 20–29 from 'various backgrounds and socio-economic classes'. While there existed many national feminist publications and several gay liberation newspapers, they believed 'no papers ... dealt with current news that is pertinent, and available, to all lesbians'. Their emphasis was on 'news and political issues ... news of court cases, festivals, cultural events, demonstrations and lesbian resources ... our mailing list will be confidential and not made available to any other group' (taken from Commemorative Issue of *LC* in February 1985).

While the homophile movement had acted as one of few information points for rural gay men and lesbians, it clearly had not encouraged personal contact nor did it appear to act as an organizer/informer for social events. In contrast, *Lesbian Connection* not only listed regional women-only gatherings but included pages and pages of 'Contact Dykes', many of whom were rural lesbians. Contact Dykes were

> lesbians who had agreed to be listed so they can provide information about their areas to travelling lesbians or new women in town ... [this] does not mean they are looking for penpals or lovers, that they're interested in 'junk' mail or chain letters, or that they're there for counselling. They do NOT want to hear from any men.
>
> (*Lesbian Connection* 1985)

By the early 1980s such was the response that a separate directory was issued listing dykes from every state. While there is no way of knowing the utility of this information for rural lesbians, the level of interest and volume of those willing to be 'contact dykes' does indicate their willingness to connect with other lesbians, as well as their decision to remain living in rural locations.

Regional newspapers sprang up from the late 1970s onwards and also provided personal/political information and contacts for rural dwellers. While these were often produced in local urban areas, they were available to country visitors and carried back to others. Below is a small sample of publications which trailblazed regional gay and lesbian communication:

Lesbian newspapers:
   from Corpus Christi, Texas – *The Lesbitarian*;
   from Fayetteville, Arkansas – *Up&Coming*;
   from Gulfport, Mississippi – *The Hericane*;
   from Lincoln, Nebraska – *Lesbian Community News*;
   from Anchorage, Alaska – *KlonDyke KontAct*;
   from Greenville, S.C. – *Upstate S.C. Women's Community Newsletter*.

Gay and lesbian newspapers:
  from Nova Scotia/Maine area – *Boonies Magazine*;
  from rural Louisiana – *Sissies in Struggle* (LaSIS) – *A Country Faggot Journal for Gay Men Everywhere*.

These archives offer not only retro entertainment but also some interesting insight into gay and lesbian rural life. Most at various times included articles acknowledging the difficulty of reaching a closeted audience. For example the *Austin Lesbian Organization Magazine* (1976) celebrates its one year anniversary by addressing the problem of 'how to inform lesbians that the ALO exists and how to contact us'. One writer offers this strategy for the future:

> 'I tossed around various ideas: bumper stickers (we'd all get our tires slashed), small stickers (people would pull them off), newspaper ads (Ha! we all know what happened with that), radio spots (already tried, no one would run the announcements), etc. Finally I came up with a brilliant idea. Bathroom Walls. ... the advantages are numerous: 1. it's free; 2. any and all of us can do it, only needing a pencil; 3. bathroom walls are cleaned and repainted infrequently; 4. graffiti is ignored by custodians, who remove things like stickers; 5. generally, no male would have the opportunity to read the notice; 6. there is no danger to the lesbian who writes the notice – likewise the woman reader can copy the address inconspicuously; 7. almost every woman uses a public restroom at one time or another ... all jokes and laughter aside, this is the best way I can think of to publicize the ALO in a hostile world.'

The writer's entertaining solution clearly constructs the social context as 'hostile', as the safety of the reader, the messenger, and the message are ensured in a women-only 'inconspicuous' environment. It is, to say the least, an interesting construction of the toilet as a safe space for contacts with other lesbians. In the 'hostile world' of the Bible Belt secrecy is a familiar cloak hiding sexual identity.

Distanced from the urban created gay and lesbian community, indeed urban constructed identity, rural non-heterosexuals did not necessarily position sexuality as the definitive characteristic of self. Some identities intertwine the 'sexual' and the 'rural'. For example, a 1977 *Lesbian Connection* reader survey of approximately a thousand readers from 48 states found that around 35 per cent lived outside the city (1977a). One question posed, 'Do you belong to any other minority group?', received the positive response, 'hillbilly'. Another question gave readers the space to identify, or label, themselves: 'Do you consider yourself lesbian feminist, lesbian, dyke, gay woman, feminist lesbian, homosexual, lesbian separatist, lesbian socialist, butch, femme.' One respondent added her own label: 'lesbian farmer' (1977b).

Of course the 'discovery' of the self-styled sexuality of non-heterosexuals existing outside post-Stonewall urban gay revolution has become a fascination of 'gay and lesbian' historians and social researchers creating our communal 'necessary fictions'.[4] But that project has been largely historical or nationally/ethnically anthropological. And when our attention has been drawn to stories of rural non-heterosexuality we are told of escape from, or the escapism to, the countryside. Rarely do we hear of the 'normal' stories of those who simply live there and get on with it, indeed enjoy it. So I want to end this discovery of rural non-heterosexuality with a brief look at a few such stories – stories not of the rural idyll where 'straights' and 'queers' live happily side by side in the peaceful pastoral, but of difficulty that one deals with and doesn't run from, of pain that doesn't consume or necessarily lead to self-hatred, of lives that reflect a 'multitude of social belongings'.

One such story emerged in the popular press about the same time as the Mattachine Society first began to organize. *Ebony* magazine, (10 November 1954), recounts the story of 'The woman who lived as a man for 15 years': Jim McHarris/Annie Lee Grant of Kosciusko, Mississippi, an African-American

> baby-faced woman of 30 with small, delicate hands and tiny earring holes in her ears … has been fooling people since her early teens when she rejected her sex and cast her lot with the men of the world … her male act was so successful that she had been scheduled for elevation to the deacon's board of her church.[5]

(*Ebony* 1954: 94)

According to this report, 'especially upset were several women who had been girl friends of Jim … one woman admitted regularly receiving money from Jim … [who] called the woman "his wife" … before his exposure Jim had been engaged to marry a high school girl' (p. 93). A long-time acquaintance noted, 'I know she's been out with men and women, but something happened to her long before she started wearing men's clothing … after this, she didn't like anything but the ladies' (p. 94). The story continues explaining that Jim/Annie had been picked up by the police for a traffic violation and when a search was attempted s/he revealed that 'he was a woman'. The policeman took Jim to the judge who reportedly stated, 'Annie Lee, if you want to prove to me you're a woman you can do it. But you don't have to unless you want to" (p. 93). For the traffic violation s/he was fined $100 or 30 days in jail.

> Within minutes after her arrest, Annie Lee was the talk of the news-hungry town. White folks gathered in the town square, fanned away flies and chuckled over the news. Farther back, along the tin-top stores of the 'Negro street' and the frame houses of the Negro section, people who

knew her well gathered and discussed the news in shocked seriousness ... Jim's ex-boss was fooled, too. [He], a proprietor of a Kosciusko filling station, said: 'I had no idea at all. He was such a good worker. Used to rush to do the roughest jobs. Sometimes a girl used to come up here and they would hug and kiss around the oil rack. He even called the girl "his wife" around here.' Having spent his/her time in jail for the traffic violation, Jim left the prison to face a cool reception in Kosciusko ... strangers gawked and grinned sheepishly; old friends avoided her eyes; white people pointed and guffawed.

(*Ebony* 1954: 98)

'Shorn of her long hair, her bust flattened by a homemade band of cloth, long-haired, soft-voiced Annie Lee became swaggering, gruff-voiced Jim' who eventually moved on to another town but vowed s/he would continue life 'as a man' (pp. 94–8). Jim had most certainly negotiated multiple social belongings. And while we may assume this encounter with the police, and subsequent 'outing', will have caused him distress, his life before and determination afterwards testify to his ability to negotiate, if not satisfy, both sexual desire and social expectation and get on with living life.

A more familiar, but none the less inspiring, story comes from a woman in Fayetteville, Arkansas, writing to *Lesbian Connection*:

After an apparently successful interview, I was called today with a job offer. However, the man asked me to remove my chin whiskers. Since I only have a dozen blond hairs (cute ones at that) on my chin, I told him I wouldn't consider removing them; would he still consider hiring me? He said no, because it could ruin his image to have me cutting his donuts with chin whiskers on my face. I told him that I hoped he could overcome his personal problem with people's appearances, wished him well in his business, and thanked him for calling. Sad, humorous, and true. I laughed.

(February 1985 Vol. 8 issue 1)

Her words are inspiring for two reasons. First, her conclusion indicates her general outlook on life – facing difficulty, noting the sadness, but not letting it hijack her positive attitude. Second, the story is inspiring in that it highlights a perhaps common reaction to heterosexual social norms – gently pointing out their oppressive nature and moving on. Of course, just as discrimination is a resident in the most diverse of cities, it likewise has a home in the country. But while heterosexism can be challenged *en masse* in anonymous city streets, one constantly challenging it in a rather tight-knit small community will inevitably lead to further marginalization. In a place where one's self is constructed publicly – at least under the watchful eye of the town's gossips – asserting one's sexuality at every opportunity can easily negate, or minimalize, other parts of one's identity.

Acknowledging the complexity and range of aspects which make up one's self allows for connections across boundaries of sexual difference. The most vivid example of this comes from an older lesbian couple in rural Texas I had the privilege of interviewing. Jo, a white woman in her late fifties, grew up in the small town in which the couple lived. Her father's family had lived in the area for many years and was amongst the respected farmers in the community. Tori, her partner, is Hispanic and also in her fifties, and moved to the town to be with Jo. Tori runs the local gas/food mart and Jo does various odd jobs. Both agree that they have met little discrimination from other local citizens. While Jo had never had anyone confront her directly, Tori had been challenged only once. Not long after moving to the town she had attended one of the local churches and a woman she didn't know walked up to her and said, 'You need to change your way of life.' A few words were exchanged but Tori insists, 'I wasn't ugly with her or used ugly words … but I was hot, really really upset.' Jo then quipped, 'Like going to church out there with them would do it!' Over the years her job has enabled her to build friendships with a large section of the community. And in turn she has become one of its respected members.

In our conversation, Jo talked about her experience of growing up gay in this small town. 'Back in the fifties that [sex with girls] wasn't necessarily just what you wanted. I don't guess I really had anything to do with anybody [sexual contact] until I was in the 7th or 8th grade (about 13 years old). And that wasn't much. The strange thing was that I never made an advance on anybody. It was always the straight girls that came on to me. Figure that out!' As a bit of a tomboy myself, I found this rather impressive. She went on to tell how her parents caught her kissing a girl in high school and that they never questioned her.

Both of them live publicly as a couple, babysit the grandkids, and are out to their family. Tori explains her feelings about being out:

> I'm not the open type. I've got my family to think about and my friends … and people are cruel. If they know about it that's fine. If they don't that's fine. But I don't bring it out. We don't bring it out to the public and say 'Yes, I'm gay'. All you're asking for is trouble. And not only for yourself but for your family. Because they're the ones that are going to have to put up with it too, not only us. And I love my family enough to not put them through that.

Jo, a good ol' country girl, recounts the time, after leaving a brief marriage, she finally told her mother: 'One night I was sitting up there talking to mother and I told her being gay is not like all this crap you see on TV or read in papers. We don't run around raping people's kids, that's straight guys … we don't wear black leather and the chains ... we're not into that stuff.' She had spent some time during her marriage living in Houston but then decided she was gay and came home 'to God's country'. Both women living in rural small town America are not just getting on with life, they are really enjoying it![6]

## Conclusion: where do we go from here?

Stories of rural exclusion or chosen isolation tell of a countryside which can be frighteningly hostile or spacially idyllic. As the accounts here testify they are very real experiences of rural marginalization for many of us now living in the urban gay and lesbian 'community'. They are the stories with which we are familiar because they have been told and retold by those with a voice and an urban audience. Over the years they have enabled us to create 'necessary fictions' cohering our stories of rural exclusion and separating us from the rural heterosexual other. In questioning the utility of necessary fictions I am not attempting to fictionalize stories of exclusion. One should never underestimate the power of a small heterosexual community to pathologize or demonize the sexual 'deviant'. Nor the need of individuals to escape it or collectively challenge it.

However, in an effort to tell of experiences of rural non-heterosexuality, perhaps we have overlooked the complexity of our 'multiple social belongings'. For example, Pharr (1994) notes the necessity for lesbian land groups to find multiple connections with those in rural towns through supporting local functions and being interested in neighbours' and the community's concerns. Furthermore, Jo and Tori remind us of the many gay men and lesbians who grew up, moved to, and remain living in small town America – and enjoy it. The benefits of rural hometown and familial ties may be as important as finding social/sexual belonging in the sexual, and usually urban, collective. Such stories challenge us to revisit our construction of the 'gay and lesbian community' in order to avoid either further marginalization – 'I'm not like them on TV' – or misrepresentation – exclusion and isolation is not always 'our' home. Even as I write, there is a part of me that wants to make accusations of 'false consciousness' – Jo and Tori just don't realize their own oppression. But this sets up a dichotomy of 'out/identity politics' or 'assimilationist/internalized homophobia'. It is worth acknowledging that rural constructions of identity are far less rooted than urban sexual identity politics. Surely in this postmodern era there is space for 'celebrating fragmentation' – the complexity of identity, the multiplicity of social belongings. The 'rural' may not be the same place left by Beebo Brinker (Bannon [1962] 1986). In fact, it may be increasingly moving toward the communal spirit reflected in the movie *In/Out* in which citizens declare 'I'm gay too' in solidarity with the ostracized local school teacher. Perhaps this is too idealistic. Nevertheless, while we should remain mindful of rural damnation, the potential power of small town loyalty and familial ties should never be underestimated. Life, as I had assumed, may not be somewhere down the road – even for gay men and lesbians it is possible to get your kicks on Route 66.

## Notes

1. A large portion of the material on lesbian land groups and backcopies of *Lesbian Connection* were found in the Lesbian Herstory Archives in Brooklyn New York. Their support and cooperation with this research has been greatly appreciated.
2. The Mattachine Society was founded in 1951 in Los Angeles. As part of the homophile movement, its purpose was to educate the public in order to spread 'accurate information about the nature and conditions of variation, and in this way eliminate discrimination, derision, prejudice and bigotry' (noted in Blumenfeld and Raymond, 1993: 94). For further information concerning the homophile movement see D'Emilio (1983a), Cutler (1956), Katz (1976), Duberman *et al.* (1989).
3. Daughters of Bilitus, established in 1955 in San Francisco, was a women's organization devoted to educating 'the variant' to 'understand herself and make her adjustment to society', including modifying her 'behavior and dress acceptable to society'. Loosely linked to the Mattachine Society by the late 1950s, many chapters had been established in other US cities (Blumenfeld and Raymond 1993: 295).
4. For example, Faderman (1981), Duberman *et al.* (1989), D'Emilio (1983a), Altman (1979), Katz (1976).
5. I positioned this story here as I believe it represents one woman's attempt to express her desire for other women, e.g. she had various girlfriends, and her awareness that in order to do so she would need to 'pass' as a man, e.g. she dressed in men's clothing and called herself 'Jim'. I cannot explicitly identify her as a lesbian, as she does not identify herself in this way. Likewise I can not identify her as a transsexual. I have attempted to note her difference simply by utilizing the label 'non-heterosexual'. I have identified her as Jim, as it is, according to the news article, her preferred name.
6. For more contemporary examples see Sears (1991) and Wilson (1999).

## References

Altman, D. (1979) *Coming Out in the Seventies*, Boston: Alyson Publication, Inc.
*Among Friends* (1986) Letters column, April, vol. 2, no. 4, newspaper from Madison Wisconsin area.
*Austin Lesbian Organization Magazine* (1976) 'Writing on Bathroom Walls', February, vol. 2, no. 1 (Austin, Texas).
Bannon, A. ([1962] 1986) *Beebo Brinker*, Tallahassee: Naiad Press.
Barry, P. (1995) *Beginning Theory: An Introduction to Literary and Cultural Theory*, Manchester: Manchester University Press.
Blumenfeld, W. and Raymond, D. (1993) *Looking at Gay and Lesbian Life*, Boston, Mass.: Beacon.
Cheney, J. (1985) *Lesbian Land*, Minneapolis: Word Weavers.
Chesler, P. (1994) 'Sister, Fear Has No Place Here', *On the Issues*, Fall.
Cutler, M. (ed.) (1956) *Homosexuals Today: A Handbook of Organizations and Publications*, Los Angeles: ONE, Inc.

D'Emilio, J. (1983a) *Sexual Politics, Sexual Communities*, Chicago: University of Chicago Press.
D'Emilio, J. (1983b) 'Capitalism and the Gay Identity', in A. Snitow, C. Stansell and S. Thompson (eds) *Desire: The Politics of Sexuality*, London: Virago.
Duberman, M., Vicinus, M. and Chauncey, G. (eds) (1989) *Hidden From History*, New York: New American Library.
Ebony (1954) 'The woman who lived as a man for 15 years', 10 November issue.
Faderman, L. (1981) *Surpassing the Love of Men*, New York: William Morrow & Co.
Friedan, B. (1963) *The Feminine Mystique*, Harmondsworth: Penguin.
Katz, J. (1976) *Gay American History: Lesbian & Gay Men in the U.S.A.*, New York: Avon Books.
Kinsey, A., Pomeroy, W. and Martin, C. (1948) *Sexual Behavior in the Human Male*, Philadelphia: Saunders.
Kinsey, A., Pomeroy, W., Martin, C. and Gebhard, P. (1953) *Sexual Behavior in the Human Female*, Philadelphia: Saunders.
*Lesbian Connection* (1977a) Newspaper survey, March, vol. 2 issue 8, national newspaper, East Lansing, Mich.: Ambitious Amazons.
*Lesbian Connection* (1977b) Newspaper survey, April, vol. 3 issue 1, national newspaper, East Lansing, Mich.: Ambitious Amazons.
*Lesbian Connection* (1979) Letters column, November, vol. 4 issue 7, national newspaper, East Lansing, Mich.: Ambitious Amazons.
*Lesbian Connection* (1985) Commemorative issue of August 1974, February, vol. 8 issue 1, East Lansing, Mich.: Ambitious Amazons.
*Lesbian Connection Directory of Land Groups* (no date listed on directory) copy found in Lesbian Herstory Archives, Brooklyn, N.Y., Lansing, Mich.: US Alliance of Lesbian and Feminist Printers.
Miller, N. (1995) *Out of the Past: Gay and Lesbian History from 1869 to the Present*, London: Vintage.
*Ozark Women on Land* (1976) May issue, Fayetteville, Ark.: Women on Land.
Pharr, S. (1994) 'Rural Organizing: Building Community across Difference', *Sojourner: The Women's Forum*, June.
Schulman, S. (1994) *My American History*, London: Cassell.
Sears, J. (1991) *Growing Up Gay in the South: Race, Gender and Journeys of the Spirit*, London: Harrington Park Press.
Valentine, G. (1997) 'Making Space: Lesbian Separatist Communities in the United States', in P. Cloke, and J. Little (eds) *Contested Countryside Cultures: Otherness, Marginalisation and Rurality*, London: Routledge.
Weeks, J. (1995) *Invented Moralities: Sexual Values in an Age of Uncertainty*, Cambridge: Polity Press.
Wilson, A. (1999) *Below the Belt: Sexuality, Religion and the American South*, London: Cassell.

# 12

# MAPPING DECOLONIZATION OF MALE HOMOEROTIC SPACE IN PACIFIC CANADA

*Gordon Brent Ingram*

It is the map that engenders the territory.

(Jean Baudrillard 1983: 2)

The nineteenth-century expansionist preoccupation with control of territory remains internalized in late twentieth-century bodies and sexualities – and well beyond the former imperial centres. This has been the case in the margins of European empires and especially where mechanisms for domination were overextended. Social spaces of 'nonmetropolitan' 'sexual outlaws' (Owens 1992: 218) have been associated with fecund though highly unstable sites of resistance and community formation. Narratives of homoeroticism, social space, and place can illuminate neglected aspects of territorial domination. Transactions within such peripheries as British Columbia did not escape Victorian controls on erotic expression in public and semi-public places. As nonmetropolitan societies, such as those in British Columbia, reproduced centre–periphery relationships through urbanization, the experience of and impacts on homoeroticized space reiterated unstable and spurious notions of race and cultural superiority. This legacy continues to constrain more conscious efforts to construct homoerotic social space that is both functional, for a range of social needs, and equitable.

Until the last decade, native English-speaking and north-western European ethnic experiences have defined and dominated the successful efforts to decriminalize homosexuality and legally counter homophobic discrimination. In British Columbia in the late 1980s and early 1990s, the emergence of 'queer nationalism' (Berlant and Freeman 1993) signalled a widespread dismantling of this cultural, linguistic and racial hierarchy. This decade's self-consciously 'multicultural' 'queer'[1] cultures in Pacific Canada have been increasingly defined by the other major demographic groups in the region, particularly 'First Nations' and those with south Chinese and south Asian heritages.

My concern in this chapter[2] is with how 'place', as in homoeroticized social space, has been constrained, contorted and sometimes expanded. I examine the transitions from colonialism to neocolonialism to nationalism to globalization and today's pressures for authentically post-colonial culture. In Pacific Canada, the social and cultural maps of public space are being redrawn across landscapes that are increasingly contentious in terms of jurisdictions, laws, effective access, and distribution of environmental benefits and costs (Ingram 1995). In this remapping, the relationships between collective cognition, use, territorialization, and architecture of homoerotic locations have been transformed. These social spaces were neocolonial from British Columbia's entry into Confederation in 1871 until the 1982 repatriation of the national Constitution and the Charter of Rights and Freedoms. In most areas of the British Columbia coast, neocolonialism lingers because of unnegotiated treaties with First Nations. In the colonial and neocolonial periods, racialization and racism dominated sexual identities and the use of public and private space. Within the shifting 'queerscapes' (Ingram 1997b) of sexual minorities, it has been difficult to separate specific peripheries, particular localities, and constraints on homoerotic communalities and expression. A historically and geographically rooted framework for charting the unevenness of contemporary 'decolonization' is needed.

The purpose of this chapter is to chart the ruptures in the racialized narratives of homoeroticism, resistance to homophobia, and place on the British Columbia coast. I am especially concerned with how various forms of colonial, neocolonial, nationalist and the more recent forms of anglocentricity have constrained the formation of 'gay' and more recently a redefined 'queer' culture and politics. Notions of 'difference' (Bhabha 1990) and marginalization become specific to particular regionalized locations and social projects. The function of this discussion is to link two assertions that have far-ranging implications for both theory and activism. My first argument is that decolonization of collective homoerotic maps is a prerequisite to confronting the disparities experienced by different groups of sexual minorities in access to public space and respective resources. I argue, second, that without more sophisticated forms of homosocial cartography, and the subsequent exchange and reconstruction of maps reflecting a fuller range of 'queer' experience, few more purposeful plans, as linked series of public policies with implications for physical aspects of communities, can be constructed. In this chapter, I also reflect on the poorly examined material in archives and how it can be used to illuminate the spatial economies of marginalized sexualities, homophobic repression, and resistance (Ingram *et al*. 2000).

## Contentious sexualities and contested sites

Even with the now waning enthusiasm for assertions and exchanges of cognitive maps as catalysts for civic activism[3] (Jameson 1984: 89; Bhabha 1994: 214–23), eroticism takes, is nurtured by, is constrained by, and is transformed by both physical space and individual and collective cognition of those places. An inherent characteristic of space, social including homoerotic, is that it can be charted along with respective human relationships and uses. Informal social mapping and resulting cartographies have a great bearing on enjoyment of such places and the nature of any collective interventions in respective locations. Social narratives around space influence priorities for civic activism, planning, economic activities and options for cultural expression. In examining the informal maps of the social spaces of sexual minorities, competing cartographies emerge: of heterosexuality and homosexuality, public and private, and the moral and the immoral. These pillars of social architecture have implications for erotic expression and communal life as well as operational notions of entitlement and citizenship.

Informal contact for the construction and exchange of individual and collective charting of origins, current locations, and directions can be thought as a kind of (cognitive) map play. In areas with highly racialized social hierarchies, such intercultural exchanges between members of sexual minorities were a way to recognize 'difference'[4] and potentials for alliances – between divergent origins, communal identifications, and class positions. For sexual minorities in sparsely populated territories such as colonial and neocolonial British Columbia, verbal contact to determine social proximities and distances was often initiated with a 'where are you from?' This exchange might have been the beginning of a conversation through which was found tolerance, communality, and erotic satisfaction. Determining what was 'pretty near'[5] was as much about intercultural cooperation as it was about spatial proximity. And 'up north' typically referred to the hinterlands not demographically dominated by European-Canadians. Reflecting the transience of many groups of non-white workers, chartings of their locations tended to be vague and their spaces more defined in terms of time and technology-based extractive activities such as logging and mining. From the vernacular of coastal British Columbia, I call this informal social mapping 'pretty-near-talk'. I argue that pretty-near-talk, reconstituted relatively segregated geographical, cultural, and political economic narratives of male homoeroticism into a neocolonial melange structured more along lines of common experience of local place and desire. In Pacific Canada until the early twentieth century, pretty-near-talk also involved a combination of English (or Cantonese or Punjabi) with terse Chinook, the regional trading language of native groups. 'From Rupert?' was partial acknowledgement of the cosmopolitan and highly transient town that grew up near the mouth of the Skeena River as the Pacific terminus of the northern railway link to Asia. Until the mid-twentieth century, 'Rupert is pretty near Metlakatla [a very old First Nations cultural centre], eh?' would have indicated that the speaker was originally from a central or eastern Canadian community where Gaelic was or had recently been spoken. And the nuanced response to the question, given that Metlakatla was light years from the town of Prince Rupert, culturally, would have indicated a great deal the speaker's intercultural perspectives. For isolated and hidden members of sexual minorities, pretty-near-talk was the precursor to the disclosure and extended erotic contact that was necessary for the cultural alliances that eventually lead to political action and today's policy-making.

In seeking to understand the formation of gay social spaces in Pacific Canada, I have come to see a number of (homo)erotic cartographies roughly corresponding to colonialism, neocolonialism, nationalist multiculturalism and the globalizing but often illusive, 'post-colonial'. These four phases of recognition of cultural differences correspond to phases of 'de-privileging' groups with British and other north-western European ethnicities and culture. The associated cartographic systems, with underlying narratives and modes of negotiation, have been largely at odds with each other. The conflicts between these contradictory responses to the legacies of colonialism constrained alliance-building between sexual minorities. In this chapter, I focus on contrasts between colonial and neocolonial cognitive maps and respective modes of homosocial contact. The associated conflicts had and continue to have tremendous implications for gay male activism and the nature of respective alliances. In beginning to map disparities in access to, along with use and control of homoerotic social space, as related to race and culture, I describe two contemporary locations. The first is a favourite portion of a gay male-populated 'clothing optional' beach at the base of a bluff adjacent to The University of British Columbia. The second site is a sidewalk café in Victoria, the island city that is the provincial capital. This touristic space is attached to a government building where anti-gay 'witch hunts' were directed at various points in the twentieth century. Both locales are highly problematic for defining and asserting homoerotic social space and illustrate the persistence and continuing mutation of colonial and neocolonial legacies in contemporary life.

'The Oasis' is a small point of land south of the main 'clothing optional' area of Wreck Beach. Sometimes referred to today as 'Glamour Beach' or 'Attitude Point', the former Salish camp site was called *Humlusum*, 'bending down to drink.' At The Oasis, I often derive a great deal of satisfaction in spending a few hours on a warm day talking with friends, reading, and walking through the forest. While the emphasis on middle-class gay male consumer and body culture can be exclusive, harkening to a men's club, The Oasis is a crossroads and meeting place for a wide array of cultural and racial groups. That section of the beach is one of the few public spaces on the West Coast, the other sites being a handful of bars, baths, cafés and outdoor cruising sites, where men from very different cultures, body types and ages can make relatively easy contact. But tensions abound.

Mike initiated a conversation with me in the summer of 1997. Both naked, there was some cognition of complex family journeys across great distances. Through body type, family information, and 'pretty-near-talk', it became clear that Mike was from the small Hawaiian community north of Victoria. In the mid-nineteenth century, the 'Kanaka' (Koppel 1995) came to the Crown Colony of Vancouver Island seafaring for the Hudson's Bay Company. Given generous land grants on the islands north of the capital, the Kanaka tended to assimilate and to marry people of Anglo-Saxon backgrounds. Whereas I am 'white' and barely suggest my mother's mix-raced background as a *franco-colombien*,[6] Mike's sexual persona is of the large polynesian male; what is termed in the contemporary Hawaiian vernacular a 'Moke'. Our pretty-near-talk functioned to establish citizenship and respective bases for residing in the area. In those first hours of our conversation, we established that our full entitlement to the territory was based on ancestral routes across the British Empire. In our conversations, Mike attempted to resist the exoticized stereotypes of the Polynesian male. But Mike remains marginalized in a consumer culture demanding hard bodies and acquisition of fetishized clothing and accessories (most of which do not come in Mike's XXXL size). We were both well-socialized in using pretty-near-talk as part of a cross-ethnic strategy for middle-class success in a fluid post-colonial but solidly neocolonial social hierarchy. Our exchange was 'neocolonial' in that it relied on validation through and privileging of at least some British ethnicity, family history as subjects of the Empire, and culture. Our pretty-near-talk celebrated a neocolonial form of what was to become the contemporary 'politics of difference' (Young 1990: 301). Mike's conversations suggested to me that it was normal for him to feel compelled to labour to establish his citizenship both as a Canadian and also as a gay man. Ironically, there was no 'natural' alliance that emerged between Mike and me. I was late for our next appointment back on the beach, apparently he had not waited, and we have lost touch. Perhaps our attempts at sharing through spatial locations were too nostalgic – or revealing. More likely, the unmet social needs, that might have been satisfied by pretty-near-talk in more repressive times, are diminishing.

In an example of a more directly colonial and singular cultural cartography of homoeroticism, I went to Victoria and the outdoor environs of its Torrefazione Italia café. In contrast to that global caffeine behemoth, Starbucks, which, while providing crucial social space for gay and bisexual males, pursues a strategy of 'eating the streets' (Smith 1996: 508), the Torrefazione Italia chain represents a 'kinder, gentler' form of privatization of public space. This ambiguity is highly attractive for revisiting aspects of colonial relations and the more genteel closeting of homoerotic desire. I met Paul in that café about the same time that I met Mike on the beach. Like me, Paul had grown up on southern Vancouver Island. But in contrast to my family's diversified set of backgrounds, Paul experienced the last gasp of what was almost a kind of British separatism in Canada. Ironically, Paul, too, is from a highly mixed set of heritages, some of which were not European. But the culture to which he was socialized was avowedly 'English' – even though it really was not. This experience apparently came to dominate Paul's sexual coming of age and aesthetics and to constrain his ability to negotiate in the post-colonial world. Instead of the alliance-building through intercultural pretty-near-talk, Paul's dwindling island world was increasingly limited. Of course his experience of a partially segregated British Columbia represented the end of an era of unsuccessful efforts for cultural hegemony. Still, there were many adjacent territories in Alberta, Washington State, Oregon, and Idaho with some of the most 'pure' populations with British heritages that remain – outside of a few remaining regions of Britain. Our sharing of maps of the homoerotic world became focused on finding the few remaining references for Canadian anglocentricity and illusions of homogeneity. Difference was framed as a problematic distance. My own experience of a highly multicultural and sometimes transracial Vancouver Island seemed to confirm to Paul his own isolation. Eventually Paul and I ran out of maps to share.

The neocolonial world of my conversations with Mike emphasized alliances around recognition of cultural difference but shared destinations and imperial allegiances. Mike's world is within the aftermath of a colonial and imperial 'system' that laid the basis for today's globalization. But his notions of propriety remain rooted in late imperial culture and political economy. Mike's maps emphasized both the diversity and the privileging of imperial routes. In contrast, Paul's more colonial cartography harked back to the ethnic hierarchy of the eighteenth-century wave of British settlement of North America. Fetishized around constructions of 'race', this relative uniculturalism, with its own unresolved tensions between British ethnic groups, continued in parts of western North America well into the twentieth century.

In hinterland regions such as British Columbia, neocolonialism did not simply replace colonialism in the cultures of sexual minorities. Rather, both sets of strategies of social contact between members of sexual minorities have continued simultaneously – and have been diffused and sometimes transformed unevenly. Hinterlands often hold quite a bit of space where various social contradictions can be played out, sometimes in relative isolation. Today, both the colonial and the neocolonial strategies, as bases for gay male space-taking and placemaking, have been exhausted. Sex and social alliances in the 'New World' of Pacific Canada (Ingram 1997a) have been transformed by demographics, AIDS, globalization, and more aggressive forms of multiculturalism. Of course, these post-colonial processes have increasingly dominated the entire English-speaking world, including Britain, though hinterlands have sometimes been slower to be affected.

Until the last decade, gay male activism in British Columbia, was constrained by the lack of translatable maps between culturally defined groups of homoerotic men. It would be simplistic to attribute this fragmentation to positioning around resistance to or complacence with racism and cultural chauvinism. Between these informal cartographies of social space, there was both a dichotomy and a continuum between the colonial and the neocolonial. Individuals tended to negotiate divergent lives in either mode. This fragmentation prompted experiences of isolation that have constrained alliance-building around public policy. For decades, most members of sexual minorities who were not British were too marginalized to feel sufficiently welcome to contribute to the building of intercultural alliances. Until the last two decades, gay/queer politics were not even conceived of as intercultural alliances. And early Pacific Canadian activists of British backgrounds were often a minority or were such a small demographic majority, within 'the gay community', that their political impacts were also limited.

Having painted a bleak picture, I remind the reader that today British Columbia has some of the most favourable conditions for sexual minorities anywhere. In the 1960s and early 1970s, Vancouver saw highly public and often raucous organizing by homophile, gay liberation, and gay and lesbian rights groups. This was at a time when few cities other than New York, Los Angeles, San Francisco, Sydney, London, and Seattle were seeing such resistance and visibility. Today, the region has some of the most effective human rights protections for sexual orientation in the world, though there remain gaps, such as around truly effective provincial government protections in employment. More than in any other hinterland on earth, sexual minorities in British Columbia have been able to claim the communal spaces as homoerotic and to resist homophobia – and to confront and to overcome racialized divisions that had seemed almost naturalized in the landscape. In the following sections, I chronicle a few of the conflicts around homoerotic social space, derived from the divergent cartographies and respective strategies for establishing social space and making tolerant places in which to live. In all of these episodes, factors of race and ethnicity have been central in significance in both the state's perception of transgression and to the extent of the gay/'queer' resistance and activism. Respective conflicts illuminate the pressures for more systematic decolonization of homoerotic social space that have led to today's more multicultural 'queer' modes of activism. In this chronicle, there is an uneven progression towards increasingly purposeful and organized impacts on public policy and environments.

## Imperial periphery and homoerotic marginalities

By the late nineteenth century, the landscapes of British Columbia were being converted from 'nature' to production; in other words, native cultural landscapes were placed under control by neocolonial and national interests. There was a corollary preoccupation, in the colonial sexual culture, between supposedly 'natural' heterosexuality and 'unnatural' homosexuality (Chapman 1983: 98). In this period, accusations of buggery were typically woven with suggestions of disloyalty to the tenuous (white supremist and pointedly sinophobic) social hierarchy. One of the first trials for buggery was in the town of Victoria in 1860. The town crier, John Butts, was a well-known figure who expanded public discussion, often satirically, in the struggling colony. As Butts became more critical of the conduct of some of the colony's politicians, including their mistreatment of women, his homosexuality became the source of newspaper-induced hostility. Local political interests took great pleasure in his subsequent humiliation. After forced labour, Australian-born Butts resorted to petty crime and was soon forced to flee the colony for China. With the scandal around Butts, a public narrative was reproduced and simultaneously established on the Pacific Coast of British North America whereby male British colonists were disloyal if they were homosexual and probably homosexual if they were disloyal. Male colonists, when exposed, were given the choice of exile rather than local punishment. Men not British were treated more harshly. For example, in 1866 two 'Greek' seamen were charged 'for committing an unnatural offence on the high seas' (British Colonist 1866b: 3). The act was later described as 'sodomy'. One sailor was sentenced to death, which later was commuted to life imprisonment, while the other was forced into two years of hard labour.

Shortages of workers in the primarily male (Perry 1995) frontier labour force necessitated a tolerance of furtive homosexual contact. As surveillance increased and police agencies become more organized, the number of trials increased while the penalties diminished. Canada had already enacted a less severe anti-buggery law in 1869 which lessened life sentences to a maximum of ten years (Chapman 1986: 279). But this liberalization came into effect slowly, after 1871, when the Crown Colony became a province of the Dominion. Prohibitions against homosexuality were further clarified in 1892. Sections 174 and 175 of the Criminal Code of Canada proscribed male homosexuality under the labels 'gross indecency' and 'indecent assault'. Maximum prison terms were from five to ten years.

As control over territory was consolidated, 'the land' – that is, First Nations political organizations – subdued, and natural resources more systematically exploited, there came a public preoccupation with the control of women and sexuality (Chapman 1986: 277). In western Canada, 'Oscar Wilde-type' (Chapman 1983: 99–101) became the code term for the unrepentant homosexual: the individual who resisted what today is called 'homophobia' and his cramped social place on the vast frontier. Highly public trials, such as the 1906 New Westminster spectacle that saw James Egan sentenced to twelve months for consensual 'indecent assault,' had a number of social functions. Trials were used as both lessons in morality and show cases of supposed judicial compassion. It was the difficulties of controlling outlawed sexualities in the public realm, no matter how furtive, that was so troubling for the nascent state. In this sense, the entire public realm in the late Victorian period became a landscape of potential immorality. But this particular periphery of the empire was rugged, isolated, and difficult to police. Difference complicated policing and miscommunication, due to language and cultural differences, was a common defence. The sharing of collective maps between members of nascent and still-hidden sexual minorities, especially between relatively segregated ethnic groups, may have had powerful and subversive results – at least in terms of the heightened satisfaction of individuals.

The state took a different tack from colonists and transient workers in its reconstruction of First Nations sexualities. In the final decades of the nineteenth century, police apparatus was increasingly used for nakedly colonial strategies of dismantling remaining claims to land and resources. What remained of traditional political economies, culture, and sexualities were attacked. One of the more substantial and intimate records of the repression of homosexuality in a north-west coast society was the biography of 'Kwakiutl' chief Charles James Nowell who was born in 1870 (Ford 1941). Nowell's generation was violently reshaped by the Canadian state as well as by resistance to repression. Nowell recalled assaults on his own culture as soon as he began attending a mission school. Through the outlawed potlatch ceremonies, heterosexual marriage had been tied in with a system of wealth accumulation and prestige. Homosexual contact was placed in the freer realm of eroticism and love.

The first aboriginals who engaged in homosexuality to be targeted by government officials and police were cross-dressing males. Nowell recalled the fate of a transgendered companion:

> I guess the Indian agent wrote to Victoria, telling the officials what she was doing. She was taken to Victoria, and the policemen took her clothes off and found she was a man, so they gave him a suit of clothes and cut off his hair and sent him back home. When I saw him again, he was a man. He was no more my sweetheart.
>
> (Ford 1941: 129–30)

A spatial narrative emerged around apprehension of the homosexual other. Homosexual and gender-ambiguous aboriginals were thought to persist in remote areas away from 'state church' missions and government agents (Christophers 1998: 44–5). When detected, these supposed deviants were taken out of their supposed 'backward' communities, transformed in the new administrative centres, and then sent back, broken, as another example of the new power of the state. In turn, police apparatus was to increasingly justify its expansion through controlling such supposedly dangerous individuals who may well have been part of networks undermining the state's control over much of the Pacific coast.

I now shift the discussion from control of native groups to that of non-European immigrants. One of the more severe periods of homophobic repression in British Columbia was in the years just before and during the First World War. Since the turn of the century, Vancouver had been booming. There was a heightened level of wealth, increased British immigration, and further class differentiation informed by ethnicity. It was in this period that the majority of Vancouver's population became of British and Irish descent heritages (often via central Canada and the United States), replacing the increasingly marginalized multiracial population which was numerically superior when the city was founded. As throughout the British Empire, inter-racial liaisons that were homoerotic were considered a threat to the stabilizing but tentative social hierarchy (Bleys 1995: 160–85). In this social landscape, the large Chinatown areas of Victoria and Vancouver were interzones of cultural fusion, prostitution, and homosexuality. It was also in this period that concerns for 'good character', a previously undervalued trait in this brash frontier, began to be used against homosexuals and as another factor in class positioning. Males found to be engaging in homosexuality were pushed down severely in the local socioeconomic hierarchy. In British Columbia, the number of court cases for buggery increased roughly tenfold in the first decade of the twentieth century. When the typical bribery was not possible, white, and particularly British, men shown to be having relations with less privileged groups, especially non-white males, were certain to lose most of their social standing. Men of 'non-white' backgrounds who were sexually aggressive to British males were considered outrageous. For example, the following trial charges against a 'Chinaman', are similar to scores of others made in those years:

> For that he the said Wing at the City of Vancouver on the 18th day
> (1) of August 1911 did unlawfully assault Sam Brewe and then and there did unlawfully attempt to wickedly and against the order of nature have a veneral affair with and to carnally know and commit and perpetrate with the said Sam Brewe that detestable and abominable crime of buggery.
> (2) for the said Wing at the time and in the place aforesaid in public or in private did attempt to procure the commission by Sam Brewe, a male person, of an act of gross indecency with himself another male.[7]

One example of the confluence of homophobia, the new preoccupation with racial and cultural superiority, and the utility of repression around supposedly deviant sexuality, was the hysteria around homosexual Sikhs. The newspapers and the state constructed a spectre of the 'East Indian' male as aggressive homosexual. Soon after the first Sikh workers arrived, there was the 1909 *Rex v. Nar Singh* case. Singh was accused of attempting to procure acts of 'gross indecency'[8] (from persons with British surnames) and later from an undercover policeman. The cross-cultural map that emerged of the events on the edge of Vancouver's Chinatown is instructive. At 2 o'clock one morning in December of 1908, Singh was waiting for sex near the Great Northern Hotel which was well established as an early meeting place for homosexuality. The detectives had clearly been instructed to entrap. A new narrative of surveillance and repression emerged, far more up close and personal, and in this way more culturally chauvinistic. It was difficult to find a place to have sex and the officer described several attempts, including in a crowded room of sleeping Sikh men. The subsequent defence revolved around questions of intoxication and intent. Singh's limited command of English was also mentioned by the defence.

The prosecution of 'oriental cases'[9] became central to the operationalization of homosexual criminality. This was one prong of a project of the nascent bourgeoisie to slow upward class mobility. One of the more transparent examples of the racism and absurdities of the early attempts to establish police apparatus was a 1915 case where charges of 'attempt [sic] buggery' were laid against two Sikh males[10]. This episode occurred in the months after the May to July 1914 crisis around the ship, the *Komagata Maru* (Johnston 1979) and its thousands of would-be Sikh immigrants. Because of racist hysteria, these British subjects were not allowed to disembark in Canada. In February of 1915, one of the defendants, wearing a white turban, tried to 'pick up' a white, and most likely homosexual driver. There was an initial two minute conversation focused on the *Komogata Maru* episode and the first defendant's activism around that event. This was not exactly light cruising talk and may have explained the driver's motivation in bringing in an undercover policeman. The driver responded to the first defendant favourably, 'he asked me if I would like to fuck. That is just what he said to me, and I said "sure any old thing".'[11] The witness may well have been planning on being paid as 'trade' and subsequently to attempt blackmail. They made 'an appoint' for later that afternoon. At one point the driver informed on the first defendant – thus becoming immune to prosecution from subsequent homosexual contact in the entrapment. The police appear to have been attempting to target a broader network of male Sikh activists. The first defendant brought a friend, a man identified in court as having a 'blue turban', while the driver brought the undercover policeman. A foursome was negotiated. The four proceeded along railroad tracks in Chinatown. Here the entrapment was botched. The other police officers commandeered for the entrapment were late for the appointment. The detailed court transcript chronicles several minutes of supposedly awkward homosexual contact. Both standing, the taller customer proceeded to attempt to penetrate the much shorter (Italian Canadian) detective whose pants were now down around his ankles. The detective later claimed that the first defendant proposed a regularized *ménage à trois* in a shack in the suburban Central Park. Upon arrival of the other police, the defendants were beaten, with the first receiving a broken jaw. What makes this case so curious, historically, is that the first defendant claimed to have known the detective and that he had been harassing Sikh activists. In the court records, there was an extraordinary level of care in attempting to confirm that a certain 75 cents was received by the two white men for the agreed upon sexual services. This suggests a backup logic whereby the detective and the informant were indicating that even if they would engage in homosexuality with non-Europeans, it was primarily for money (to be deposited with the state). Oddly, there is no longer 75 cents in the envelope of the carefully archived trial transcript – if the sum was ever paid. Clearly there were major differences in the (homo)erotic and geopolitical maps of these Sikh and European-Canadian males – particularly as they pertained to sex, citizenship, and entitlement. That time, the Europeans prevailed.

By the Cold War, a political economy of homophobia emerged. On the Pacific

Coast, there appear to have been two purges of sexual minorities. Within a year of the end of the Second World War, numerous lesbians and gay men who worked in the communications unit of the Empire's North Pacific fleet, headquartered in Esquimalt west of Victoria, were court-marshalled under the secrecy of the War Measures Act.[12] With the economic pressures to decommission military personnel quickly, and the fiscal constraints on providing benefits to all honourably discharged, sexual minorities were easy targets for swift discrediting and removal. With the military benefits, such individuals were pushed downward class-wise. The charges had some historical similarity to many of the anti-homosexual purges in the British navy in the nineteenth century. It was also in this period, from 1947 to 1949, that east Asians, south Asians and some aboriginals were fully enfranchised. Soon after, public establishments, such as beer parlours and hotels, some with furtive meeting places for homosexuals, began to be desegregated. The second purge, again centred in Victoria, was in the 1958–65 period and roughly coincided with the Progressive Conservative federal government, 'the Diefenbaker years'. In 1958, Leo Anthony Mantha, a former naval officer discharged for his homosexuality, murdered his lover in a jealous rage on the naval base. Such a crime of passion involving lovers was no longer grounds for the death penalty. But Mantha was Québec-born, bilingual and was of a mixed-raced background. In terms of the typical prejudices of English-speaking Canada, Mantha was perfect for demonizing. He was soon to be one of the last Canadians executed by the state. In the early years of the Cold War, the Canadian government was under pressure from the United States military to apprehend subversives. In British Columbia, the strength of the trade unions precluded imprisonment of most communists and apprehension of homosexuals was substituted. After he confessed to the murder, three times, Mantha was portrayed in the media, as something of a predatory masculine 'Homo Sexual'. A significant factor in Mantha receiving the death penalty was the prosecutor's portrayal of him as amoral and a monster of cultural hybridity. This was part of the now Canada-in-Commonwealth reconstruction of the superiority of relatively unadulerated Anglo-Saxon culture – of which little actually remained in the region. The hanging of Leo Mantha was a watershed event in the political economy of homophobia in Cold War British Columbia. In subsequent years, the hysteria led to such a 'witch hunt' against gay men that scores were entrapped, were removed from employment, were forced to leave the region, and were driven into such despair that several of those targeted committed suicide. The purges in the military and in the government probably went on as late as the mid-1960s.

By the mid-1960s, the laws that criminalized homosexuality were in crisis. 'Gross indecency', the cornerstone of Canadian homosexuality law since the Wilde trials, was not well-defined (Sanders 1967: 25). Unresolved legal questions were forcing police to shift the emphasis in arrests to control of sex in open areas of public space

(Ingram 1997c). By 1965, Vancouver became an early centre in the international movement to decriminalize homosexuality. The first homophile organization in Canada, the Association for Social Knowledge, was formed in Vancouver in 1964 (Kinsman 1996: 230–5) after a year of police harassment in the city's gay bars. While purges were still going on, some of the more liberal churches as well as the legal profession began to talk about state repression of homosexuals and the need for greater tolerance. ASK sponsored parties, social spaces, and public discussions on 'homosexual marriages', 'lesbians', 'drag and transvestitism', and 'sadism, masochism, and fetishism'. By mid-1965, even the right-centrist *Vancouver Sun* was running guest editorials from theologians calling for decriminalization. The movement in British Columbia to decriminalize homosexuality was virtually all-white. An ironic discourse was constructed of supposed liberal and 'modern' whiteness versus homophobic and 'primitive' ethnicity (as in groups formerly colonized). The landmark year for the Canadian homophile and decriminalization movements was 1967. Canadian Prime Minister Trudeau's federal Liberal Party announced its plans to decriminalize homosexuality (Bill C-150). As the overtly homophobic state apparatus began to be dismantled, at the end of the 1960s, police remained preoccupied with homosexual males of colour and those who engaged in public sex.

Gay liberation, youth culture and the counterculture framed sexuality, more overtly, in terms of collective resistance to the state. But in decolonizing homoerotic space, the gay liberation movement reproduced new forms of cultural chauvinism and a continued privileging of anglophile Canadian culture. Gay liberation that erupted in the years after the 1969 Stonewall Riots marked the transition from neocolonial to nationalist social maps. Its short-lived location is enigmatic. Vancouver's Chinatown was formed by a series of riots by racist whites, a substantial portion of which were United States citizens, in the late-1880s and 1890s. Today the opium dens of Vancouver's Shanghai Alley have been replaced by residential towers often financed with Hong Kong capital. At the corner of Pender Street is a century-old brick building: 509 Carrall Street. This was the site of the 1970–71 Vancouver Gay Liberation Front (GLF) drop-in centre shared with the Youth International Party (the Yippies), along with one of the city's first Women's centres. The building is a prime example of nineteenth-century Chinatown architecture with a collapsing and a meagre apportionment of the spaces of the social other. The now turquoise-coloured building represents an imperial accommodation between British capital and Asian labour mediated through Canadian and overseas Chinese entrepreneurial classes. There is the hidden second floor to avoid the crippling, anti-Chinese taxes. There is also the classic balcony that may have seen much theatricality – well before the 'genderfuck' in the euphoria of gay liberation. The 'drag' duo, The Ephemerals, who performed there in 1970 and 1971, 'specialized in street theatre that ... mocked traditional male–female roles and stereotypes' (McLeod

1996: 54). But while it might have seemed like the white men from the balcony were telling the Chinese 'below' how to loosen up on their rigid sexual world-views, the opposite had been more the case over the previous two centuries. That supposedly 'countercultural' world-view is still influential. But the GLF had virtually no relevance to or impact on Chinese-Canadian gay males. The GLF simply had appropriated the exoticized space of Chinatown in order to disavow the remnants of imperial Victorianism – without reflecting on its own unresolved cultural relationships with Victorian imperialism.

The renewal of leftist politics in the 1970s saw an awkward framing of disparities around race and ethnicity that was overshadowed by early twentieth-century notions of class. Vancouver's Gay Alliance Towards Equality (GATE), was one of the country's most influential and broadly based gay rights groups. But GATE was effectively all-white and overwhelmingly male. GATE's preoccupation with the working-class also functioned as a foil for avoiding any recognition of racial and ethnic-based disparities in vulnerability to homophobia. GATE's inability to embody 'difference' and to address cultural chauvinism was rooted in a nationalism and a limited multiculturalism that continued to privilege English and French-speaking cultures. Problematic as were its politics, the formation of GATE represented the genesis of local strategizing for reconstructing public space through confronting institutional homophobia and racism. The August 1971 national demonstrations in front of the Canadian Parliament thrust gay and lesbian rights into Canadian national consciousness and inspired a smaller demonstration on the steps of Vancouver's courthouse. The older political economy of homophobia was crumbling at a dizzying pace. For example, a high school in New Westminster saw gay organizing in 1972 to the chagrin of conservative politicians. The first gay pride rally in commemoration of the Stonewall riots was organized by GATE in June of 1972. GATE attempted to work in broad coalitions of the left but was constantly having to fight homophobia, especially from Stalinist and Maoist-allied factions. In 1972, GATE was demonstrating around the war in Indo-China declaring that the 'common enemy' of both the Vietnamese and Canadian homosexuals was the government of the United States. As well as developing the *Gay Tide* as the first Western Canadian newspaper to theorize on the remaking of public space by sexual minorities, GATE further pushed the state to decolonize through finding more gaps in constitutional law. The GATE campaign that had national significance was the case against the *Vancouver Sun* for not printing an advertisement in 1973. This struggle was eventually lost in the Supreme Court of Canada but the legal challenge prefigured a decade of interpretations of the 1982 Charter of Rights and Freedoms around the rights of minorities (Smith 1998: 301–3).

In 1980 GATE dissolved itself, noting that 'The lesbian and gay movement in Vancouver has advanced to the point where there are numerous and diverse organizations'[13]. The dissolution of GATE was two years before the first human rights protections for sexual orientation, in the City of Vancouver (The Body Politic 1982), and three years before the first organizing against AIDS. GATE's achievements were perhaps the most substantial of any single organization of sexual minorities in Canadian history. And GATE was the first Canadian organization of sexual minorities to recognize and to begin to confront racism. But GATE remained, throughout its history, a white organization in a multicultural region. The position of the organization was typically that racism was considered to be so pervasive with people of colour so 'colonized' that gay rights were not always the priority. GATE was also denied participation in some anti-racist coalitions because of overt homophobia.[14] The maps of non-white homosexuality and the opportunities posed by gay rights were still obscured – at least for eurocentric organizations.

The ravages of AIDS illuminated the persisting disparities between groups of gay men in access to public resources as rooted in 'difference'. Whatever gains were made for gay rights and in options for freedom of expression in public space were undermined by the homophobic hysteria around HIV. The homosexual body in British Columbia was reinscribed as diseased just as the older stigmas were being discredited. The experience of and vulnerability to this disease varied greatly in terms of race, ethnicity, and language. As HIV infections in Pacific Canada soared in the mid-1980s (Brown 1994: 877), there was cultivated government indifference in a highly centralized socialized system of health care delivery. The first AIDS-related services organization, AIDS Vancouver, was formed in 1984 and developed a coalition or umbrella model of administration that allowed for affiliations with smaller organizations. In the rightist homophobia of the late-1980s, the provincial government was forced to effectively launder modest levels of funding for badly needed services. In this collaborationist bureaucracy, boundaries were increasingly blurred between 'the gay community', nongovernmental service agencies, and the state (Brown 1995). There were 'tremendous external pressures on the white gay male community to form a sort of shadow state' (Brown 1994: 876). Compounding the new wave of homophobia was a devastating fiscal 'restraint' programme from 1983 to 1985 by the conservative provincial. The covert hostility became overt in 1987 when the provincial government read into law the Health Statutes Amendment Act. This legislation provided the legal basis for putting into quarantine people suspected of testing positive for HIV. The bill developed the notion of a health hazard deriving from sexually active gay men. There were even politicians in ruling circles privately calling for 'a special ghetto' in Vancouver and the use of a former leper colony for quarantine.

The AIDS bureaucracy was even more racialized than the federal and provincial governments at the time. The neocolonial model of service delivery, emphasizing nongovernmental organizations, harked to the nineteenth-century Christian missions that functioned as surrogate states. These semi-political entities were forced to recognize cultural difference as a matter of life and death as well as for self-validation. For gay men of colour, AIDS generated additional opportunities for alliances with heterosexuals with similar ethnic experiences. The primacy of whiteness and the exoticization of the other (as in supposedly not belonging to the locale) began to be effectively contested in gay male environments. By the late-1980s, groups that eventually became ASIA for east Asians and the Black AIDS Network (BAN) had formed – often with as much if not more support for heterosexuals from respective ethnic communities as from white gay men.

It is only in the last decade that the colonial (racist) versus neocolonial (anglocentric) 'choice' in homoerotic contact has broken down. Today the divergence in homoerotic cartographies is shifting to nationalist multiculturalism versus globalist post-colonialism. The widespread resistance to the provincial AIDS Quarantine bill and the 1990 Gay Games in Vancouver inscribed, tentatively, cross-gender and 'multicultural' alliances around sexuality. ACT UP Vancouver came to be the harbinger of queer nationalism and a style of gender and culturally specific coalitions. There was more cultural space for acknowledgement of disparities related to race and culture in relationship to erotic difference and homophobia. ACT UP Vancouver was formed in July of 1990 three years after the celebrated New York chapter emerged and well after there were functioning chapters in most large North American cities. Originally, this relatively small chapter consisted of a telephone tree of 80 people with consensus decision-making at semi-regular meetings. As well as appropriations of public space, such as 'die-ins', there were demonstrations at the constituency offices of the provincial Minister of Health. ACT UP Vancouver sparked queer nationalism in Vancouver because it was one of the first coalitions of sexual minorities not controlled by white, middle-class gay men. In the words of co-founder Kevin Robb, 'surprisingly, few people coming to meetings are white, middle-class gay men. I think a lot of the disapproval we're getting is coming from that community' (Buttle 1990: A17). Short-lived, ACT UP Vancouver became one of the few venues in which to express public rage especially for PWAs. ACT UP Vancouver emerged as much from a century of western Canadian traditions of activism on the left, with strategizing to occupy public space, as from the globalizing network of activism to fight AIDS. Much of the local precedents for civil disobedience and other forms of resistance demanding social services, which laid the basis for ACT UP Vancouver, had emerged in the previous century in the women's, labour, and environmental movements.[15]

ACT UP Vancouver was one of the front line groups that highlighted the bankruptcy of the social programmes of the corrupt and draconian ruling party in the provincial government. Sexual minorities and PWAs provided the spectacle to illuminate the final fall from the public confidence of the last Social Credit Party government. The party had been in power for all but three and half years out of the last four decades. In the year after the formation of ACT UP Vancouver, a social democratic provincial government came into power. A year later, British Columbia's human rights code was amended to include protections from discrimination on the basis of sexual orientation. After years of broad public pressure, the federal government similarly amended its human rights protections in 1996. Continuing problems with ineffectual implementation aside, it is finally possible, legalistically, to examine social inequities in a matrix that acknowledges gender, ethnicity, race, language, and sexuality. It was also in this period that the provincial government resumed negotiations for treaties with most of the First Nations on the coast after the government of British Columbia broke with London on its policy of engagement thirteen decades before.

## Multiple voices and divergent maps

The late-1980s saw the beginning of the dismantling of the nineteenth-century social and cultural hierarchies that put British Columbia on the map. It was no coincidence that a 'queer' politics, that was self-consciously multicultural and antiracist, finally emerged. Whites recognized the ascendance of globalization over neocolonialism, the inevitability of multiculturalism, and an increasingly diverse nature of Pacific Canadian culture. People of non-European heritages developed new strategies for confronting effective disparities, tied to race and culture, in access to and impact on public space. There emerged a popular awareness that Canadian political and cultural nationalism had sometimes been used as foil for latent xenophobia (Ng 1993).

On the West Coast, gay and lesbian aboriginal groups began organizing in 1977. The distinct, 'two-spirited' identity, linked more directly to native spirituality around gender ambiguity and homoeroticism, emerged publicly in the 1980s. Much of the focus of early organizing was on providing peer support to urbanized aboriginal people and assistance around obtaining social services including those for substance dependence. While originally marginalized by mainstream aboriginal organizations, two-spirited and First Nation feminist groups became active in broader coalitions around native self-determination. In recent years there has been a growing interest in building links to and presences in often more rural First Nations institutions.

In the early-1980s, lesbians 'of colour' began to articulate themselves. This was years earlier than their gay male counterparts. The Spring 1983 issue of the Canadian feminist journal, *Fireweed*, signalled that racial disparities between groups of sexual minorities could be talked about on the West Coast. By the late-1980s, the implications of racism, to the public lives of gay men, was finally being more seriously, and sometimes more humorously, discussed. Lingering racism became identified with an unsuccessful historical project of erasure and censorship. Young artists, such as Paul Wong, framed discussions of censorship of homoeroticism within broader, increasingly global, cultural terms. The struggle around the 1984 censoring of his video, 'Confused: Sexual Views', by the Vancouver Art Gallery left an indelible mark on culture on the West Coast (MacKillon 1984; Wong 1998). In Vancouver's communities of sexual minorities, the public recovery of the experiences of the Native, the Chinese-Canadian, the South Asian and the African-Canadian began to hasten as the older anglophile world-views (and regional views) lost credence. The last decade has seen a growing assertion of the eroticization of Chinese-Canadian males and the contesting of a largely eurocentric body culture (Koo 1994: 17). The Lotus Root Conference, in March 1996, created new cultural spaces for gay men and lesbians of east Asian heritages. Vancouver, along with Montréal and Toronto, became a major international destination for political refugees, with flight from homophobic prosecution being one basis for sanctuary. Barriers to immigration by same-sex partners were only dismantled in the mid-1990s. The shift away from family-oriented immigration to entry of more appropriately trained individuals has allowed more settlement by single adults, some of whom have quickly asserted their particular homosexualities. Today, perhaps truly post-colonial homoerotic maps of Pacific Canada have begun to be articulated around, and inscribed in, public space.

## Conclusions: new cartographies and emerging designs

Homoerotic life in Pacific Canada, particularly as long it is still called 'British Columbia', remains a long way from being truly decolonized and post-colonial. Even with a large portion of the gay male population made up of individuals with non-European heritages, the culture of homoerotic public space, and how it marks bodies and the body politic, remains overwhelmingly white, anglocentric, and almost neocolonial. Without more sophisticated forms of homosocial cartography and the sharing and reconstruction of maps reflecting a fuller range of 'queer' experiences, few new maps can be constructed that will lead to effective collective plans. The prerequisites for an activist 'queerscape architecture' (Ingram *et al*. 1997) are only partially in place.

The internal pressures to redesign public space with recognition of a wide range of cultural experiences of eroticism, in relatively safe and affluent cities such as Vancouver, continue to intensify (Bombardier *et al*. 1995). But the continued weakness of the 'dialogue' (Debord 1994: 127) around culture and sexuality limit possible 'environmental planning' and design responses. Multiple maps may better define territories in which to intervene but they do not constitute plans. New maps are being constructed if only to begin to engender badly needed consensus for construction of diversifying spaces for communal well-being, survival, consumption, and pleasures. In the coming decades, it will be the work of many people, who are members of sexual minorities in Pacific Canada, to chart authentically post-colonial and homoeroticized possibilities. And the sharing of the underlying maps for these new collectivities and social projects, the search for new forms of 'pretty-near', will become more central to regional culture.

## Notes

1 The label 'queer' was largely used as a pejorative in Pacific Canada until 1990. Since then, a growing group, perhaps today a majority of sexual minorities, now use the term to include any person engaged in homoeroticism or gender transgression.
2 The research for this article was funded by grants 2550–95–0008 and 5680–97–0002 for architecture criticism from The Canada Council for the Arts. Access to some of the trial files was through agreement 97–0043 with the British Columbia Archives. Thanks to its staff, especially Mac Culham.
3 Jameson did not substantiate his 1984 enthusiasm for cognitive mapping. In his 1989 clarification (Jameson 1989) of his earlier assertions, he began to distance himself from more literal use of cognitive mapping in activism.
4 The discourses of 'difference' have expanded greatly in recent years and there are numerous and in many cases divergent interpretations now being articulated. For example of the kinds of critical frameworks of difference, that lay the basis for charting the fluid relationships of race, gender and sexuality in class-defined hierarchies and related utilization of social space, see Haraway (1991: 200), Terry (1991), and Warner (1993: vii–xxxi).
5 In one nineteenth-century vernacular on the West Coast of Canada (and parts of the adjacent United States), 'pretty-near' was the common phrase for determining relative location. The phrase was pronounced as one word, 'pri-ti-near', with the first two syllables short, the first syllable longer than the second, and with the third syllable lengthened.
6 *Franco-colombien* is a recent term for British Columbians of French-speaking ethnicities, a substantial portion of which in the nineteenth-century had *Métis* or creole/'mulatto' heritages.
7 Charge Book Provincial Gaols in Vancouver. November 1908–December 1911. On file British Columbia Archives (BCA) (Victoria) Gr 0602 V.3 (C1816). See pp. 131–2.
8 The alleged incident occurred on 12 December 1908 and the guilty verdict appears to have been reached on 5 May 1909. (Attorney General of British Columbia. 1909. Copy of Depositions – *Rex v. Nar Singh* (Attempt Gross Indecency). Crown brief – compiled 5 May 1909. On file BCA – BC Attorney General documents GR 419, V. 134, file 50 (1909)).
9 Letter to A.H. McNeill, Crown Prosecutor, Vancouver, from E.M.N. Woods, Barrister, May 6th to May 20th, 1915 included in the dossier with the Crown Brief. *Rex v. D—p S—g*, *Rex v. N—a S—g* [names deleted by requirement of the BC Freedom of Information Act]. Offence: Attempt Buggery. 1915. On file, BCA, BC Attorney General documents GR 419, V. 197, file 31 (1915).
10 Ibid.
11 Ibid., court transcript point 16.
12 Ron Dutton, BC Gay and Lesbian Archives, Vancouver, 1997, pers. comm. Dutton was contacted by a woman whose gay father was purged from his job in the Communications Office of Naden soon after the end of the Second World War.
13 GATE. 24 June 1980. Press release: The dissolution of GATE Vancouver and Gay Tide. On file Canadian Lesbian and Gay Archives, Toronto (GATE 82 005/10 (Vancouver)). 2 pp.
14 Don Hann, pers. comm., 1998.
15 This analysis diverges markedly from that in Brown (1997). In 1999 conversations with Brown on the topic, he indicated that he based his conclusions on interviews as he was not in Vancouver at the time of the 1990–91 events. In contrast, I witnessed many of the events and saw similarities in those tactics to ones employed in labour, women's and environemntal activism in British Columbia in the previous two decades.

## References

Baudrillard, Jean (1983) 'The Precision of Simulacra', in *Simulations*, trans. Paul Foss, Paul Patton, and Philip Beitchman, New York: Semiotext(e).

Berlant, Lauren and Elizabeth Freeman (1993) 'Queer Nationality', in Michael Warner (ed.) *Fear of a Queer Planet: Queer Politics and Social Theory*, Minneapolis: University of Minnesota Press: 193–229.

Bhabha, Homi K. (1990) 'The Other Question: Difference, Discrimination and the Discourse of Colonialism', in Russell Ferguson, Martha Gever, Trinh T. Minh-ha, and Cornel West (eds) *Out There: Marginalization and Contemporary Cultures*, New York: New Museum of Contemporary Art, and Cambridge, Mass.: MIT Press, 70–87.

Bhabha, Homi K. (1994) *The Location of Culture*, New York: Routledge.

Bleys, Rudi C. (1995) *The Geography of Perversion: Male-to-Male Sexual Behavior Outside the West and the Ethnographic Imagination 1750–1918*, New York: New York University Press: 160–85.

Body Politic, The (1982) 'Vancouver's Pre-election Surprise', *The Body Politic* (Toronto), 89: 7.

Bombardier, Sylvain, Anne-Marie Bouthillette, Michael Carroll, Trolley Bus, Michael Hoeschen, Jeff Gibson, Michael Howell, Gordon Brent Ingram, Bryan Langlands, Ian Pringle and Kathleen Morrissey (1995) 'Queers in Space Vancouver Manifesto', *UnderCurrents: Critical Environmental Studies* (Toronto) 7: 56–7.

British Colonist, The (1866a) (for trial) *The British Colonist* (Victoria) 15(50) (8 February): 3.

British Colonist, The (1866b) 'Regina vs. Mat Rosid and Andrew Patrico, Sodomy', *The British Colonist* 15(67) (28 February): 3.

Brown, Michael (1994) 'The Work of City Politics: Citizenship Through Employment in the Local Response to AIDS', *Environment and Planning A: Society and Space* 26: 873–94.

Brown, Michael (1995) 'Sex, Scale and the "New Urban Politics" HIV-prevention Strategies from Yaletown, Vancouver', in David Bell and Gill Valentine (eds) *Mapping Desire: Geographies of Sexualities*, London and New York: Routledge: 245–63.

Brown, Michael (1997) 'Radical Politics Out of Place?: The Curious Case of ACT UP Vancouver', in Steve Pile and Michael Keith (eds) *Geographies of Resistance*, London and New York: Routledge: 152–67.

Buttle, Jeff (1990) 'AIDS Protestors Won't Stop Confrontations, Protests', *Vancouver Sun* (13 September): A17.

Chapman, Terry L. (1983) '"An Oscar Wilde type": The Abominable Crime of Buggery in Western Canada, 1890–1920', *Criminal Justice History* 4: 97–118.

Chapman, Terry L. (1986) 'Male Homosexuality: Legal Restraints and Social Attitudes in Western Canada, 1890–1920', in Louis Knafla (ed.) *Law and Justice in a New Land: Essays in Western Canadian Legal History*, Toronto: Carswell: 277–92.

Christophers, Brett (1998) *Positioning the Missionary: John Booth Good and the Confluence of Cultures in Nineteenth-century British Columbia*, Vancouver: University of British Columbia Press.

Debord, Guy (1994) *The Society of the Spectacle*, trans. Donald Nicholson-Smith, New York: Zone Books.

Ford, Clellan (1941) *Smoke From Their Fires: The Life of a Kwakiutl Chief*, New Haven, Conn.: Yale University Press.

Haraway, Donna J. (1991) *Simians, Cyborgs, and Women: the Reinvention of Nature*, London and New York: Routledge.

Ingram, Gordon Brent (1995) 'Landscapes of (Un)lawful Chaos: Conflicts around Temperate Rain Forest and Biological Diversity in Pacific Canada', *RECIEL: Review of European Community & International Environmental Law* (London) 4(3): 242–9.

Ingram, Gordon Brent (1997a), 'Sex Migrants: Paul Wong's Video Geographies of Erotic and Cultural Displacement in Pacific Canada', *FUSE* (Toronto) 20(1): 17–26.

Ingram, Gordon Brent (1997b) 'Marginality and the Landscapes of Erotic Alien (n)ations', in G.B. Ingram, A.-M. Bouthillette and Y. Retter (eds) *Queers in Space: Communities | Public Places | Sites of Resistance*, Seattle: Bay Press: 27–52.

Ingram, G.B. (1997c) '"Open" Space as Strategic Queer Sites', in G.B. Ingram, A.-M. Bouthillette and Y. Retter (eds) *Queers in Space: Communities | Public Places | Sites of Resistance*, Seattle: Bay Press: 95–125.

Ingram, Gordon Brent, Yolanda Retter and Anne-Marie Bouthillette (1997) 'Strategies for (Re)constructing Queer Communities', in *Queers in Space: Communities | Public Places | Sites of Resistance*, Seattle: Bay Press: 447–57.

Ingram, Gordon Brent, Anne-Marie Bouthillette and Cornelia Wyngaarden (2000) *Vancouver (as queer)scape: The Construction of Public Space by Sexual Minorities in Pacific Canada*, Toronto: University of Toronto Press.

Jameson, Frederick (1984) 'Postmodernism, or the Cultural Logic of Late Capitalism', *New Left Review* 146 (July–August): 53–92.

Jameson, Frederick (1989) 'Marxism and Postmodernism', *New Left Review* 176 (July–August): 44.

Johnston, J.M. (1979) *The Voyage of the Komagata Maru: The Sikh Challenge to Canada's Colour Bar*, Delhi: Oxford University Press.

Kinsman, Gary (1996) *The Regulation of Desire: Homo and Hetero Sexualities*, Montréal: Black Rose Books.

Koo, Henry (1994) 'Caucasian and Asian Men Together in Lotusland', *Xtra West* (March 25) 16: 17.

Koppel, Tom (1995) *Kanaka: The Untold Story of Hawaiian Pioneers in British Columbia and the Pacific Northwest*, Vancouver: Whitecap.

MacKillon, Michael (1984) 'Gallery Politics Kill Sexuality', *Angles* (Vancouver) (April): 26.

McLeod, Donald W. (1996) *Lesbian and Gay Liberation in Canada: A Selected Annotated Chronology, 1964–1975*, Toronto: Homewood Books and ECW Press.

Ng, Roxana (1993) 'Sexism, Racism, and Canadian Nationalism', in Himani Bannerji (ed.) *Returning the Gaze: Essays on Racism, Feminism and Politics*, Toronto: Sister Vision: 183–4.

Owens, C. (1992) 'Outlaws: Gay Men in Feminism', in S. Bryson, B. Kruger, L. Tillman and J. Weinstock (eds) *Beyond Recognition: Representation, Power, and Culture*, Berkeley: University of California Press: 218–35.

Perry, Adele (1995) '"Oh I'm so Sick of the Faces of Men": Gender Imbalances, Race, Sexuality and Sociality in Nineteenth Century British Columbia', *BC Studies* 105–106 (Spring/Summer): 27–44.

Sanders, Douglas E. (1967) 'Sentencing of Homosexual Offenders', *Criminal Law Quarterly* 10 (November): 25–9.

Smith, Michael D. (1996) 'The Empire Filters Back: Consumption, Production, and the Politics of Starbucks Coffee', *Urban Geography* 17(6): 502–24.

Smith, Miriam (1998) 'Social Movements and Equality Seeking: The Case of Gay Liberation in Canada', *Canadian Journal of Political Science* XXXI(2): 285–309.

Terry, Jennifer (1991) 'Theorizing Deviant Historiography', *Differences: A Journal of Feminist Cultural Studies* 3(2): 54–74.

Warner, Michael (1993) Introduction to Michael Warner (ed.) *Fear of a Queer Planet: Queer Politics and Social Theory*, Minneapolis: University of Minnesota Press: vii–xxxi.

Young, Iris Marion (1990) 'The Ideal of Community and the Politics of Difference', in Linda J. Nicholson (ed.) *Feminism/Postmodernism*, New York: Routledge: 300–23.

Wong, Paul (1998) (in interview with Richard Fung) 'Misfits Together: Paul Wong on Art, Community and Vancouver in the 1970s and '80s', *FUSE* 21(3): 41–6.

# Part IV

DEVOLVING SEXUALITIES

# 13

# DEVOLUTIONARY DESIRES

*Lynne Pearce*

This chapter – part reflection, part prognosis – will explore some of the ways in which devolutionary politics relate to, and impact upon, our romantic desires and sexual relations. Its focus is specifically upon Britain – and even more specifically upon British fiction written between 1979 and 1997: these being the dates of when the people of Scotland and Wales were last, and most recently, given the opportunity to vote for limited self-government in a referendum. The swing by both nations from an uncertain 'no' in 1979 to an overwhelming 'yes' in 1997 has set the scene for the most far-reaching constitutional reform Britain has known since the 'Act of Union' in 1707. Furthermore, in May 1998, the people of Northern Ireland also voted 'yes' for their own Assembly: supposedly in the hope that *this* act of devolution would facilitate 'the road to peace' in what remains our most desperate centre–margin conflict.

Needless to say, this brief overview of British devolution has been written primarily for non-British readers who may, indeed, find it extraordinary that a country as small as Britain should be on the point of breaking up into even smaller parts. They may also be amazed that this investment in 'regional' identities should give rise to desires, fears, resentments and hostilities as powerful as those I am about to describe. And they may question, too, the relevance of such provincial feuding to 'world politics', sexual or otherwise.

What I would like to argue, however, is that British devolution *does* represent something rather more than another centre–margin 'case-study'. Quite aside from the more general insights that can be gained from this particular articulation of sexuality and space (of imperialist centrism, marginal resistance, and the dependence of *both* on heterosexist orthodoxies), this chapter may also be seen as a modest contribution to recent attempts to re-write the history of British colonialism by 'starting at home'. The cultural and political legacy of this (post)colonialism 'overseas' is now of huge academic interest, whilst anything focusing on Britain *per se* is not. This, I feel, is a mistake, because the centre–margin politics which enabled Britain to effect such change throughout the world clearly does have (and continues to have) its origins *within* these islands. Furthermore, the intensity of resistance –

both national/regional *and* sexual — that I am about to describe can *only* be understood as the effect of the multiple differences (e.g., culture, language, ethnicity, class) brought into 'unnatural union' by an imperial centre with (other) margins far beyond its shores.

## National desires

Whatever else the General Election of May 1997 may or may not have achieved, the constitutional reform effected by the New Labour's 'commitment' to British Devolution has set in motion legislation that at least gestures towards a redistribution of power from 'centre' to 'margin'. How far this gesture is taken, and to what extent it becomes meaningful, of course remains to be seen: as one of the more sceptical characters in Robert Watson's *Rumours of Fulfilment* (1982) observes: 'That was what devolution meant … it meant delegating bits and pieces of something to subordinates … It was a word victors could throw at the defeated' (Watson 1982: 198). And now that Northern Ireland has been pitched into the devolutionary fray, we have even more cause to be suspicious. What exactly is it that the centre *is* granting the margins? Perhaps no more than a recognition, finally, that the colonies closest to home, like the ones further away, are ultimately more trouble than they are worth.

But these suspicions are, for the most part, being swept aside on a tide of euphoric relief that the despotic rule of the centre — culminating in eighteen years of Thatcherism — is finally over. This, at least, is the situation in Scotland, where no amount of scaremongering about the 'cost' of the new parliament, or the suggestion that this is the inevitable first step towards full-scale independence, seems able to dampen the spirits or commitment of the majority of Scottish citizens. Having failed to 'go with their hearts' once, there seems little danger that they will make the same mistake again. And although the buoyancy of the nation is presently built on cultural rather than economic capital, the opinion polls consistently suggest that its people are prepared to bear the cost (they did, after all, vote 'yes' not only for consititutional self-rule but also tax-raising powers). So, for the moment, at least, Scotland represents an emphatic rejection of its former 'union' — even if this is sometimes a cold comfort to the other 'Celtic' nations — Ireland, Wales and Cornwall — for whom the possibility of divorce may be seen to have come too late.

The fact that I have set up this re-mapping of the British Isles in a vocabulary that is expressly gendered, hetero/sexual and matrimonial is not, I would argue, as contrived as it might at first seem. As other contributors to this volume (e.g. Vincent Quinn) have also observed, the rhetoric of colonialization has depended upon these tropes exhaustively and problematically (inasmuch as it has sometimes signalled a crippling lack of political as well as sexual imagination). But it is the discourse of *desire itself* that I see to be most inevitable when attempting to understand the enduring affiliations of peoples to their nations or homelands. Prevailing (Western) ideology decrees that such peoples love (and are expected to love) their countries with a passion which is comparable to romantic or sexual passion. And, by extension, they are prepared to (and are expected to) die for their countries. Countries – as post-colonial theory continually reminds us – are often gendered and sexualized (female). They inspire acts of devotion: not only in the form of taking up arms or laying down one's life but in terms of cultural gifts also. Thus it is often not the people of a country, but the land itself that artists address their work to: a space that is both supremely abstract, and supremely material.

Armed with even a little psychoanalytic theory it is not difficult to begin positing explanations for these connections between the dynamics of sexual desire and of national affiliation, as has, indeed, been made clear in some of the most sophisticated post/colonial theorizing (Bhabha 1990). It is now common theoretical currency for us to think about the more 'irrational' excesses of colonial oppression in terms of 'othering', for example, though for the purposes of this discussion I am more interested in viewing the operation from the other side and thinking about what it is that causes individuals – and then *groups* of individuals – to 'devote' themselves to a country or a region in the way that they do. In as much as all acts of devotion are (admittedly convoluted) expressions of desire, 'commitment' to one's country (however defined) must also be predicated upon an act of othering: the individual's need, one would guess, to guarantee or validate his/her identity through an 'act of union' with 'an other'. This paradox of 'finding oneself' through 'losing oneself', which is such a well-figured dynamic within romantic discourse and its attendant narratives, is also a neat way of reminding ourselves why individuals have been prepared to commit themselves to their countries or nations in the way that they have. It is the classic 'relief' of the sublimation of self in other – an impulse that temporarily quells the troubling insecurities of the ego by directing it *outwards* and enabling it to take up residence elsewhere: usually in 'an other' (person/nation/collectivity/faith) that is considered 'greater' than the individual. Thus romantic love, in its first 'rapture', depends utterly upon a wild aggrandisement of the 'loved object' who becomes (typically) the rolling sea, the stars and heavens, and numerous other 'infinities' (Barthes [1977] 1990). In psychoanalytic terms, this impulse can, of course, be neatly interpreted as a classic expression of the adult subject's insatiable need to regain his/her sense of 'oceanic' merger with a m/other that encompasses themselves fully, and finally.

By reminding ourselves, then, of psychological dynamics that offer some sort of explanation for the excesses and irrationalities of our interpersonal relations we can, perhaps, also go a small way to explaining both the nature and the extent of national desire/s. The main purpose of the association, for me, however, is to decree the futility of *denying* our wish for community or national affiliations. Whilst history undoubtedly shows us that national, like religious, identifications have been the primary generator of all manner of xenophobic violence, often linked to acts of unspeakable atrocity, their predication upon a principle of desire commensurate with the sexual one means that they are unlikely to disappear. And whilst the analogy of nation with religion reminds us that such identifications might, in time, be displaced (i.e., it need not necessarily be the concept of 'country' or 'nation' *per se* that we dedicate ourselves to), the inference is that there is a strong tendency for identifications and loyalties to be spatially defined.

But beyond the fundamental, if problematically universal, psychic drives that help explain how national and sexual desires are linked, there are a plethora of attendant cultural and political riders that actually work to *dis*-articulate the two terms. Extensive as the vocabulary linking sex and nation has been, it has been largely in the context of a repressed and 'invisibilizing' heterosexual orthodoxy which encourages 'normal' individuals to 'identify' with their nation and forget about their sexuality. As Andrew Parker, citing Benedict Anderson, reminds us, 'nation-ness is the most universally legitimate value in the political life of our time' (Parker *et al.* 1992: 8). In other words, it remains the identity of which it is perhaps most *easy* to be proud; the 'love' that it is least embarrassing to own up to. It is much easier, indeed, than proclaiming an identity that has been consistently, and historically, *de*-legitimated: like being gay, or even 'feminist'. And despite the many hopeful visions of a more sexually liberated future promised by our newly devolving nations, one senses – or suspects – something of this in the 'identifications' of their most high-profile authors. Contemporary Scottish women writers like Liz Lochhead (1990), Janice Galloway and A.L. Kennedy (Bell 1995: 101–2) have repeatedly shown themselves more prepared to 'identify' (or, indeed, to 'market') themselves as 'Scottish' than 'feminist', for example; though the implicit/explicit rationale here is that it is 'limiting' to be read as 'feminist' and/or politically *strategic* to be read as 'Scottish'. Lochhead, indeed, has made the conscious decision to change her affiliation on these grounds, admitting:

> Ten years ago I liked being called a feminist writer because feminism was a new and helpful thing to be writing about and I was surprised to find how feminist my writing was. Now I'm happy to be called a Scottish writer because I'm surprised how Scottish it is ... For some reason 'a Scottish poet' sounds as if its something they're saying about you, whereas 'a feminist poet' tells a lot of people not to bother listening.
>
> (Lochhead 1990: 10–11)

We must therefore conclude that for all the structural similarities in the desire/identification underpinning our sexual and national identification/s, it is undoubtedly easier to *legitimate* the latter – especially when our sexual desires threaten the heterosexual or heterosocial norm. Moreover – and in so far as I have plunged in with examples from Scotland – this prioritization of national over gendered or sexual identity must be seen to apply to the 'marginalized' as well as the 'centralized' nations. Indeed, as the Lochhead quotation suggests, it is a prioritization which may be seen as crucial to the strategic liberatory cause of the oppressed nation: something that Vincent Quinn also touches upon in Chapter 14 in this volume in which he speaks of a 'deviant sexual identity' being seen as a 'rival identification' at a time when a country (or, in the case of Northern Ireland, a sectarian party) can ill afford it.

From such a juncture, and simultaneously bringing to mind all the political, social and anthropological theory that shows us that the history of the nation-state is inextricably linked to the heterosexual family, it is easy to doubt whether national and sexual desires *can* speak to one another in any more radical or subversive way. Certainly there is no guarantee that what Etienne Balibar calls the 'nationalisms of liberation' (often emerging *in response to* colonial oppression) will be any less orthodox than the 'nationalisms of domination' (Balibar and Wallerstein 1991: 46). Not only might the emerging nation require its subjects to prioritize their national identification, but so might it also demand evidence of a more material commitment in the form of an explicitly *procreative* sexual politics. For, notwithstanding all the layers of complexity now attending our thinking about what actually constitutes 'a national identity', there is no escaping the fact that *ethnicity* is still a key factor – and with it some investment, however residual, in the heterosexual nuclear family (Balibar and Wallerstein 1991: 96–103).

I shall therefore begin my speculations on the sexual/political future British Devolution might bring with it with reference to this most reactionary of responses, before passing on to some more liberating, and possibly utopian, scenarios. In anticipation of the latter, it is only fitting that I should end this preliminary theoretical overview with the reminder (implicit in some of my earlier comments) that devolution is seen by many as our great *hope* in redrawing the sexual–political map of the British Isles. Instead of the erstwhile margins replicating the politics of the centre, here is an opportunity to do things differently – and, in particular, to allow the experience and identity of *having been marginal* to enable us to rethink the negative and destructive forces of 'othering' in favour of a more dialogic, though no less charged, dynamic of 'us' and 'them'. But first, back to the 'worst-case' scenario.

## Un/desirable others

As we have already established, national identity, liberatory or otherwise, is inevitably linked with some form of ethnic othering which, in the history of the British Isles, has been starkly conceptualized in terms of margins and centre. In terms of the discourse of 'British' colonialism, the Scottish, Welsh, Irish and, indeed, Cornish (my own 'nation') have all been depicted as ethnically 'other': not only in terms of their residual Celtic languages but also 'racially' in terms of their physiology and colouring (e.g., dark-haired/light skinned) and their 'barbarous' ('heathen'/

'pagan') cultures. From a position of centralized *strength*, these features of ethnic difference and marginality have, of course, been re-packaged as romantically *desirable*: there is no shortage of dark, handsome and rebellious heroes – and occasionally heroines – in the literatures of all these countries. But the racism – viewed through a post-colonial lens – is none the less blatant: those from the margins of the UK, like black people throughout the world, are both elevated and oppressed in terms of their sexual cachet.

When we turn this particular table on its head, however, and consider how our erstwhile 'marginal', and now devolving, nations have themselves characterized their sexual political relations with the 'centre', we see that it is a relationship that has been similarly ethnically defined. But where for English writers the creation of a Celtic hero or heroine has been regarded as unproblematically 'romantic', the novelists of Scotland, Wales and Ireland have long struggled with the serious national and territorial implications of whether their peoples' sexual relations should be with their 'ain folk' or not. In the crudest, most heterosexist/racially defined terms, the choice of one's sexual partner might determine the future of one's country. It might determine (or, at least, it might *appear* to determine) whether one's country as a linguistic-ethnic unity is likely to survive. In the case of my own 'country' of Cornwall, indeed (and thinking in terms which I do not wholly subscribe to), it could be argued that it is already too late. The county has been so 'swamped' with middle-English incomers that its own indigenous (working-class) population is now reduced to the small ghetto of Redruth–Camborne. All the 'young people' (like myself!) either left or married 'outsiders'. Not only is the Cornish language consequently long gone, but the region's distinctive dialect is also fast disappearing. Cornwall is a nation subsumed and colonized out of existence.

Reading this 'result' from this perspective it is therefore not surprising that we should find contemporary Scottish and Welsh writers advocating, however indirectly, sexual endogamy – and preferably that which is heterosexual and reproductive. The two Welsh texts which I have focused on for the purposes of this chapter both represent this logic – though both also problematize it. If we take Robert Watson's *Rumours of Fulfilment* (1982) first, we find a text which initially appears to endorse a commitment both to country and 'traditional family values'. Set in rural Wales at the time of the last Devolution referendum, it tells the story of two sisters: of Ruth, who is unambitious, home-loving, and who marries a local lad at the age of 16 and promptly begins a family; and of Rhiannon, who is the opposite of all those things, and whose affair with her English art teacher makes her own 'rite of passage' much more grief-striken and confused. The end of the novel, moreover, which sees Rhiannon burning down her (dead) father's house in an act of Nationalist solidarity (it will prevent the incursion of more English 'incomers'), might be seen as her simply coming round to her sister's position. A veil of irony hangs over this central narrative, however. For example: 'Ruth's white wedding was a great success, despite the fact that Zion was too small for all the guests … It was a marvellous day which no-one spoiled, and at the end they moved into their nice new council house and that was that' (Watson 1982: 146). Similarly, there is little attempt to modify or excuse the extreme and violent xenophobia of the characters most hostile to Rhiannon's 'betrayal' of family and nation: 'And don't think I haven't noticed her in the corner, neither. Off with bloody teachers! Ought to be horse-whipped, the pair of 'em. Fancy letting me hear it from Madox the meat's wife – if I'd of been on my feet I'd of kicked her down' (Watson 1982: 141). For all its primitive logic, then, the future of a nation based on the advocation of strict endogamy is quickly seen to have its dark and ugly side; and, indeed, the 'black blood' [sic] associated with *too much* 'in-breeding' is a symbolic subtext of both Watson's novel (Rhiannon's father's affair with the 'native' Eileen produces the autistic Donald) and Alice Thomas Ellis's *Unexplained Laughter* (1985).

Although romance is not the central focus of Ellis's sharp-tongued tale about 'natives' and 'incomers' in the Welsh valley of Ty Fach, the sexual relations of all the protagonists – not only Lydia – *do* comment shrewdly on the centre–margin dynamic, and effect a complex mesh of sexual and locational desires. Whilst, on the surface, the valley represents a claustrophobically conventional and heterosexist community in which sexual relations are reduced to families and procreation, many of the inhabitants (Elizabeth, Beuno, Dr Wyn) all reach out to the world beyond the valley. This does not make them any 'better', or happier characters (far from it); it is merely the text's acknowledgement that the relationship between 'margin' and 'centre' is a constant two-way traffic, in which 'both sides' fear and envy the other. The festering envy of the rural for the metropolitan is given its most explicit embodiment in the character of Dr Wyn who taunts Lydia with salacious innuendoes about his 'visits' to 'her' city ('"Guess where I'm going this weekend," he invited her … "London"' (Ellis 1985: 65)). Meanwhile, Lydia is brought closer and closer to an acknowledgement of what the people of Ty Fach have that she has not: a sense, however miserable and suffocating, of home as a *fixed* place and location (Ellis 1985: 148). Yet whilst it effectively communicates the 'otherness' that makes rural Wales, and its men, attractive to an incomer like Lydia, this novel's principal achievement lies in its evocation of the stultifying pressures of belonging to such a closed, defensive community – and the reality of this in terms of relationships. It gives rise, first of all, to all sorts of repressed fantasies, cruelties and punishments that are usually visited by the men upon the women, as in the case of Dr Wyn and Elizabeth; and it allows for no version of sexual desire other than a strictly heterosexual and procreative one. It is a mindset that Beuno, the (gay?) priest sums up with the indulgence and irony of one that also, and forever, 'belongs':

> Sometimes in a small community – and ours is very small – passions which in a wider context would be dissipated become distilled and reduced to

poison. A trivial slight, a threat to self-esteem, which might cause you a moment's irritation, here give rise to resentments which might fester for centuries ... But I'm one of them, so I know what they do, and even when I'm away the things that I do are the same things that they're doing.

(Ellis 1985: 146)

This sense of the inescapability of certain national/regional/rural backgrounds is something with which I also identify, and which I feel is supremely important in any discussion of the politics of location: namely, the sense that some identities, or some aspects of identity, are effectively *non-negotiable*. The fact that Beuno has both 'gone away' from Ty Fach and yet *has not* seems to me to sum up perfectly the way in which marginal communities combine stoical and embattled attitudes to 'the outside world' with cycles of existence and associated institutions (marriage, the family) so effectively that escape *is* impossible. Subsequent identities which we might affect to choose (including sexual identities) must always, therefore, contend with those visited upon us. Thus Beuno might, for all we know, live his life outside of Ty Fach as a gay man; but in Ty Fach he will always remain an eligible bachelor, waiting for the right (Welsh) girl to come along.

This sort of scenario is, I would suggest, the bleakest prospect of what Devolution holds out for us in terms of our sexual, family, and community relations: countries or regions which retain a sense of themselves as threatened margins instead of re-located centres; a suspicion of 'outsiders' which translates back into prescribed endogamous sexual relations; a continued reification of the heterosexual nuclear family; no tolerance of what Quinn (Chapter 14) calls 'rival identities'.

In these two Welsh novels, then, a sympathetic understanding of what inclines marginal and colonized regions towards sexual endogamy is combined with a perceptive and decidedly *unromantic* vison of its 'lived' consequences. It could be argued, however, that it is precisely those novels that represent mono-ethnic relations *less* self-consciously that are ultimately more problematic in political terms. Under this heading I must, of course, include the long tradition of Cornish romances and family sagas that Ella Westland writes so well, and so tolerantly, about in *Peripheral Visions* (Bell 1995), and a large swathe of contemporary Scottish writing which, although far more politically aware in other respects (class, gender, race) may nevertheless be seen to promote a heterosexual, family-oriented orthodoxy in which the principal protagonists just 'happen' to breed amongst themselves.

For there is, I feel, something very double-edged to this particular casualness. Although, on the one hand, the unselfconscious, un-spelt-out way in which both the new, national culture and its people are being represented will be seen as a welcome sign of a *secure* identity, on the other it is allowing certain orthodoxies and assumptions to go unquestioned. Iain Banks's celebrated novel, *The Crow Road* (1993) may be seen as a classic case in point. Whilst dealing with a broad spectrum of finely realized, 'sympathetic' characters who show an awareness and tolerance of all manner of social issues and lifestyle choice (apart from the baddies and bigots like Uncle Fergus, that is), the novel's 'heart' remains 'the family': and in particular, the *Scottish* family whose continuance is guaranteed, at the novel's end, with the birth of Lewis and Verity's child (a son, named after his dead grandfather), and the union of Prentice and Ashley Watt – a relationship whose protracted inevitability is unquestionably linked to its ethnic and genetic appropriateness. Although nowhere made explicit, it is clearly 'right' that Prentice should honour his Scottish, socialist father's memory by marrying a Scottish, working-class girl – with the promise of offspring that will carry forward not only the family name but also the 'new nation'.

At this point a personal coda is necessary. Whilst it might seem, from the preceding comments, that I dislike and disapprove of Banks's *Crow Road*, nothing, in fact, could be further from the truth. It has been one of the novels I have *most* enjoyed reading this year, and one of the ones I have most engaged with, notwithstanding the ambivalence of my own positioning. What this reminds us of is the often 'queer' dynamics engendered by the 'emotional politics' of reading (Pearce 1997): the fact that we can become involved with texts and their protagonists quite against the grain of our own (sexual/textual) positioning. And so it is for me with Banks's *Crow Road*: the sneaking acknowledgement that, in other circumstances, this is a 'family' that I should *like* to belong to. For all its problematic political implications, Banks's portrayal of a vibrant, robust Scottish culture and community – which looks back to the Scottish renaissance of Lewis Grassic Gibbon's *Scots Quair* ([1946] 1998) and forward to that world 'after Independence' – is an overwhelmingly attractive devolutionary future. The power of such visions should, moreover, remind us that the full complexity of our positioning within a devolving nation will never be understood if we keep ourselves permanently behind the ring fence of political correctness. Our own slips should be used to remind us, once again, of the desires which underpin all surges of national/ist identification and which, in full flood, *necessarily* forget that the moment of inclusion for some is also a moment of exclusion for others.

## Romancing the margins

This coda on my own maverick and inconsistent positioning within endogamous/heterosexual cultures leads me directly to some of the other ways in which the sexual relations of those living in the newly devolving nations are being imagined and, indeed, *re*-imagined. As the subheading implies, these relationships are often *doubly* romantic: relationships whose romance stems, either directly or indirectly, from the marginalized, 'outlawed', or even pro-revolutionary positioning of the central protagonists; and relationships which consequently contribute to the glamour or kudos of those nations and cultures 'on the margins'.

In the texts I have read and re-read for the purposes of identifying the different forms such devolutionary desires might take, it is striking that the majority represent alliances between individuals united, either explicitly or implicitly, against the 'English' centre, with a dearth of texts imagining positive outcomes for relationships involving Scottish, Irish or Welsh protagonists in *alliances* with English lovers. If we fix UK Devolution within the wider post-colonizing moment this is, of course, hardly surprising: for years to come England and its government will remain part of a historical nightmare from which these nations are trying to awake (see James Joyce's *Ulysses* ([1922] 1993)), and relationships which 'cross the border' are thus hardly the easiest to legitimate or defend. On this issue, too, I think it is vital to see how Scotland, Wales and (the North of) Ireland are all very differently positioned in terms of the historical moment (i.e. 'now'), with the latter having the most extensive collection of texts dealing with bilateral romances — though often, of course, through a further sectarian refraction. The stark truth here (and it was one that pulled me up short when I first determined to include texts from the North of Ireland within my devolutionary remit) is that 'England' has long been a different order of 'enemy' for the (Republican) Irish than it is for the Scottish, Welsh or other marginalized regions of the UK. It is, in short, a *military* enemy as well as a cultural and economic one, with the consequence that Irish/English (and, within this, Catholic/Protestant) relationships, being more obviously transgressive, are also, if paradoxically, more likely to be written about than collusions with a colonizer still too monolithically present to be given any particular focus.

In contemporary Scottish literature, indeed, the trend seems much more to 'write the English out' altogether, with texts like the Banks novel I have already described representing a quiet celebration of the 'all-Scottish' romance. Although I have already pointed to the rather problematic endogamous and, by inference, heterosexist proclivity of such imaginings, there is no doubt that they also hold the seeds of the best of futures in which one's national identity, like one's sexual identity, can remain visible, but be worn lightly, with non-aggressive pride. The texts that fall into this category are, indeed, the ones that I am most envious of as a 'non-validated' regional subject: the healthy glut of novels and short stories which have recently fallen off the Scottish presses, and which proclaim their Scottishness in the most various, and ever more subtle, of ways (incidental but well-recognized locations; linguistic figurations, which may be *very minor*; jokes, expletives, and other marks of address). The current, expansive model of Scottish identity (the SNP's 'civic nationalism') has, moreover, meant that the texts included in, say, Polygon's *Scottish Love Stories* (1995) do not have to have been written by Scottish-born writers (it is enough that they are merely resident there), or, conversely, that they do have to be explicitly 'about Scotland', if their author/literary history locates them in a Scottish tradition *in some way*. There is a tendency for A.L. Kennedy's recent texts to eschew the more obvious trappings of Scottish identity, for example, by looking outwards to European locations and, indeed, romantic heroes (*So I am Glad*, 1995; *Original Bliss*, 1997), but one small allusion to a Glaswegian location or the casual use of 'Ach!' will be enough to provide the necessary specificity. For other writers like James Kelman, Liz Lochhead (1991) and Janice Galloway (1991, 1992, 1995, 1996) the Scottishness of their texts is of course more consistently there in their use of the Scots language, but, again, chat 'about' the characters' identity has become emphatically non-dogmatic. As with issues of sexual identity, there seems to be a 'settled will' to move on to a more contextualized vision – which is not to say, of course, that these things have ceased to matter. It is here that we should remind ourselves again that for all the European lovers in these texts there are few *English* ones, either heterosexual *or* gay!

From the coolness and confidence of the 'new Scotland', I turn now to a consideration of those texts in which the national identities of the protagonists impact rather more self-consciously upon their relationships. In this respect, Watson's *Rumours of Fulfilment* written, it will be remembered, in the wake of the last Welsh Referendum, is certainly the most politically schematic: a feature that, according to Tony Bianchi, severely 'strains the realist terms in which the novel is framed' (Bell 1995: 53). Whilst it is true that, in the course of its two hundred pages, the novel appears to 'try out' every possible combination of Welsh/Anglo-Welsh relationship, this formulaic perception of the novel does not do justice to the complexity with which these identities and positionings are understood: in particular the quiet subtext which asks, are we really 'born' Welsh and English, or is it something that we 'become' or, alternatively, 'unbecome'?

This last possibility is certainly hinted at in the relationship of Rhiannon and Felix, which, although starting from such unpromising beginnings (he is not only English, but ten years older than her, married *and* her teacher), worms its way round to becoming the surprise 'romantic' conclusion to the novel. What is most nuanced about the terms of their relationship, however, is the way in which it '*becomes* Welsh', in spite of Felix's English birth, and Rhiannon's early anti-Nationalist sentiments. Although somewhat clichéd, great efforts are made to connect their love-making with the Welsh landscape in a generally positive way (a good deal of it takes place in the open air), and by the time of the referendum, both Felix and Rhiannon (now at university in England) find themselves surprisingly aligned with the country they have, temporarily, left behind. At this moment, Felix is given maximum ideological 'brownie points' for expressing love for a country he nevertheless feels he has no 'right' to:

> Rhiannon had liked his remark about not having the right to be in Wales. She was sure he meant it, though she knew his motive for driving out. His convictions were as generous as they were sentimental, and they usually involved him in quiet decisions of conscience ... He was nice, and part of

what she liked about Wales. It didn't matter that he happened to be English, because his was the courteous and affectionate nature, the dry humour and the gentle sensuality of the best of Wales. Like her father. Like Tim. Like the sounds of the [Welsh] song. He was a man she could love.

(Watson 1982: 160–3).

Felix, then, is slowly earning the right to a Welsh identity, and there is the attendant suggestion that, at the end of the day, his relationship with Rhiannon might be no less 'legitimate' than that of Ruth and Daffyd. True, these protagonists have discovered their love-of-country by travelling away, crossing the border, and 'coming home', rather than simply by 'staying put', but their commitment proves true nevertheless. Indeed, in terms of the dynamic being explored in this chapter, Felix and Rhiannon could be seen as evidence that it is *only* by moving between margin and centre that we can really understand the values that make national and regional affiliations 'affairs of the heart'. In Rhiannon's case, of course, love of Felix and love of country miraculously coalesce: 'There was something marvellous about the way Felix had re-entered her heart' (Watson 1982: 165).

Another, more recent, text which uses exile in England to explore the protagonist's abiding ties to his regional/national 'other' is Glen Patterson's *Fat Lad* ([1992] 1993): the story of a Protestant Irishman returning to Belfast after ten years in Manchester. Here, again, the turbulent dynamics between margin and centre are explored *vis-à-vis* the protagonist's sexual relationships, which seem incidental at first (like, it must be said, his Northern Irishness), but then steadily gain in significance until they reach crisis proportions.

The hero of Patterson's text, Drew Linden, has three significant relationships with women in the time span covered by the novel. There is also passing reference to the attraction his 'accent' held for women when he first arrived in Manchester as a university 'fresher'. Kelly (herself claiming 'Irish descent') falls for him right away, and this most explicit marker of national location becomes an ironic symbol of the sexual glamour attached to a 'marginal' identity. But Drew himself is significantly turned off by this particular dynamic: like many of the other 'ex-Pats', he has come to university in England precisely in order to 'get away', and his long-term relationship with the 'Middle-English Melissa comes to represent all that he values most about this decision. Theirs is a liberal, tolerant and apparently 'mature' relationship: each partner has affairs, but ultimately comes back to a 'home' which is safe, comfortable, and promisingly upwardly mobile.

Throughout the time-scheme of the novel, Drew's actions and behaviour are predicated upon the assumption that he can escape back to Melissa, and England, whenever he wants. He *imagines* this to be his primary commitment. Only retrospectively does he realize that he is *involuntarily* committed elsewhere: that, as for many of us who were brought up far away from the cosmopolitan centres, his national and sexual desires are bound up in something profoundly *non*-negotiable. Of his other two relationships, Kay (another upwardly mobile Protestant living in Belfast) represents nothing especially Irish (their casual sexual relationship purposefully avoids discussion of their families and former lives), but her sister Anna – transformed into a tragic, yet glamourous icon of the Irish 'troubles' through the violent death of her former (Catholic) lover – is another matter. Although she and Drew come together only once, the event is earth-shatteringly meaningful: it is more meaningful than any other encounter in Drew's life, largely because all the freight and weight of politics and history (personal and national) is implicated in it:

> And in the sure and certain knowledge that the moment would never be repeated, they very slowly, very deliberately, and as though recognising what was involved, very carefully made love to one another.
> What was involved was a supporting cast of family, lovers, friends, disposed collusively about this island and the next and the continent beyond; a conspiracy of events both local and global ...
> Vast movements of people were communicated in the silence of a single kiss. Borders were crossed, identities blurred. Land masses rose and fell with their bodies.
>
> (Patterson [1992] 1993: 249)

One of the factors that makes the relationship between Drew and Anna both so romantic and yet so tragic in political terms is their largely *involuntary* involvement in the centre–margin dynamic. As with the lovers in Bernard MacClaverty's classic, *Cal* (1983), neither Drew nor Anna are *directly* involved in the war themselves, but are *implicated* to the hilt: Drew, because of his own protestant inheritance (symbolized by his Loyalist father), and Anna because of her own 'turncoat' relationship with the Catholic, Con. As with Cal and Marcella, the lovers are thus inadvertently positioned both alongside *and* against the British Centre: through several 'removes', but to an extent that still makes their respective relationships 'impossible'. At this point we must remember, too, that the 'impossible' for these players is not simply an abstract concept, but one predicated upon the fear of violent reprisal and death.

With respect to our more general enquiry into how devolutionary, or centre–margin, politics impact upon our ability to 'imagine' sexual relationships, these texts offer a predictably tragic–romantic conclusion, with the romance inextricably bound up in the tragedy. Mutual attractions are finally declared and consummated, but not permitted to survive in the 'real world' where the divisions (themselves *inciting of* desire) remain intractable. The formula is thus wonderful for romance – where national/religious/ethnic difference has been one of the great engines of romantic narrative (Pearce and Stacey 1995) – but rather less helpful in imagining more long-term relationships (both personal and national).

Pitching the literature of the North of Ireland into the devolutionary remit of this project was, as I have already indicated, something of a sobering experience. After several years spent 'enjoying' the literature of the 'New Scotland' – in which the promise of Independence has translated itself into an often cheeky, but generally good-humoured, dialogue with the old, culturally bankrupt, indentity-floundering 'English' centre – it was indeed *shocking* to be reminded of the blood that has been, and has yet to be, spilt in the enfranchisement of one of Britain's last-remaining colonies. Whilst the writings of Lochhead, Banks and Galloway may thus help us understand what the quest for national/regional identity is all about (a vision of a heterogeneous community nevertheless united by a common location, history, language, destiny, etc.), the writings of 'the Troubles' (an admittedly problematically defined genre: Patten, in Bell (1995: 128–48)), reminds us of how it can all go so dreadfully wrong. This is not to suggest that either the past struggles of Eire, or the present ones of the North of Ireland, could ever be directly compared with the present and future prospects of Scotland or Wales (they are, alas, too painfully unique), but we should never forget how easily the processes of independence can spill over into ethnic polarizations, hatreds and bloodsheds. Whilst it is not inevitable that the 'liberation' of ex-colonies should take this form, the threat lingers, and with it the most serious implications of with whom we should be *allowed* to fall in love.

## Making devolution desirable

In the preceding sections I have used some of the recent fiction written from the devolving margins of the UK to help us imagine what form romantic/sexual relationships are likely to take during this major constitutional upheaval. I have also hinted at the ways in which the dynamics of these relationships can help us better understand the national/ist desires themselves. What we find, predictably, is a mixture of both the utopian and the dystopian: of emerging nations taking the opportunity to re-think new models of self–other relations at both a personal and international level, and of besieged provinces that feel they can 'hold on' to their cultural identities only by maintaining a fiercely endogamous policy – both at the level of the family and the nation.

It was noticeable, however, that even amongst the more utopian visionaries, there was a tendency to valorize heterosexual relations and the nuclear family (Watson, Banks). This, I would argue, is not simply a problem of representation (the fact that these authors have excluded homosexual relationships in their imaginings), but rather that no obvious connection has been made between the *structural* problems of colonial/nationalist discourses and heterosexism. This connection – inspired, of course, by the epistemological breakthroughs of 'Queer Theory' – is, I feel, far more important in helping us imagine the devolutionary future than erstwhile attempts to *align* marginal groups (Wollaston 1992: 35–9; Whyte 1995). Nationalism, as theorists like Balibar have shown, depends (in both its 'liberatory' and 'dominatory' modes) upon a process of othering in which the 'the racial–cultural identity of the "true nationals" remains invisible, but [it] can be inferred (and is ensured) *a contrario* by the alleged, quasi-hallucinatory visibility of the "false nationals"' (Balibar and Wallerstein 1991: 60). This is precisely the mechanism that theorists like Eve Sedgwick (1991, 1994) have long since identified as the *a priori* of heterosexuality, and it therefore stands to reason that any more radical vision of our national futures invites a similar sort of scrutiny: an analysis of how different, but comparable, orthodoxies are maintained and always threaten to reproduce themselves. Without this extra level of self-reflexivity it is all to easy to see how liberatory nationalisms will convert into dominatory ones by simply repositioning themselves within the invisibilizing 'us'/'them' binary.

As I have argued elsewhere with respect to romance, structural and cultural hegemonies cannot be transformed simply through the multiplication ('permission') of alternatives which nevertheless leave the defining orthodoxy in place (Pearce and Wisker 1998: 1–19). This is certainly the case with heterosexuality, for which the literature of devolution sampled here becomes a telling case in point. Whilst this writing includes depictions of gay relationships (besides specific lesbian and gay collections like Winning's *The Crazy Jig* (1992) there is a judicious spattering of gay relationships in all the Scottish anthologies – e.g. Ritchie 1996), its situation in, and alongside, texts in which marriage and the family are still largely unproblematized makes homosexuality little more than a liberal 'choice'. Whilst this inclusivity is, of course, a major improvement on the homophobic exclusions and silences of the past, there must always be the suspicion that the 'tolerance' of neither nations nor publishers can be trusted to be permanent.

A similar threat – or, at very least, a wasted opportunity – will attend our emerging nations if they *too easily* take up their place alongside their erstwhile centre. Whilst the majority of us will desperately hope that these transitions can be made without violence, it nevertheless seems imperative that we keep up a vigorous rhetorical and discursive interrogation *of that centre*: a relentless probing as to what enabled its particular hegemomy to persist so effectively, and for so long. And it is here, I believe, that an abiding attention to how national and sexual desires *interrelate* is of the utmost importance. How a nation (or its literary representatives) configures its personal, sexual, and family relationships is a clear barometer of the nature, and direction, of its (inter)national relationships: a link as incontrovertibly material (sexual choices = reproductive choices) as it is ideological (besieged nations think endogamously, empowered ones exogamously). And whilst colonial oppression and assimilation might have given rise to some great 'classic romance' predicated upon exquisitely 'impossible' circumstances, it is clear that nations, no more than individuals, cannot live in the moment of *ravissement* forever, but must begin looking for new ways of writing 'the sequel'

(Pearce 1997: 85–186). Moreover, if we reposition this challenge within the wider global context with which I opened this chapter, there must surely be the possibility that we could take a lead from the nations (and their literatures) later colonized, and sooner liberated, than our own. Somehow we, too, have to begin to imagine how to live without that centre ('England', 'London'/'Westminster'/ 'The South') as our defining point of reference, whilst never forgetting its powers of reproduction, mutation and (re)assimilation.

## References

Balibar, Etienne and Wallerstein, Immanuel (1991) *Race, Nation, Class: Ambiguous Identities*, trans. Chris Turner, London: Verso.
Banks, Iain (1993) *The Crow Road*, London: Abacus.
Barthes, Roland ([1977] 1990) *A Lover's Discourse: Fragments*, London: Penguin.
Bassnett, Susan (ed.) (1995) *Studying British Cultures*, London: Methuen.
Bell, Ian A. (1995) *Peripheral Visions: Images of Nationhood in Contemporary British Fiction*, Cardiff: University of Wales Press.
Bhabha, Homi (ed.) (1990) *Nation and Narration*, London: Routledge.
Ellis, Alice Thomas (1985) *Unexplained Laughter*, Harmondsworth: Penguin.
Galloway, Janice (1991) *The Trick is to Keep Breathing*, London: Minerva.
—— (1992) *Blood*, London: Minerva.
—— (1995) *Foreign Parts*, London: Jonathan Cape.
—— (1996) *Where You Find It*, London: Jonathan Cape.
Grassic Gibbon, Lewis ([1946] 1998) *A Scots Quair*, London: Penguin.
Joyce, James ([1922] 1993) *Ulysses*, Oxford: Oxford University Press.
Kennedy, A.L. (1993) *Looking For The Possible Dance*, London: Secker & Warburg.
—— (1994) *Now That You're Back*, London: Jonathan Cape.
—— (1995) *So I am Glad*, London: Jonathan Cape.
—— (1997) *Original Bliss*, London: Jonathan Cape.
Lochhead, Liz (1990) Interview, in Gillean Somerville-Arjat and Rebecca E. Wilson (eds) *Sleeping with Monsters: Conversations with Scottish and Irish Women Poets*, Edinburgh: Polygon: 8–17.
—— (1991) *Bagpipe Muzak*, Harmondsworth: Penguin.
MacClaverty, Bernard (1983) *Cal*, London: Jonathan Cape.
Maguire, Susie (ed.) (1995) *Scottish Love Stories*, Edinburgh: Polygon.
Parker, Andrew, Russo, Mary, Summer, Doris and Yaeger, Patricia (1992) *Nationalisms and Sexualities*, London: Routledge.
Patterson, Glen ([1992] 1993) *Fat Lad*, London: Minerva.
Pearce, Lynne (1997) *Feminism and the Politics of Reading*, London: Arnold.
Pearce, Lynne and Stacey, Jackie (1995) *Romance Revisited*, London: Lawrence & Wishart.
Pearce, Lynne and Wisker, Gina (1998) *Fatal Attractions: Re-scripting Romance in Contemporary Literature and Film*, London: Pluto.
Ritchie, Harry (ed.) (1996) *New Scottish Writing*, London: Bloomsbury.

Sedgwick, Eve Kosofsky (1991) *Epistemology of the Closet*, Hemel Hempstead: Harvester-Wheatsheaf.
—— (1994) *Tendencies*, London: Routledge.
Watson, Robert (1982) *Rumours of Fulfilment*, Glamorgan: Seren Books.
Winning, Joanne (ed.) (1992) *The Crazy Jig: Gay and Lesbian Writing from Scotland*, Edinburgh: Polygon.
Wollaston, Graeme (1992) 'Lesbians and Gays in the Scottish Republic', in Joanne Winning (ed.) *The Crazy Jig: Gay and Lesbian Writing from Scotland*, Edinburgh: Polygon: 33–9.
Whyte, Christopher (1995) *Gendering the Nation: Studies in Modern Scottish Literature*, Edinburgh: Edinburgh University Press.

# 14

# ON THE BORDERS OF ALLEGIANCE

## Identity politics in Ulster[1]

*Vincent Quinn*

If gay space exists what does it look like? Shops and houses marked with distinctive emblems? Banners bearing provocative slogans? Marches? Demos? Clubs and bars with particular clienteles? Flags? Bodies declaring their allegiances via dress codes and styles of personal adornment? Resistance? Pride? A statement of identity in the face of public hostility?

The chances are you will recognize some or all of the above. Even if you have never been in such a space the images will be familiar from television footage, newspaper articles, and lesbian and gay fiction. Since Stonewall these are the displays that have given public expression to gay liberation. The symbols may change from time to time – note the emergence of the rainbow flag – but their deployment has been surprisingly stable. Despite queer revisionism, these are still the strategies by which lesbian and gay visibility is figured.

Although such tactics are increasingly contested[2] they are hardly unique to same-sex communities. Many subcultural groups use similar signals to mark out their psychic and material territories. So if the gay community is a ghetto, it isn't the only one in contemporary Britain. I can think of other communities with distinctive emblems – things like the Shamrock and the Red Hand of Ulster. These groups have more marches than one would think possible – so many of them that a Parades Commission has been set up to monitor their routes. Naturally the marchers have favourite slogans ('Troops Out' or 'No Surrender') as well as instantly recognizable modes of dress (sashes, bowler hats). They probably live in neighbourhoods where businesses cater for a particular section of people and where the streets are adorned with flags – although these ones tend to have only *three* colours of the spectrum. These communities manifest a potent mixture of group loyalty and suspicion of the state. They have a prevailing sense of grievance, of being hard-done-by. But they continue to insist that their demands are natural and just, even if their enemies say otherwise. And yes, there's a great deal of *pride* here as well.

I begin in this way, not because I believe that Ulster sectarianism is 'the same as' lesbian and gay pride, but because I want to think about the politics of identity, and how they function in Northern Ireland. As a gay man from a largely Nationalist background I find the rituals of Unionism both alien and threatening, but I'm aware that some of these strategies are generically similar to those employed by gay activists. I'm also aware that gay Loyalists are likely to have the same response to Republicanism that I have towards Unionism. So while subcultural resistance is a mode of survival – a way of finding a voice, a way of being listened to – its processes can seem oppressive to those on the outside (as, perhaps, they are meant to). Moreover, subcultural allegiances can cut across other forms of self-definition. Should I define myself as a gay man first and a Nationalist second? Are the identities compatible? And are Loyalism and Nationalism equally difficult to combine with a gay identity?

These questions matter, not least because they reveal the asymmetry between metropolitan discussions of identity politics and the rather specific identity culture that pertains in Northern Ireland. Academic and journalist critiques of fixed sexual identities take two main lines of attack. First, it's said that postmodernism has destabilized the notion of an essential self, thus making it harder to maintain the boundaries that define a fixed identity; while second, the rise of gay consumerism has undermined the left-wing agenda that powered the politically based identities of the late 1960s and 1970s. For instance Mark Simpson has recently asked us to

> Pity the leftist gay Utopian. The workers abandoned the revolution in the Sixties, so in the early Seventies you became New Left and turned to other gays who, after a dalliance with street theatre and 'zaps' in the form of the Gay Liberation Front, also abandoned the revolution ... in the Eighties the New Right made you feel the lash of the market and turned your precious gays into the shock-troops of Thatcherism. No group in society benefited more from Eighties' individualism, consumerism, hedonism and assaults on family values than gays.
>
> (Simpson 1998)

As a result, the 'leftist gay Utopian' of the 1990s is 'still clinging desperately on to the pitiful idea that gays still represent some kind of radical "progressive" potential ... [a] mixture of victimhood, sensitivity and subversion' (Simpson 1998).

It's possible to admire the verve of Simpson's writing while questioning his historical analysis. (Was Section 28 intended to benefit lesbians and gay men?) But what's most striking is his assumption that 'Thatcherism' had an identical effect throughout the whole of Britain. The consumerism he describes is indeed a familiar aspect of contemporary gay life, but it's rather more common in Soho than it is in Antrim or Armagh. Perhaps politically based identities have more valency than Simpson concedes – especially in places lacking a large commercial scene. Similarly, while the Thatcher years produced a drift, in certain quarters, from community-based politics towards an unapologetic individualism, this was hardly the case in Northern

Ireland where Thatcher's policies galvanized mass resistance from both the Unionist and Nationalist communities. The outrage resulting from her handling of the Anglo-Irish Agreement and the 1981 Hunger Strikes (or, for that matter, the Miners' Strike) suggests that her administration provoked political activism in the provinces even while it eroded oppositional structures in the capital. Granted these are not *gay* identities, but they hint, none the less, at the metropolitan assumptions underlying Simpson's analysis – after all, one of the key strands in latter-day Republicanism is a movement towards the Marxist Utopia that Simpson's workers are supposed to have given up in the 1960s.

Simpson's generalizations are symptomatic of a tendency (within both journalism and the academy) to ignore the regional circumstances that inflect the formation of political and sexual identities.[3] For example, most genealogies of Gay Liberation rightly emphasize models such as the Black Civil Rights Movement, CND, and anti-Vietnam War demos. However, queer revisionists who claim that these structures have lost their contemporary relevance ignore the fact that Northern Ireland had its *own* Civil Rights Movement, and that *this* 1960s organization remains a part of the Irish popular imagination in a way that, say, CND does not. Identity politics therefore have a currency in Northern Ireland that they lack in London (or, for that matter, Dublin). Moreover, the identities that dominate Ulster are ones that derive, at least nominally, from religious categories. As a consequence, Northern Irish political discourse is epitomized by a dogmatic fundamentalism that's a million miles removed from the jolly hedonism that Simpson represents as universal. You don't need to be paranoid to feel marginalized from such a culture; indeed if anyone has a right to feel victimized it's the lesbians and gay men who have been persistently targeted by Nationalist and Unionist extremists, as well as by the Northern Ireland legislature.

It would be dangerous, however, to valorize identity politics at the expense of all other forms of personal organization. After all, Northern Ireland offers a stark example of what can happen when a politics of identity becomes overly emphatic – when faced by hard-line sectarianism, with its discourses of exclusion and ethnic purity, a selfhood based on fluidity and inclusivity seems highly attractive. But surely sectarianism is not the whole story? Oughtn't there to be a way of expressing a religious affiliation without collapsing into an antagonistic relationship to rival churches? Unionism and Republicanism both have long, and in many ways heroic, pasts. Couldn't there be a way of celebrating these traditions without perpetuating the divisions that they have produced?

These aren't questions I can answer unilaterally, but perhaps a more nuanced approach to sexual politics might also provide new ways of thinking about Northern Ireland. For example, somewhere between gay and anti-gay is the notion that fixed sexual identities can be strategically useful provided that they are also open for renegotiation.[4] Or as Jeffrey Weeks has put it, they are 'points of alignment' which 'are both precarious and essential, historically shaped and personally chosen'. As such, they help us 'to negotiate the hazards of everyday life, and to assert our sense of belonging in an ever more complex social world' (Weeks 1997: 47). Northern Ireland could certainly learn from this willingness to view identity as historically contingent – and therefore mutable. But this chapter will also argue that 'coming out' in Northern Ireland involves a bargaining process which throws light both on sectarianism *and* on the identity debate more generally. After all, the issues which reverberate in current discussions of (homo)sexuality – such as history, amnesia, selfhood, and authenticity – are also at the heart of the Irish question. Although such an argument runs the risk of collapsing into 'the pitiful idea that gays ... represent some kind of radical "progressive" potential', the observation shows, none the less, that the traffic between the provinces and the metropolis isn't one-sided, and that metropolitan commentators, such as Mark Simpson, ought to be able to learn from the provinces – and not just the other way round.

Thus far the discussion has been fairly general: now for more detail. First of all I want to look at the binary structures of Northern Irish political discourse; the chapter will relate these to the gendering of national identity and will argue that myths of Irishness (and Ulsterness) have marginalized lesbian and gay voices. I will also discuss Derry/Londonderry, a city which occupies a key position in Unionist and Republican mythology and which has often been taken as a microcosm of the Northern Irish conflict. By looking at the sexualized narratives that have grown around Derry/Londonderry, I hope to show the negative effect that gender-based narratives have had on the production of lesbian and gay identities in Northern Ireland.

## Derry/Londonderry

Despite its remoteness from Belfast, London and Dublin, Derry/Londonderry seems to carry important messages for both Britain and Ireland. In a period when European integration and regional devolution are said to be threatening the stability of Britain, the city's double name and border status reveal the *dis*unities of the so-called 'United Kingdom' while also hinting at the impossibility of a truly 'United' Ireland. It's ironic that a province which was routinely pathologized by metropolitan commentators in the 1970s should now represent the more general tensions of the British state. However these days England's version of the North–South divide looks starker than ever, and if the Union seems even more shaky than before, it's because Scottish and (to some extent) Welsh activists have started to read 'Britain' as a quasi-imperial construct. One needn't share this view of history to see that Irish debates over the Union are now part of a wider picture in which 'Britain' can no longer be construed as a natural and unified state.[5] (And this is even before we get into disputes over class, race and employment.) In such a context, Derry/Londonderry is both an emblem of neglect and a reminder that the metropolis *depends* on the provinces even as it marginalizes them. After all, the city was placed in Northern Ireland (rather than the Republic) because it was deemed indispensable to Britain's defences.

Events such as Bloody Sunday and the Siege of 1689 ensure that Derry/Londonderry plays a crucial role in the Irish political imagination. The Siege – in which the town stayed loyal to William III despite being surrounded by James II's Catholic forces – has become a founding myth of Unionist resistance. Bloody Sunday (30 January 1972) – in which British paratroopers shot dead fourteen unarmed civil rights protesters – has come to symbolize Nationalist suspicion of the security forces and the Stormont and Westminster governments. This intertwining of the recent past and the distant past is perpetuated via Unionist and Nationalist commemorations. Key events from the Siege are celebrated with annual marches organized by the Apprentice Boys of Derry, while the Orange Order holds parades honouring the Battle of the Boyne, at which William III decisively beat James II. Meanwhile, Nationalist marches mark Bloody Sunday, the imposition of internment without trial, and the 1981 Hunger Strikes.[6] And a relic of the old Bogside – a free-standing gable wall bearing the words 'You Are Now Entering Free Derry' – is as potent to Republicans as the city walls are to Unionists.

In Derry/Londonderry such landmarks have a double meaning: besides marking the sites of specific physical confrontations they also embody the wider ideological conflicts that have characterized Irish history. Indeed there's an active relationship between these two forms of reality. In Northern Ireland, material confrontations have arisen out of ideological conflict; these material disputes have in turn been mythologized, hoarded, and retold as part of the region's struggle over cultural identity. This process can be traced in the murals and graffiti which mark Derry/Londonderry's topography. Partly commemorative and partly provocative, these remind the viewer that discursive battles have produced material conflicts and vice versa. As a result, city residents are constantly surrounded by signifiers demanding repudiation or acceptance.[7] Indeed sectarian conflict even extends to the city's name since media wisdom has it that Derry/Londonderry is 'Derry' to Catholics and 'Londonderry' to Protestants – a sign of divided attitudes to James I's decision to give control of the city to a group of London guilds.

However, it's worth asking if this Derry/Londonderry split is as universal as people claim. Just before the unrest of the 1970s, the 1967 *Blue Guide* to Ireland was able to refer confidently to 'Londonderry, always spoken of as Derry' (Muirhead 1967: 130) while as far back as 1849 Samuel Lewis's *Topographical Dictionary of Ireland* noted that 'It was originally and is still popularly called Derry ... The English prefix, London ... was for a long time retained by the colonists, but has ... fallen into popular disuse' (Lewis 1849: 259). It's indicative of the traumatic events of the last thirty years that 'Londonderry' has reasserted itself despite the fact that descendants of the original colony had abandoned the usage by the mid-nineteenth century – which was itself a period of sectarian conflict.[8] As a result, 'Derry' and 'Londonderry' have lost all semblance of neutrality. Like disputed parades, these names have become part of Unionist and Republican self-definition and self-assertion; they're not just symptoms of certain cultural allegiances, they're also constitutive of those allegiances.

There are several ironies in this situation, however, not least the fact that the Loyalist society most associated with Siege commemorations is called the Apprentice Boys of *Derry*, and that one of Unionism's most favoured songs is '*Derry*'s Walls'. Even more tellingly, the Anglican diocese in which Derry/Londonderry is situated 'retains its ancient name of Derry' (Lewis 1849: 266). These slippages suggest that 'Derry' is not an exclusively Catholic usage and that 'Londonderry' is by no means universal among Protestants. Loyalists who use the term are therefore identifying themselves with the town's original planters in order to signal that they once again feel besieged. While it's possible to have sympathy for this position, the revivification of 'Londonderry' as a marker of resistance has none the less created a situation where citizens are forced to participate in a sectarian discourse even if they don't want to. Indeed they are projected into that discourse simply by naming their place of residence. Short of calling the place 'Stroke City' (*pace* 'Derry-stroke-Londonderry') it's impossible to find a term for it that isn't loaded with historical baggage.[9]

But what has all this got to do with sexuality? Well for one thing it's worth asking what it means to form a sexual self in a place where religious and ethnic identities are charged with so much significance. What space exists – materially or psychically – for the exploration of sexual identity when other forms of identity are already so over-determined? The problem is twofold. For one thing, the discourses which produce these fixed identities are hostile to any attempt to *opt out* of sectarianism. As the Derry/Londonderry issue shows, neutrality is rarely possible in Northern Ireland, where even atheists and agnostics are read in terms of their assumed ethnic origin. So while a homosexual identity might in theory represent an evasion or a qualification of ethnic division, the culture of sectarianism is unlikely to accept such an elision.

More crucially, sexuality is itself a highly regulated aspect of Northern Irish life. It's not accidental that mixed-religion couples (whether gay or straight) present a favoured target for paramilitary groups – such alliances are not only an inadmissible rejection of sectarian polarities, they are also seen as tribal betrayals.[10] Theories of ethnic and moral purity have also powered paramilitary attacks on lesbians and gay men. A deviant sexual identity is therefore doubly dangerous in Northern Ireland; as well as being a rival identification it has also been actively proscribed by the discourses which shape sectarianism.

Moreover, even 'mainstream' Nationalist and Unionist groups have accused lesbians and gay men of anti-social behaviour. In the 1970s, Unionist politicians consistently resisted attempts to bring the 1967 Homosexual Law Reform Act into force in

Northern Ireland, a process which culminated in Ian Paisley's 1981 campaign to 'Save Ulster From Sodomy'.[11] Notwithstanding Sinn Fein's positive policy on lesbian, gay and bisexual equality,[12] it's easy to find similar distancing moves within Nationalism. Few Republicans have been able to deal effectively with Patrick Pearse's homoerotic poetry or Roger Casement's diaries.[13] More recently, Brendí McClenaghan has written of the obstacles impeding his attempt to define himself simultaneously as a Republican and a gay man,[14] while the Ancient Order of Hibernians – a Nationalist society modelled on the Orange Order – has tried to prevent lesbians and gay men participating in St Patrick's Day parades in Boston and New York.[15]

It's also true that however one reads the ideologies of Unionism and Nationalism, their material embodiments – the Irish Republic and the post-partition Stormont Government – have tended to oppose sexual liberalization. Recently things have changed for the better (especially in the Republic) but the historical picture is not encouraging. The vital point is that Nationalism and Unionism have been founded on mythologies that have marginalized homosexuality, and as a result the cultures associated with Loyalism and Republicanism are at best heterosexist and at worst homophobic. There are numerous instances of these exclusively heterosexual narratives, but the one I want to look at brings us back to the Derry/Londonderry division.

## The Maiden City

In the popular consciousness the Derry/Londonderry split is read as an echo of an equivalent Catholic/Protestant dichotomy. This is in turn supposed to mirror the Loyalist/Republican and Unionist/Nationalist dichotomies. The dominance of these polarities (and their tendency to produce rigid ethnic and sexual categories) becomes apparent when one tries to evade the Derry/Londonderry split. Because the town's name is a site of conflict, the Northern Irish Tourist Board and various business organizations have searched for alternative designations such as 'Foyleside' or 'the Gateway to the Northwest', but the name that they most often invoke is 'the Maiden City.' Hence a local hotel boasts of offering 'a serene, relaxing environment where every request is met with the warmth and charm the Maiden City is famous for' (Trinity 1997). Likewise, the express bus between Belfast and Derry/Londonderry has been re-named 'the Maiden City Flier', a move which is designed to enable passengers to buy their tickets without seeming to reveal their religion. I'm not in principle antagonistic to this move but I think it's important to realize that the term 'the Maiden City' is in fact far from euphemistic when applied to Derry/Londonderry. After all, the reason that the town is a 'maiden' is that 'she' remained 'untaken' in the siege of 1689. Thus the supposed euphemism actually propels its user right back to the cultural conflict that it is supposed to elide. Here, the modern binary of 'Derry/Londonderry' has been replaced by an older narrative in which defenders of 'the Maiden City' fight off the vulgar natives who want to possess her by force. (*Very* warm and charming.)

There are numerous literary and popular representations of this tradition. One example, chosen at random, is *Lillibulero*, Denis Johnston's 1938 radio play about the Siege. One of Johnston's narrators refers to the city's inhabitants as 'dour, embattled farmers' and to the town itself as 'A maiden city manned by their forefathers' (Johnston 1992: 44). Another of the narrators refers to 'The great Post Road that leads across the wooded hills / Through which her ravishers will come' (Johnston 1992: 44). This is followed by an anonymous woman describing how 'a holy temple' crowned the city:

> And commerce graced her street,
> A rampart wall was round her,
> [With] the river at her feet.
> And here she sat alone, Boys,
> And looking from the hill
> Vowed the maiden on her throne, Boys,
> [That she] would be a maiden still.
> (Johnston 1992: 44–5)

Johnston's text aptly demonstrates the interplay between the gender of the fortified maiden and that of her defenders – the 'Boys' in question being the twelve apprentices who unilaterally closed the city gates against the Jacobite army. The Apprentice Boys of Derry commemorate their actions with annual marches marking the opening and closing of the gates. As their name suggests, the Apprentice Boys are an all-male organization and the rituals of their marches tend to underscore their masculine defence of a 'female' city. Indeed this division of masculine and feminine identities is frequently accompanied by a desire to police *gender* boundaries as well as territorial ones. Thus, in his research into Northern Irish youth culture, Desmond Bell quotes a 14-year-old boy from Derry/Londonderry who objects to girls marching alongside boys because it's 'too cissy lookin''. The youngster remarks that 'if you're goin' te have a flag carrier you'd be better having a young fellah carrying it with dark glasses or something ... better than a crowd of wee girls wavin' the flag, disgrac[ing] themselves with [it]'. When pressed he adds that male flag-carriers look 'More military ... more *Protestant* like!' (Bell 1990: 103–4; the emphasis is Bell's). Such statements suggest that the rituals of the marching season are as much about domestic power as they are about state power. In this context, men and boys patrol the public sphere, protecting it from female incursions while simultaneously upholding an ideal of masculinity untainted by effeminacy. The irony, of course, is that this policing of gender is done in the name of a female heroine – the Maiden City herself.

With her unpierced defences and her cry of 'No Surrender' – a seventeenth-century version of 'No means No' perhaps? – this maiden calls to mind a long line of besieged Protestant virgins, including Elizabeth the First, in whose reign Ireland was first planted. Another analogue to the Maiden City is provided by Edmund Spenser. Besides being replete with martial virgins bent on protecting their Protestantism as well as their purity, Spenser's *The Faerie Queene* (1590–1609) allegorizes the Elizabethan campaigns in Ireland by representing Irena as the spirit of an ideal, anglicized Ireland whose position is imperilled by the savageries of existing Irish culture. In the poem, Irena seeks help from the Faerie Queene because she is being pursued by Grantorto (who represents Catholicism).[16] The relationship between Irena and the Faerie Queene (which naturalizes Elizabethan involvement in Ireland) is echoed in much subsequent writing, as well as in several nineteenth-century political cartoons where the figure of Hibernia goes to her sister Britannia for help with the annoying savages who are oppressing her. In *Women and Nation in Irish Literature and Society*, C.L. Innes reproduces one such image from an 1866 issue of *Punch*. Entitled 'The Fenian-Pest', the cartoon shows a meek and submissive Hibernia approaching a much more martial Britannia, and asking 'O my dear sister, what *are* we to do with these troublesome people?' Britannia, who is crushing rebellion underfoot, replies: 'Try isolation first, my dear, and then —' (Innes 1993: 13).

There are several interesting things about these images, not least the way in which they represent cultural difference in terms of gender difference. However, they also have a complicated relationship to Nationalist representations of Ireland as a woman oppressed by male invaders. Again this is a vast area involving a large range of personifications which have been deployed for different reasons at different times in Irish history. And – like Loyalist commemorations of the Siege – the tradition is still alive. Seamus Heaney, for example, has spoken on more than one occasion of Ireland as female and Ulster/England as male. In his essay, 'Feeling into Words' (1974) Heaney writes that the conflict in Ireland might be viewed as

> a struggle between the cults and devotees of a god and a goddess. There is an indigenous territorial numen, a tutelar of the whole island, call her Mother Ireland, Kathleen Ní Houlihan, the poor old woman, the Shan Van Vocht, whatever; and her sovereignty has been temporarily usurped or infringed by a new male cult whose fathers were Cromwell, William of Orange and Edward Carson.
>
> (Heaney 1980: 57)

Heaney's mythic project is well-intentioned, although not above criticism.[17] For one thing, female embodiments of Ireland are more multiple and contradictory than Heaney acknowledges. Besides the ones he mentions, there are also figures such as Roisin Dubh, Erin, Hibernia, and – dare one say it? – the Blessed Virgin Mary, who has of course appeared in Ireland, and whose statues have moved on more than one occasion. While these figures have much in common, they are not coterminous. Furthermore, Heaney's narrative implies that female personifications are solely the preserve of Nationalists although this, in fact, is not the case. C.L. Innes and Belinda Loftus have shown that nineteenth-century Nationalist and Unionist propaganda both gender the Ireland/England relationship.[18] All that changes in these representations is the nature of the perceived oppressor; in Nationalist discourse the ravisher is England, while for Unionist commentators the oppressors are either Fenians or Home Rulers. Moreover, Derry/Londonderry's incarnation as the Maiden City is a towering instance of a Loyalist myth that derives much of its force from the *feminization* of a particular location.

Heaney's conceptualization of the Irish situation is therefore in danger of establishing yet another binary relationship between the so-called 'two communities' of Northern Ireland; like other such polarities, Heaney's formula sacrifices cultural complexity in favour of a schematic map. And the map, moreover, is gendered – hence its collapse into a binary opposition. These genderings in turn project a heterosexual narrative onto Irish history and culture. And as the next section shows, not only are the myths on offer always male/female, they also tend to valorize heterosexual masculinity, even at those points at which masculine force appears to be at fault.

## The gendering of cultural production

Seamus Heaney's 'The Ocean's Love to Ireland' appeared the year after his essay 'Feeling into Words'. The poem allegorizes the plantation of Ireland via Sir Walter Raleigh's seduction of an Irish servant, an act in which the maid is backed 'to a tree/As Ireland is backed to England'. Raleigh's power, like his nation's, is expressed in terms of liquids:

> He is water, he is ocean, lifting
> Her farthingale like a scarf of weed lifting
> In the front of a wave.
>             (Heaney 1975: 46)

However Raleigh returns to Elizabeth the First ('His superb crest inclines to Cynthia'), leaving his ruined maid to '[complain] in Irish'. The maiden's fall is exacerbated by the failure of her countrymen and their allies to gain compensation, and Heaney tellingly represents these failures as sexual mis-functions which contrast with the 'superb crest' of Raleigh/England:

> Ocean has scattered her dreams of fleets,
> The Spanish prince has spilled his gold
> And failed her. Iambic drums
> Of English beat the woods where her poets
> Sink like Onan.
> 
> (Heaney 1975: 47)

Here Heaney construes the sinking of the Spanish Armada as a premature ejaculation ('spilled his gold/And failed her') while representing the decay of Gaelic culture as a form of masturbation/*coitus interruptus* ('her poets/Sink like Onan'). By contrast, Raleigh's sexuality is as powerful as it is profligate.

The metaphors are eye-catching but I wonder if they ought to be endorsed given that they pay implicit homage to a fantasy of monolithic heterosexual masculinity. The poem may satirize Raleigh's unregulated sexuality, but it's also fascinated by his heterosexual power – indeed it seems to imply that things would have worked out better if only the Spanish Prince and the Irish poets had been as technically adept as Raleigh. Moreover, even if one accepts Heaney's analysis of the Ireland/England relationship, one is still left with a set of metaphors that are overwhelmingly heterosexual. The volume from which this poem comes is full of similar images – most notably in 'Act of Union' where the speaker is 'imperially/Male' and where he leaves his lover 'raw, like opened ground' (Heaney 1975: 49–50). Although this poem is a self-conscious exploration of imperial and sexual power, the project – like much of *North* – is shot through with identification fantasies in which Heaney's narrator occupies a position of masculine domination. I'm not necessarily opposed to such uses of fantasy (they might, in some cases, be therapeutic) but in this instance Heaney seems to invoke a monolith of hetero-normative masculinity without thinking through the implications of the construction. Indeed, far from using fantasy to challenge the limits of familiar roles Heaney's usages represent an uncritical reification of masculine force.

The exclusively heterosexual nature of these metaphors is confirmed in 'Belfast' (1972), an autobiographical essay published three years before *North*. Here Heaney argues that the process of writing poetry is

> a kind of somnambulist encounter between masculine will and intelligence and feminine clusters of image and emotion. I suppose the feminine element for me involves the matter of Ireland, and the masculine strain is drawn from the involvement with English literature.
> 
> (Heaney 1980: 34)

There is much to pause over in this passage – not least the tired gendering of intelligence as male and emotion as female. (A metaphor, yes, but surely an outmoded one?) Here England and Ireland are once again gendered as masculine and feminine, and are brought together in a night-time *rendezvous*. But most interesting of all is Heaney's comment that 'the feminine element *for me* involves the matter of Ireland, and the masculine strain is drawn from the involvement with English literature'. I emphasize the words '*for me*' because they suggest that Heaney's genderings of Ireland and England are separate from a larger notion that all poetry – *not just his own* – is the product of a meeting between 'masculine will and intelligence' and 'feminine ... emotion'. Therefore besides gendering intelligence as male and emotion as female, Heaney establishes an intrinsically heterosexist theory of poetic production. His notion that poetry is the product of a male/female encounter doesn't *wholly* disallow lesbian and gay cultural interventions, but it makes it difficult to imagine a lesbian or gay poetics. And if one looks at this conceptualization alongside the relentless male/female unions of his political poetry, then Heaney's stance begins to look actively, if unintentionally, disabling for lesbian or gay readers and writers.

As I write this I wonder if I'm being too exacting; after all, Heaney is writing about poetry, not sexuality. There's no reason to expect him to adopt a queer perspective. Perhaps I shouldn't complain, perhaps I should just enjoy the poetry. Well I *do* enjoy the poetry – or some of it at least – but writers have to take responsibility for the metaphors that they use: it's a condition of what Adrienne Rich has called 'verbal privilege' (Rich 1986: 33). And in this instance, Heaney has set up a myth of creativity which makes a claim on universality while simultaneously suppressing the voices of gay men and lesbians. Indeed his formulation makes any writing by women – whether they're gay or straight – more difficult.

These are familiar marginalizations – Heaney is hardly the only one to enact them. But his reproduction of them undermines his view (expressed in 'Feeling into Words') that poems are 'elements of continuity, with the aura and authenticity of archaeological finds' and that they can therefore be 'a restoration of the culture to itself' (Heaney 1980: 41). The problem here is that Heaney blurs what ought to be a sharp distinction between found objects and constructed texts. A given poem may be 'true' to a poet's experience, but that doesn't mean that the constructed voice of the poem should be taken as more representative, natural or 'authentic' than any other cultural artefact. (In any case, who decides which poems are 'authentic' and which ones are not? And don't found objects also have to be interpreted? Their 'aura' may mean different things to different people.) Moreover, Heaney's stress on 'continuity' implies that there is an underlying Irish culture waiting to be rediscovered and that this 'culture' is a unified whole. In fact even though Heaney is suggesting that Gaelic culture has been displaced by an imperially English canon, he seems unaware that his essentialist version of indigenous culture runs the risk of marginalizing large swathes of Irish experience.

To be fair, these texts are not necessarily representative of Heaney's current thinking – *North* has always been a controversial and somewhat anomalous volume in his body of work. Nor is Heaney responsible for the high level of public scrutiny which has given his interventions more weight than those of his contemporaries. (Indeed he has been rightly suspicious of any attempt to co-opt him as a general spokesperson for 'Ireland'.) Even so, his conceptualizations of literary creativity perpetuate narrow versions of gender and nationhood, and ought to be queried. The shortcomings of these contributions remind one that there is a pressing need to rethink categories such as 'English', 'Irish', and 'Ulster' and to find fresh ways of construing their inter-relations while simultaneously re-thinking the gender binaries that have marked Irish history. I'm aware of the difficulties of such a project and of the pressure to lapse into an unconsciously sexualized discourse. (Even 'relations', which I use above, can be read as an erotic metaphor.) However, even if it's impossible (given their historical symbiosis) to divorce metaphors of sex and gender from political discussions, such frameworks ought to be used with care and with a willingness to think through their implications.

To summarize: so far I've been arguing that Irish history has usually been represented in terms of polarities rather than multiplicity or diversity. Combined with this is a tendency to invoke a male/female binary as a template for the supposed dichotomies of Irish culture. One of the many debilitating results of this is that same-sex stories have been consistently written out of Irish life. Now it's time to consider the spaces within which it might be possible to produce the new metaphors that I'm advocating. In particular I want to look at how 'coming out' represents a challenge to the received formations of Northern Irish life.

## Utopian sexualities?

'Coming out' is a contentious concept, one which Alan Sinfield (Chapter 1 in this volume) describes as quintessentially metropolitan. Moreover some queer writers have complained that the ideology of 'coming out' enacts and maintains the gay/straight divisions of identity politics.[19] How, then, can 'coming out' undermine set categories? Well, for one thing, Ulster lesbian and gay identities are not exact replicas of the models circulating elsewhere in Britain and their difference ought to make us re-think the assumption that 'coming out' is a single mode. Moreover, 'coming out' in Northern Ireland creates identities which supplement and refigure sectarian loyalties: it forces a reconsideration (though not necessarily a rejection) of the Nationalist/Unionist map. The resulting selves are mixtures of gay and Republican, lesbian and Unionist; they can be seen as hybrid identities, *un*fixed categories.

Information and advice circulated by lesbian and gay groups in the North often have graphic representations of these inter-identifications. For example the letterhead of the Queen's University Belfast Lesbian, Gay and Bisexual Society has a rainbow flag alongside the University arms. The potentially alienating Red Hand of Ulster (which features in the University crest) is therefore re-inflected by being juxtaposed with a symbol of inclusion and alliance. The result is a space in which supposedly contrary identities are allowed to co-exist, thus reconciling the ghettos with which I began this chapter. Similarly, the Foyle Friend Homepage is dominated by a huge rainbow flag carried aloft during a Pride Parade and the accompanying text refers to the group's location in the 'North West of Ireland' rather than in 'Derry' or 'Londonderry'. Besides avoiding disputed names, this places the city in a wider geographical context, thus undermining the border's power to enforce division. (That is, the 'North West' includes Co. Donegal, which is in the Republic, as well as Co. Londonderry, which is in the North.)

A slightly different approach is taken by Belfast's Queer Space Project, which aims to create

> a lesbian, gay, bisexual, transgender (LGBT) community space. It is for the promotion of LGBT visibility, resources, networking and communication within the community. Queer Space aims to form a collective, where participation by all members of the LGBT population is welcome on all levels, from administration of space to attendance in it.
>
> (Queer Space 1998)

The project's website has a stylized picture of the group's meeting place: green walls with a purple easy-chair and well-stocked bookshelves. (The books are a mixture of colours, including green and orange, but shades of lavender predominate.) A rainbow flag hangs from the window. The accompanying policy statement rejects all forms of inequality – including discrimination on grounds of religion, nationality and ethnicity. It stresses the four principles of accessibility, communality, non-commercialism and non-judgementalism.

The language here is a striking mixture of old and new. Contemporary queerness (with its emphasis on inclusivity and multiplicity) meshes with concepts from 1970s identity politics (collectivity, community, economic self-sufficiency).[20] Responsibility towards the group exists alongside individual subject positions, but no attempt is made to erase the *differences* between the project's various constituencies. Significantly, 'members of the community will not be asked to hide or change any element of their identity within Queer Space.' This recognition of multiple loyalties allows for diversity without imposing censorship. The resultant 'queer family space' supplements Ulster's 'two communities' and creates, at least in theory, a multicultural locale.

Like sectarianism, the Queer Space Project operates simultaneously on a discursive and a material level. Its rhetoric is obviously shaped in part by postmodernism – hence the use of queer terminology and spatial metaphors. But there's an obvious danger in placing too much faith in the virtual reality of Utopian postmodernism: crucially, a discourse of inclusion does not *in itself* create a 'safe space' even if it helps us to envisage one. This is in no way a criticism of the Belfast project (which seems exemplary); rather, it's a reminder that however much language shapes materiality discourse alone cannot change societies. Culture, after all, consists of competing and opposed discourses, and queer inclusivity cannot, alas, vanquish sectarian conflict in anything more than a fleeting (though none the less valuable) way.

Therefore although the Ulster gay scene could be described as a Foucaldian heterotopia, we should be wary of attributing magical powers to it just because it's 'a space that is other' (Foucault 1986: 27). The cross-identifications of Northern Irish queer life also evoke Homi Bhabha's theory that hybridity is 'the third space' which 'displaces the histories that constitute it, and sets up new structures of authority, new political initiatives, which are inadequately understood through received wisdom' (Bhabha 1990: 211). What could be more hybrid, one wonders, than queer Unionism or lesbian Catholicism? However, I share the scepticism that several commentators have shown towards theories of hybridity. Sally Munt writes that 'models such as Homi Bhabha's Third Space and hybridity have a tendency to be applied as though any kind of instability, like "difference", is an end in itself, and intrinsically progressive' (Munt 1998: 170–1). Having made a similar point, Alan Sinfield remarks that 'it is easier than we once imagined to dislocate language and ideology; and harder to get such dislocations to make a practical difference' (Sinfield 1998: 34).

This is certainly apposite to Northern Ireland, where the recent cease-fires have been marred by an *increase* in violence towards gay men and lesbians.[21] All the same, if hybridity 'has to be addressed not in the abstract, but as social practice' (Sinfield 1998: 34), Ulster has lessons for the rest of Britain, if only because Northern Irish queer identities are hybrid in a conspicuous and *specific* way. In this context, one 'comes out' to a series of balancing acts rather than to a single, rigid, born-again self. The particularities of the Northern Irish situation in turn suggest that 'coming out' (even in a *metropolitan* location) is an ongoing transaction that continues to provoke reformulations of identity: it's a process, not a once-in-a-lifetime act.

'Coming out' clearly isn't the only way of unsettling sectarianism and nor is it always successful in doing so. (There are gay paramilitaries as well as gay moderates.) But the central point is that identities based on sexual oppression can counter-weigh religious or cultural grievances and create agendas which compete with ethnic identifications. And as a result it may be possible to evolve new narratives for and about life in Northern Ireland. Such an enterprise is inevitably utopian, with all the problems that utopianism brings. But even though the Belfast Queer Space Project is vulnerable to attack (from its members as well as from outsiders) it's none the less an investment in the idea of *positive* change, as opposed to sectarian stagnation or the 'instability' as 'an end in itself' identified by Munt. Indeed, even if such a space only existed on a metaphorical level (which is not the case), it would still countermand the gendered myths examined earlier in this chapter. Instead of claiming to be unified and natural, the Queer Space Project acknowledges its own diversity – and by doing so it reveals the excluding and constructed nature of Heaney's supposedly 'authentic' culture. This doesn't eliminate the existing myths of Irish and Ulster identity, but it allows several different subcultures to *re-imagine* their relation to dominant ideologies.

One example of how this process might work is provided, ironically, by the border. This – the most contested line in Ireland – is the zone which defines 'Northern Ireland' and keeps it in uneasy relation to 'the South'. (Until very recently the Republic's constitution has laid claim to the six counties, thus refusing the legitimacy of partition.)[22] Contemporary Republicanism is structured around opposition to the border while Ulster Unionism is predicated on its maintenance. So the border is both a physical entity and a symbol of wider disputes. Moreover, by creating the political units that lie on either side of it, the border has been an agent of cultural production; the different routes taken by North and South since 1920 have arisen, to a large extent, from their contradictory responses to partition. As a result Ireland has been conditioned socially, as well as geographically, by the border.

Given that it is *literally* divisive, the border is hardly a promising place in which to look for ways forward. It could of course be redeemed through postmodernism: the liminal zone, like the twilight zone, might be a place where freaky things take place. Unfortunately, however, Ireland's border zone continues to be a site of violence rather than of playful inversion. A fake traffic sign saying 'Sniper at Work' may be witty (and semiologically sophisticated) but it is underpinned with the threat of concrete violence – a bullet in the brain would be rather less droll. Furthermore, living on the border does not in itself unfix rigid loyalties; if anything it strengthens them. Three-quarters of the Derry/Londonderry secondary school Protestants interviewed by Desmond Bell in 1985 had either never crossed the border, or had only done so 'a few times' (Bell 1990: 150). Mirroring this, Derry/Londonderry Catholics tend to identify themselves with the land *across* the border in Donegal, rather than with the rest of Northern Ireland. The polarities encoded in Derry/Londonderry's name are not, therefore, deconstructed through the city's borderline status.

This assumes, however, that all Nationalists and Loyalists feel the same way about the border – which is surely not the case. Subcultural groupings within Republicanism and Unionism are likely to have particular responses which may not tally with the responses of other Unionists and Republicans. In particular, what might happen if queer Irish people began to contemplate the border in a new way? In certain contexts it could be an enabling line rather than a dividing one.

Although this is partly a postmodern gambit, it's also based on social actualities. Take the recent (though incomplete) liberalization of life in the Irish Republic. Interesting questions arise for a gay Unionist when one considers that between 1993 and 1998 the legal age of consent for homosexual sex was lower in the Irish Republic than in the North. And although the legal age of consent in the North is soon likely to become 16 (as opposed to 17 in the South),[23] the Irish Republic can still boast an array of anti-discrimination legislation that's singularly lacking in Britain. (Sexual orientation is included in the Republic's Unfair Dismissals Act and extremes of homophobic (and/or sectarian) rhetoric can be challenged under the Prohibition of Incitement to Hatred Act. Irish law does not recognize the category of 'gross indecency', and there is no ban on gay men and lesbians serving in the Irish armed forces.)

So how might these factors cut across existing cultural and religious suspicions? Do they represent a temptation to younger gay Unionists? The question is rhetorical. Given my own identity as an expatriate lapsed Catholic, I'm hardly in a position to speak for Ulster Loyalists; in any case Jeff Dudgeon (whose action against the British Government brought the 1967 Homosexual Law Reform Act into force in Northern Ireland) is a committed Unionist.[24] Besides which, the Irish Republic is not yet as modern a state as is sometimes claimed. The improved position of gay men in the South is not matched by an equivalent advance in the status of women, whether gay or straight. Confronted by a Republican tradition that's ambivalent about homosexuality, and by a state that's still associated with a homophobic church, emigration to England, not the Republic, remains a compelling choice for many Northern Nationalists.

There's no reason why lesbian or gay Unionists should have to abandon their traditional allegiances in favour of a queer United Ireland. Nor should Nationalists have to leave the North to evade the homophobic attentions of the RUC. But the discrepancies between North and South provoke unique dilemmas for Irish gay men and lesbians. So much so that their identities represent a different sort of boundary. If living on the physical North/South border does not necessarily create plurality and fluidity, what about the psychic borderland of being gay *and* a Nationalist, or lesbian *and* a Unionist? This involves a stronger form of agency – it's a *choice* of identity (and a double one, at that) rather than the acceptance of a single, pre-ordained cultural category. Those inhabiting it are therefore ideally placed to produce new ways of thinking about nationality and sexuality. Like 'Ulster' itself[25] – which is composed of nine counties, of which six are in the North and three in the South – this is a location which crosses boundaries and *need not* be subject to sectarian divisions, even if those divisions have hitherto structured political and cultural debate in Ireland.

## Notes

1 I would like to thank the editors of this volume for their comments and advice; thanks are also due to Louise Hudd and Alan Sinfield.
2 Affrica Taylor's 'A Queer Geography' analyses the difficulties as well as the enticements of so-called 'gay spaces' (Taylor 1997: 3–12).

3  For a critique of globalizing accounts of identity politics see Ng (1997: 216–21).
4  'Anti-gay' was coined by Mark Simpson in his edited collection of the same name (Simpson 1996).
5  An early account of this process can be found in Nairn (1977).
6  It should be noted, however, that there are many fewer Nationalist marches than Unionist ones.
7  Loyalist and Republican murals are reproduced in Rolston (1992, 1995); other murals are analysed in Rolston (1987). Further symbolic material is examined in Loftus (1990, 1994).
8  See Bell (1990: 72–84).
9  'Stroke City' was coined by Radio Foyle presenter Gerry Anderson to poke fun at 'Derry-stroke-Londonderry'. Of course Radio *Foyle* is itself a canny avoidance of Derry/Londonderry.
10 One savage instance of this was the murder by Loyalist paramilitaries of Bernadette Martin, an 18-year-old Catholic, while she was in bed with her Protestant boyfriend. See Streeter (1997).
11 Although the campaign was unsuccessful, Paisley and his supporters managed to gather 70,000 signatures on their petition (Rose 1994: 38).
12 See Sinn Fein (1996).
13 Public opinion ran against Casement when leaked extracts from his diaries revealed extensive homosexual activities; Nationalists insisted that the diaries were forged and that 'this most gallant gentleman' (Yeats 1984: 306) could not have harboured such vile preoccupations. The issue is still debated; Mitchell supports the forgery theory in Casement (1997b) while Sawyer opposes it in Casement (1997a). In a sense, the authenticity of the diaries is a red herring: Nationalist unease at Casement's supposed homosexuality is indicative of underlying homophobia, even if the allegations made against him can be shown to be false. See Kilfeather (1994) for an account of Casement's trial. Walshe (1997: 3–5) discusses Casement and Pearse as homosexual influences on the formation of the Irish Republic. For the homoerotic poetry see Pearse (1993).
14 See McClenaghan (1995).
15 For Gerry Adams's equivocal response to the controversy, see Katz (1996). See Rose (1994: 31–4) for the role of the Ancient Order of Hibernians. See Davis (1995) for a cultural geographer's account of these parades.
16 See Spenser (1984: 727–8).
17 See Longley (1994: 189–90) and Cullingford (1990).
18 See Innes (1993) and Loftus (1990).
19 See Simpson (1996: 5–6).
20 The homepage also makes it clear, however, that these principles are themselves open for negotiation; it will be interesting to see how this group, and others like it, change in response to recent social and political developments in Ireland.
21 See Section Three of Smyth (1996).
22 Earlier this year (1998), the Dublin government signed the Good Friday Agreement which stipulated, subject to a subsequent referendum, that clauses two and three should be removed from the Republic's constitution.
23 In 1993 the Irish government decriminalized homosexual acts and set a common age of consent for gay and straight sex. In 1994 the Westminster government lowered the age of consent for gay sex in mainland Britain from 21 to 18. The fact that Northern Ireland had been initially excluded, for tactical reasons, from this legislation did not prevent Ian Paisley from opposing the measure in the House of Commons. In June 1998 the British House of Commons voted to lower the age of consent to 16; so far, however, the House of Lords has

failed to ratify this decision. Reform of the Upper Chamber makes it likely, however, that the age of consent (at least in mainland Britain) will eventually be lowered to 16.
24 See Woolaston (1991b: 40).
25 The ancient province of Ulster comprised the counties now in Northern Ireland, plus Cavan, Monaghan and Donegal.

# References

Bell, D. (1990) *Acts of Union: Youth Culture and Sectarianism in Northern Ireland*, Basingstoke and London: Macmillan.

Bhabha, H.K. (1990) 'The Third Space', in J. Rutherford (ed.) *Identity: Community, Culture, Difference*, London: Lawrence & Wishart.

Casement, R. (1997a) *Roger Casement's Diaries: 1910 – the Black and the White*, ed. R. Sawyer, London: Pimlico.

Casement, R. (1997b) *The Amazon Journal of Roger Casement* (1910–11), ed. A. Mitchell, London: Anaconda.

Cullingford, E.B. (1990) '"Thinking of Her ... as ... Ireland": Yeats, Pearse and Heaney', in *Textual Practice* 4: 1.

Davis, T. (1995) 'The Diversity of Queer Politics and the Redefinition of Sexual Identity and Community in Urban Spaces', in D. Bell and G. Valentine (eds) *Mapping Desire: Geographies of Sexualities*, London and New York: Routledge.

Dublin Lesbian and Gay Men's Collectives (1986) *Out for Ourselves: The Lives of Irish Lesbians and Gay Men*, Dublin: Women's Community Press.

Foucault, M. (1986) 'Of Other Spaces', trans. J. Miskowiec, in *Diacritics*, vol. 16.

Heaney, S. (1975) *North*, London: Faber.

—— (1980) *Preoccupations: Selected Prose 1968–1978*, London: Faber.

Hughes, E. (ed.) (1991) *Culture and Politics in Northern Ireland 1960–1990*, Milton Keynes: Open University Press.

Innes, C.L. (1993) *Woman and Nation in Irish Literature and Society 1880–1935*, Hemel Hempstead: Harvester-Wheatsheaf.

Johnston, D. (1992) 'Lillibulero' (1938) in vol. III, *The Dramatic Works of Denis Johnston* (3 vols), Gerrards Cross: Colin Smythe.

Katz, I. (1996) 'Adams Treads Lightly in Big Apple', *The Guardian*, 18 March.

Kilfeather, S. (1994) 'Remembering Pleasure and Pain: Roger Casement's Diaries', in *perversions* (Summer).

Kirkland, R. (1996) *Literature and Culture in Northern Ireland Since 1965*, Harlow: Longman.

Lewis, S. (1849) *A Topographical Dictionary of Ireland*, vol. II, 2nd edn (2 vols), London: S. Lewis and Co.

Loftus, B. (1990) *Mirrors: William III and Mother Ireland*, Dundrum: Picture Press.

—— (1994) *Mirrors: Orange and Green*, Dundrum: Picture Press.

Longley, E. (1994) *The Living Stream: Literature and Revisionism in Ireland*, Newcastle upon Tyne: Bloodaxe.

McClenaghan, B. (1995) 'Letter from a Gay Republican: H-Block 5', in I. O'Carroll and E. Collins (eds) *Lesbian and Gay Visions of Ireland*, London: Cassell.

Muirhead, L.R. (1967) *The Blue Guides: Ireland*, 3rd edn, London and Chicago: Ernest Benn and Rand McNally & Co.

Munt, S.R. (1998) *Heroic Desire: Lesbian Identity and Cultural Space*, London: Cassell.

Nairn, T. (1977) *The Break-Up of Britain: Crisis and Neo-Nationalism*, London: NLB.

Ng, V. (1997) 'Race Matters', in A. Medhurst and S.R. Munt (eds) *Lesbian and Gay Studies: A Critical Introduction*, London: Cassell.

Pearse, P. (1993) *Selected Poems/Rogha Dánta*, ed. D. Bolger, introd. E. McCabe, trans. M. Davitt, Dublin: New Island Books.

Queer Space (1998) www.geocities.com/WestHollywood/Heights/7124/

Rich, A. (1986) 'North American Time', in *Your Native Land, Your Life*, New York and London: Norton.

Rolston, B. (1987) 'Politics, Painting and Popular Culture: the Political Wall Murals of Northern Ireland', *Media, Culture and Society* 9: 5–28.

—— (1992) *Drawing Support: Murals in the North of Ireland*, Belfast: Beyond the Pale.

—— (1995) *Drawing Support 2: Murals of War and Peace*, Belfast: Beyond the Pale.

Rose, K. (1994) *Diverse Communities: The Evolution of Lesbian and Gay Politics in Ireland*, Cork: Cork University Press.

Sales, R. (1997) *Women Divided: Gender, Religion and Politics in Northern Ireland*, London and New York: Routledge.

Simpson, M. (ed.) (1996) *Anti-Gay*, London: Cassell.

—— (1998) 'Sing If You Cringe To Be gay', *The Independent on Sunday Magazine*, 25 January, p. 26.

Sinfield, A. (1998) *Gay and After*, London: Serpent's Tail.

Sinn Fein (1996) 'Moving On: a Policy for Lesbian, Gay and Bisexual Equality', http://www.serve.com/rm/sinnfein

Smyth, M. (ed.) (1996) *A Public Hearing on Minority Experiences in Derry Londonderry*, Derry Londonderry: Templegrove Action Research Ltd.

Spenser, E. (1984) *The Faerie Queene* [1590–1609], Harmondsworth: Penguin.

Streeter, M. (1997) 'Ulster Grieves for Teenager Shot as She Slept', *The Independent*, 18 July.

Taylor, A. (1997) 'A Queer Geography', in A. Medhurst and S.R. Munt (eds) *Lesbian and Gay Studies: A Critical Introduction*, London: Cassell.

Trinity (1997) 'Trinity Hotel Homepage', www.trinity-hotel.co.uk

Walshe, E. (1997) 'Introduction: Sex, Nation and Dissent', in E. Walshe (ed.) *Sex, Nation and Dissent in Irish Writing*, Cork: Cork University Press.

Weeks, J. (1997) 'Sexual Values Revisited', in L. Segal (ed.) *New Sexual Agendas*, Basingstoke and London: Macmillan.

Woolaston, G. (1991a) 'Come Dance with Me in Ireland', *Gay Times* (September).

—— (1991b) 'The Green, the Orange, and the Pink', *Gay Times* (October).

Yeats, W.B. (1984) 'Roger Casement' (1937) in R. Finneran (ed.) *W. B. Yeats: The Poems. A New Edition*, London: Macmillan.

# 15

# TRANSGRESSION IN GLASGOW

## A poet coming to terms

*Edwin Morgan*

When I was young I always thought of Glasgow as being some sort of metropolis. It was quite a large city, with well over a million inhabitants. If it was a metropolis, it was a strange one, very unlike Edinburgh, full of incongruities and surprises, offbeat, brash, politically aware and restless, open to change, trying to live down, or alternatively live up to, its rather gamy and violent image. I remember seeing Fritz Lang's film, *Metropolis* in the early 1930s, and saying to myself, Mm, yes, that's the sort of thing! – darkness and light, machines, smoke, social conflict, crowds of people milling about, a sense of the modern. So if you can subtract the idea of dominance from the metropolitan, I like a metropolis, and that may be no more than to say that I like cities, and indeed the larger the better.

Glasgow, notoriously, was 'no mean city', to use the title of that crude but indestructible novel by Alexander McArthur which has never been out of print since 1935, has sold millions of copies, and is readily available in paperback today. This story of Johnnie Stark the Razor King, and the gang warfare of the 1920s and 1930s, was probably more influential than any other book in giving Glasgow its image of danger and dread, the place of the hardman and the blade. The women in the story often use the word 'manly' as a term of praise, but manly means able to fight, capable of violence. Even when they themselves are the recipients of violence, the women uphold the unwritten right of a man to be macho. Well, I was 15 when that novel came out, and I know the world it describes; the descriptions may be lurid, but they are not untruthful to the facts. A hard world, you might say, for anyone growing up and trying to come to terms with being gay. But of course it's not the whole story, and it's not the whole Glasgow. That it's not the whole story is very nicely shown in a poem by Tom Leonard, written in Glasgow dialect, called 'The Hardmen':

noa sumhm

see Calvinism
see Catholicism
shame a thi body

> sex
>
> aw this bevvyin
> aw this hardman stuff
> stull tiedty thir muthirz
> straight up
> eevnthi wey they tok
> stifflike yi no
> no moovna muscle
> cowboyz
>
> n they aw hate queerz
> arssbandits they caw thim
> thi wan thing they canny stand
> poofs
>
> geeyi a tip sun
> fyirivir stucknthi dezirt
> stuckwia Glasweejin
> a *hard*man
>
> noa sumhn
> wotchyir bawz
>
>    (Leonard 1984: 58)

There's a lot of truth in that, and I can assure you that you don't have to be 'stuck in the desert' to prove it. Glasgow has never been short of tough little men, or tough big men, who would not dream of calling themselves gay, and who in all probability have wives or girlfriends, but who nevertheless engage readily, and even regularly, in gay sexual activity. If this sounds like a godsend for gays who are looking for 'real men', you have to remember that such men are potentially dangerous, and if you fail to please them you may be sorry you met them. But still, there they are, a part of the scene, and they make their wants known.

But there are other Glasgows, and always were. I recall one incident from the time when I was about ten – it would be around the end of the 1920s – of my mother and my aunt taking me to one of Glasgow's splendid tearooms, near Charing Cross, with real pictures in gilt frames on the walls, highly polished silver cakestands, and waitresses in crisp black and white. A woman came in, sat down, and in a gruff voice asked for a pot of tea. She had short hair brushed back, she wore a man's suit with collar and tie, and she started smoking a cigarette in a long cigarette-holder. The room was quite crowded, and people were trying hard, though not very successfully, not to look. My mother whispered, Don't stare! It's rude! But I strongly remember what my aunt said: I'm always sorry for people like that. I didn't understand at the time what she meant, but clearly she saw this wasn't just someone dressing up, or cross-dressing, it was someone who belonged to a group, a group of 'people like that' who were somehow cut off from the majority but whom she didn't regard with disgust or contempt. Though they never talked about it, my mother and her sister would have know about lesbianism from the fact that Radclyffe Hall's novel *The Well of Loneliness* had been published not long before, amid great publicity. Later I learned that the woman was well known in the centre of Glasgow, and the city seemed to accept her in its generally all-embracing way. But what struck me was her solitariness, and when I began writing poems a few years later I think I was to some extent haunted by the idea of a solitary figure not in the mainstream of society. One of my earliest poems, written at school when I was 15 or 16, was called 'The Opium-Smoker' – I wasn't into opium!, but this was an imaginary picture of a man in the last stages of addiction in a Chinese opium-den, but he wasn't Chinese, I made him a Polynesian, so that he was a double exile from his own country and from normal behaviour. How far I projected myself into the opium-smoker is hard to say. I already felt myself to be 'different', and had had gay experiences, but without having the word 'gay' and without having much knowledge of the things I was increasingly drawn to. It was a time of silences and inhibitions and guilts and quests and mistakes and very gradual understanding.

So what was Glasgow like to a young gay writer in that period from say the late 1930s through to the 1950s (I can't speak about wartime Glasgow because I wasn't there, I was abroad in the army from 1940 to 1946 – that's another story, of which perhaps a little, later on). Physically, visually, the city was very different from what it is today after the massive stone-cleaning, smoke abatement, and general refurbishment of recent years. It was a dark city. I'd like to quote from a little article I recently wrote about this. The piece was written for a public brochure about Glasgow, but I quote it because it has some coded homosexual references. It's called 'Fog City':

> Without being nostalgic about it, I have a strong recollection of the great Glasgow fogs of the decade after the Second World War. In the spruced-up city of today, these are now no more than memories, and no doubt thought of as a good riddance, but to a writer (or indeed any artist) dark cities can be as attractive as bright ones. At the end of the 1940s, Glasgow was still heavily industrialized, with many soot-blackened and grime-encrusted buildings, and with smoke pouring from thousands of coal-burning chimneys. It was also a city of unabashed and prolific smokers. And of course it is a northern city of early winter evenings. So its fogs could be spectacular. One night in 1947 or 1948 I was returning by train from London, and when I got into Central Station I could not understand why such a crowd of people was massed at the entrance. I soon found out why. Gordon Street was a silent wall of impenetrable grey. There were no buses, trams, taxis or cars to be seen or

heard. It was a stricken, immobile place. No one could get home. I booked a room in the Central Hotel, and as I slipped between the sheets I reflected it was the first time I had stayed at a hotel in my own town: an experience! These fogs penetrated everywhere; in the cinemas each film looked like *Quai des brumes*, and the Golden Divans in Green's Playhouse were more than usually seductive. The long cinema queues of those pre-booking days, snaking round whole blocks, huddled together as if afraid some segment might break off and be lost for ever. We did not curse the fog: it was simply one recurring phase of the environment. Half-sinister, half-romantic wanderings by the River Kelvin seemed incomplete unless the nose-prickling waves of an oncoming fog combined with the acrid but haunting smell of the scummy effluent on the water to fix a future memory unmodified by anything politically correct.

(Burgess 1996: 23)

The reference to Green's Playhouse in that passage is to a huge cinema, advertised as 'the largest in Europe', which was famous as a place of gay resort for many years; people came to it from far and near, and on a foggy night, when you could hardly see the screen, anything could and did happen. The management would periodically conduct a sudden blitz on the activities, using some of their better-looking staff as *agents provocateurs*, who would sit beside you, make advances, and if you responded would march you out to the foyer and declare that you were barred. You left it for a week or two, came back, and no one noticed. It was a great Glasgow institution, and there must have been many sad hearts when the building was demolished. Another reference in the article which would say more to some people than to others is the night scene by the River Kelvin: Kelvingrove Park was (and is) one of the main trolling areas after dark, and also, perhaps inevitably, a haunt of muggers, so my description of it as half-romantic and half-sinister contains or conceals that other resonance.

Perhaps the fog that I used in that passage, though perfectly real, can also be taken as a metaphor. Gay contacts, gay friendships, were by no means unobtainable but took place in an atmosphere of secrecy, of deception and pretence and machination. Information was by word of mouth; there were no gay clubs or magazines or videos, and if any establishment such as a pub attracted a gay clientele it could never advertise the fact. The shadow of illegality, of the severe penalties of being caught (not only imprisonment, but also social ostracism), hung like a cloud in the background all the time. I don't forget how I happened to be in a cinema (not Green's Playhouse!) at a time shortly after Sir John Gielgud had been arrested and charged with persistent importuning of male persons, and when his name appeared on the screen of a film that was being shown the audience uttered a hiss of disapproval. That was the climate of the period, and it meant that most gays, whether they wanted to or not, were leading double lives. And can I remind you that this situation lasted not until 1967, when the law was changed in England and Wales, but until 1980, when the separate Scottish legal system at last got round to a degree of liberalization. So it was an oppressive time, and if you are a writer, a poet, you have to find ways and means of dealing with it. You don't go silent. You circumvent, you encode, you enfabulate, you invent parallel or analogous worlds. You work by methods not unlike those used by dissidents in authoritarian regimes. From the 1950s onwards, I knew that I wanted somehow to write about that side of my life, and that side of my life in Glasgow and Scotland, and I developed my own strategies for doing so. I didn't want to become a 'gay poet'; it was only a part of my experience, not the whole; but it was an important enough part for me to feel I had to come to terms with it and somehow communicate it in forms of art, in publishable poetry – even in unpublishable poetry if that was the case at that time.

I sometimes used what today we would call gay icons. I wrote a poem called 'Je Ne Regrette Rien' about Edith Piaf, in the first person, imagining myself into her life as someone who although she became famous was always on the edge of society and was never really absorbed by the establishment, and I used her promiscuous heterosexual love-life as if it could provide a gay subtext, since the poem came from a male author. As for example, in one passage:

> his broad shoulders
> glisten through the rain
> I can see
> the dead cigarette
> in his firm mouth
> he throws it aside
> it begins and
> I regret nothing
> We sway in the rain,
> he crushes my mouth.
> What could I regret
> if a hundred times
> of parting struck me
> like lightning if this
> lightning of love
> can strike and
> strike
> again!
> (Morgan 1990: 148)

I made use of this dramatic projection in other poems in different ways. I wrote a poem about Jack London, again in the first person, inhabiting him as closely as I could, and bringing out, almost explicitly, the homoerotic element in his personality which I have always found very fascinating, an idealization of male companionship which may or may not have been sexual. And I suggested the darker side of things in a poem called 'Grendel', a dramatic monologue from the totally alienated anti-hero of the Anglo-Saxon epic *Beowulf*, exiled from normal human society and prowling round the lighted hall where all the normal enjoyments of eating and drinking and singing and lovemaking are going on; like the Glasgow hardman, he finds his closest friend is his mother, and she is a monster too! I made it a fairly grim poem, expressive of a mood that probably wouldn't be so commonly felt today – an anger against the triumphalism of normality. Here are a few lines from the poem:

> It is being nearly human
> gives me this spectacular darkness.
> The light does not know what to do with me.
> I rise like mist and I go down like water.
> I saw them soused with wine behind their windows.
> I watched them making love, twisting like snakes.
> I heard a blind man pick the strings, and sing.
> There are torches everywhere, there are faces
> swimming in shine and sweat and beer and grins and greed.
> There are tapers confusing the stacked spears.
> There are queens on their knees at idols, crosses, lamps.
> There are handstand clowns knocked headlong by maudlin heroes.
> There are candles in the sleazy bowers, the whores
> sleep all day with mice across their feet.
>                                             (Morgan 1990: 427)

That feeling of 'being nearly human', as Grendel says, goes with a sense of the dominance and oppression of another group, but I think that Grendel's knowledge of rejection is moving forward into an area of critical anger and even pride. 'The light does not know what to do with me', he says. So perhaps there's a case for darkness?

Another area where it was possible to 'come out' in a disguised way was translation. I translated many poems by gay foreign poets, including Lorca, Genet, Michelangelo, and Platen. I was particularly pleased to discover the last of these, partly because he was so little known in Britain but also because I shared many of his problems – the inhibitions, the dangers and difficulties of speaking out, the desire to conceal and reveal at the same time, the choice of such a universal human theme as love which must somehow not be untrue to the special experience of gay love. His full name is August, Graf von Platen-Hallermünde, and he lived from 1796 to 1835. His poetry has great formal control but is often all the more moving because of that. In the latter part of his life he went to Venice, and fell in love with a gondolier. He wrote a very fine sequence of *Venetian Sonnets*, and I'd like to quote my translation of one of these, No.14, 'Wenn tiefe Schwermut meine Seele wieget':

> When I am deeply burdened, desolate,
> My soul is drawn to the Rialto, to haunt
> The stalls in dying daylight – not a jaunt
> For trifles, but for the mind's ease I await.
>
> A shadow on the bridge, I've often gazed
> Down where the dull waves quiver sluggish and cold,
> Where old half-crumbled walls are overscrawled
> With branches of laurel, from bushes wild and crazed.
>
> And there, where time has turned the posts to stone,
> I stand and stare till all things disappear
> In the dark doge-widowed sea that sleeps alone;
>
> And in that silent space my listening ear
> Catches at times a faint cry that is blown
> Here from the far canals. Ah, gondolier!
> (Morgan 1996: 321)

My own love-poems, those that were written in my own person and not through a translation or through a character in monologue, had various degrees of disguise, the commonest being the use of the indeterminate pronoun 'you' instead of 'he', but must sometimes have been virtually transparent. I knew that some would be taken by most readers as heterosexual, though they weren't. I knew that some would be perceived as ambiguous, which might or might not be worrying to the reader, depending on his or her interest in gender. And the ones I personally worried about at the time, wondering how they would be received when the climate of opinion was still fairly hostile to homosexuality, were poems I was determined to write and to publish, perhaps in the spirit of seeing what could be done, what the barriers, if any, were. There's one poem which is not exactly a love-poem, though it is a poem about a sexual encounter, that I have always thought of as being an important moment in my aim to take such material into serious poetry, especially in a Scottish and indeed a Glasgow context, and to ask people to think about it. This is the poem called 'Glasgow Green', written in 1963, while gay activity was still illegal. It describes physical events in a physical scene, but on a more philosophical level it was a plea for gay liberation before there was a gay liberation movement. The action it presents is nightmarish, and to some readers it may not at the time have seemed clear, but when looked at closely it can only be a homosexual rape – and this links back, if you remember, to what I said earlier about the dangers in finding hardmen attractive. This poem also links back, by the way, to the article on 'Fog City' which I quoted before. So here is 'Glasgow Green' (Glasgow Green is a large open park in the east end of the city which can't be closed at night because there are roads running through it):

Clammy midnight, moonless mist.
A cigarette glows and fades on a cough.
Meth-men mutter on benches,
pawed by river fog. Monteith Row
sweats coldly, crumbles, dies
slowly. All shadows are alive.
Somewhere a shout's forced out – 'No!' –
it leads to nothing but silence,
except the whisper of the grass
and the other whispers that fill the shadows.

'What d'ye mean see me again?
D'ye think I came here jist for that?
I'm no finished with you yet.
I can get the boys t'ye, they're no that faur away.
You wouldny like that eh? Look there's no two ways aboot it.
Christ but I'm gaun to have you Mac
if it takes all night, turn over you bastard
Turn over, I'll — '
           Cut the scene.
Here there's no crying for help,
it must be acted out, again, again.
This is not the delicate nightmare
you carry to the point of fear
and wake from, it is life, the sweat
is real, the wrestling under a bush
is real, the dirty starless river
is the real Clyde, with a dishrag dawn
it rinses the horrors of the night
but cannot make them clean,
though washing blows
       where the women watch
by day,
     and children run,
          on Glasgow Green.

And how shall these men live?
Providence, watch them go!
Watch them love, and watch them die!
How shall the race be served?
It shall be served by anguish
as well as by children at play.
It shall be served by loneliness
as well as by family love.
It shall be served by hunter and hunted in their endless chain
as well as by those who turn back the sheets in peace.
The thorn in the flesh!
Providence, water it!
Do you think it is not watered?
Do you think it is not planted?
Do you think there is not a seed of the thorn
as there is also a harvest of the thorn?
Man, take in that harvest!
Help that tree to bear its fruit!
Water the wilderness, walk there, reclaim it!
Reclaim, regain, renew! Fill the barns and the vats!
Longing,
      longing
            shall find its wine.

Let the women sit in the Green
and rock their prams as the sheets
blow and whip in the sunlight.
But the beds of married love
are islands in a sea of desire.
Its waves break here, in this park,
splashing the flesh as it trembles
like driftwood through the dark.

                              (Morgan 1990:168–9)

That poem probably has something of the spirit of the 1960s, which I found a genuinely liberating decade, despite the fact that there was no change in the Scottish law until 1980. After the bleak, leaden 1950s, there was a much freer atmosphere of discussion. There was exciting new music, new poetry. The American Beats had quite an influence in Scotland; Burroughs and Ginsberg came to visit us. Alexander Trocchi, our Glasgow Beat, brought drugs into the central agenda and had his novel *Cain's Book* publicly burned in Sheffield. There was a definite shift, at that time, away from centres and monoliths and establishments, and sexual minorities, like other minorities (including national minorities, for example Scotland) began to stir and speak and tingle and start a long search for empowerment. As a poet, I felt that pretty well everything could be expressed, though the state of the law meant that life itself was still far from liberated. I say 'pretty well everything' because it would be unwise to forget the blasphemy case which Mary Whitehouse successfully instigated against James Kirkup and *Gay News* in respect of Kirkup's poem 'The Love that Dares to Speak its Name', where he suggests that Jesus and his disciples were no strangers to homosexuality. But during the 1970s I published quite a few poems which were unmistakably gay, one of them for example, called 'Christmas Eve', being about a proposition from a young tough, slightly drunk, on a Glasgow bus. Glasgow still provided plenty of material that was subversive of good order and discipline! I also wrote, at long last, about my experiences during the Second World War, when I served in the Middle East, in the North African campaign, and also in Palestine and Lebanon; these were poems of memory, of very vivid memory, and I included snapshots of the intense homoerotic friendships wars are known to produce, plus the sexual encounters which are not so commonly acknowledged but which occur all the same, perhaps especially in the sweat-trickling half-naked circumstances of a desert environment. Maybe I should quote two short pieces, both written in Glasgow in the 1970s but looking back to the 1940s; one wholly platonic, one wholly non-platonic: they are from a long sequence called *The New Divan*:

> Not in King's Regulations, to be in love.
> Cosgrove I gave the flower to, joking, jumping down
> the rocky terraces above Sidon, my heart bursting
> as a village twilight spread its tent over us
> and promontories swam far below
> through goat-bells into an unearthly red.
> He dribbled a ball through shrieking children and
> they laughed at our bad Arabic, and the flower. To tell
> the truth he knew no more of what I felt than of tomorrow.
> Gallus, he cared little of that. I've not lost
> his photograph. Yesterday, tomorrow
> he slumbers in a word.
>                           (No.86) (Morgan 1990: 325)

> You came under my mosquito-net
> many times, till you were posted far off.
> I was innocent enough
> to think the posting was accidental.

> When you left, it was my studious
> avoidance of you that said goodbye.
> It was enough, the body, not the heart.
> We'd our black comedy too —
> the night you got up, on Mount Carmel,
> with a dog's turd flattened on your shirt-front:
> not funny, you said.
> Well, it was all a really unwashable laundry
> that finally had to be thrown away.
> (No. 98) (Morgan 1990: 329)

The fact that I published these poems and others like them during the 1970s and into the 1980s meant of course that people would generally regard them as coming from an author who was gay, even if he had not declared himself as such. Increasingly, through the 1980s, as more and more journalists and critics were interviewing me or writing reviews and articles about my work, I felt that not coming out was rapidly becoming an untenable position. If you ask me why it took me so long to come to this decision, I can only plead the inhibitions and insecurities and apprehensions of my early years; these had a lasting effect, as I think on most people of my 1920s generation. Anyhow, I took the plunge in 1988 by giving a series of long interviews to Christopher Whyte which told the whole story, and this story came out publicly, very publicly, in broadcasts and books and newspaper spreads, in 1990, when Glasgow had its moment of glory (disputed glory!) as European City of Culture. I felt that the coincidence was good. I was still living in the city, I was committed to it, and I was changing ever so slightly the cultural image of Glasgow by bringing into the open something which really was there but had been dumb or muffled or marginalized for too long. The decision to come out was personal, not civic, but it clearly had a civic dimension, or civic reverberations, and I don't regret that. I wrote a lot during the 1980s, on both personal and public subjects, and felt confident about switching from the one to the other — writing poems about the break-up of the Soviet Union, about Glasgow becoming post-industrial, about the Gulf War, on the one hand, and on the other hand I found a new freedom in trying to make riskier subjects just as good material for genuine poetry: 'Il Traviato' was a poem about a rent-boy, 'Stein on Venus' was about the lesbian Gertrude Stein, 'Eros' about a gay demonstration in Piccadilly Circus, 'Head' about a blowjob, and 'A Memorial' about cottaging. Despite their shameful subjects, these poems were published, presented to a general readership, as poems like any other, as well made as I could make them, but presented in a deliberately non-ghettoized way, dropped like strange little nuggets into an amalgam, a collection of straightforward poetry on recognizably acceptable themes. And although I don't object to gay anthologies, I still think that is the best way to do it. Let readers stub their toes on these queer poems, and then hopefully begin to say,

Well, I hadn't thought of that, or Good God, is that right? is it really like that?, or is there really anything impossible in poetry? And I encouraged people to ask such questions, to extend their gamut of the acceptable. In 'Head', for example, I have a play on words in the last line, which reads '[I] brought that head back here for all.' It, the head, the poem, is meant not for specialized tastes but for everybody.

Let me quote one of these poems, 'Il Traviato', which in its way is a Glasgow poem. I was standing waiting for a bus, opposite the Theatre Royal, home of Scottish Opera. A big poster was advertising *La Traviata*, Verdi's famously affecting story of the tragic prostitute Violetta. I had a long wait for the bus, and my mind set off on an equally long train of thought, thinking about the title and its meaning, 'the lost one', 'the one who has gone astray'. Suppose it was not feminine but masculine, Il Traviato, with the same meaning. Could I write about such a person? Not following Verdi's story but inventing something parallel to it, suggested by it? This is the result:

> That's my eyes at their brightest and biggest.
> It's belladonna. I've a friend who. Not that
> I'd ever use too much, did once, came out of
> delirium after a week of sweats, you learn. But
> I'm so pale now, some men like the contrast
> as I stand in the park with my eyes burning,
> or glide among the poplars, they're thin as I am
> but seem to manage, get their light, get nourished
> as I get trade although the Wraith's my nickname.
> I ought to be in bed, probably, maybe.
> In any case my lover sends me out now,
> he says it's all I'm good for, bring some money.
> He hides my razor till I'm 'interesting',
> a chalky portrait ruffed in my black stubble.
> I mustn't be too hard on him. The years we.
> It all comes down to what kind of constant
> you believe in, doesn't it, not mathematics
> but as if you had the faintest brilliance
> that was only yours, not to let any sickness
> douse it, or despair creeping with a snuffer.
> I sometimes think I wish it could be ended
> – those hard-faced brutes that hit you at the climax –
> but then I go on, don't I, as everyone
> should, pressing through the streets with glances
> for all and everything, not to miss crumbs of
> life, drops of the crowded flowing wonder.
> 
> (Morgan 1994: 51)

To me, there's a lot of Glasgow in that poem – standing in the park with your eyes burning, the hard-faced brutes that hit you at the climax, pressing through the streets with glances for all and everything – but it's also in a more general way an attempt to express solidarity with all those who are not so 'gay' in the old sense, whose lives are on the brink, who need encouragement, determination, survival medicine which can only be bought in the mind, not from a shop, can be conjured by poetry, by words, by the sympathetic magic of the imagination. The couple in the poem are imaginary, but the imagination works on things known and seen, and I can recognize, as I think others will recognize, the reality of the two men and their strangely unbreakable relationship.

Glasgow in the 1990s seems a bit uncertain about what role it wants to play. It has lost its heavy industry and gained a batch of luxury hotels. We recently put up, or put up with, a Rotary conference of 30,000. The Emporio Armani does its best trade outside London. We are erecting a vast shopping mall, the Buchanan Galleries, which will abut onto the Glasgow Royal Concert Hall – commerce and culture could not be more intimately connected. The peripheral housing estates have been improved, but have still a long way to go. The City Council has been very supportive of minorities, and gave its blessing to the setting up of a Gay and Lesbian Centre which was opened by George Galloway MP and launched by my reading of a poem written for the occasion. At the moment the city is gearing itself up for 1999, when it will have to live up to the accolade of its Year of Architecture and Design. There seems to be some determination to mark this event not by putting up some monumental buildings but rather through a series of community projects which will be pointed towards people's everyday lives and will be suggested and discussed and voted on by local communities. If it does happen in this way, it will be very much in accord with the city's traditions of social concern, which have slipped a bit recently and could do with a shot of refurbishment.

But before 1999, Glasgow may have to reckon with something else – a Scottish Parliament in Edinburgh.[1] If this body is delivered as the government has promised (assuming that the referendum hurdle is successfully passed), it seems to be generally assumed that it will sit in Edinburgh. Considerable if unquantified consequences will follow. Edinburgh will gain an expansion of population, housing, offices, shops, spending power, and kudos. No one knows yet just what powers the parliament will have, but it is already being proleptically lobbied by various pressure groups, including Outright Scotland, who want to ensure that lesbian and gay rights are written into what they call a Claim of Right. Whatever its powers and political complexion turn out to be, it will inevitably change perceptions of Scotland from both within and without. Will Edinburgh values – professional, traditional, conservative – dominate? Or will Edinburgh be forced to broaden its base if it wants to claim to be the 'capital' – which it does at the moment, if improperly, since only independent nations have capitals. Perhaps it will force the rest of us to be consigned to non-metropolitan status? – a double bind, first London and then Edinburgh! Well, I can't see Glasgow going into terminal decline. It is a very resilient place. My feeling is that it will be quite happy to let the other place have the pomp and the trappings and whatever the Scottish equivalent of Black Rod is. Glasgow will become the joker in the pack, the Xanadu, the Vegas. It seems to be shaping up to this role already. A big event called Pure Glasgow is planned for the end of August this year, to celebrate the end of the Edinburgh Festival (and you can take that how you like): there will be music, theatre, fireworks; seven new double-decker-bus-sized sculptures will be transported through the streets to Glasgow Green; a great parade will be issued with red flags to show that the city has not gone all New Labour and lost its radical roots. And there will almost certainly be some pink flags among the red. But what I like best about the show is its snook-cocking aspect: the poster advertising it has a picture of the equestrian statue of the Duke of Wellington which stands on a plinth in the city centre, and the Duke's head is crowned with a traffic cone. This is not a piece of gratuitous fantasy: it is an event which happens every weekend, when someone at the dead of night climbs the statue and carefully places a traffic cone on the Duke. There is something very Glaswegian about this constructively anarchic spirit.

In a place with this spirit, poets can certainly live, gay poets among them. A place of many unexpectednesses, a place of streets and the drama of the streets, a place of much tolerance despite its history of violence, a place of undogmatic bisexuality which gives it a special flavour – these are all characteristics that I feel at home with, though 'at home with' does not mean I am unaware of the desperate transgressions of the past or of the fact that things can change for the worse as well as for the better. But at present I feel confident for the city and its writers.

## Editors' note

1 This paper was delivered at the Non-Metropolitan Sexualities Conference at the University of Wales, Aberystwyth, in July 1997. Later the same year the Scottish electorate voted for a Scottish Parliament.

## References

Burgess, Moira (1996) *Reading Glasgow*, Edinburgh: Book Trust Scotland.
Leonard, Tom (1984) *Intimate Voices*, Newcastle upon Tyne: Galloping Dog Press.
Morgan, Edwin (1990) *Collected Poems*, Manchester: Carcanet.
—— (1994) *Sweeping Out the Dark*, Manchester: Carcanet.
—— (1996) *Collected Translations*, Manchester: Carcanet.

# AUTHOR INDEX

Aaron, J. 53, 58
Abelove, H. 85, 95
Aldrich, R. 134
Alexander, M.J. 184
Altman, D. 37, 38, 215
Amnesty International 170
Antler 194
Appleton, J. 157

Bachelard, G. 157–8
Baldwin, J. 143
Balibar, E. and Wallerstein, I. 245, 255
Ballard, J. 38
Ballaster, R. 152
Bannon, A. 214
Barrett, H. and Phillips, J. 79
Barry, P. 199
Barthes, R. 243
Baudelaire, C. 130
Baudrillard, J. 217
Bech, H. 84, 85, 95
Bell, D. 86, 87, 196, 265, 273, 275; and Valentine, G. 1, 85, 95
Bell, I.A. 244, 254
Bell-Metereau, R. 28
Bellos, L. 32
Benjamin, W. 130
Bennett, M.R. 186
Bentley, 70
Berlant, L. and Freeman, E. 184; and Warner, M. 182
Berman, S. and Jiménez, M.A. 168
Bersani, L. 34
Bérubé, A. 191
Bhabha, H.K. 1, 218, 243, 272
Bjelke-Petersen, J. 38
Blainey, G. 40
Bland, L. 104, 109
Blumenfeld, W. and Raymond, D. 215

Bombardier, S. et al. 234
Bonnett, A. 96
Brand, A. 128
Brandth, B. 84
Brett, J. 38
Bristow, E. 104, 106, 109, 110
Bristow, J. 131, 134
Brown, M. 102, 231
Brown, R.M. 42
Buchanan, J. 46
Bunce, M. 84, 86
Burgess, M. 281
Burnett, J. 79
Butler, J. 74, 109
Butler, S. 149

Cardenas, N. 177
Carey, J. 69, 79
Carrier, J.M. 168, 169
Case, S.-E. 30
Castle, T. 151
Castro, Y.M. 174
Cavaliero, G. 86
Chan, C.S. 22
Chapman, T.L. 223, 224
Charity Commission 118
Chavez Leyva, Y. 179
Chedgzoy, K. 132
Cheney, J. 95, 96, 125, 207
Chinchilla, N. 167, 171
Ching, B. 85, 98
Cibber, T. 103
Clayre, A. 149
Cleland, J. 103
Cloke, P. and Little, J. 148
Clover, C. 86, 87
Cooper, E. 136
Corona, M. de J. 175
Creed, G. and Ching, B. 83, 85, 86, 87, 98

# AUTHOR INDEX

Crowe, R. 50
Cullingford, E.B. 275
Cutler, M. 215

Dahl, J. 90
Davidoff, L. and Hall, C. 150
Davidson, M. 31
Davies, M. 53
Davies, R. 102
Davis, T. 275
Deakin, M. and Willis, J. 111, 113–17
Debord, G. 234
Defoe, D. 149
Dellamora, R. 134
D'Emilio, J. 204, 215
Demos, J. and Demos, J. 122
Dessaix, R. 37
Dibblin, J. 113, 119
Dollimore, J. 131, 132
Donoghue, E. 125, 153; *et al* 147
Douglas, J. *et al* 85, 93, 94
Douglas, M. 1–2
Dowling, L. 134
Drucker, P. 46
Dubermanet, M. *et al* 215
Dyer, R. 51–2

Edelman, L. 56
Edgeworth, M. 149
Eliot, T.S. 69
Ellis, A.T. 247–8
Empson, W. 131
Eng, D.L. 196
Enríquez, V. 168
Epstein, S. 26

Faderman, L. 96, 147, 153, 191–3, 196
Fellows, W. 1, 187, 189
Finch, M. and Kwietniowski, R. 142
Finkelhor, D. 113, 117–18, 122
Fisher, G. 31
Flynt, L. 90
Fone, B.R.S. 85, 95, 127–8
Ford, C. 225
Foucault, M. 1, 83, 97, 151, 272
Freeman, B.C. 56
Furbank, P.N. 137, 139
Fuss, D. 184

Gaard, G. 93, 97
Galloway, J. 251
Genet, J. 126
Genovese, E.D. 54

Grassberger, R. 91
Grassic Gibbon, L. 249
Green, M. 149, 150
Greve, J. *et al.* 114
Grey, A. 110
Grieg, N. 95
Griffiths, A. 53–4
Grosskurth, P. 134
Gutierrez, T. 172–3

Hall, R. 143
Halperin, D.M. 129
Haraway, D.J. 235
Harper, P.B. 184
Hart, L. and Dale, J. 34
Hartigan, J. Jr 88
Harvey, J. 125, 142, 144
Heaney, S. 15, 266–70
Hirschfeld, M. 129
Hoare, P. 137
Hogarth, W. 103
Hoggart, R. 65, 79
Hopkins, E. 107
Houlton, D. and Short, B. 84
Howells, C.A. 7
Huyssen, A. 79
Hyam, R. 1

Ines de la Cruz, S.J. 172
Ingram, B. 1
Ingram, G.B. 218, 222, 229; *et al.* 218, 234
Innes, C.L. 266, 275

Jackson, A. 79
James, H. 136, 137
Jameson, F. 218, 235
Jarman, D. 126
Jeffrey, S. 30
Jewell, T.L. 194
Jiménez, M.A. 168
Johnson, L. 188
Johnston, J.M. 227
Jones, O. 84
Jordan 70
Joyce, J. 150
Julien, I. 31

Kanievska, M. 141
Katz, I. 275
Katz, J.N. 95, 98, 134, 143, 215
Kennedy, A.L. 150
Kett, J. 122
Kilborn, R. 112, 118

293

# AUTHOR INDEX

Kilfeather, S. 275
King, R. and Taylor, H. 86
Kinsman, G. 229
Kipnis, L. 89, 90
Koo, J. 234
Koppel, T. 220
Kramer, J.L. 85
Kroetsch, R. 6

Labbe, J.M. 158
Lacan, J. 77
Lawrence, D.H. 143
Lawrence, M. 97
Leavitt, D. 22–3, 25, 28
Lebeau, V. 64, 79
Leonard, T. 279
Levi-Calderon, S. 168
Lewis, S. 262
Liddington, J. 147, 148, 149–50, 154, 159, 160
Light, A. 79
Lind, C. 109, 123
Little, J. and Austin, P. 84
Lo-Johansson, I. 91
Lochhead, L. 244, 251
Loftus, B. 275
Longley, E. 275
Luibheid, E. 167, 176–7

MacClaverty, B. 253
McClenaghan, B. 275
McClintock, A. 1
McCluskey, J. 119
McKenna, N. 46
MacKillon, M. 233
McLean, H. and Ngcobo, L. 29
McLeod, D.W. 229
MacMurraugh-Kavanagh, 112, 119
Madden Arias, R.M. 171
Mains, G. 34
Manalansan IV, M.F. 22, 33
Marsh, J. 84, 95
Martin, B. 51, 52, 188, 192
Martin, R.K. and Piggford, G. 137, 138
Mason, M. 102
Mason-John, V. and Khambatta, A. 32, 33
Matless, D. 85
Mavor, E. 148–9
Medhurst, A. 80
Medina, L.M. 170
Mercer, A. 32, 33
Meyer, R. 89
Miller, N. 111, 201–2

Milligan, B. *et al*. 179
Mingay, G. 84
Moore, S. and Rosenthal, D. 122
Moraga, C. 29–30
Morgan, E. 282, 283, 284, 285–9
Morris, M. 46
Mosse, G.L. 85, 94, 130, 139
Moya, P.K.L. 30
Muirhead, L.R. 262
Mullaney, S. 71
Munt, S. 272

Nairn, T. 275
Nestle, J. 30
New, W. 5
Newitz, A. 88
Ng, R. 233
Ng, V. 275
Norton, R. 127

Ocana, P. 168, 169
O'Carrol, I. and Collins, E. 1
Oliver, P. *et al*. 79
Oosterhuis, H. and Kennedy, H. 129
Ortega, R. 178
Owens, C. 217

Paget, D. 112, 118
Pantycelyn, W.W. 49, 52, 54
Parker, R. 46
Pearce, L. 249, 256; and Stacey, J. 253; and Wisker, G. 255
Pearse, P. 275
Penley, C. 89–90
Pérez Ocana, 173, 175, 178
Perry, A. 224
Pfeil, F. 96
Pharr, S. 207–8, 214
Polsky, N. 46
Ponsonby, E. 149
Porter, R. 71
Probyn, E. 98
Prosser, J. 30
Pyke, M. 72

Quiroz, S.H. 176–7

Reed, J. 88
Reid, F. 135–6
Renault, M. 143
Rich, A. 134, 147, 269
Riesman, D. 79
Riordan, M. 1

# AUTHOR INDEX

Ritchie, H. 255
Roffiel, R. 168
Rose, K. 275
Rowan, L. and McName, J. 47
Rugoff, R. 93, 94

Sanchez-Crispin, A. and Lopez-Lopez, A. 168, 170
Sandell, J. 85
Sandford, J. 114
Savage, J. 70, 79
Sayle, C. 137
Schulman, S. 214
Schults, R. 104, 105
Scott, B. 105
Sears, J. 215
Segal, L. 27
Seidman, S. 185
Short, B. 84
Short, J. 103
Silverstone, R. 80
Simmons, R. 32
Simpson, M. 259, 275
Sinclair, R. 68
Sinfield, A. 26, 31, 128, 130, 135, 139
Smalls, J. 31
Smith, M.D. 221
Sontag, S. 131
Steakley, J.D. 139
Stein, G. 69
Stoppard, T. 122
Streeter, M. 275
Sturgess, B. 111
Styrene, Poly 71

Tarantino, Q. 86–7
Taylor, A. 274
Terry, J. 235
Thompson, M. 95–6
Thoreau, D. 95, 134, 143

Tolkien, J.R.R. 79
Trinity 264
Tsuzuki, C. 95
Tuke, H.S. 136

Valentine, G. 85, 95, 200, 205, 207
Vicinus, M. 147

Wadsworth, E. 150
Walker, C. 150
Walkowitz, J. 104, 105, 106–7
Walshe, E. 275
Ward, J. 93
Warner, M. 55, 56, 185, 192, 235
Webster, A. 55, 61
Weeks, J. 30, 95, 122, 129, 135, 199
Weiskel, T. 55–6, 60
Wells, P. 37
Weston, K. 85
Whatling, C. 58
Whitbread, H. 147, 148, 149, 150, 151–3, 155, 157, 158
White, R.L. 185
Whyte, C. 254
Whyte, W. 79
Williams, G.R. 79
Williams, R. 102, 112, 120, 129, 135, 139
Williamson, J. 84, 86, 89, 98
Wilson, A. 143, 215
Wilson, E. 79
Wollaston, G. 254
Wolschke-Bulmahn, J. 94
Woods, G. 46, 85, 95, 128, 138
Woolaston, G. 95, 276
Wotherspoon, G. 47
Wray, M. and Newitz, A. 86, 98

Yeats, W.B. 275
Young, I.M. 221

# SUBJECT INDEX

ACT UP Vancouver 232
Adlon, Percy 7–8
age of consent 103–4; for boys 110–19; for girls 104–10
AIDS 24–5, 38, 231–2
AIDS Quarantine bill 232
Allen, Claudia 193–4
Allison, Dorothy 61–2
*Angelic Conversation* (film) 170
*Anna Karenin* (Tolstoy) 6
Anzaldúa, G. 173–4, 178
*Aqui Estamos* 166
Arcadians 134
assimilationist model 9–10
Association for Social Knowledge 229

Banks, Iain 248–9
*Bastard out of Carolina* (Allison) 61–2
*Beautiful Thing* (film) 125–6, 141–3
*Beowulf*, as inspiration for poem 283
*Between the Body and the Flesh* (Hart) 57, 61–2
'Bitter Cry' campaign 105
Black AIDS Network (BAN) 232
Boorman, John 87
*Brokeback Mountain* (Proulx) 2–5, 8, 9
*The Buddha of Suburbia* (Kureishi) 11, 66–8, 71, 72–9
*Butterfly Kiss* (film) 49, 57–61
Butts, John 223–4

*Cal* (MacClaverty) 253
Camp Sister Spirit 207
Campaign for the Homeless and Rootless (CHAR) 118
Carpenter, Edward 86, 137–9
Cather, Willa 186, 188
*Cathy Come Home* (TV documentary) 118
centre–margin conflict 39–41, 45–6; and colonialism 245–6; and devolution 241, 242, 248, 254–6; and emerging nations 255–6; and identity 154, 159–60; involvement with 253; and romance of the margins 249–54
Charity Commission 118
*The City and the Pillar* (Vidal) 140–1
coastal/heartland split 191–2, 193, 195
colonialism/neo-colonialism 14, 15, 218, 220–3; and oppression 243; post- 241, 243; sexual culture of 223–4
*The Construction of Homosexuality* (Greenberg) 27
*Corydon: Four Socratic Dialogues* (Gide) 133–4
*The Country and the City* (Williams) 103
Criminal Code of Canada 224
Criminal Law Amendment Act (1885) 11, 105, 109–10
*The Crow Road* (Banks) 248–9
cultural cringe 37, 40, 41
cultural difference 220–3, 222
cultural production 267–70

*Dancer from the Dance* (Holleran) 25–6
*Daphnis and Chloe* 133
Daughters of Bilitus (DOB) 203
Dekkers, Midas 91–2
Delany, Samuel R. 24
*Deliverance* (film) 87
Department of Health and Social Security (DHSS) 118
Department of Prices and Consumer Protection 118
Derry/Londonderry split 261–2; and border zone 273; Catholic/Protestant identification with 263; as Maiden City 264–7; parades/marches in 262, 264; as site of physical/ideological conflict 262–3; *see also* Ireland
desire, national/sexual 242–5
devolution: and centre–margin politics 241–2, 245–6; as desirable 254–6; and Ireland

296

252–4; and national desires 242–5; and perceptions of England 250; and romancing the margins 249–54; and Scotland 250–1; un/desirable others 245–9; and Wales 251–2
*Doing It With You Is Taboo* 33

Edward Carpenter Community 95, 96
egalitarian model 27–33
Ellis, Alice Thomas 247–8
*Encuentro* 172–3, 179
*Enlace Lésbico* 12, 167, 175, 180
Ephemerals 229

*The Faerie Queen* (Spenser) 266
Fairie movement 95–6, 97
*The Farewell Symphony* (White) 28
*Fat Land* (Patterson) 252–3
Fellows, W. 187, 189
Female Friendly Societies 150
femininity: corruption theory of 106–7; rural simplicity/purity of 107–8; as vulnerable 107–9
feminism: and lesbians 167, 169, 172–3; and nationalism 244; and utopian rural collectives 205
Firbank, Ronald 131–2, 143
Forster, E.M. 135, 136–7, 138, 139
Foyle Friend Homepage 271
Frente Zapatista de Liberacion Nacional (FZLN) 175–6

*The Garden God: a Tale of Two Boys* (Reid) 135–6
Gay Alliance Towards Equality (GATE) 230–1
Gay Games (1990) 232
Gay Liberation Front (GLF) 95, 229–30, 259
gay liberation movement 229–32, 260
gay/lesbian community: building 199; and choice of identity 274; and coming out 272; construction of 214; and creation of necessary fictions 199, 208, 211; and exclusion 203–4; impact of capitalism on 204–5; and importance of Second World War 201; in Northern Ireland 261, 263–4, 270–4; publications 206, 208–10; rural life of 210–11; and Thatcherism 259–60; as urban led 202; urban migration/rural exclusion 199–200; violence against 272
gay/lesbian/queer community 41, 42–3; centre/periphery change 46; growth of identity 43–4
gays: activism of 222–3; American influence on 26, 41–2; changed attitude towards 41, 43; coming out 43; dominated by white middle-class 192; egalitarian model 27–33; formation of social spaces 220–3; literature on 168, 255; and marriage 177–8; Midwest identity 186–96; multiple/anonymous partners 24–5; poems about 282–9; rite-of-passage 125–6; triple marginality of 10, 37; visibility of 168, 169
*Getting His Goat* (film) 90
Gide, André 133–4
*Giving Up the Ghost* (Moraga) 29–30
Glasgow: described 278–80, 288, 290–1; homosexuality in 280–2; poetry about 289–90
*The Glass Menagerie* (Williams) 23
globalization 14, 15–16, 42–3, 44, 45, 46, 222
Greenberg, David F. 27, 122
Gunn, Thom 25

Halberstam, Judith 27, 30, 34
Hart, Lynda 57, 61–2
Health Statutes Amendment Act (1987) 231
Heaney, Seamus 266–70
heterosexism 212–13, 214; and cultural production 267–70
hillbilly horror 87–9, 96
Holleran, Andrew 25–6
Homeless Young People, Working Group on 118
homoerotic space 217–18; contentious 218–23; decolonization of 218, 229, 230; marginality of 223–33; meeting places 220–1; multiple voices/divergent maps 233–4; new cartographies/emerging designs 234
homophobia: and control of native groups 223–5; and control of non-European immigrants 225–8; crumbling of 230; new wave of 231; political economy of 227–8
Homosexual Law Reform Act (1967) 263–4, 274
Homosexual Liberation Front (FHAR) 174
homosexuality: aboriginal 225; and age of consent 110–19, 273–4; and appropriation of manliness 139; Arcadian references 127–8; and coming out 283, 288; and corruption/exclusion 117; as crime 110, 217, 228–9; Fog City metaphor 280–1; information required on 202–3; (in)visibility of 203; and marginalization 173–4; as metropolitan identity 129–32; moral panic concerning 202; and morality laws 170; pastoral 131–2; poems

## SUBJECT INDEX

concerning 282–90; purges of 228–9; as rural fantasy 134–5; and trials for buggery 223–4; as unnatural 223
Housing (Homeless Persons) Act (1977) 118–19
*Hustler* magazine 90
hybridity theory 272

identity 25; central/marginal 154, 159–60; choice of 260–1, 274; complexity of 201, 214; deviant 245; as dichotomous 72–3; discovering 43–4, 51–2; and environment 156–9; gendered 15–16, 261; homosexual 129–32; metropolitan 74; Midwest gay/lesbian 186–96; national/sexual 244–9, 259; national/social 15, 44–5; problems of 78–9; queer 183–4; rural constructions of 214; as self assertion 66–7; two-spirited 233; *see also* politics of identity
image/reality difference 102
imperialism 21, 33–4, 229–30; peripheral 223–33
International Lesbian and Gay Association (ILGA) 33, 170
International Lesbian Information Service (ILIS) 179
Ireland: and devolution 252–4; gay/lesbian community in 261, 263–4, 270–4; images of 266–70; north/south border zone 273; *see also* Derry/Londonderry split

*Johnny Go Home* (documentary) 11, 104, 110–19
Johnston, Denis 265
Julien, Isaac 31

Kinsey, A. 86, 87–8, 91, 97, 201, 202
Kinsey Report 13
*Kiss of the Spider Woman* (Puig) 28
Kramer, Larry 24–5, 28
Kureishi, Hanif 11, 66–8, 71, 72–9

La Asociacion Nacional Civica Feminina 171
Ladies of Llangollen 149, 151–2
Lambda 174
Latin American Lesbian Archive 166, 167
Leavitt, David 22–4, 25
Lee, Annie/Jim McHarris 211–12
lesbian sublime 10
lesbian-feminist communities 193
Lesbian-Homosexual Movement 174
lesbians: butch/fem model 30; of color 233; coming out 51, 166; communes 14; egalitarian model 26–7, 29–30; and enjoyment in rural life 213–14; and feminism 167, 169, 172–3; and gender hierarchy 29; history 147; homophile movement 208–9; and identity 147–8, 156–9; and influence of landscape 156–9; information concerning 209–10; and the left 174–6; literature on 167–8, 169, 178–9; looking for 166–70; marginalization of 12–13, 169–70, 172–3, 177; and marriage 177–8; and media bias 177–8; metropolitan bias of 168–9; Mexican 166–80; Midwest identity 186–96; and pastoral self-discovery 200–1; and power through separatism 202, 208; presence of 168; relationship with US 176–7; social exclusion/isolation of 207–9; and subversion of Catholic church 171–2; treatment of 170–1; US/colonial influence 178–80; US/European models 177–8; and utopian rural collectives 205–8; visibility of 166, 168, 169, 177; in the workforce 192
*Lesbians Talk: Making Black Waves* 32
Lesbos 172
*Lillibulero* (Johnston) 265
Lister, Anne 12, 147–8; appearance of 153; attitude to marriage 159; background 148; as consistent/rational 160; diary entries 148–9, 155–6; as employer 149–50; her crypt-hand alphabet 155–6; landscaping/building fantasies 156–9; lesbian tendencies 148–9, 150–3; status of 153–5
Loach, Ken 118
location: and boundaries 274; as crucial 8; as gendered 6–7; and identity 156–9
London: as corrupt 106, 108, 112, 116–17; as place of falling 115–16
*Looking for Langston* (film) 31
*The Lost Language of Cranes* (Leavitt) 22–4, 25, 26, 28
Lotus Root Conference (1996) 234
*Loving in the War Years* (Moraga) 29

McHarris, Jim/Annie Lee 211–12
machismo 173–4
'Maiden Tribute of Modern Babylon' campaign (1885) 104–10, 112–13, 120, 121
*Maiden Voyage* (Welch) 30–1
male/female binary: and cultural production 267–70; and the Maiden City 264–7
*The Man with Night Sweats* (Gunn) 25
*Mandragora* (film) 103
Mantha, Leo Anthony 228

# SUBJECT INDEX

Mapplethorpe, Robert 31, 132
marginality 8–9, 37, 218; Australian 40–1; based on geography/distance 39–41; centre/periphery 39–41, 45–6; contexts 166–70; contradictory sources of 165–6; end of 43; homoerotic 223–33; of lesbians 169–70, 172–3, 177, 179–80; and national identity 245–9; resistance by Women's Movement 172–3; of sexual minorities 221, 222–3, 269; in small communities 212–13, 214; speaking from 174–6; struggle against by homosexual movement/the left 173–4; subversion by religion 171–2; surviving sources of 170–6
Mattachine Society 202–3, 215
*Matter of Life and Sex* (Moore) 24
*Maurice* (Forster) 135, 136, 138, 139, 140, 141–2
metropolitan model: and coming out 21–2; contrast with suburbia 67–8, 76; as egalitarian 33–4; fantasies of 73, 77; and gay marriage 24, 25; gay/lesbian concepts of 22–6; and homosexuality 129–32; migration to 11, 12–14, 202; moves away from 9–10; as object of desire 11; as powerful/imperialist 21, 33–4; scope of 21
metropolitan/non-metropolitan 83–4, 88, 98, 103, 125; as corrupt/uncorrupt 104–5, 106–10, 112–13, 120–1; and ideas of homelessness/home 114–15; imagined 102–3, 120–1; *see also* non-metropolitan sex-gender systems
metrosex 11
Mexico: lesbians in 165–6; global context 176–80; looking for 166–70; surviving sources of marginalization 170–6
Midwest America: agrarian myth of 185–6; gay/lesbian identity in 186–96; influence of 186; literature on 185; as socially constructed landscape 185–8; and specificity of landscape 194–5
mirror stage model 77
Mogrovejo, N. 166–8, 171, 173, 174, 179, 180
Moore, Oscar 24
Moraga, Cherríe 29
*The Motion of Light in Water* (Delany) 24
multiculturalism 42–3, 44, 222, 230
Murray, Stephen, O. 27
*My Beautiful Launderette* (film) 32

National Front for the Liberation of Women's Rights 172

National Vigilance Association (NVA) 109
neo-colonialism *see* colonialism/neo-colonialism
Nijinsky 137
non-metropolitan sex-gender systems 27; and class/race hierarchies 30–3; and difference 27–30; and power differentials 33–5; *see also* metropolitan/non-metropolitan
*The Normal Heart* (Kramer) 24–5, 28
Nowell, Charles James 225

Oikabeth 172, 174
*On the Beach* 89
Other 77–8

paedophilia 117–18
*Pall Mall Gazette* 104, 121–2
pastoral discourse: academic arcadias 134–5; authentic 132–4; dreams/lonely bars 140–1; garden gods to gamekeepers 137–9; as gay heritage 12, 141–3; as Greek ideal 128; and homosexual isolation 13–14; motifs 127; queer 127–9, 141–3; and rite-of-passage 125–7; and romantic friendship 125; and stories of panic 135–7; as transformative 12
Patterson, Glen 252–3
Piaf, Edith, poem about 282
pilgrimage 49–50; politicized understanding of 54; queer 57–61; as religious/sexual experience 11, 55–6
*Places Far From Ellesmere* (van Herk) 5–7, 8, 9
poetry: about Glasgow 289–90; on being nearly human 283; on coming out 283; on gay liberation 284–6; homoerotic elements 282–3; influence of American Beat on 286–7; on love 284; queer 288–9; on war experiences 287–8
politics of identity 258–61; and Derry/Londonderry split 261–4; and the gendering of cultural production 267–70; and the 'Maiden City' 264–7; and utopian sexualities 270–4; *see also* identity
Pool, Gary 193
pornography 89–90
power: as sexy 27, 28–9, 33–4; and SM 34
PRD group 174–5
pretty-near-talk 14, 219, 220–2
Pro-Vida 171
Proulx, Annie 2–5, 8, 9
Puig, Manuel 28
*Pulp Fiction* (film) 86–7
purity movement 109, 110

## SUBJECT INDEX

Queen's University (Belfast) 270–1
queer 218; activism 223; assimilation/ resistance struggle 193–4; coastal experience 191–2, 193, 195; contemporary 271–2; culture 192; and identification of common attributes 184; identity 183–4; literature 193–5; marginalization of 184; metropolitan bias 182–3; Midwestern 185–96; and the military 192; and nature 93, 95; pastoralist 126, 127–9, 141–3; and pilgrimage 57–61; and resistance to oppression 188; as undesirable 191
queer child: alternative role models for 189–91; myth of 182–3
Queer Space Project (Belfast) 271–3

race/sex relations 31–3, 178–9, 233–4
racism 14, 40
Reeder, Jennifer 89
Reform Act (1832) 150
Reichard, William 191
Reid, Forrest 135–6
religion: and homosexuality 171–2, 177–8; and impact of hymns 52–5; motifs 10; oceanic metaphor 60–1; and salvation/ redemption 61–2; and sexual desire 50–1, 53, 55–7, 61–3; and the sublime 55–6, 60, 61
*A Restricted Country* (Nestle) 30
Riggs, Marlon 31–2
Rockhampton: described 38–9; gay life in 39–40
Rodi, Robert 190
*Rumours of Fulfilment* (Watson) 246–7, 251–2
rural erotic 11; bestiality 85–6, 90–2; natural/ unnatural 97–8; naturism 86, 92–7; white trash 85, 86–90
rural places: enjoyment in 213–14; as hostile/ idyllic 201, 214; as idealized women's space 205–8; representations of 84–5; and self-discovery 200–1; and social exclusion 203–4, 207–8; as uncorrupt 104, 106–19
rural/urban distinction *see* metropolitan/non-metropolitan

s/m: as internalization of domination 76; and power 34
*Salmonberries* (film) 7–8
Seaton, Maureen 193
Secret Commission 107
Sedgwick, Eve 67, 128, 139, 189–90, 255
Sexual Offences Act (1967) 110

sexuality: ambiguous 74; as consumer choice 74; contentious 218–23; and corruption 119; de-centring 1–2; discursive constructions 102; effect of devolution on 254–6; and ethnicity 246–8; as highly regulated 263; and human rights 232–3; journeys 103–4, 120–1; and national identity 244–9, 259; as performance 74–7; politics/representation beyond the metropolis 9–16; power and danger 2–9; public policy on 14; and religion 50–1, 53, 55–7, 61–3; and self 74; and the sublime 55–6; utopian 270–4; village 84
Sikhs 226–7
space: attempts at sharing 221–2; conflicting dualities in 261–4; formation of gay 219–23; gendered 264–7; as ghetto 258; informal maps of 219–23; symbols of 258
Spenser, Edmund 266
Stead, W.T. 11, 104–10
Stonewall Riots (1969) 1, 202, 229, 230, 258
'The Story of Panic' (Forster) 137
subcultures 65
suburban subject 66, 77
suburbia 10–11; absence of 67; blind spot concerning 65; contrast with metropolitan 11, 67–8; critique of 72; described 64; as gendered 70; growth of 68–9; as (in)authentic 68, 71, 73; as marginal space 64–6; and punk 70–1; simulations of 72–9; as site of ambiguity 69–70, 71, 76; as theatricalized subversion 71–2
*Sucking Feijoas* (Buchanan) 46
Symonds, John Addington 134

Tarantino, Quentin 86–7
Telemanita 167–8
*Teleny: or the Reverse of the Medal* (Wilde and others) 132–3
*Thelma and Louise* (film) 89
Tolstoy, Leo 6
*Tongues Untied* (film) 31–2
*Towards Democracy* (Carpenter) 139
transgressive model 9–10
Tsui, Kitty 195
Tuxtla Gutierrez Gay and Transvestite Group 170

*Un Chant D'Amour* (film) 126
*Unexplained Laughter* (Ellis) 247–8
urban/male rural/female dichotomy 205
urban/rural distinction *see* metropolitan/non-metropolitan

# SUBJECT INDEX

*Valmouth* (Firbank) 131–2
van Herk, Aritha 2, 5–7, 8, 9
Vidal, Gore 140–1

Watson, Robert 242, 246–7, 251–2
*The Wedding Banquet* (film) 32
Welch, Denton 30–1
White, Edmund 28, 42, 186, 187, 188
Whitman, Walt 26, 138–9

Wilde, Oscar 130–1, 132–3, 136
Williams, Tennesse 23
Willis, John 11, 110, 119
Wolfenden Report (1957) 110, 111, 117
Women's Movement 14, 172–3

Youth International Party (Yippies) 229

Zapatistas 175–6